Maritime Security and Indonesia

Indonesia is the largest archipelago state in the world, comprising 17,480 islands, with a maritime territory measuring close to 6 million square kilometres. It is located between the two key shipping routes of the Pacific and Indian Ocean. Indonesia's cooperation in maritime security initiatives is vitally important because half of the world's trading goods and oil pass through Indonesian waters, including the Straits of Malacca, the Strait of Sunda and the Strait of Lombok.

This book analyses Indonesia's participation in international maritime security cooperation. Using Indonesia as a case study, the book adopts mixed methods to assess emerging power cooperation and non-cooperation, drawing from various International Relations theories and the bureaucratic politics approach. It addresses not only the topic of Indonesia's cooperation but also engages in debates across the International Relations, political science and policy studies disciplines regarding state cooperation. Based on extensive primary Indonesian language sources and original interviews, the author offers a conceptual discussion of the reasons underlying participation or non-participation of emerging middle powers in cooperation agreements. The analysis offers a fresh perspective on the growing problems of maritime terrorism and sea robbery and how an emerging power deals with these threats at unilateral, bilateral, regional and multilateral levels.

The book fills a significant gap in the literature on Indonesian foreign policy making in the post-1998 era. It provides the first in-depth study of Indonesia's decision-making process in the area of maritime security and will thus be of interest to researchers in the field of comparative politics, international relations, security policy, maritime cooperation, port and shipping businesses and Southeast Asian politics and society.

Senia Febrica is a researcher at the American Studies Center, Universitas Indonesia, and a Gerda Henkel Stiftung post-doctoral scholar.

Routledge Contemporary Southeast Asia Series

72 **Human Trafficking in Colonial Vietnam**
Micheline Lessard

73 **Conflict Resolution and Peacebuilding in Laos**
Perspective for Today's World
Stephanie Stobbe

74 **Urbanization in Vietnam**
Gisele Bousquet

75 **Social Democracy in East Timor**
Rebecca Strating

76 **The Politics of Aid to Myanmar**
A Humanitarian Struggle on the Thai–Burmese Border
Anne Décobert

77 **Animism in Southeast Asia**
Edited by Kaj Århem and Guido Sprenger

78 **Brunei – History, Islam, Society and Contemporary Issues**
Edited by Ooi Keat Gin

79 **Political Institutions in East Timor**
Semi-Presidentialism and Democratisation
Lydia M. Beuman

80 **Religious Violence and Conciliation in Indonesia**
Christians and Muslims in the Moluccas
Sumanto Al Qurtuby

81 **Identity Politics and Elections in Malaysia and Indonesia**
Ethnic Engineering in Borneo
Karolina Prasad

82 **Rethinking Power Relations in Indonesia**
Transforming the Margins
Edited by Michaela Haug, Martin Rössler and Anna-Teresa Grumblies

83 **Indonesia and the Politics of Disaster**
Power and Representation in Indonesia's Mud Volcano
Phillip Drake

84 **Nation-Building and National Identity in Timor-Leste**
Michael Leach

85 **Visual Media in Indonesia**
Video Vanguard
Edwin Jurriëns

86 **Maritime Security and Indonesia**
Cooperation, Interests and Strategies
Senia Febrica

87 **The King and the Making of Modern Thailand**
Antonio L. Rappa

Maritime Security and Indonesia

Cooperation, Interests and Strategies

Senia Febrica

LONDON AND NEW YORK

First published 2017
by Routledge
2 Park Square, Milton Park, Abingdon, Oxon OX14 4RN

and by Routledge
711 Third Avenue, New York, NY 10017

Routledge is an imprint of the Taylor & Francis Group, an informa business

© 2017 Senia Febrica

The right of Senia Febrica to be identified as author of this work has been asserted by her in accordance with sections 77 and 78 of the Copyright, Designs and Patents Act 1988.

All rights reserved. No part of this book may be reprinted or reproduced or utilised in any form or by any electronic, mechanical, or other means, now known or hereafter invented, including photocopying and recording, or in any information storage or retrieval system, without permission in writing from the publishers.

Trademark notice: Product or corporate names may be trademarks or registered trademarks, and are used only for identification and explanation without intent to infringe.

British Library Cataloguing in Publication Data
A catalogue record for this book is available from the British Library

Library of Congress Cataloging in Publication Data
Names: Febrica, Senia, author.
Title: Maritime security and Indonesia : cooperation, interests and strategies / Senia Febrica.
Description: New York : Routledge, 2017. | Series: Routledge contemporary Southeast Asia series ; 86 | Includes bibliographical references and index.
Identifiers: LCCN 2016044685| ISBN 9781138688438 (hardback) | ISBN 9781315541815 (ebook)
Subjects: LCSH: Merchant marine–Security measures–Indonesia. | Shipping–Security measures–Indonesia. | Piracy–Indonesia–Prevention. | Sea control–Indonesia. | Sea control–International cooperation. | Maritime terrorism–Indonesia–Prevention.
Classification: LCC VK203 .F43 2017 | DDC 359/.0309598–dc23
LC record available at https://lccn.loc.gov/2016044685

ISBN: 978-1-138-68843-8 (hbk)
ISBN: 978-1-315-54181-5 (ebk)

Typeset in Times New Roman
by Wearset Ltd, Boldon, Tyne and Wear

To my parents
Santje Takalamingan and Julien Lucas

Contents

List of figures ix
List of tables x
A note on the author xi
Acknowledgements xii
List of abbreviations xiii

Introduction 1

*Locating Indonesia in the literature on international
 cooperation 4*
The significance of Indonesia in the study of maritime security 11
Outline of this book 13

1 Maritime security and Indonesia 25

Introduction 25
*The trends of maritime terrorism and armed robbery against
 ships 26*
The importance of Indonesia in maritime security 33
Conclusion 52

2 Domestic politics 64

Introduction 64
Domestic politics dynamics and maritime cooperation 64
Indonesia's assigned bureaucratic politics model 69
*The limitation of bureaucratic politics in explaining Indonesian
 cooperation 70*
Conclusion 86

3 When the hegemon is leading   102

Introduction 102
Fully cooperative on the bilateral front 103
Cases of non-cooperation: the hegemon did not bark 107
The United States unilateral initiatives: the public–private partnership model 113
Conclusion 119

4 When shared identity does not matter   130

Introduction 130
The ASEAN Way 131
The ASEAN Way and history of maritime security cooperation in ASEAN 132
Debunking the ASEAN Way? Cooperation with extra-regional states 137
Conclusion 141

5 Gains and losses   148

Introduction 148
Relative gains' lack of explanatory purchase 148
Calculating absolute gains 151
Conclusion 184

6 Conclusion   206

Findings 206
Conclusion 216
Future work 217

Index   222

Figures

1.1	Armed robbery attacks and attempted attacks in Indonesian waters (excluding the Straits of Malacca and Singapore) 1991–2015	31
1.2	Armed robbery attacks and attempted attacks in the Straits of Malacca and Singapore 1991–2015	32
1.3	Map of Indonesia	34
1.4	The Indonesian ministry of defence maritime security budget	45

Tables

I.1	List of all cooperation cases	2–3
I.2	Categories of cooperation partners, based on comparison of defence expenditure	7
1.1	Indonesia's national initiatives to address armed robbery against ships	46–47
1.2	Overfished fishery stocks in Indonesia	49
1.3	Status of Indonesia's maritime boundaries agreements with neighbouring states	50
1.4	List of Indonesia's outermost islands	51
6.1	Cooperation to address maritime terrorism: variables and negotiated outcomes	208–209
6.2	Cooperation to address sea robbery: variables and negotiated outcomes	210

A note on the author

Dr Senia Febrica is a researcher at the American Studies Center, Universitas Indonesia, and a Gerda Henkel Stiftung post-doctoral scholar. She is also a university teacher at the Universitas Indonesia, an associate principal at the Adyatmika Sakti Nusantara, and the director of the Maritime Affairs Programme at the Indonesian Institute of Advanced International Studies, Jakarta. She was a visiting fellow at the Scottish Centre for International Law, the University of Edinburgh, Scotland, and the International Master Program in International Studies, National Chengchi University, Taiwan. She received her PhD from the University of Glasgow, Scotland, in 2014. Febrica holds an MSc in International Politics from the University of Glasgow. She graduated with distinction in 2008 and was awarded the John Peterson Prize for the best dissertation and overall performance during her Master. She has taught at the Universitas Indonesia and the University of Glasgow. Febrica was a Taiwan Fellowship recipient, a United Nations–the Nippon Foundation of Japan research fellow and a Haruhisa Handa–Worldwide Support for Development non-residential fellow. Her past and current research is characterised by the themes of international security and maritime cooperation. She has published in peer-reviewed journals, including *Asian Survey, Perspectives on Terrorism* and *Asian Politics and Policy* and in edited volumes published by university press and academic publishers.

Acknowledgements

I have received enormous support from various people and institutions to complete this book. I am deeply indebted to my PhD supervisors Dr Cian O'Driscoll and Professor Alasdair Young for their guidance and advice during and after my doctoral study at the University of Glasgow. I thank Suzie Sudarman MA, my former undergraduate dissertation supervisor, for inspiring me to pursue an academic career and providing tremendous support.

I thank the American Studies Center, Universitas Indonesia, the Department of International Relations, Universitas Indonesia, and the International Centre for Political Violence and Terrorism Research, Rajaratnam School of International Studies for facilitating and hosting my fieldwork.

The Indonesian Ministry of Education, the School of Social and Political Sciences, University of Glasgow, the Gilbert Murray Trust, the United Nations Division for Ocean Affairs and the Law of the Sea, the Nippon Foundation of Japan and the Gerda Henkel Stiftung have provided scholarship, fieldwork and conference funding that made the completion of this book possible.

During my field trips in Southeast Asia and New York, a number of government officials, academics and business representatives were willing to share their time, ideas and knowledge with me. I thank them for their invaluable cooperation and insights.

To my friends and colleagues in Indonesia and Scotland, thank you for your warm friendships. A special thanks to Ima, Nara, Kajol, Lenny, Irene, Vidia, Dr Hariyadi Wirawan, Utaryo, Mba Diana, Mba Vita, and Mas Roni for their kind help and encouragement during my field work in Indonesia and Singapore. I thank Dr I Made Andi Arsana for his assistance in designing maps for this book.

My most profound debt is to my parents Julien and Santje, and my brother Michael. Thank you for keeping me grounded.

Most of all, I thank my husband, Daniel, for his understanding and assistance in reading early drafts of this book, cooking, baking, organising various trips and holidays, and introducing me to the wonderful Hammond family.

Abbreviations

AEO	Authorised Economic Operator
AFP	Australian Federal Police
AIS	Automatic Identification System
AMF	ASEAN Maritime Forum
APEC	Asia–Pacific Economic Cooperation
APEC TRP	Asia–Pacific Economic Cooperation Trade Recovery Programme
APT	ASEAN Plus Three
ARF	ASEAN Regional Forum
ASEAN	Association of Southeast Asian Nations
ASF	Asian Shipowners' Forum
BIMP-EAGA	Brunei Darussalam–Indonesia–Malaysia–the Philippines East ASEAN Growth Area
CBP	Customs and Border Protection
CSI	Container Security Initiative
C–TPAT	Customs–Trade Partnership Against Terrorism
DCA	Defence Cooperation Agreement
DGST	Directorate General of Sea Transportation
EAMF	Expanded ASEAN Maritime Forum
EEZ	Exclusive Economic Zone
EiS	Eyes in the Sky
GAM	Gerakan Aceh Merdeka
GDP	Gross Domestic Product
IMB	International Maritime Bureau
IMCP	Indonesia–Malaysia Coordinated Patrol
IMO	International Maritime Organization
IMSS	Integrated Maritime Surveillance System
IPS	International Port Security
ISC	Information Sharing Centre
ISCP	Indonesia Singapore Coordinated Patrol
ISPS	International Ship and Port Facility Security
JCLEC	Jakarta Centre for Law Enforcement Cooperation
JI	Jamaah Islamiyah
JWC	Joint War Committee

MFA	Ministry of Foreign Affairs
MITA	Mitra Utama
MoD	Ministry of Defence
MoT	Ministry of Transportation
MoU	Memorandum of Understanding
MPA	Malacca Patrol Agreement
MSP	Malacca Straits Patrol
MSSP	Malacca Straits Sea Patrol
NCIS	Naval Criminal Investigative Service
NGO	Non-Governmental Organisation
NPT	Non-Proliferation Treaty
PSI	Proliferation Security Initiative
ReCAAP	Regional Cooperation Agreement on Combating Piracy and Armed Robbery against Ships in Asia
RMSI	Regional Maritime Security Initiative
SLOC	Sea Lanes of Communication
SOLAS	International Convention for the Safety of Life at Sea
SUA	Suppression of Unlawful Acts Against the Safety of Maritime Navigation
TAC	Treaty of Amity and Cooperation
UN	United Nations
UNCLOS	United Nations Convention on the Law of the Sea
UNCTAD	United Nations Conference on Trade and Development
UNHCR	United Nations High Commissioner for Refugees
US CBP	United States Customs and Border Protection
WCO	World Customs Organization
WMD	Weapons of Mass Destruction

Introduction

Indonesia is a critical state in maritime security. Almost half of the world's traded goods and oil navigates through the key Indonesian straits of Malacca, Sunda and Lombok (Carana, 2004, p. 14; US Department of Homeland Security, 2005). These strategic sea routes are threatened by possible maritime terrorism attacks and armed robbery against ships. Since 2013 close to 40 per cent of worldwide armed robbery attacks against ships have taken place in Indonesian waters (IMB, 2014). Despite the growing threats in its waters, Indonesia's participation in maritime security cooperation continues to vary. Indonesia participates in a number of international cooperative endeavours to deal with maritime terrorism and sea robbery, for instance the World Customs Organization SAFE Framework of Standards to Secure and Facilitate Global Trade (WCO SAFE Framework), and has even actively initiated a selection of measures and convened multiple meetings to improve maritime security cooperation, such as the Malacca Straits Patrol (MSP) agreement among others (*Jakarta Post*, 2005; Singapore Ministry of Foreign Affairs, 2005).[1] Yet it has also refrained from participating in a number of other cooperative arrangements, such as the Convention for the Suppression of Unlawful Acts against the Safety of Maritime Navigation (SUA convention), also designed to tackle maritime terrorism and sea robbery. Given Indonesia's rigorous response towards some cooperation initiatives to address maritime terrorism and armed robbery against ships, but not towards others, I pose the question: why does Indonesia join or not join a cooperation agreement?

The study of maritime security I develop in this book makes a valuable empirical contribution by offering a comprehensive account of the measures being taken by Indonesia to address two serious threats to maritime security: maritime terrorism and armed robbery against ships. As Indonesia is an important player in maritime security, and as the security of Indonesia's sea lanes are crucial to global trade, this is worthy of our attention. This book covers a much broader set of Indonesia's unilateral measures and maritime cooperation arrangements. It compares Indonesia's participation in all maritime security cooperation to address maritime terrorism and armed robbery against ships. In total there are twenty-six cooperation arrangements dealing with maritime terrorism and armed robbery against ships, capturing both cooperation and non-cooperation (see Table I.1).

2   *Introduction*

Table I.1 List of all cooperation cases

	Subject of cooperation	
Outcome	Maritime terrorism	Parties
Cooperation	The US–Indonesia Defence Framework Arrangement, 10 June 2010	Indonesia and the US
	The Indonesia–Japan Joint Announcement on Fighting against International Terrorism, 24 June 2003	Indonesia and Japan
	Three Bilateral Arrangements with Australia: Australia MoU on Counter-Terrorism, 7 February 2002; Lombok Treaty, 13 November 2006; and the Defence Cooperation Arrangement, 5 September 2012	Indonesia and Australia
	The Brunei Darussalam–Indonesia–Malaysia–the Philippines East ASEAN Growth Area MoU on Sea Linkages, 2 November 2007 and the MoU on Transport of Goods, 25 June 2009	Indonesia, Brunei, Malaysia and the Philippines
	The Agreement on Information Exchange and Establishment of Communication, 7 May 2002	Indonesia, Malaysia and the Philippines
	The ASEAN Convention on Counter-Terrorism, 13 January 2007	ASEAN member states (10 states)
	The International Ship and Port Facility Security (ISPS) Code, 12 December 2002	148 states who are contracting parties to the Safety of Life at Sea (SOLAS) Convention including ASEAN and non-ASEAN states
	The World Customs Organization SAFE Framework of Standards (WCO SAFE Framework), 23 June 2005	164 out of 179 WCO member states including ASEAN and non-ASEAN states
	The Asia–Pacific Economic Cooperation Trade Recovery Programme (APEC TRP), 9 September 2007	7 ASEAN member states and 14 extra-regional states
Non-cooperation	The Convention for the Suppression of Unlawful Acts against the Safety of Maritime Navigation (SUA Convention), 10 March 1988	6 ASEAN states and 155 non-ASEAN states
	The Proliferation Security Initiative (PSI), 31 May 2003	3 ASEAN states and 69 extra-regional states
	The Container Security Initiative (CSI), 20 January 2002	3 ASEAN states and 33 extra-regional states
Outcome	Armed Robbery against Ships	Parties

	Subject of cooperation	
Outcome	Maritime terrorism	Parties
Cooperation	Indonesia–Singapore Coordinated Patrol Arrangement, 8 July 1992	Indonesia and Singapore
	Indonesia–Malaysia Coordinated Patrol Arrangement, July 1992	Indonesia and Malaysia
	Indonesia–the Philippines Defence Agreement, 27 August 1997	Indonesia and the Philippines
	Indonesia–India Defence Agreement, 11 January 2001	Indonesia and India
	The MoU on Maritime Cooperation between Indonesia and China, 25 April 2005	Indonesia and China
	The Malacca Straits Patrol (MSP) Agreement, 21 April 2006	Indonesia, Malaysia and Singapore
	Two ASEAN Initiatives: The ARF Statement on Cooperation against Piracy and Other Threats to Maritime Security, 17 June 2003 and the ASEAN Maritime Forum, 23 July 2005	ASEAN member states and 16 extra-regional states including the US, China, the European Union and Australia
Non-Cooperation	Defence Cooperation Agreement with Singapore, 27 April 2007	Indonesia and Singapore
	The Regional Maritime Security Initiative (RMSI), November 2004	It was intended to include all 20 countries in East Asia and Pacific
	The Regional Cooperation Agreement on Combating Piracy and Armed Robbery against Ships in Asia (ReCAAP), 11 November 2004	ASEAN member states (excluding Malaysia and Indonesia) and 11 extra-regional states

Cooperation in both policy areas is important because of two reasons. First, the two issues have become the focus of international maritime security cooperation. Armed robbery against ships is not a new security concern for either Indonesia or the international community. It has been a recurring maritime security challenge in Southeast Asia since AD 414 (Chalk, 1998, p. 87). Although armed robbery at sea is not new, this issue has received a lot of attention since 9/11. Similarly, concern over maritime terrorism attacks began to rise as an international security concern in the wake of 9/11. Consequently, there is now extensive regional and multilateral cooperation on both issues.

Second, maritime terrorism and armed robbery against ships have the potential to impact the international economy and security significantly. If the three international Sea Lanes of Communication (SLOC) that overlap with Indonesian territory – the Straits of Malacca and Singapore, the Strait of Lombok and the Strait of Sunda – were closed, the additional transport costs for detouring around Australia would cost an extra US$8 billion per year based on 1993 trade flows in

4　*Introduction*

these straits (Noer and Gregory, 1996, p. 47). The closure of adjacent ports in Singapore, Malaysia and Indonesia that are located around the three SLOCs would impede the transport of cargo worth around US$232 billion (Noer and Gregory, 1996, p. 47). Acts of maritime terrorism and sea robbery would bring devastating consequences, not only in terms of economic and financial damage to affected countries and industries, but also in human losses (Ho, 2006, p. 563). Acts of maritime terrorism carried out by the Abu Sayaff Group on board the MV Super Ferry in the Sulu Sea in the Philippines caused the death of 116 of the 900 passengers and crew (Monje, 2013). Concerns have been raised over the possibility of terrorists hijacking a super tanker in a busy sea lane.

In addition to providing valuable empirical contributions, I also contribute to the theoretical debate on international cooperation. It shows that Indonesia's decision to join or not to join a cooperation agreement is informed by the absolute gains calculation. Indonesia signed agreements only if it anticipated that the benefits of cooperation would exceed the costs. Indonesia is seeking core benefits such as burden sharing, equipment, access to maritime training and exercises to improve the country's maritime security measures; it is also seeking ancillary benefits, including agreement from its cooperation partners to negotiate other treaties or assistance to develop its undeveloped areas. In assessing the costs of cooperation, Indonesia takes into account the sovereignty costs that refer to the degree of limitation that an agreement poses to national autonomy, and the implementation costs that point to the costs incurred in implementing the cooperation requirements. By analysing why Indonesia did or did not join a cooperation agreement, I contribute to theoretical debates on cooperation in international relations by bringing in discussion of middle power participation in international cooperation. The international relations literature on cooperation tends to focus on great power bargaining. Whether, why and how middle powers decide to join international initiatives over which they have little influence has been overlooked.

Locating Indonesia in the literature on international cooperation

Indonesia's participation in maritime agreements informs analytical and empirical debates on the study of international cooperation. Scholars have indicated that states in the international system have different capacities and opportunities to influence the outcome of interactions between nations (Keohane, 1969; Ping, 2005, p. 1). Academic work categorises the various states in this fluid international system into three groups: great powers, middle powers and small powers (Keohane, 1969; Ping, 2005, p. 1). The burgeoning international relations cooperation literature, however, tends to focus on cooperation between major powers (see Axelrod, 1981; Axelrod and Keohane, 1985; Gowa, 1986; Grieco, 1988; Jervis, 1978, 1988; Keohane, 1984; Krasner, 1982; Lipson, 1984; Martin and Simmons, 1998; Mearsheimer, 2001; Moravcsik, 1993; Oye, 1985; Singer, 1958; Snidal, 1985; 1991; Waltz 1979). Little attention has been given to the study of middle power participation in cooperation arrangements, some of which they have little influence on.

By focusing solely on Indonesia's participation in maritime security cooperation, I provide a starting point for a new research agenda to search for the reasons underpinning emerging middle power participation in cooperation arrangements. Most literature on middle power focuses on explaining traditional middle power leadership at international organisations such as the United Nations (Behringer, 2005, especially p. 305; Chapnick, 1999; Fox, 1980; Glazebrook, 1947; Granatstein, 1973, 2011; Higgott and Cooper, 1990; 2000; Holmes, 1976; Otte and Greve, 2000, pp. 7–8; Ravenhill, 1998). These works primarily centre on Canadian and Australian foreign policy (Behringer, 2005, especially p. 305; Chapnick, 1999; 2000; Fox, 1980; Glazebrook, 1947; Granatstein, 1973; 2011; Higgott and Cooper, 1990; Holmes, 1976; Ravenhill, 1998).

Very little attention has been given to discussing the behaviour of emerging middle powers such as Indonesia. Some of the literature has specifically referred to Indonesia as a rising middle power in the international system (Emmerson, 2012; Frigo, 2013; Halimi, 2014; *Jakarta Post*, 2014; Laksmana, 2011; Ping, 2005; Roberts and Habir, 2014, p. 6). This primarily surveys Indonesia's key attributes as a middle power – including population, geographic area, military expenditure, Gross Domestic Product (GDP), value of exports, gross national income per capita, trade as percentage of GDP and life expectancy at birth in comparison to other states – and examines the implications of Indonesia's rise towards regional and global order (Frigo, 2013; Halimi, 2014; *Jakarta Post*, 2014; Laksmana, 2011; Ping, 2005; Reid, 2012; Roberts *et al.*, 2015). It does not account for the middle power's varying participation in international cooperation. The existing studies on middle powers show a lack of theoretical discussion on factors that inform state decisions in approaching different cooperation settings (see Efstathopoulos, 2011; Jordaan, 2003; Neufeld, 1995; Pfister, 2005; Ping, 2005; Westhuizen, 1998).

Some of the literature on Indonesia cooperation only implicitly draws inspiration from international relations accounts of international cooperation (constructivism, neoliberalism and neorealism) and foreign policy analysis (the bureaucratic politics approach). A number of works on Southeast Asia have echoed the constructivist explanation of the origin of cooperation. Ball, Acharya, and Johnston point to the role of the so called 'ASEAN spirit' or 'ASEAN Way' that mainly relies on discussion, consensus and accommodation at the high political level in solving disputes among member states and advancing security cooperation among them (Acharya, 1992; 1995; 1997, pp. 328–329; 1998, p. 80; 2004, pp. 249, 256; Acharya and Tan, 2006, pp. 42, 53; Ball, 1993, p. 53; Johnston, 1999, pp. 294–295). The 'ASEAN Way' that is embraced by Southeast Asian states can explain the growing cooperation and the avoidance of inter-state conflict in the region. As Acharya explains, the dense networks of regional military security cooperation in Southeast Asia were started from bilateral border security arrangements that have evolved into 'an overlapping and interlocking network' of a regional security system (Acharya, 1992, p. 10, 1995, p. 191).

Ball, Acharya and Johnston advance the constructivist argument that states that share similar identities are more likely to cooperate with each other (Acharya, 1997, pp. 320, 324, 327, 328–333; Ball, 1993, pp. 46–47, 53, 55, 59–60; Johnston, 1999, pp. 290–291, 295–297; see also Hemmer and Katzenstein, 2002, pp. 575–576, 588–589, 592–593; Wendt, 1995, p. 77, 1992, pp. 400–401, 417–418). They develop a collective identity that refers to positive identification with the well-being of others (Wendt, 1994, p. 386). Collective identity provides an important foundation for cooperation by increasing willingness for states to diffuse reciprocity and act on the basis of 'generalised principles of conduct, that is, principles which specify appropriate conduct for a class of actions, without regard to the particularistic interests of the parties or the strategic exigencies that may exist in any specific occurrence' (Ruggie, 1992, p. 571; see also Wendt, 1994, p. 386). According to this line of argument, Indonesia should be more likely to cooperate with ASEAN member states. In order to incorporate the constructivist argument on the reasons affecting a state's willingness to cooperate, I use ASEAN membership as a proxy for shared identity.

The existing literature does not provide much insight on the neorealist conception of relative gains. To find plausible explanations for Indonesia's participation in international cooperation, this review of the literature proceeds with the neorealist account of the role of relative gains. According to neorealism, states are preoccupied with their survival and uncertainty about other states' future intentions and actions. This circumstance compels states to emphasise relative gains in cooperation (Waltz, 1979, p. 105). States not only consider how much they gain in the deal, but also how much they obtain in comparison to the other side (Krasner, 2002, p. 139). Giving serious attention to the gains of cooperation partners addresses the concerns about survival and uncertainty, as states can achieve a more comprehensive and accurate understanding of distribution of benefits and capabilities (Grieco, 1988, p. 487; Krasner, 1991, p. 362). A state will refuse to join, will leave, or will limit its commitment to a cooperation agreement if it deems that its partners are achieving relatively larger gains (Grieco, 1988, p. 499). The lack of neorealist accounts in the existing literature on maritime cooperation is surprising, given that neorealism claims to explain security particularly well (Krasner, 1992, p. 40).

Given Indonesia's status as a middle power, neorealists would expect Indonesia to cooperate with either much larger or smaller states, because the vast power inequality between Indonesia and these states would be less detrimental to Indonesia's survival (Elman, 1996, p. 24; Krasner, 1992, p. 39; Waltz, 2000, p. 38). In contrast, Indonesia would be expected to refuse to cooperate with its near-peer competitors due to the insignificant power disparity between them. If a cooperation arrangement brings greater gains for its near-peer competitors, the competitor would be in a position to challenge and threaten Indonesia (Christiansen, 2001, p. 8).

In assessing relative gains concerns, I look at Indonesia and its cooperation partners' positions in the power spectrum (Christiansen, 2001, p. 6). Indonesia's cooperation partners will be put into three categories: larger, near-peer and smaller states. Following convention, military spending is used as a proxy for power (see Table I.2; Christensen, 2001, p. 6; Handberg, 2013, p. 209; Kurth, 2007, p. 597).

Some works have implicitly made reference to the neoliberal absolute gains argument (Bradford, 2004, pp. 480–505; Sato, 2007, pp. 1–10). For neoliberals, it is absolute gains rather than relative gains that matter for states (Keohane, 1984, p. 80). States will cooperate if that would make them better off than if they had not cooperated (Keohane and Martin, 1995, pp. 44–45). The costs and benefits of cooperation are influenced by the institutional design of each agreement. Bradford and Sato draw attention to the importance of the calculation of aggregate costs and benefits in informing Indonesia's non-cooperation in the ReCAAP. They claim that Indonesia did not join the ReCAAP because of perceived low benefits and high costs of cooperation (Bradford, 2004, pp. 497–498; Sato, 2007, pp. 6–7). This literature only mentions the costs and benefits in passing and tends to overemphasise sovereignty costs without specifying why the agreement brought with it high sovereignty costs or assessing the institutional design of the ReCAAP agreement. Nevertheless, the expectation would be for Indonesia to join a cooperation arrangement only if the aggregate benefits provided by the agreement outweighed the costs.

I define the term 'benefit' as the net advantage obtained by a participant from cooperation (See Oxford dictionary, 2006). As is extensively explained in the literature on maritime security, some benefits gained from cooperation arrangements contribute directly to Indonesia's efforts to counter maritime terrorism and sea robbery. These benefits include burden sharing with neighbouring countries to secure important sea lanes and opportunities to gain maritime capacity-building training and new equipment from other cooperation partners (Djalal 2009a, pp. 21–22; 2009b, pp. 327–329; Ho, 2007a, pp. 213–216; 2007b,

Table I.2 Categories of cooperation partners, based on comparison of defence expenditure

Larger states	Near-peer states	Smaller states
United States	Singapore	The Philippines
China	Malaysia	Brunei
Japan	Thailand	Cambodia
India		Laos
South Korea		
Australia		

Source: Military Balance 2013: 548–554.

Notes
1 Larger states are countries in the world's top 15 defence budgets in 2012. The defence budgets of these states are at least 300 per cent higher than Indonesia's defence budget.
2 Near-peer states are countries with defence budgets that deviate by less than plus or minus 50 per cent from Indonesia's total defence budget.
3 Smaller states are countries with defence budgets that deviate by more than minus 50 per cent from Indonesia's total defence budget.

pp. 29–30; Sjaastad, 2007, pp. 11–12; Sondakh, 2006, pp. 88–89; Stryken, 2007, p. 135). The existing literature also acknowledges the existence of some side benefits, such as developing undeveloped border areas, facilitating negotiation of other treaties and developing the country's military industry (Bakti, 2010, p. 300; Elisabeth, 2008, pp. 43–44; Kristiadi, 2007). The benefits of cooperation are categorised as high or low. High benefits emerge when the incentives of cooperation are tangible/concrete and are not available elsewhere. In contrast, low benefits occur when there are no identifiable benefits or if the benefits of cooperation are available elsewhere.

As argued by some international relations scholars, the costs of cooperation consist of sovereignty and implementation costs (Abbott, 1999; Abbott and Snidal, 2000; Kahler, 2000; Raustiala and Slaughter, 2002). The sovereignty costs are the symbolic and material costs that are associated with the lessening of national autonomy (Abbott, 1999, p. 375). In assessing sovereignty costs, I categorise sovereignty costs as high or low. Under the condition of high sovereignty costs, states have to accept external authority over significant decisions making or, in more extreme conditions, interference from external authorities in the relations between the state and its citizens or territory (Abbott and Snidal, 2000, p. 437). The cooperation agreement may explicitly or implicitly insert international actors into national decision procedures or may require states to change domestic legislation and structures of governance (Abbott and Snidal, 2000, p. 437). In this regard, in assessing sovereignty costs the degree of costs are considered high if the cooperation agreement explicitly limits a state's rights to govern its territory, delegates authority to settle disputes to an international tribunal or gives a third party authority to monitor compliance with a cooperation arrangement. Under the condition of low sovereignty costs, a state is not required to make significant legal and governance changes at domestic level or accept external authority in its decision-making process (Abbott and Snidal, 2000, p. 437).

The second component of costs that need to be considered is the implementation costs. This type of cost is incurred in 'the process of putting international commitments into practice: the passage of legislation, creation of institutions (both domestic and international) and enforcement of rules' (Raustiala and Slaughter, 2002, p. 539). Accordingly, implementation costs can be divided into two categories: high and low. High implementation costs occur when a state needs to carry out extensive policy changes, create new legislation and institutions at a domestic level and therefore exhausts economic resources to meet cooperation requirements. Low implementation costs occur when the international commitment is already compatible with a state's current practice. Thus, adjustment is 'unnecessary and compliance is automatic' (Raustiala and Slaughter, 2002, p. 539).

A number of studies also touch upon the theme of neorealist and neoliberal hegemonic leadership. The hegemonic leadership concept suggests that the presence of a hegemon is sufficient to affect whether other states cooperate (Gilpin, 1975, p. 85; 1981, p. 30; Keohane, 1984, p. 49; 1982, pp. 326, 330; Krasner,

1976, p. 322; Lipson, 1984, p. 19; Strange, 1987, p. 555). King, Byers, Stryken, Rosenberg and Chung discuss US efforts to promote new maritime security cooperation, including the Customs–Trade Partnership against Terrorism, the PSI, the CSI, and the RMSI (Byers, 2003, pp. 171–190; 2004; King, 2005, pp. 236, 241; Rosenberg and Chung, 2008, pp. 53–54, 63–64; Stryken, 2007, pp. 136–137, 141–142). Some authors point out that the US was willing to enforce the PSI and the CSI rules by interdicting vessels suspected of carrying weapons of mass destruction (WMD) and placing US Customs and Border Protection (CBP) monitoring teams in foreign ports and, therefore, to bear the enforcement costs of cooperation (Byers, 2004, pp. 527–528; King, 2005, p. 241; Rosenberg and Chung, 2008, pp. 53–54). Authors also note that the US was willing to provide selective incentives – in the form of equipment and capacity-building assistance – to other states in order to encourage participation (Stryken, 2007, pp. 135–136; Rosenberg and Chung, 2008, p. 64). In the case of maritime security cooperation, it is arguable that the US is willing to gain less relative to others in order to secure its objectives of establishing and promoting maritime security initiatives, as suggested by US offers to bear the enforcement costs and provide selective incentives. This literature, however, focuses exclusively on what the US did, not how it influenced the considerations of other states. Nonetheless, the expectation would be that states are more likely to participate when there is hegemonic leadership.

The assessment of hegemonic leadership is made by examining whether the US advanced and promoted cooperation initiatives, was willing to bear enforcement costs or provided incentives such as training and equipment to encourage participation (Rosenberg and Chung, 2008, p. 64; Stryken, 2007, pp. 135–136). Hegemonic leadership is considered high when the US proposes and promotes a maritime security initiative, bears the enforcement costs and/or offers selective benefits. Low hegemonic leadership takes place when the US does not carry out much action in a cooperation initiative that it is involved in.

Some scholarly works have used bureaucratic politics to understand Indonesia's foreign policy making (Emmerson, 1983, pp. 1220, 1223; Jackson, 1978, p. 395; 1980, pp. 10–11; Liddle, 1985, p. 70; Nabbs-Keller, 2013, pp. 56, 68; Suryadinata, 1998, pp. 48–55). Although these works do not refer to the influence of bureaucratic politics in informing Indonesia's maritime security policy, they provide useful insight on bureaucratic politics accounts of Indonesia's foreign policy more generally (Emmerson, 1983, pp. 1220, 1223; Jackson, 1978, p. 395; 1980, pp. 10–11; Liddle, 1985, p. 70; Nabbs-Keller, 2013, pp. 56, 68; Suryadinata, 1998, pp. 48–55). Liddle, Jackson, Suryadinata and Emmerson, for instance, claim that during Suharto's rule (1966–98) the military, particularly the army, held the most power in the decision-making process and carefully controlled those parts of the bureaucracy connected to security, including the Ministry of Defence, the Ministry of Home Affairs, the Ministry of Information, the Ministry of Justice, and the Ministry of Foreign Affairs (MFA) (Emmerson, 1983, pp. 1223, 1228, 1230; Jackson, 1978, pp. 10–11; Liddle, 1985, pp. 70–71; Suryadinata, 1998, pp. 50–51). Nabbs-Keller draws attention to the important role of the Indonesian MFA in formulating Indonesia's foreign policy and redefining Indonesia's image as the 'world's third largest democracy' following political reform in 1998 (Nabbs-Keller, 2013, pp. 56, 68). This suggests that bureaucratic politics may explain Indonesia's decisions to cooperate, but this proposition has not been systematically tested. This book seeks to address that gap.

The bureaucratic politics approach to the analysis of foreign policy, first introduced by Allison, focuses on assessing interaction among governmental actors in bargaining games (Allison and Zelikow, 1999, p. 255; Carlsnaes, 2006, p. 338). Bureaucratic politics focuses on the process of the formulation and reformulation of a policy decision through the interaction of various actors' competing preferences (Allison and Zelikow, 1999, p. 255). Each actor is involved in the 'deadly serious games' of bargaining to advance their conception of national, organisational, group and personal interests (Allison and Zelikow, 1999, pp. 295, 302). Therefore, the bureaucratic politics approach suggests that cooperation is most likely to occur when it serves the interests of the governmental actors that prevail in the internal decision-making process.

Among government ministries, the Indonesian MFA plays a central role in foreign policy formulation. Nabbs-Keller explains that the Indonesian foreign ministry is the main actor responsible for formulating foreign policy, managing Indonesia's external relations and carrying out the country's diplomacy (Nabbs-Keller, 2013, pp. 56, 58). Ruland (2009, p. 399) confirms that, despite much reform, the Indonesian foreign ministry views treaty-making as an executive prerogative (Juwana, 2008 p. 450; Parthiana, 2008, p. 470; see also Dosch, 2006, p. 62; Indonesian Parliament, 25 September 2006, 25 January 2007, 26 February 2007, 28 May 2007, 25 June 2007, 9 July 2007; Sherlock, 2003, p. 20; Suhartono, 2001, p. 165).[2] In the Reform Era, the government issued a series of laws that provides the MFA with the authority to formulate and implement national policies in the field of foreign policy (Indonesian MFA, 2006, p. 13; 2009).[3] In this context, the MFA is the leading institution in international maritime security diplomacy, although other ministries have input (Indonesian Coordinating Ministry for Political, Legal and Security Affairs, 2007, p. 31; Indonesian MFA, 2005a, p. 21; 2005b, p. 19). The MFA organises inter-ministerial meetings to settle Indonesia's decisions on international security cooperation.[4] The inter-ministerial meetings involve other government agencies, including the Ministry of Defence (MoD), Navy, the Ministry of Transportation (MoT), the Ministry of Marine and Fisheries, Customs and Excise and the Coordinating Ministry for Political, Legal and Security Affairs.[5] As is often the norm with maritime security, when international cooperation concerns activities that fall under the remit of this ministry the MFA shares leadership, both in representing the government internationally and in discussing them domestically (Juwana, 2008, p. 449).[6] The MFA would likely share leadership with other relevant government institutions if a cooperation initiative covered technical matters, for instance regulation of security in ports or on board vessels registered under Indonesian flags, interdiction at sea, customs laws or naval patrol coordination.

Discussion regarding governmental actors' preferences in this book is based on the literature on Indonesia's bureaucratic politics, which highlights the importance of leading governmental actors in informing Indonesia's decision (Emmerson, 1983, pp. 1220, 1223; Jackson, 1978, 395; Liddle, 1985, p. 70; Nabbs-Keller, 2013, pp. 56, 58; Suryadinata, 1998, pp. 48–55). Governmental actors' preferences are clustered into two categories: 'in favour' and 'not in favour'. The 'in favour' category means that the government actors leading the negotiation at the international level and deliberations at national level stated their support for the cooperation initiative and carried out programmes to promote Indonesia's participation in it. The 'not in favour' category means that the government actors that were assigned principal tasks as leading agencies stated their opposition to Indonesia's participation in a cooperation initiative.

In conclusion, there are five plausible explanations offered by constructivism, neorealism, neoliberalism and the bureaucratic politics approach to understand Indonesia's participation in maritime security cooperation:

- First, following the constructivist argument on collective identities, Indonesia would be more likely to cooperate with other ASEAN states.
- Second, in line with the neorealist argument on the importance of relative gains consideration Indonesia would likely refuse to cooperate with its near-peer(s) and agree to cooperate with larger and smaller states.
- Third, according to the neoliberal claim on the role of the absolute gains calculation, Indonesia would only join a cooperation arrangement where the benefits of cooperation outweighed the costs.
- Fourth, the neorealist and neoliberal idea of hegemonic leadership implies that the presence of a hegemon would increase the likelihood that Indonesia would cooperate.
- Finally, the bureaucratic politics approach suggests that Indonesia is most likely to cooperate when the arrangement benefits key government actors.

The significance of Indonesia in the study of maritime security

The study of Indonesia's participation informs analytical and empirical debates in the study of maritime security. In the period after 11 September 2001, the potential for maritime terrorism and sea robbery in the Straits of Malacca and Singapore grabbed headlines in the media. The Straits are an area of enormous significance. The majority of Middle East oil exports to Asia and most commerce between Asia and Europe pass through this 610-mile-long strait (Coutrier, 1988, p. 186). At least 600 ships navigate through the Straits of Malacca and Singapore every day (Indonesian MFA, 2006, p. 14). This includes 72 per cent of super tankers and other vessels plying between the Indian and Pacific Oceans, making these Straits the busiest sea lane of communication and for the oil trade globally. At its narrowest point, the Straits are only 1.7 miles wide and 25 meters deep at its shallowest point, creating a natural bottleneck and making it vulnerable to potential collisions, grounding, oil spills or terrorist attack (Reuters, 2010; United States Energy Information Administration, 2011). Understanding how Indonesia, the largest littoral state of the Straits, deals with maritime terrorism and armed robbery against ships is crucial, given the country's engagement in maritime cooperation is a matter of some import for the international community. This is deemed important, as the number of armed robbery attacks in the Straits has been on the increase since 2011. By 2014 Indonesian waters accounted for more than 40 per cent of worldwide armed robberies against ships (IMB, 2014). The increase in attacks on ships in Indonesian waters has generated enormous concern among states such as Singapore who are concerned about the security of the archipelagic sea lanes.[7]

By focusing on Indonesia's policies to deal with maritime threats, this book also provides a fresh perspective on the varying cooperation instruments that a developing country can use to address the two maritime security threats. The existing literature on maritime security cooperation is largely descriptive and focuses on piracy in East Africa and Southeast Asia. Scholarly works that touch upon Indonesia's efforts to secure its sea lanes (notably the Straits of Malacca and Singapore) is fragmented, considering only one or a few cases of cooperation at a time (Anggoro, 2009, pp. 59–80; Djalal, 2007, 51–58; 2009; Nasrun, 2009, pp. 115–133; Purdjianto, 2009, pp. 27–42; Purnomo, 2004, pp. 27–40; Sondakh, 2004, pp. 1–26). The explanations suggested by the descriptive literature for Indonesia's participation in cooperation can be grouped into three categories: functional motivations, concerns about sovereignty costs, and economic disinterest.

The, usually implicit, functional argument describes the presence of maritime terrorism and sea robbery threats and identifies a series of policy responses. This group of scholarly works focuses on the maritime security problems to be solved. They explain that Indonesia has been involved in bilateral, trilateral and regional maritime cooperation to secure key waterways, particularly the Straits of Malacca and Singapore and the Indian Ocean (Djalal, 2004, pp. 419–440; 2007, pp. 51–58; 2009a, pp. 8–26; 2009b, pp. 315–332; Sondakh, 2004, pp. 3–26; 2006, pp. 79–90; Wisnumurti, 2009, pp. 333–352). These descriptive works on Indonesia's maritime cooperation elaborate on the existing maritime security threats, policies to deal with these issues and the limitations and constraints faced by the country (Anggoro, 2009, pp. 59–80; Nasrun, 2009, pp. 115–133; Purdjianto, 2009, pp. 27–42; Purnomo, 2004, pp. 27–40; Sondakh, 2004, pp. 1–26; Wisnumurti, 2009, pp. 115–133). They only focus on successful cases of cooperation. Implicitly, these works show how Indonesia assesses the costs and benefits of cooperation. Their argument overstates the benefits of cooperation relative to costs, suggesting that Indonesia should always cooperate. Therefore, the functional motivations argument cannot offer a satisfactory explanation of Indonesia's non-cooperation in a number of cases such as the SUA convention and the ReCAAP.

Those that focus on non-cooperation overstate sovereignty costs. Bradford, Huang, Valencia, Shie, Bateman, Hassan, Bingley, Sittnick and Murphy point to concerns over sovereignty infringement as the reason underpinning Indonesia's non-cooperation in a number of agreements including the RMSI, the ReCAAP, the SUA convention, the CSI and the PSI (Bateman, 2007, p. 109; 2009, p. 118; Bingley, 2004, pp. 363–364; Bradford, 2005, pp. 73–75; 2008, p. 489; Huang, 2008, p. 93; Murphy, 2009, pp. 169, 174; Shie, 2006, p. 178; Sittnick, 2005, pp. 752, 754; Valencia, 2006, p. 89). The notion of sovereignty in their works refers to government's concern and sensitivity over potential breaches of sovereignty, which they do not define. Their works highlight the possibility of US warships patrolling Indonesian waters as the main source of concern about sovereignty generated by the RMSI (Huang, 2008, p. 93; Murphy, 2009, p. 174; Sittnick, 2005, pp. 754–755). The placement of US officials in foreign ports under the CSI and the PSI's interdiction activity against ships suspected of carrying WMD materials is cited as the main sovereignty concerns raised by the two US-led initiatives (Rosenberg and Chung, 2008, p. 62). These works implicitly point to the way Indonesia calculates its costs and benefits. However, by over emphasising sovereignty concerns, these scholarly works overstate the importance of the costs of cooperation and neglect the benefits. As a consequence, they overlook Indonesia's willingness to participate in maritime security cooperation including that which involves cross-border sea and air patrols and to provide to other states access to its port facilities, airspace and land territory.

The third line of argument found in the descriptive literature argues that Indonesia's lack of economic interest limits its willingness to join maritime cooperation. Raymond, Mak, Huang, Mo, Ho, Desker, and Stryken explain that Indonesia's interest in pursuing international cooperation to secure the straits is the lowest among the three littoral states that border the Straits of Malacca. They argue that this is because, in comparison to Singapore and Malaysia, Indonesia has a smaller economic stake in the Straits of Malacca because it is the least dependent on seaborne international trade (Ho, 2009, p. 734; Huang, 2008, p. 91; Mak, 2006, pp. 135–136, 152, 156–157; Mo, 2002, p. 351; Raymond, 2007, p. 88; Stryken, 2007, 139). These works pay attention to how Indonesia weighs costs and benefits but they have understated the benefits of cooperation and implied that Indonesia should always be less cooperative. As a result, they can only explain Indonesia's non-cooperation.

These descriptive works, therefore, cannot explain why Indonesia cooperates sometimes, but not others. They are, nonetheless, a valuable resource for this book because they provide a detailed account of various international agreements, including those which Indonesia chose to join or not to join, how they were established and what Indonesia could receive in exchange for participating in these initiatives. I, therefore, use the descriptive literature on Indonesia's maritime cooperation as a point of departure.

Outline of this book

Chapter 1 emphasises the main question that this book seeks to address. It provides detailed background for the chapters that follow. This chapter explains the problems posed by maritime terrorism and armed robbery against ships. It then establishes the importance of Indonesia in maritime security and describes Indonesia's unilateral policies, including the allocation of resources, to address maritime terrorism and sea robbery. This chapter also details the various maritime threats faced by Indonesia to contextualise maritime terrorism and armed robbery against ships against the wider issues that Indonesia faces.

Chapter 2 outlines two important points for understanding the limit of bureaucratic politics in cooperation. First, this chapter shows the limitation of a bureaucratic politics approach for understanding Indonesia's participation and non-participation in maritime security arrangements. Allison's bureaucratic politics focuses on the process of the formulation and reformulation of policy decisions through the interaction of various actors' competing preferences. This chapter demonstrates that Indonesia has a distinct bureaucratic politics, different from Allison's focus on competing preferences of various government institutions involved in the policy process. Given the Ministry of Foreign Affairs's dominant role in Indonesia's foreign policy, competitive bargaining among self-interested actors as expected by the bureaucratic politics literature does not take place. Second, this chapter provides detailed background information on Indonesia's domestic political dynamics. It highlights the political practices that have changed and what remains the same in post-authoritarian Indonesia. This chapter elaborates on the specifics of Indonesia's bureaucratic politics. Drawing on documents and interview sources, this chapter identifies key actors and the institutional process of Indonesia's foreign and security policy making.

Chapter 3 is grounded theoretically in the neorealist and neoliberal argument regarding the role of the hegemon in inducing cooperation. This chapter first explains Indonesia's close cooperation with the US at bilateral level. Second, it explores unsuccessful cases of cooperation, including the SUA convention, the PSI, the CSI and the RMSI. Using government documents, newspaper articles and research by Indonesian scholars, this chapter argues that US leadership was not enough to change Indonesia's calculation of gains sufficiently for it to cooperate. This chapter also examines the behaviour of the US in maritime security cooperation. Indonesia's participation in US-led initiatives was important to the US objectives of halting the proliferation and transportation of WMD and securing important sea lanes from terrorist and sea robbery attacks; yet, the US did not coerce Indonesia to join cooperation initiatives that Jakarta has rejected, such as the SUA convention, the PSI, the CSI and the RMSI. In order to explain US behaviour towards Indonesia, this chapter offers a comprehensive explanation of Indonesia's cooperation in US unilateral initiatives, such as the International Port Security Programme and the US Customs–Trade Partnership against Terrorism, that have sufficiently induced changes at the domestic level.

Chapter 4 questions the dominant view amongst scholars that the ASEAN Way, as a form of shared identity among Southeast Asian states, played an important role in shaping cooperation. This chapter challenges theoretically the constructivist argument that states which share similar identities are more likely to cooperate with each other. Constructivism deems that these states develop a collective identity that refers to positive identification with the well-being of others. To begin with, this chapter familiarises readers with the notion of the ASEAN Way, which emphasises the role of consensus and accommodation to settle disputes and advance security cooperation among ASEAN member states. Given that the ASEAN Way identity is believed to be embraced by ASEAN states, it is argued that ASEAN membership is an appropriate proxy for shared identity. This chapter argues that shared identity did not inform Indonesia's decision to cooperate or not cooperate with its neighbouring states. To support this argument, it first explains Indonesia's cooperation and non-cooperation when dealing with fellow ASEAN states. This chapter finishes by examining Indonesia's extensive cooperation with non-ASEAN states.

Chapter 5 explains how the calculation of absolute gains trumps concern over relative gains. This chapter is based theoretically on the neorealist and neoliberal debate regarding the calculation of costs and benefits. The first part of this chapter examines the calculation of relative gains across all cooperation initiatives dealing with maritime terrorism and sea robbery. The second part of this chapter explores the calculation of costs and gains in absolute terms. It assesses both the sovereignty and implementation costs of various agreements. This is important since the burgeoning literature on Indonesia's maritime security overstates the sovereignty costs. As a consequence, they overlook Indonesia's willingness to participate in maritime security cooperation including that which involve cross-border sea and air patrols and to provide to other states access to its port facilities, airspace and land territory.

The concluding chapter brings together the threads of the argument and the main findings presented in the core chapters. It reiterates the place that this research has in the current literature and its contribution both to the IR literature on cooperation and the middle power literature. It then proceeds with a section that identifies areas for future research.

Notes

1 Interview with a high government official in the Indonesian Navy (Jakarta, 14 July 2010).
2 Despite this existing legislation requiring the government to seek agreement from the Parliament on international agreements, particularly those related to defence and security, a large proportion of such agreements have been implemented at national level without prior ratification by the Parliament. The Parliament tends to focus on problems related to preservation of territorial integrity, including separatist movements in Aceh, the Moluccas and West Papua, and a number of issues that reflect deep anti-Israeli and anti-American sentiments among the Moslem-majority public, such as the relation between Arab nations and Israel, responses to the 9/11 attacks and the 2002 Bali bombings. This point was confirmed in interviews with an Indonesian government official (Jakarta, 4 November 2011) and an Indonesian foreign and security policy expert at the University of Indonesia (Depok, 11 October 2011) and email correspondence with a former expert member of staff of the Indonesian Parliament, 24 April 2013).

16 *Introduction*

3 These laws are the Presidential Regulation No. 9 of 2005 regarding the position, duties, roles, structure, and work procedure of the state ministries of the Republic of Indonesia (Articles 31 and 32); Law No. 39 of 2008 on state ministries (Article 7) and Law No. 37 of 1999.
4 Interviews with an Indonesian government official (Jakarta, 4 November 2011); a high government official at the Indonesian MoD (Jakarta, 7 July 2010); a high government official in the Indonesian Navy (Jakarta, 14 July 2010); an Indonesian security policy expert at the University of Indonesia (Depok, 11 October 2011); and an Indonesian foreign and security policy expert at the University of Indonesia (Depok, 11 October 2011).
5 Interviews with an Indonesian government official (Jakarta, 4 November 2011); a former high government official at the MoD (Depok, 8 October 2011); and a high government official at the Indonesian Maritime Security Coordinating Board (Jakarta, 2 July 2010).
6 Interviews with a high government official at the Indonesian MoD (Jakarta, 7 July 2010); and two high government officials at the Indonesian MoT (Jakarta, 3 September 2010).
7 Interview with a Singaporean official (Singapore, 11 August 2015).

References

Abbot, Kenneth W. (1999). 'International Relations Theory, International Law, and the Regime Governing Atrocities in Internal Conflicts'. *The American Journal of International Law* 93:2, pp. 361–379.

Abbot, Kenneth W. and Snidal, Duncan. (2000). 'Hard and Soft Law in International Governance'. *International Organization* 54:3, pp. 421–456.

Acharya, Amitav. (1992). 'Regional Military-Security Cooperation in the Third World: A Conceptual Analysis of the Relevance and Limitations of ASEAN (Association of Southeast Asian Nations)'. *Journal of Peace Research*, February 29, pp. 7–21.

Acharya, Amitav. (1995). 'A Regional Security Community in Southeast Asia?' *Journal of Strategic Studies* 18:3, pp. 175–200.

Acharya, Amitav. (1997). 'Ideas, Identity and Institution Building: From the "ASEAN Way" to the "Asia–Pacific Way"?' *The Pacific Review* 10:3, pp. 319–346.

Acharya, Amitav. (1998). 'Culture, Security, Multilateralism: The "ASEAN Way" and Regional Order'. *Contemporary Security Policy* 19:1, pp. 55–84.

Acharya, Amitav. (2004). 'How Ideas Spread: Whose Norms Matter? Norm Localization and Institutional Change in Asian Regionalism'. *International Organization* 58:2, pp. 239–275.

Acharya, Amitav and Tan, See Seng. (2006). 'Betwixt Balance and Community: America, ASEAN and the Security of Southeast Asia'. *International Relations of the Asia Pacific* 6:1, pp. 37–59.

Allison, Graham and Zelikow, Philip. (1999). *Essence of Decision: Explaining the Cuban Missile Crisis*, 2nd edition. New York: Wesley Longman.

Anggoro, Kusnanto. (2009). 'Strategi Pertahanan Kepulauan, Diplomasi Kelautan dan Kekuatan Matra Laut Indonesia'. *Jurnal Diplomasi* 1:2, pp. 59–83.

Axelrod, Robert. (1981). 'The Emergence of Cooperation among Egoists'. *American Political Science Review* 75:2, pp. 306–318.

Axelrod, Robert and Keohane, Robert O. (1985). 'Achieving Cooperation under Anarchy: Strategies and Institutions'. *World Politics* 38:1, pp. 226–254.

Bakti, Ikrar Nusa. (2010). 'Bilateral Relations between Indonesia and the Philippines:

Stable and Cooperative', in *International Relations in Southeast Asia: Between Bilateralism and Multilateralism*, N. Ganesan and Ramses Amer (eds). Singapore: ISEAS.

Ball, Desmond. (1993). 'Strategic Culture in the Asia–Pacific Region'. *Security Studies* 3:1, pp. 44–74.

Bateman, Sam. (2007). 'Building Good Order at Sea in Southeast Asia: The Promise of International Regimes', in *Maritime Security in Southeast Asia*, Kwa Chong Guan and John K. Skogan (eds). New York: Routledge, pp. 97–116.

Behringer, Ronald M. (2005). 'Middle Power Leadership on the Human Security Agenda'. *Cooperation and Conflict* 40:3, pp. 305–342.

Bingley, Barrett. (2004). 'Security Interests of the Influencing States: The Complexity of Malacca Straits'. *The Indonesian Quarterly* 32:4, pp. 353–383.

Bradford, John F. (2004). 'Japanese Anti-Piracy Initiatives in Southeast Asia: Policy Formulation and the Coastal States Responses'. *Contemporary Southeast Asia* 26:3, pp. 480–505.

Bradford, John F. (2005). 'The Growing Prospects for Maritime Security Cooperation in Southeast Asia'. *Naval War College Review* 56:3, pp. 63–86.

Bradford, John F. (2008). 'Shifting the Tides against Piracy in Southeast Asian Waters'. *Asian Survey* 48:3, pp. 473–491.

Byers, Michael. (2003). 'Preemptive Self-defense: Hegemony, Equality and Strategies of Legal Change'. *Journal of Political Philosophy* 11:2, pp. 171–190.

Byers, Michael. (2004). 'Policing the High Seas: The Proliferation Security Initiative'. *The American Journal of International Law* 98:3, pp. 526–545.

Carana. (2004). *Impact of Transport and Logistics on Indonesia's Trade Competitiveness*, available at www.carana.com/images/PDF_car/Indonesia%20Transport%20and%20 Logistics%20Report.pdf. Last accessed 20 January 2011.

Carlsnaes, Walter. (2006). 'Foreign Policy', in *Handbook of International Relations*, Walter Carlsnaes, Thomas Risse and Beth A. Simmons (eds). London: Sage Publications.

Chalk, Peter. (1998). 'Contemporary Maritime Piracy in Southeast Asia'. *Studies in Conflict and Terrorism* 21:1, pp. 87–112.

Chapnick, Adam. (1999). 'The Middle Power'. *Canadian Foreign Policy* 7:2, pp. 73–82.

Chapnick, Adam. (2000). 'The Canadian Middle Power Myth'. *International Journal* 55:2, pp. 188–206.

Christensen, Thomas J. (2001). 'Posing Problems without Catching up: China's Rise and Challenges for US Security Policy'. *International Security* 25:4, pp. 5–40.

Coutrier, P.L. (1988). 'Living on an Oil Highway'. *Ambio* 17:3, pp. 186–188.

Djalal, Hasjim. (2004). 'Piracy In South East Asia: Indonesia and Regional Responses'. *Indonesian Journal of International Law* 1:3, 419–440.

Djalal, Hasjim. (2007). 'The Strategic Values of the Indian Ocean to Indonesian Diplomacy, Law and Politics', in *The Security of Sea Lanes of Communication in the Indian Ocean Region*, Dennis Rumley, Sanjay Chaturvedi and Mat Taib Yasin (eds). Kuala Lumpur: Maritime Institute of Malaysia.

Djalal, Hasjim. (2009a). 'The Regime of Managing Safety and Security in the Straits of Malacca and Singapore'. *Jurnal Diplomasi* 1:2, pp. 8–26.

Djalal, Hasjim. (2009b). 'Regulation of International Straits'. *Indonesian Journal of International Law* 6:3, pp. 315–332.

Dosch, Jorn. (2006). 'The Impact of Democratization on the Making of Foreign Policy in Indonesia, Thailand and the Philippines'. *Journal of Current Southeast Asian Affairs* 25:5, pp. 42–70.

Efstathopoulos, Charalampos. (2011). 'Reinterpreting India's Rise through the Middle Power Prism'. *Asian Journal of Political Science* 19:1, pp. 74–95.
Elisabeth, Adriana. (2008). *The Role of the Philippines in the BIMP-EAGA Growth Triangle and the Dynamics of ASEAN Political Economy*, PhD Thesis, Department of History and Politics, University of Wollongong, 2008, available at http://ru.uow.edu.au/theses/52. Last accessed 20 November 2012.
Elman, Colin. (1996). 'Horses for Courses: Why Not Neorealist Theories of Foreign Policy?' *Security Studies* 6:1, pp. 7–53.
Emmerson, Donald K. (1983). 'Understanding the New Order: Bureaucratic Pluralism in Indonesia'. *Asian Survey* 23:11, pp. 1220–1241.
Emmerson, Donald K. (2012). 'Is Indonesia Rising? It Depends', in *Indonesia Rising: the Repositioning of Asia's Third Giant*, Anthony Reid (ed.). Singapore: ISEAS.
Fox, Annette Baker. (1980). 'The Range of Choice for Middle Powers: Australian and Canada Compared'. *Australian Journal of Politics and History* 26:2, pp. 193–203.
Frigo, Michael. (2013). 'Indonesia: A Rising Economic Power', *Jakarta Post*, 5 August 2013, available at www.thejakartapost.com/news/2013/08/05/indonesia-a-rising-economic-power.html. Last accessed 12 July 2016.
Gilpin, Robert. (1975). *US Power and the Multinational Corporation: The Political Economy of Foreign Direct Investment*. New York: Macmillan Press.
Gilpin, Robert. (1981). *War and Change in World Politics*. Cambridge: Cambridge University Press.
Glazebrook, G. De T. (1947). 'The Middle Powers in the United Nations System'. *International Organizations* 1:2, pp. 307–315.
Gowa, Joanne. (1986). 'Anarchy, Egoism, and Third Images: The Evolution of Cooperation and International Relations'. *International Organization* 40:1, pp. 167–186.
Granatstein, J.L. (1973). *Canadian Foreign Policy Since 1945: Middle Power or Satellite?* 3rd Edition. Toronto: The Copp Clark Publishing Company.
Granatstein, J.L. (2011). 'Can Canada Have a Grand Strategy?', presented at a Grand Strategy Symposium, 6–7 April 2011, at the Canadian Forces College, Toronto, available at www.cdfai.org/PDF/Can%20Canada%20Have%20a%20Grand%20Strategy.pdf. Last accessed 26 April 2013.
Grieco, Joseph M. (1988). 'Anarchy and the Limits of Cooperation: A Realist Critique of the Newest Liberal Institutionalism'. *International Organization* 42:3, pp. 485–507.
Halimi, Abdul-Latif. (2014). 'The Regional Implications of Indonesia's Rise', *The Diplomat*, 10 April 2014, available at http://thediplomat.com/tag/indonesian-military-spending/. Last accessed 12 July 2016.
Handberg, Roger. (2013). 'Crowded and Dangerous Space: Space Navigation System Proliferation's Impact on Future Security Operations'. *Comparative Strategy* 32:3, pp. 207–223.
Hemmer, Christopher and Katzenstein, Peter J. (2002). 'Why Is There No NATO in Asia? Collective Identity, Regionalism, and the Origins of Multilateralism'. *International Organization* 56:3, pp. 575–607.
Higgott, Richard A. and Cooper, Andrew Fenton. (1990). 'Middle Power Leadership and Coalition Building: Australia, the Cairns Group and the Uruguay Round of Trade Negotiations'. *International Organization* 44:4, pp. 589–632.
Ho, Joshua. (2006). 'The Security of Sea Lanes in Southeast Asia'. *Asian Survey* 46:4, pp. 558–574.

Ho, Joshua. (2007a). 'Securing the Seas as a Medium of Transportation in Southeast Asia', in *The Security of Sea Lanes of Communication in the Indian Ocean Region*. Kuala Lumpur: Maritime Institute of Malaysia.

Ho, Joshua. (2007b). 'The Importance and Security of Regional Sea Lanes', in *Maritime Security in Southeast Asia*. New York: Routledge.

Ho, Joshua. (2009). 'Recovering After a Maritime Terrorist Attack: The APEC Trade Recovery Programme'. *Marine Policy* 33:4, pp. 733–735.

Holmes, John W. (1976). *Canada: A Middle-Aged Power*. Ottawa: McClelland and Stewart and The Institute of Canadian Studies, Carleton University.

Huang, Victor. (2008). 'Building Maritime Security in Southeast Asia: Outsiders Not Welcome?' *Naval War College Review* 61:1, pp. 87–105.

Indonesian Coordinating Ministry for Political, Legal and Security Affairs. (2007). *Kumpulan Pidato Menteri Koordinator Bidang Politik Hukum dan Keamanan Republik Indonesia*. Jakarta: Kementerian Koordinator Bidang Politik Hukum dan Keamanan Indonesia.

Indonesian MFA. (2005a). *Diskusi Panel tentang Studi Kebijakan Kelautan Indonesia Dalam Rangka Mendukung Pembangunan dan Integritas Nasional, Surabaya 7–8 April 2005*. Jakarta: Badan Penelitian dan Pengembangan Kebijakan.

Indonesian MFA. (2005b). *Pertemuan Kelompok Ahli: Kebijakan Terpadu Pengelolaan Keamanan Selat Malaka, Medan 19–20 Juli 2005*. Jakarta: Badan Penelitian dan Pengembangan Kebijakan.

Indonesian MFA. (2006). *Pertemuan Kelompok Ahli Membahas Aspek Strategis Diplomasi Kelautan Dalam Mendukung Pembangunan Nasional*. Jakarta: Indonesian MFA.

Indonesian MFA. (2009). 'The Duty of the Ministry of Foreign Affairs', 1 August 2009, available at www.deplu.go.id/Pages/Polugri.aspx?IDP=3&l=en. Last accessed 3 January 2011.

Indonesian MFA. (2009). 'The Role of the Ministry of Foreign Affairs', 6 September 2009, available at www.deplu.go.id/Pages/Polugri.aspx?IDP=13&l=en. Last accessed 3 January 2011.

Indonesian Parliament. (2006). 'Rapat Kerja Komisi I DPR RI dengan Menteri Pertahanan dan Panglima TNI', 25 September 2006, available atwww.dpr.go.id/id/komisi/komisi1/report/95/Rapat-Kerja-Komisi-I-DPR-RI-dengan-Menteri-Pertahanan-dan-Panglima-TNI. Last accessed 24 April 2013.

Indonesian Parliament. (2007). 'Rapat Kerja Komisi I DPR RI dengan Menteri Luar Negeri', 25 January 2007, available at www.dpr.go.id/id/komisi/komisi1/report/89/Rapat-Kerja-Komisi-I-DPR-RI-dengan-Menteri-Luar-Negeri. Last accessed 24 April 2013.

Indonesian Parliament. (2007). 'Rapat Kerja Komisi I DPR RI dengan Menkopolhukam', 26 February 2007, available at www.dpr.go.id/id/komisi/komisi1/report/88/Rapat-Kerja-Komisi-I-DPR-RI-dengan-Menkopolhukam. Last accessed 24 April 2013.

Indonesian Parliament. (2007). 'Rapat Kerja Komisi I DPR RI dengan Menteri Pertahanan dan Panglima TNI', 28 May 2007, available at www.dpr.go.id/id/komisi/komisi1/report/143/Rapat-Kerja-Komisi-I-DPR-RI-Dengan-Menteri-Pertahanan-dan-Panglima-TNI. Last accessed 24 April 2013.

Indonesian Parliament. (2007). 'Rapat Kerja Komisi I DPR RI dengan Menteri Luar Negeri', 25 June 2007, available at www.dpr.go.id/id/komisi/komisi1/report/149/Rapat-Kerja-Komisi-I-DPR-RI-Dengan-Menteri-Luar-Negeri. Last accessed 24 April 2013.

20 Introduction

Indonesian Parliament (2007). 'Rapat Dengar Pendapat Komisi I DPR-RI dengan Gubenur Lemhanas dan Sekjen Wantannas', 9 July 2007, available at www.dpr.go.id/id/komisi/komisi1/report/150/Rapat-Dengar-Pendapat-Komisi-I-DPR-RI Dengan-Gubernur-Lemhannas-dan-Sekjen-Wantannas. Last accessed 24 April 2013.

International Maritime Bureau. (2014). *Piracy and Armed Robbery against Ships Annual Report January 1st–December 31st, 2014*. Kuala Lumpur: IMB.

Jackson, Karl D. (1978). 'The Prospects for Bureaucratic Polity in Indonesia', in *Political Power and Communications in Indonesia*, Karl D. Jackson and Lucian W. Pye (eds). Berkeley, CA: University of California Press, pp. 395–398.

Jackson, Karl D. (1980). 'Bureaucratic Polity: A Theoretical Framework for the Analysis of Power and Communications in Indonesia', in *Political Powers and Communication in Indonesia*, Karl D. Jackson and Lucian W. Pye (eds). Berkeley, CA: University of California Press, pp. 3–22.

Jakarta Post. (2005). ' "The Eyes in the Sky" Patrol over Malacca to Start Soon', 9 September 2005. Accessed from the Newsbank database.

Jakarta Post. (2014). 'Analysts Excited By Asia's Rising Power But Warn of Economic and Political Downside Risks', 4 July 2014, available at www.thejakartapost.com/news/2014/07/04/analysts-excited-asia-s-rising-power-warn-economic-and-political-downside-risks.html. Last accessed 12 July 2016.

Jervis, Robert. (1978). 'Cooperation under the Security Dilemma'. *World Politics* 30:2, pp. 167–214.

Jervis, Robert. (1988). 'Realism, Game Theory and Cooperation'. *World Politics* 40:3, pp. 317–349.

Johnston, Alistair Ian. (1999). 'The Myth of the ASEAN Way? Explaining the Evolution of the ASEAN Regional Forum', in *Imperfect Unions: Security Institutions over Time and Space*. New York: Oxford University Press.

Jordaan, Eduard. (2003). 'The Concept of A Middle Power in International Relations: Distinguishing Between Emerging And Traditional Middle Powers'. *Politikon* 30:2, pp. 165–181.

Juwana, Hikmahanto. (2008). 'Catatan atas Masalah Aktual dalam Perjanjian International'. *Indonesian Journal of International Law* 5:3, pp. 443–451.

Kahler, Miles. (2000). 'Conclusion: The Causes and Consequences of Legalization'. *International Organization* 54:3, pp. 661–683.

Keohane, Robert O. (1969). 'Lilliputians' Dilemmas: Small States in International Politics'. *International Organizations* 23:2, pp. 291–310.

Keohane, Robert O. (1984). *After Hegemony: Cooperation and Discord in the World Political Economy*. Princeton, NJ: Princeton University Press.

Keohane, Robert O. and Martin, Lisa L. (1995). 'The Promise of Institutionalist Theory'. *International Security* 20:1, pp. 39–51.

King, John. (2005). 'The Security of Merchant Shipping'. *Marine Policy* 29, pp. 235–245.

Krasner, Stephen D. (1976). 'State Power and the Structure of International Trade'. *World Politics* 28:3, pp. 317–347.

Krasner, Stephen D. (1982). 'Regimes and the Limits of Realism: Regimes as Autonomous Variables'. *International Organization* 36:2, pp. 497–510.

Krasner, Stephen D. (1991). 'Global Communications and National Power: Life on the Pareto Frontier'. *World Politics* 43:3, pp. 336–366.

Krasner, Stephen D. (1992). 'Realism, Imperialism and Democracy: A Response to Gilbert'. *Political Theory* 20:1, pp. 38–52.

Krasner, Stephen D. (2002). 'Chapter 7: Sovereignty, Regimes and Human Rights', in *Regime Theory and International Relations*, Volker Rittberger and Peter Mayer (eds). Oxford: Clarendon Press.

Kristiadi, J. (2007). 'Nasib Kerjasama Pertahanan RI-Singapura', 17 July 2007, available at www.csis.or.id/Publications-OpinionsDetail.php?id=633. Last accessed 17 January 2013.

Kurth, James. (2007). 'The New Maritime Strategy: Confronting Peer Competitors, Rogue States and Transnational Insurgents'. *Orbis* 51:4, pp. 585–600.

Laksmana, Evan A. (2011). 'Indonesia's Rising Regional and Global Profile: Does Size Really Matter'. *Contemporary Southeast Asia* 33:2, pp. 157–182.

Liddle, R. William. (1985). 'Soeharto's Indonesia: Personal Rule and Political Institutions'. *Pacific Affairs* 58: 1, pp. 68–90.

Lipson, Charles. (1984). 'International Cooperation in Economic and Security Affairs'. *World Politics* 37:1, pp. 1–23.

Mak, J.N. (2006). 'Unilateralism and Regionalism: Working Together and Alone in the Malacca Straits', in *Maritime Terrorism and Securing the Malacca Straits*. Graham Gerard Ong-Webb (ed.). Singapore: ISEAS Publishing.

Martin, Lisa L. and Simmons, Beth A. (1998). 'Theories and Empirical Studies of International Institutions'. *International Organization* 52:4, pp. 729–757.

Mearsheimer, John J. (2001). *The Tragedy of Great Power Politics*. New York: W.W. Norton & Company.

Mo, John. (2002). 'Options to Combat Maritime Piracy in Southeast Asia'. *Ocean Development and International Law* 33, pp. 343–358.

Monje, Theresa Guia. (2013). 'Maritime Enforcement in the Philippines: Issues and Challenges', Presentation for the UN Division for Ocean Affairs and the Law of the Sea, the UN-Nippon Fellowship Programme, New York, 25 January 2013.

Moravcsik, Andrew. (1993). 'Armaments among Allies European Weapons Collaboration, 1975–1985', in *International Bargaining and Domestic Politics: Double Edged Diplomacy*. Berkeley, CA: University of Californian Press.

Murphy, Martin. (2007). 'Piracy and UNCLOSL: Does International Law Help Regional States Combat Piracy?' in *Violence at Sea Piracy in the Age of Global Terrorism*, Peter Lehr (ed.). New York: Routledge.

Nabbs-Keller, Greta. (2013). 'Reforming Indonesia's Foreign Ministry: Ideas, Organization and Leadership'. *Contemporary Southeast Asia* 35:1, pp. 56–82.

Nasrun, Rezal Akbar. (2009). 'The Importance of Promoting the Image of Indonesian Maritime Continent for Strengthening Territorial Integrity'. *Jurnal Diplomasi* 1:2, pp. 115–135.

Noer, John H. and Gregory, David. (1996). *Chokepoints: Maritime Economic Concerns in Southeast Asia*. Washington DC: National Defense University Press.

Neufeld, Mark. (1995). 'Hegemony and Foreign Policy Analysis: The Case of Canada as Middle Power'. *Studies in Political Economy* 48, pp. 7–29.

Oye, Kenneth A. (1985). 'Explaining Cooperation under Anarchy'. *World Politics* 38:1, pp. 1–24.

Otte, Max and Greve, Jurgen. (2000). *A Rising Middle Power? German Foreign Policy in Transportation, 1989–1999*. New York: St. Martin's Press.

Oxford Dictionary of English. (2010). Oxford: Oxford University Press.

Parthiana, I Wayan. (2008). 'Kajian Akademis (Teoritis dan Praktis) atas Undang-Undang Nomor 24 Tahun 2000 Tentang Perjanjian Internasional Berdasarkan Hukum Perjanjian Internasional'. *Indonesian Journal of International Law* 5:3, pp. 460–487.

Pfister, Roger. (2005). *Apartheid South Africa and African States: From Pariah to Middle Power, 1961–1994*. London: Tauris Academic Studies.

Ping, Jonathan H. (2005). *Middle Power Statecraft: Indonesia, Malaysia and the Asia Pacific*. Aldershot, Hampshire: Ashgate.

Purdjianto, Tedjo Edhy. (2009). 'Peran TNI Angkatan Laut dalam Penegakan Kedaulatan Negara dan Keamanan di Laut'. *Jurnal Diplomasi* 1:2, pp. 27–48.

Purnomo, Y. Didik Heru. (2004). 'Pengamanan Wilayah Laut RI Bagian Barat'. *Indonesian Journal of International Law*, pp. 27–40.

Raustiala, Kal and Slaughter, Anne-Marie. (2002). 'International Law, International Relations and Compliance', in *Handbook of International Relations*, Walter Carlsnaes, Thomas Risse and Beth A. Simmons (eds). London: Sage Publications.

Ravenhill, John. (1998). 'Cycles of Middle Power Activism: Constraint and Choice in Australian and Canadian Foreign Policies'. *Australian Journal of International Affairs* 52:3, pp. 309–327.

Raymond, Catherine Zara. (2007). 'Piracy in the Waters of Southeast Asia', in *Maritime Security in Southeast Asia*, Kwa Chong Guan and John K. Skogan (eds). New York: Routledge, pp. 62–77.

Reid, Anthony (ed.). (2012). *Indonesia Rising: The Repositioning of Asia's Third Giant*. Singapore: Institute of Southeast Asian Studies.

Reuters. (2010). 'Security Raised in Malacca Strait after Terror Warning', 4 March 2010, available at www.reuters.com/article/2010/03/04/us-malacca-threat-idUSTRE62335120100304. Last accessed 15 March 2011.

Roberts, Christopher B. and Habir, Ahmad D. (2014). 'Australia's Relations with Indonesia: Progress Despite Economic and Socio-Cultural Constraints?' Australian National University National Security College Issue Brief No. 1, available at http://nsc.anu.edu.au/documents/issue-brief-1-roberts-habir.pdf. Last accessed 12 July 2016.

Roberts, Christopher B., Habir, Ahmad D., and Sebastian, Leonard C. (eds). (2015). *Indonesia's Ascent: Power, Leadership and the Regional Order*. London: Palgrave.

Rosenberg, David and Chung, Christopher. (2008). 'Maritime Security in the South China Sea: Coordinating Coastal and User State Priorities'. *Ocean Development and International Law* 39:1, pp. 51–68.

Ruggie, John Gerard. (1992). 'Multilateralism: The Anatomy of an Institution'. *International Organization* 46:3, pp. 561–598.

Ruland, Jurgen. (2009). 'Deepening ASEAN Cooperation through Democratization? The Indonesian Legislature and Foreign Policymaking'. *International Relations of the Asia-Pacific* 9:3, pp. 373–402.

Sato, Yoichiro. (2007). 'Southeast Asian Receptiveness to Japanese Maritime Security Cooperation', The Asia-Pacific Center for Security Studies, Honolulu (A research center under the US Department of Defense), available at http:www.dtic.mil/cgi-bin/GetTRDoc?AD=ADA472466. Last accessed 7 December 2013.

Sherlock, Stephen. (2003). *Struggling to Change: The Indonesian Parliament in an Era of Reformasi*. Canberra: Centre for Democratic Institutions, available at https://cdi.anu.edu.au/CDIwebsite_19982004/indonesia/indonesia_downloads/DPRResearchReport_S.Sherlock.pdf. Last accessed 24 April 2013.

Shie, Tamara Renee. (2006). 'Maritime Piracy in Southeast Asia: The Evolution and Progress of Intra-ASEAN Cooperation', in *Maritime Terrorism and Securing the Malacca Straits*, Graham Gerard Ong-Webb (ed.). Singapore: ISEAS Publishing.

Singapore Ministry of Foreign Affairs. (2005). 'The Batam Joint Statement of the 4th Tripartite Ministerial Meeting of the Littoral States on the Straits of Malacca and Singapore', 2 August 2005, available at http://app.mfa.gov.sg/2006/press/view_press.asp?post_id=140602/08/2005. Last accessed 20 September 2010.

Singer, David J. (1958). 'Threat-Perception and the Armament–Tension Dilemma'. *The Journal of Conflict Resolution* 2:1, pp. 90–105.

Sittnick, Tammy M. (2005). 'State Responsibility and Maritime Terrorism in the Strait of Malacca: Persuading Indonesia and Malaysia to Take Additional Steps to Secure the Strait'. *Pacific Rim Law and Policy Journal* 14, pp. 743–769.

Sjaastad, Anders C. (2007). 'Southeast Asian SLOCs and Security Options', in *Maritime Security in Southeast Asia*, Kwa Chong Guan and John K. Skogan (eds). New York: Routledge, pp. 3–13.

Snidal, Duncan. (1985). 'Coordination versus Prisoners' Dilemma: Implications for International Cooperation and Regimes'. *American Political Science Review* 79:4, pp. 923–942.

Snidal, Duncan. (1991). 'Relative Gains and the Pattern of International Cooperation'. *American Political Science Review* 85:3, pp. 701–726.

Sondakh, Bernard Kent. (2004). 'Pengamanan Wilayah Laut Indonesia'. *Indonesian Journal of International Law*, pp. 1–26.

Sondakh, Bernard Kent. (2006). 'National Sovereignty and Security in the Straits of Malacca', in *Building A Comprehensive Security Environment in the Straits of Malacca*. Kuala Lumpur: Maritime Institute of Malaysia, pp. 79–110.

Strange, Susan. (1987). 'The Persistent Myth of Lost Hegemony'. *International Organization* 41:4, pp. 551–574.

Stryken, Christian-Marius. (2007). 'The US Regional Maritime Security Initiative and US Grand Strategy in Southeast Asia', in *Maritime Security in Southeast Asia*. New York: Routledge, pp. 134–145.

Suhartono. (2001). 'Hubungan Indonesia-Timur Tengah Era Pemerintahan Abdurrahman Wahid', in *Analisis Kebijakan Luar Negeri Pemerintahan Abdurrahman Wahid (1999–2000)*. Jakarta: Dewan Perwakilan Rakyat Republik Indonesia.

Suryadinata, Leo. (1998). *Politik Luar Negeri Indonesia di Bawah Soeharto*. Jakarta: LP3ES.

United States Department of the Homeland Security. (2005). 'The National Strategy for Maritime Security', 20 September 2005, available at http://georgewbush-whitehouse.archives.gov/homeland/maritime-security.html. Last accessed 13 March 2011.

United States Energy Information Administration. (2011). 'World Oil Transit Chokepoints: Malacca', available at www.eia.doe.gov/cabs/world_oil_transit_chokepoints/malacca.html. Last accessed 28 March 2011.

Valencia, Mark J. (2006). 'The Politics of Anti-Piracy and Anti-Terrorism Responses in Southeast Asia', in *Piracy, Maritime Terrorism and Securing the Malacca Straits*. Singapore: ISEAS.

Waltz, Kenneth N. (1979). *Theory of International Politics*. New York: McGraw-Hill.

Waltz, Kenneth N. (2000). 'Structural Realism after the Cold War'. *International Security* 25:1, pp. 5–41.

Wendt, Alexander. (1992). 'Anarchy is what States Make of it: The Social Construction of Power Politics'. *International Organization* 46:2, pp. 391–425.

Wendt, Alexander. (1994). 'Collective Identity Formation and the International State'. *The American Political Science Review* 88:2, pp. 384–396.

Wendt, Alexander. (1995). 'Constructing International Politics'. *International Security* 20:1, pp. 71–81.
Westhuizen, Janis Van Der. (1998). 'South Africa's Emergence as a Middle Power'. *Third World Quarterly* 19:3, pp. 435–455.
Wisnumurti, Nugroho. (2009). 'Maritime Security Issues in Southeast Asia: An Indonesian Perspective'. *Indonesian Journal of International Law* 6:3, pp. 333–352.

1 Maritime security and Indonesia

Introduction

The 9/11 attacks have raised the profile of armed robbery against ships and maritime terrorism. The attacks have driven the maritime sector to re-evaluate its vulnerability against the probability of attacks or other forms of sabotage. Heads of state, media and analysts' statements that often conflated the threat of sea robbery and maritime terrorism had raised public attention and enabled more resources to be put into countering sea robbery and maritime terrorism (Lee, 2005; Powell, 2004; Richardson, 2005; *Sunday Times*, 2005; Urquhart, 2004; Young and Valencia, 2003, p. 269). As various ships pass through Indonesian waters, the act of sea robbery and the potential for maritime terrorism attacks constitute a number of threats to the international community. They pose direct threat to the life and safety of citizens of various flag states, serve to increase insurance premiums, and have the potential to cause environmental pollution if the attacks take place in busy sea lanes against super-tankers (Chalk, 1998a, pp. 90–91).

In the years after 9/11, international attention turned to three specific maritime areas – the vast Indonesian archipelago, the busy Strait of Malacca and the poor coast of Bangladesh – as homes to groups of sea robbers who were responsible for carrying out three-quarters of maritime hijackings (Chandrasekaran, 2001). Various elements of the international maritime community, such as shipping businesses, international shipping insurance companies and international maritime organisations such as the International Maritime Bureau (IMB), the International Maritime Organization (IMO) and user states, exercised pressure on the littoral states of the Strait of Malacca and Singapore to crack down on armed robbery in their waters. At present, the piracy attacks in East Africa and the Indian Ocean have grabbed headlines in the media, but there is a growing concern in the maritime community over the increase in armed robberies in Indonesian waters. In 2014, sea robbery attacks in Indonesia accounted for over 40 per cent of worldwide incidents (IMB, 2014).

This chapter provides detailed background for the chapters that follow. For this purpose, this chapter is structured as follows. The second section explains the problems posed by maritime terrorism and armed robbery against ships, which the international community focuses on and which are ultimately the focus of maritime security cooperation. It explains the trends of maritime terrorism and armed robbery against ships. The term 'trends' as used in this chapter refers to patterns and changes in maritime terrorism and sea robbery incidents. This section also examines the changes in the way that the international community engages with these two issues over time.

The next section establishes the importance of Indonesia for international maritime security and examines Indonesia's unilateral policies, including the allocation of resources, to address maritime terrorism and sea robbery. Focusing primarily on maritime terrorism and armed robbery against ships, it identifies how Indonesia prioritises its security threats and notes that Indonesia's prioritisation differs from that of the international community

The fourth section maps the various maritime threats faced by Indonesia, to contextualise maritime terrorism and armed robbery against ships against the wider issues that Indonesia faces. It analyses Indonesia's perception of each security issue and compares it with Indonesia's perception of the threat posed by maritime terrorism and sea robbery. This discussion of Indonesia's perception of threat and its security priority will provide the basis for analysing Indonesia's participation in maritime security cooperation, which will be the focus in the following chapters.

The concluding section highlights key points to take away from this chapter. It points out that the development of maritime security cooperation does not coincide with Indonesian concerns over maritime terrorism and sea robbery. The concluding section also draws attention to Indonesia's national efforts to deal with maritime terrorism and sea robbery.

The trends of maritime terrorism and armed robbery against ships

In the aftermath of the 9/11 attacks, maritime terrorism and sea robberies have received greater worldwide attention and generated various international arrangements to deal with the two security threats. Maritime terrorism itself is a recently developed concept (Power, 2008, p. 121). A common legal definition of maritime terrorism does not yet exist (Power, 2008, pp. 121–122; Tiribelli, 2006, p. 136). In the absence of an agreed definition, Tiribelli defines maritime terrorism as 'the systematic use or threat to use acts of violence against international shipping and maritime services by an individual or group to induce fear and intimidation on a civilian population in order to achieve political ambitions or objectives' (Tiribelli, 2006, p. 145). The Council for Security Cooperation in the Asia–Pacific at its working group on maritime cooperation in 2002 provided another broad definition of maritime terrorism as follows:

> the undertaking of terrorist acts and activities (1) within the maritime environment, (2) using or against vessels or fixed platforms at sea or in port, or against any one of their passengers or personnel, (3) against coastal

facilities or settlements, including tourist resorts, port areas and port towns or cities.

(Quoted in Ong, 2004, p. 17; Power, 2008, p. 122; Quentin, 20 January 2003)

Both definitions of maritime terrorism explicitly point to the use of violence that can take place in vessels, ports and coastal facilities to serve the perpetrators' political objectives (Ong, 2004, p. 17; Power, 2008, p. 122; Tiribelli, 2006, p. 145).

The first incident which generated international attention on the danger posed by maritime terrorism occurred in 1985. Four Palestinian terrorists hijacked an Italian-flag cruise ship the *Achille Lauro* with 454 passengers in Egyptian territorial waters (*Times*, 1985). The terrorists initially had planned to attack the Israeli port of Ashdod but later decided to change their plan when a crew member discovered them (Clough, 1985). They demanded the release of Palestinian prisoners detained by the Israeli government (Greaves and Hill, 1985). The terrorists killed one American passenger in this incident before surrendering to Egyptian authorities (Greaves and Hill, 1985). Fifteen years later, on 12 October 2000, an attack on the USS *Cole* brought maritime terrorism back to the world's attention. Two suicide bombers used a small boat to come alongside the Navy warship, which was calling at the Yemeni port of Aden to refuel, and later detonated a high explosive bomb killing six and injuring thirty-six US sailors (Brodie *et al.*, 2000). Although these two maritime terrorism attacks were widely reported by the media, it was only after the 9/11 attacks that this issue began to draw international attention (Raymond, 2006, p. 240).

Although a maritime terrorist attack has never taken place in Indonesian territory, terrorism is not a new security issue (Chalk, 1998b, pp. 122–124). Since the hijacking of the Indonesian aeroplane registered by Garuda Airline in its flight from Jakarta to Bangkok in 1980, a number of terrorist attacks have taken place in Indonesia (Indonesian MoD, 2008, p. 19). At least thirty-four bomb attacks have happened in Indonesia since the resignation of Suharto in May 1998 (DKPT, 2008, p. 40). Despite Indonesia's experience of a long history of terrorist incidents, only after 9/11 did governments around the world began to highlight the possibility of a terrorist attack in Indonesian waters. Although, in the immediate aftermath of the 9/11 attacks, international attention focused on the security of air transport, soon after it began to turn to the vulnerability of port facilities and marine transport to terrorist attacks (Raymond, 2006, p. 239). The US began to express its concern about 'Muslim extremists in Indonesia, Malaysia, the Philippines and Thailand' as a possible threat to world trade navigating through Southeast Asian waterways (Valencia, 2006, p. 97).

Parallel to this the US rapidly embarked on a global campaign against terrorism. Identifying and intercepting maritime terrorist threats way before they reached the US became the goal of US maritime strategy in the war on terror (US Coast Guard, 2002, p. i). Thus, under this extensive global campaign, the US promoted a number of international cooperation arrangements to improve the security of maritime transport, including the PSI and the CSI. A number of the US-led cargo security initiatives that require direct government involvement were introduced one to two years after 9/11. The CSI was launched in 2002 and the PSI was introduced in 2003. There was no long delay between the 9/11 attacks and the launching of international maritime arrangements, and by the end of 2002, mainly as a response to the 2002 Bali bombing, Indonesia already had a number of anti-terrorism measures in place and they had started to show positive results (DKPT, 2008, p. 41; Indonesian Coordinating Ministry for Political, Legal and Security Affairs, 2006a, pp. 25, 38; 2007, p. 132; Singh, 2004, p. 59).[1]

After the 2002 Bali bombing that killed 202 people, Indonesia adopted numerous counter-terrorism measures at national level to prevent terrorist attacks on its key ports and offshore facilities, and to improve the security of its maritime supply chains (DKPT, 2008, p. 41; Singh, 2004, p. 59).[2] Currently there are 141 ports and over 1000 special terminals mainly serving mining and oil drilling companies involved in both domestic and export–import activities (ASEAN, 2009, p. 153).[3] By May 2003 as a result of Indonesia's counter-terrorism efforts, the arrest of the bombing suspects and members of the JI (*Jamaah Islamiyah*) had reached thirty-three people (National Institute for Defense Studies, 2004, p. 126). By 2008, the anti-terrorism coordinating body the *Desk Koordinator Pemberantasan Terorisme* reported that 325 terrorists had been detained, 200 of them had undergone legal process, 5 persons had received the death sentence, 85 suspects were freed and 1 had been killed (DKPT, 2008, p. 33). By 2012 the Indonesian government had arrested 750 terrorist suspects and successfully prosecuted 500 of them (Australian Department of Defence, 2012).

As the level of threat posed by terrorism has fallen, there has, from the Indonesian perspective, been a corresponding fall in the benefits of cooperation. The benefits of cooperation for Indonesia are further reduced because, although the issue of maritime terrorism attracts international attention, Indonesia has been struggling to deal with other maritime issues. An Indonesian official confirmed this, as he characterised the threat of terrorism as not being the major security threat to Indonesia (Febrica, 2010, p. 582). There are four maritime issues that sit at the top of the national security priorities list. These issues are highlighted in almost every government document and government official's statement (Bakorkamla, 2010, pp. 6, 8; Dewan Maritim Indonesia, 2007a, pp. 4–4, 4–9; 2007b, pp. 2, 17; Indonesian Coordinating Ministry for Political, Legal and Security Affairs, 2008, pp. 51–52; 2006b, p. 35; Indonesian MFA, 2006, p. 6; Indonesian MoD, 2008, pp. 28, 145; Indonesian Ministry of State Secretariat, 2004).[4] These are illegal fishing, border disputes, illegal seaborne migrants, and smuggling. An Indonesian Navy official named maritime terrorism as the fifth most dangerous threat to Indonesia's maritime security, following illegal fishing, illegal migrants, potential border disputes and smuggling.[5] The government official's claim over the nature of maritime terrorism is also reflected in an Indonesian shipowner's statement. The chairman of the Indonesian shipowners' association suggested that 'as long as there are sovereign littoral states surrounding the strategic waterways like the Straits of Malacca and Singapore such incidents would never materialise'.[6]

Adding to the puzzle of this book, a number of interviews carried out with international shipping lines, international chambers of commerce and international marine insurance and re-insurance companies corroborated the perception of maritime terrorism of the Indonesian government and businesses. For instance, a chief executive of a Singapore-based international chamber of commerce claimed that 'regional governments have improved the ability to work together. The threat [of maritime terrorism] is real, yet there is the ability of government to contain it'.[7] This is also confirmed by a senior marine underwriter of an international re-insurance company. As he put it: 'the littoral states have been active to mitigate the threat of maritime terrorism. The threat becomes minimal and at reasonable level'.[8] The perception of maritime terrorism of the Indonesian government and businesses, as elaborated on above, shows that there has been a discrepancy not only between Indonesia and the international community but also among various stakeholders within the international maritime community. For the shipping lines, shipping operators, insurance and re-insurance companies, and non-governmental organisations that are concerned with shipping issues, the risk posed by maritime terrorism is not the highest level risk.[9]

For the shipping businesses, the issue related to the safety of navigation is deemed as of more immediate concern, because the risk of collision, grounding, and near misses, particularly at the shallow and narrow Straits of Malacca and Singapore, are higher than of potential maritime terrorist attacks.[10] This shows a disjuncture between the perception of maritime terrorism within the shipping businesses and the US, which puts maritime terrorism high on its security agenda.

In the wake of 9/11, the issue of maritime terrorism has received a lot of attention. As a consequence, concern over armed robbery against ships, or, as it is often referred to, sea robbery, also began to rise as an international security concern. The US especially conveyed its concern that, if sea robbery attacks in Southeast Asia were not addressed properly, terrorist groups in the region would take advantage of the situation and copy the sea robbers' method of operations.[11]

The International Maritime Organization Code of Practice for the Investigation of Crimes of Piracy and Armed Robbery against Ships (Resolution A. 1025(26)) defines armed robbery against ships as any of the following acts:

1   any illegal act of violence or detention or any act of depredation, or threat thereof, other than an act of piracy, committed for private ends and directed against a ship or against persons or property on board such a ship, within a State's internal waters, archipelagic waters and territorial sea;
2   any act of inciting or of intentionally facilitating an act described above.[12]

The introduction of international cooperation to address armed robbery attacks against ships has been driven by a significant change in the international community's response to sea robbery. Prior to 9/11, Japan was the only user state actively seeking for greater involvement to address armed robbery against ships in Southeast Asia. In the late 1990s to 2001, among all the user states, Japan was the one that played the most assertive role in addressing armed robbery against ships in Indonesian waters and the Straits of Malacca and Singapore. The Japanese Prime Minister Keizo Obuchi in 1999 articulated an idea to set up a regional framework to address armed robbery against ships and piracy. At the 1999 ASEAN Plus Three (APT) Summit in Manila, Obuchi proposed 'a meeting of coast guards of Asian countries to discuss possible counter-measures' to fight sea robbery (*Straits Times*, 2000a). In March 2000, Japan hosted a meeting which involved coast-guard officials from Brunei, Cambodia, India, Indonesia, Japan, South Korea, Laos, Malaysia, Myanmar, the Philippines, Singapore, Thailand and Vietnam to discuss the possibility of joint anti-sea robbery patrols in the region (*Straits Times*, 2000a). At the 2000 APT Summit in Singapore, Obuchi's successor Prime Minister Yoshiro Mori proposed a similar counter-piracy measure. Mori proposed to start a joint anti-sea robbery patrol of the Straits of Malacca and Singapore. The parties involved would include Japan, China, South Korea, and the three littoral states of Indonesia, Malaysia and Singapore (*Straits Times*, 2000a). Indonesia opposed this idea of joint patrols.

In the aftermath of the 9/11 attacks, there was a growing interest among extra-regional states, particularly the US, in taking a bigger part in securing the strategic sea lanes. The international community maintained that armed robbery attacks in Indonesian waters remained at a worrying level, since they still accounted for almost 30 per cent of all incidents globally. Apart from Japan, other extra-regional states, including the US, India and China, showed growing interest in this issue and sought a bigger role when engaging in counter-sea robbery efforts (Rahman, 2007, p. 195; Rekhi, 2006).

Among the extra-regional actors, a significant change could be seen from the US reaction to sea robbery in the Straits of Malacca and Singapore after 9/11. Since pulling out of Vietnam in 1973–75, the US maintained only a low profile engagement in the region (Dittmer, 2007, p. 530). Prior to 9/11, the US government did not pay much attention to the issue of sea robbery in Indonesian waters. A number of elements within the US administration including the Navy, the Maritime Administration, the Department of Energy and the Defence Mapping Agency response to sea robbery in Southeast Asia had been limited to developing a number of databases and communication links that were made available to ship masters, ship owners and operators who requested them (Chalk, 1998a, p. 101). In addition, these agencies issued advisories periodically to all US-flag merchant ships navigating through Southeast East Asian waters, including Indonesian territorial waterways (Chalk, 1998a, p. 102). In the aftermath of 9/11, the US revised this practice. In 2004, the US proposed the RMSI, to play an active role in safeguarding the key Straits of Malacca and Singapore. However, as shown in Figure 1.2, the number of sea robbery incidents in the Straits has declined since 2001. At bilateral level, maritime security issues became one of the main topics during US Defence Secretary Donald Rumsfeld's discussions with Indonesian President Susilo Bambang Yudhoyono, Foreign Minister

Hassan Wirayuda and Defence Minister Juwono Sudarsono in 2006 (Rekhi, 2006). The US also provided assistance to Indonesia in setting up a radar system across the Strait of Malacca, Singapore and the Sulawesi Sea. Adding a piece to the puzzle, Indonesia rejected the US RMSI with sovereignty concerns cited as its main reason, but cooperated extensively with the US through bilateral defence arrangements.

Armed robbery against ships itself is not a new problem and has been a recurring maritime security challenge in Southeast Asia that dates back to AD 414 (Chalk, 1998a, p. 87). The early 1990s were a critical period for trends of armed robbery against ships incidents in Indonesian waters. From 1981 to 1988, the number of piratical incidents in Indonesian waters was very low. During this period, with 1982–83 as an exception, no more than a dozen incidents a year took place in the Strait of Malacca and the Strait of Singapore through to the southern part of South China (Vagg, 1995, p. 69). This trend changed in the early 1990s, as armed robbery at sea attacks increased from 1990 to 1992 (IMB, 1992, pp. 5–6; Renwick and Abbott, 1999, p. 184; 2007, p. 49; Vagg, 1995, p. 70). The most sea robbery-prone areas at that point in time were the Philip Channel, the Strait of Malacca and around the whole Indonesian Riau archipelago with its main islands of Batam and Bintan (IMB, 1992, p. 6; Renwick and Abbott, 1999, p. 184).

By 1999 Indonesian waters accounted for more than one third of the reported sea robbery incidents in the world. As can be seen from Figure 1.1, in 1999, Indonesian waters accounted for 38 per cent of worldwide incidents. A close

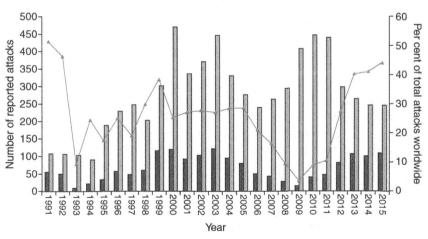

Figure 1.1 Armed robbery attacks and attempted attacks in Indonesian waters (excluding the Straits of Malacca and Singapore) 1991–2015.

Sources: IMB, 2001, 2005, 2009, 2010, 2014, 2015.

32 *Maritime security and Indonesia*

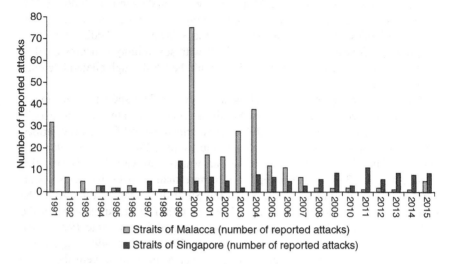

Figure 1.2 Armed robbery attacks and attempted attacks in the Straits of Malacca and Singapore 1991–2015.

Sources: IMB 2001, 2005, 2009, 2010, 2014, 2015.

observation of the increase in incidents during this period is interesting because it shows that armed robberies had been on the rise many years prior to the introduction of maritime cooperation to address sea robbery.

The evidence of an increased level of violence used in armed robberies from 1996 to 2000 is even more striking. During the end of the 1990s and 2000, the degree of violence inflicted upon ships' crews during the act of robbery had reached an alarming level. From 1996 to 1997, there was a 96 per cent increase in the number of crews murdered by sea robbers and from 1997 to 1998 there was a 52 per cent rise. Although the number of crew killed dropped significantly from seventy-eight crews in 1998 to three crews in 1999, this number increased dramatically in 2000 to seventy-two seamen killed (IMB, 2001). Yet, despite the increased level of violence, during this period there were no international cooperation initiatives launched to halt sea robbery. There was a lag of several years before the introduction of international initiatives to counter sea robbery, such as the RMSI and the ReCAAP.

Adding to the puzzle of this book, in recent years there has been a steady increase of sea robbery attacks in Indonesian waterways. As shown in Figure 1.1, from 2011 to 2012 there was a 76 per cent increase in the number of robbery attacks in Indonesian waters. In 2013, 40.1 per cent of armed robbery incidents in the world took place in Indonesia. This number increased to 40.8 per cent in 2014. Yet, despite the recent sharp rise in armed robbery attacks in the archipelago, Indonesia has not joined a number of international cooperation agreements dealing with this issue such as the ReCAAP and the SUA convention. Indonesia has cited sovereignty concerns as its main reason for non-participation.

However, Jakarta has taken various cooperative measures that allow cross-border air and sea patrols with regional and extra-regional states.

The importance of Indonesia in maritime security

Indonesia has always been important in international maritime security. Almost half of the world's trading goods and oil supply pass through key Indonesian straits including the Straits of Malacca and Singapore, the Strait of Sunda and the Strait of Lombok (Carana, 2004, p. 14; US Department of Homeland Security, 2005). This largest archipelago state in the world, which comprises 17,480 islands with a maritime territory measuring close to 6 million square kilometres, is located between the two key shipping routes of the Pacific and Indian Ocean, and between two continents, Asia and Australia (Indonesian MoD, 2008, p. 145). It also sits at the crossroads of busy maritime traffic between Europe and the Far East, between Australia and Asia, and between the Persian Gulf and Japan (Coutrier, 1988, p. 186).

Three major sea lanes in Southeast Asia overlap with Indonesia's maritime jurisdiction (Ho, 2007, p. 205). These are the archipelagic sea lanes I, II and III (see Figure 1.3). Archipelagic sea lane I facilitates navigation from the Indian ocean through the Sunda Strait to the Natuna Sea and eventually reaches the South China Sea (Djalal, 2009, p. 63). Archipelagic sea lane II assists the flow of maritime transport from the Indian Ocean through the Lombok Strait to the Makassar Strait and then finally to the Sulawesi Sea, the Pacific Ocean and Philippine waterway (Djalal, 2009, p. 63). Finally, sea lane III links the Timor Sea and Arafuru Sea to the Pacific Ocean through the Sawu Sea, the Banda Sea, the Seram Sea and the Moluccas Sea (Djalal, 2009, p. 63).

The region's major sea lanes are centred on key straits such as the Malacca, the Singapore and the Lombok Straits (Ho, 2007, p. 205). Of these three straits, the Straits of Malacca and Singapore are the most important trading route. The majority of Middle East oil exports to Asia and most commerce between Asia and Europe pass through this 610-mile-long strait (Coutrier, 1988, p. 186; US Department of Homeland Security, 2005). At least 600 ships navigate through the Straits of Malacca and Singapore every day (Indonesian MFA, 2006, p. 14). This includes 72 per cent of super-tankers and other vessels plying between the Indian and Pacific Oceans, making these Straits the busiest global sea lane of communication (Indonesian MFA, 2006, p. 14; US DoD, 2006, p. 33; 2005, p. 33; 2007, p. 8; US Energy Information Administration, 2012). Most of the imported oil for Asia–Pacific countries, including around 80 per cent of Japan's and China's imported oil originating from the Persian Gulf, transits through the Straits of Malacca and Singapore (US DoD, 2006, p. 33; 2005, p. 33; 2007, p. 8; US Energy Information Administration, 2012). This is because this sea lane is the shortest sea route between the Middle East and Asia (US DoD, 2006, p. 33; 2005, p. 33; 2007, p. 8; US Energy Information Administration, 2012). Currently, 45 per cent of the world's annual merchant fleet tonnage passes through the Straits of Malacca and Singapore, the Sunda Strait and the Lombok

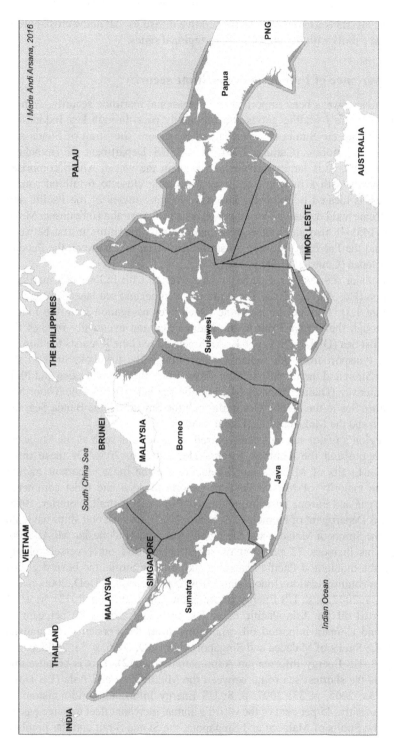

Figure 1.3 Map of Indonesia.

Strait (Carana, 2004, p. 14; US Department of Homeland Security, 2005). The total value of goods transported via these waters reaches US$1.3 trillion annually (Bakorkamla, 2010, p. 34). Indonesian waters also serve as an important sea lane for the oil trade. Half of the world's oil navigates through Indonesian waterways (Carana, 2004, p. 14; US Department of Homeland Security, 2005). The significance of Indonesia's sea lanes was clear in July 2007: when the supply of tankers decreased on all major shipping routes because of limited cargo availability, the Indonesia–Far East route did not experience any decline (UNCTAD, 2008, p. 73).

As the Strait of Malacca, the Strait of Lombok and the Strait of Sunda overlap with Indonesia's maritime jurisdiction, Indonesia has great importance in securing these maritime passages. According to the United Nations Convention on the Law of the Sea (UNCLOS), the responsibility for security and safety of navigation lies with Indonesia as a coastal state (Oegroseno, 2006, p. 30). The UNCLOS Part III Article 34 (1) provides a legal basis for the sovereignty and jurisdiction of the coastal states bordering straits used for international navigation. This article states as follows:

> The regime of passage through straits used for international navigation established in this Part shall not in other respects affect the legal status of the waters forming such straits or the exercise by the States bordering the straits of their sovereignty or jurisdiction over such waters and their air space, bed and subsoil.[13]

Indonesia's status as a coastal state not only implies Indonesia's responsibility to secure its waterway but also suggests an international community expectation for Indonesia to take the responsibility seriously.

Indonesia's importance in maritime security also lies in its role as a flag state. Indonesia is amongst the thirty-five flags of registration, with the largest registered deadweight tonnage (UNCTAD, 2008, p. 46). Indonesia's position as one of the largest states of registration or flag states indicates three important points. First, Indonesia's status as a flag state provides legal and diplomatic leverage, since the flag state has pre-dominant, or even exclusive, jurisdiction over all vessels flying its flag on the high seas (Suchharitkul, 2006, p. 415). Consequently, the international community expects Indonesia to exercise its jurisdiction thoroughly to improve maritime security, including interdiction of suspected vessels in the high seas. The UNCLOS Part IX Article 92 stipulates flag-state jurisdiction over a vessel flying its national flag.[14]

Second, the flag state is also the primary enforcer of international standards (Vorbach, 2001, p. 34). The flag state's role to ensure that ships comply with international rules at different levels – sub-regional, regional and global – is clearly articulated in UNCLOS Article 94 on duties of the flag state (Suchharitkul, 2006, p. 420).[15] As a result, Indonesia is a key state in the success of the implementation of maritime security initiatives. Third, Indonesia's position as one of the main flag states in the world suggests that there are strong economic reasons to participate in maritime security cooperation. In addition to a significant proportion of vessels registered under the Indonesian flag, Indonesian ship-owners also have significant control of the world merchant fleet. Out of the total world merchant fleet of 1.12 billion deadweight tons (dwt) in 2008, ship-owners from Indonesia control 7.3 million dwt (UNCTAD, 2008, p. 44). This implies the presence of economic reasons for the Indonesian government to address sea robbery and maritime terrorism.

In conclusion, the importance of Indonesian waterways as routes of global trade and oil, and its rights and responsibilities both as a coastal and a flag state, have established Indonesia as a key player in international maritime security. The role that Indonesia plays in international maritime security arrangements, therefore, can be seen as a key to the success of maritime regulations and significant for the achievement of the protection of the international maritime domain. Given the expectation of the international community over Indonesia's role to secure its waterways and the ships flying its flag, Indonesia's responses to maritime terrorism and sea robbery are very important. The next section examines Indonesia's policy responses to deal with the two issues.

Indonesia's responses to maritime terrorism and armed robbery against ships

The increase of armed robbery against ships in Indonesian waters and the potential for maritime terrorism in this archipelagic state have become the main concern for international businesses and foreign governments, as these illicit activities pose dangers to the safety and security of navigation. Indonesia's preoccupation with other maritime issues, as mentioned above, does not suggest that Indonesia denies the existence of a maritime terrorism threat or does nothing to prevent armed robbery against ships.

The government has not discounted the possibility of maritime terrorism. A Navy official claimed that: 'there is only a small possibility of maritime terrorism attacks in Indonesian waters. Nevertheless, Indonesian authorities remain cautious'.[16] A particular concern is the security and safety of the Straits of Malacca and Singapore, the world's busiest sea lane. Around 60 to 70 per cent of vessels plying through the Straits of Malacca and Singapore are tankers carrying oil from the Middle East to East Asia (Dewan Maritim Indonesia, 2007b, p. 25). A terrorist attack on a tanker navigating through this water would have a devastating impact, harming Indonesia's inter-island and international supply chains. The Indonesian Maritime Security Coordinating Board and the Navy have anticipated a number of worst scenario maritime terrorism incidents that may take place in Indonesian key waterways (Bakorkamla, 2004, p. 5; 2010, p. 99; DKPT, 2008, p. 11; Sondakh, 2004, p. 7). These include: sea robbery and hostage-taking carried out by terrorist groups to generate funding; terrorists hijacking and exploding a super tanker to block the key Strait or to use it as a floating bomb to be directed at a nearby port city or sunk at the Strait of Malacca's narrowest part; the destruction of undersea pipelines and communication cables; and the spreading of sea mines in Indonesia's strategic waterways (Bakorkamla, 2004, p. 5; Sondakh, 2004, p. 7; for explanation of a number of worst scenario maritime terrorism incidents in the Straits of Malacca and Singapore, see also Richardson, 2004; US Energy Information Administration, 2012).

Indonesia's policies to address maritime terrorism comprise five important aspects: first, the establishment of a new security structure and policy; second, the making of new legislation; third, counter-terrorism training exercises; fourth, the implementation of container security programmes; and finally, the launch of counter-terrorism operations. These now will be discussed in more detail.

First, Indonesia's efforts to improve its counter-terrorism ability can be seen from the establishment of new institutions. To deal with terrorism, Jakarta established an anti-terrorism task force that comprises the Ministry of Justice, the Ministry of Home Affairs, the Ministry of Foreign Affairs, the Ministry of Finance, the Attorney General's Office, the Armed Forces, and the National Intelligence Agency (Indonesian Coordinating Ministry for Political, Legal and Security Affairs, 2007, p. 132; International Crisis Group, 2002). The purpose of the task force is to coordinate action and share information from the intelligence units of various government institutions. Parallel with the establishment of the task force, the government strengthened the Maritime Security Coordinating Board (Bakorkamla) to coordinate the country's maritime security policy. The coordinating board serves as a focal point to coordinate government institutions involved in maritime security, including the Ministry of Foreign Affairs, the Ministry of Home Affairs, the Ministry of Defence, the Ministry of Justice, the Ministry of Finance, the Ministry of Transportation, the Ministry of Marine and Fisheries, the District Attorney, the Armed Forces, the Police and the National Intelligence Agency (Bakorkamla, 2010, p. 18).

A high government official responsible for determining the security budget claimed that there has been a significant increase in the government allocation of funding to deal with terrorism since 9/11.[17] The government has allocated substantial resources for the development of Bakorkamla from 2005 to 2015. By 2011, the allocation of resources for this institution had increased by more than 99 per cent (Bappenas, 2011).

Second, Indonesia's response to maritime terrorism can also be traced from the launch of new legislation. Following the Bali bombing, Jakarta promulgated a Presidential Emergency Decree on the Prevention of Terrorism, and implemented a new anti-terrorism law (Singh, 2004, p. 59). Although the legislation does not empower the Indonesian central government to the same degree as Singapore's Internal Security Act empowers the Singapore government, it enables security personnel to detain suspected terrorists for twenty days, which could be extended for another six months based on preliminary evidence reported by the intelligence services (Tan and Ramakrishna, 2004, p. 96). In addition, government legislation from 2002 on combating criminal acts of terrorism deals with maritime terrorism-related issues including the proliferation of WMD and acts of terrorism on Indonesian flagged ships.[18] Article 4 of the 2002 anti-terrorism legislation empowers the Indonesian central government to detain terrorists that carry out attacks on board ships that fly the Indonesian flag.

Responding to the bombing of the parliament building on 14 July 2006, the Ministry of Political, Legal and Security Affairs issued the Ministry Instruction on Prevention, Detection and Prosecution of Acts of Terrorism in Indonesia (DKPT, 2008, p. 6). The Ministry Instruction highlights two important points. First, it points to the need to improve the security of government premises and public facilities, including ports, and the monitoring of weapons and explosive devices. Second, the instruction underlined the importance of cooperation between the police, intelligence agencies, immigration, customs and local government, particularly in Central Java, Jakarta, Bogor, Tangerang and Bekasi (DKPT, 2008, p. 7). The Ministry Instruction highlighted that cooperation between these agencies was deemed crucial, as terrorists are likely to begin their operation by entering main gateways such as ports (DKPT, 2008, p. 7). As part of the government's efforts to safeguard its territory, Indonesia has also introduced the shipping law 17/2008. Article 276 of the shipping law provides a legal basis for the establishment of the Sea and Coast Guard. The new agency assists the Navy in port security, naval counter intelligence and coastal patrol and in protecting the country's offshore facilities (Indonesian DGST, 2010, pp. 1–3). Currently, Indonesia is still in process of establishing its Sea and Coast Guard. The Ministry of Transportation has been assigned with a task to form this new institution (Indonesian DGST, 2010, pp. 1–3).[19]

Third, the government conducted counter-terrorism training exercises to improve government agencies' capabilities in responding to the terrorism threat. The training exercises included intra-agency training and combined exercises. The combined exercises involve a number of government agencies, including the Marine Police, Navy, Customs, MoT, Search and Rescue Unit, and Immigration agency (Supriyadi, 2010, pp. 48–49).[20]

Fourth, as part of the government efforts to safeguard its maritime supply chains, Indonesia has also introduced container security policies, including harmonisation of advance electronic cargo information and adoption of a risk management approach. To achieve the harmonisation of advance electronic cargo information, Indonesia has adopted the WCO data model for its customs clearance system (APEC Desk of the Indonesian Customs, 2011, p. 19). Indonesia's advance electronic information programme requires all ships carrying import goods bound for an Indonesian port to provide manifest information 24 hours prior to their arrival (APEC Desk of the Indonesian Customs, 2011, p. 27).

In terms of employing a risk management approach, Indonesia has developed a database of importers, exporters, customs brokers, criminal records and transport units (APEC Desk of the Indonesian Customs, 2011, p. 21). Through this database, Customs developed a profiling system for shippers, customs brokers and forwarders (APEC Desk of the Indonesian Customs, 2011, p. 21). The Indonesian Customs simplifies customs' procedures for economic actors that have a good record of compliance with Customs regulations. The risk management principles were adopted in the inspection of import and export cargo, packages delivered through the mail service, passengers' goods, post clearance audit, as well as the inspection of ships and other vehicles (APEC Desk of the Indonesian Customs, 2011, p. 20). In terms of the risk-profiling system, the government issued decrees from the Director General of Customs and Excise to improve the security of maritime trade (Polner, 2010, p. 33). The risk-profiling systems are determined by the shippers' previous track records, the nature of the commodity, the nature of their business and the Customs' intelligence information.

To complement these risk-profiling systems, Indonesia also uses non-intrusive cargo inspection devices, including Hi-Co, Gamma and X-ray scanners, in its major international ports. Non-intrusive devices such as X-ray scanners have been used in a number of major ports from before 1990.[21] In 2009–10 Indonesia installed more advanced instruments to carry out inspections. These include a number of new Gamma ray and Hi-Co Scan devices. Indonesia had six Gamma ray devices in 2010. These devices are installed in the three international ports of Tanjung Priok, Tanjung Emas and Tanjung Perak.[22] In comparison to other type of scanners, Hi-Co devices provide a more accurate scan result. Indonesia purchased four of these and operated them in Tanjung Priok and Tanjung Perak ports. These two ports are Indonesia main international gateways. Tanjung Priok port alone is responsible for managing 65 per cent of Indonesia's export and import activities.[23] The X-ray devices are used to scan imported cargos. The Gamma ray scanners have higher accuracy in comparison to X-ray scanners and are used in export cargo inspection.

Finally, in the operational domain the government has also been undertaking a thorough investigation to unravel terrorist activities. Indonesia's counter-terrorism efforts have been low key and largely focused on intelligence operations (*Jakarta Post*, 2002b). For counter-terrorism operations the government has equipped and set up counter-terrorism units in the armed forces and police. The specialist counter-terrorism units are detachment eighty-one of the army elite force, detachment Jala Mengkara of the navy, detachment Bravo Paskhas of the air force and detachment eighty-eight of the national police (DKPT, 2008, p. 2; Indonesian Coordinating Ministry for Political, Legal and Security Affairs, 2007, p. 132). Indonesia has also responded quickly to international warnings on possible maritime terrorism attacks, as exemplified in the March 2010 incident. In early March 2010, the IMB had sent out warnings to Indonesian maritime authorities noting that Islamic extremists in Indonesia planned to carry out attacks on two petroleum super tankers and five very large crude carrier (VLCC) vessels which pass through the Strait of Malacca.[24] Responding to the IMB warning on the possible terrorist attacks, Indonesia increased security and stepped up patrols in that area (Reuters, 2010).[25] This provides a counter argument to the widespread perception that Indonesia has not done enough in the war against terrorism (Chow, 2005, p. 309; Emmers, 2003, p. 429; Singh, 2004, p. 59; Sittnick, 2005, pp. 752–755).

The economic costs for the national counter-terrorism initiatives are high. Indonesia has allocated substantial resources to support its policies (Bappenas, 2011; Indonesian Coordinating Ministry for Political, Legal and Security Affairs,

2006a, pp. 25, 37–38).[26] An official in charge of the country's foreign and security policy budget claimed that concern over maritime terrorism has an impact on the state's allocation of resources.[27] She explained: 'we do not know whether terrorist only use maritime gateways to operate. Nevertheless, we identified that there are indications that they are travelling through maritime passages to enter our territory. The budget for countering terrorism is currently increasing'.[28] The costs incurred cover the expenses to improve counter-terrorism institutions, including the Indonesian Maritime Security Coordinating Board and the Anti-Terrorism Desk that later become the Counter-Terrorism Coordinating Body (*Badan Nasional Penanggulangan Terorisme*). They enhance the existing institutions, purchase new inspection devices such as X-ray, Gamma ray and Hi-Co scanning devices, and improve risk management systems through the implementation of MITA. The government bears the costs of financing the development of these counter-terrorism measures.

Indonesia has also carried out unilateral and bilateral attempts to address the surge in armed robbery. In 1992 Indonesia established a series of bilateral arrangements with Malaysia and Singapore to crack down on armed robbers in the areas where incidents were concentrated (IMB, 1992, p. 9). As can be seen from Figure 1.1, these attempts successfully reduced the number of attacks in 1993 to one fifth of that of the previous year. Nevertheless, as seen in Figure 1.1, as early as 1994 the statistics on armed robbery in Indonesia showed a relatively slow and steady increase. As Figures 1.1 and 1.2 show, the twin problems of the Asian 1997 economic crisis and rebel military operations in Aceh from 1998 fuelled a surge of armed robbery attacks in Indonesian waters. The Aceh separatist group Gerakan Aceh Merdeka (GAM) had been reported to be carrying out maritime robberies in the Strait of Malacca to fund their movement (Burton, 2006; Chen, 2007, pp. 139, 148; Mak, 2007, pp. 206–207; Power, 2008, p. 117; Ong-Webb, 2007, p. 78; Siregar *et al.*, 2004, p. 14; Sudrajat, 2005, p. 82).[29] At the same time, Indonesia was facing various issues on the domestic front. In the late 1990s to early 2000s, the Indonesian government was faced with not only the Aceh separatist movement at the western end of the archipelago but also a number of domestic challenges, including: the Papua separatist movement at its eastern end; the upsurge of religious conflict in Maluku and Poso; as well as ethnic violence elsewhere which had left thousands of people dead and injured and many others as internally displaced persons (Halloran, 2003). The economic crisis had forced the Indonesian defence force to tighten its budget, putting pressure on an already undermanned, ill-equipped and overstretched force (Meredith, 2000).

Government officials are aware of sea-robbery incidents in Indonesian waters but do not perceive this as a main threat. Currently, the main concern about sea-robbery attacks is in Palembang, the Berhala Strait, the South China Sea, particularly in the triangle between Indonesia's island of Natuna, Anambas, and up to off Tioman, and Eastern OPL (Outside Port Lines) of Singapore.[30] The Indonesian waterways surrounding Anambas and Natuna are gateways for ships to enter and exit the Malacca Straits.[31] The waterways near Anambas and Natuna are situated in one of the most important sea lanes of communication connecting the South China Sea via Indonesia's territory of the Karimata Straits, the Java Sea, and the Sunda Straits to the Indian Ocean (Dewan Maritim Indonesia, 2007b, p. 18).[32]

Although the Indonesian government acknowledges the threat of sea robberies in its waters, the issue was no longer a primary security concern in 2010. This was due to the decline in the number of sea-robbery attacks in Indonesian waterways, including the Strait of Malacca and Singapore. According to an official from the Indonesian Navy, the issue of piracy and armed robbery at sea has declined significantly. He suggested, 'even in 2009 there was no incident of armed robbery against ships, and so far there has been no incident reported in 2010',[33] although the IMB Piracy Reporting Centre noted fifteen incidents had taken place in Indonesian waters in 2009 and sisxteen incidents from January to June 2010 alone (IMB, 2010, p. 5). In addition, businesses in Indonesia did not deem sea robbery a serious concern. A representative of the Indonesian National Shipowners' Association described the Strait of Malacca and Singapore as a 'safe waterway' because the number of piratical incidents had dropped significantly. To quote him: 'Most of the incidents only take the form of petty thefts. The armed robbers in these cases do not seize the ship for ransom'.[34]

The peace process between the Indonesian government and GAM, in particular after the 26 December 2004 tsunami, further contributed to the decreasing number of armed robbery attacks in the Strait of Malacca. The 2004 tsunami brought tremendous devastation to Aceh province. It was reported that 166,080 people were killed in Aceh and 617,159 Acehnese became internally displaced persons (Indonesian Ministry of Health, 2013). Under this circumstance, the Indonesian government and GAM opted to restart peace negotiations in May 2005 to enable Aceh's reconstruction efforts (Chen, 2007, p. 143). Successful peace talks between the two parties have put an end to the separatist group's armed robbery activities in the Strait of Malacca (Kurniawan, 2008).[35] As a representative of the Indonesian ship-owners' association put it: 'In the past, seizure of freight ships in the Straits are often linked with GAM supporters ... the successful peace settlement between the Indonesian government and GAM has significantly reduced the seizures against ships in the Straits'.[36] Moreover, there is a widespread perception among government officials that Indonesia has shown sufficient cooperation and commitment to combatting sea robbery. Government officials perceive that Indonesia's national measures and cooperation with the other littoral states of the Straits of Malacca and Singapore have managed to secure the waterways. As the Indonesian Minister of Defence Juwono Sudarsono put it, 'Indonesia believes that it is under no pressure to ratify [any agreement to counter sea robbery]. Currently Indonesia, Malaysia and Singapore undertake coordinated patrols to secure the Malacca Strait' (BBC, 2006). The chairman of the Indonesian National Shipowners' Association echoed this stance. He claimed that armed robbery against ships is no longer a main threat; the security of waterways has improved after the littoral states carried out coordinated patrols.[37]

However, over time there has been a disjuncture between Indonesia's perception of the threat and the way the international community perceives it. As can be seen in Figure 1.1 and Figure 1.2, in 2005 armed robbery activities in Indonesian waters and the key Straits of Malacca and Singapore were already declining. Nevertheless, in 2005, the London-based Lloyd's Market Association's Joint War Committee (JWC) declared the Strait of Malacca as a war risk zone, together with Iraq, Lebanon and Nigeria, despite the incidents of sea robbery in the Strait of Malacca showing a declining trend (*Jakarta Post*, 2005). This point is confirmed in an interview with a Singaporean local ship-owner who was actively involved in protesting and lobbying the JWC to remove the Strait of Malacca from the war-risk list. He pointed to the JWC decision as a unilateral decision. According to the shipowner, when the JWC made the announcement, the sea-robbery incidents in the Strait of Malacca and Singapore had already 'calmed down', since Indonesia, Malaysia and Singapore had taken action to combat armed robbery at sea.[38] Sustained efforts to secure the Straits and protests from the Indonesian, Singaporean and Malaysian governments and their shipping associations against Lloyd's JWC finally resulted in the removal of the Strait of Malacca from its list of war and related perils areas in 2006 (Lloyds, 2006).[39] The removal of the Strait of Malacca and Singapore from the JWC list can be seen as an external validation of Indonesia's assessment of the problem.

Although the Indonesian government officials claim armed robbery against ships is no longer a problem for Indonesia and the JWC decision to remove the Strait of Malacca and Singapore validates Indonesia's perception, sea robbery in Indonesian waters has continued to be of international concern. The international community is still concerned over a sustained spate of armed robbery against ships that continues to take place in its territorial waters, in particular in the Strait of Malacca and Singapore and tri-border areas (bordered by Indonesia, Malaysia and the Philippine) in the Sulawesi sea (Intertanko, 2005; *Straits Times*, 2010; Young and Valencia, 2003, p. 271).[40] A Singaporean official claimed that the increased number of sea-robbery attacks in recent years is of significant concern for all maritime nations.[41] Non-governmental organisations that have concerns over the security and safety of navigation, scholars, international shipping lines, government officials and the media point to the increased levels of violence and degrees of sophistication, taking into account 'faster and more military-type craft and weapons', even though the use of violence from 2001 onwards has begun to show significant decline in comparison to the use of violence employed in armed robbery against ships in 1998 to 2000 (Intertanko, 2005; Sittnick, 2005, p. 744; *Straits Times*, 2010; Young and Valencia, 2003, p. 271). Despite the growing international concern regarding the rise of robbery attacks in Indonesian waters from 2010, Indonesian officials seemed to play down the threat posed by sea robbery. A high government official from the Indonesian Sea and Coast Guard, for instance, stated that 'one should not believe everything being reported by media or international organisations dealing with this issue'.[42] Officials characterised sea robbery incidents that took place in Indonesia as merely low-scale theft activities.[43] They suggested that the issue of rampant misreporting by international organisations had portrayed Indonesia in a bad light.[44]

At national level, responding to the first surge of sea robbery in 1990–92, the Indonesian Navy infiltrated a number of local sea-robber communities, which successfully resulted in arrests throughout 1992. The operation resulted in the arrest of 86 to 133 suspects in May, June and July 1992 (Chalk, 1998a, p. 98; Vagg, 1995, p. 77). During the second surge of armed robberies from 1996 to early 2001 propagated by the 1997 financial turmoil and military operations in Aceh, Indonesian authorities responded in several ways. At national level, Indonesia intensified its patrols. The Indonesian Navy dedicated fifteen Special Forces boats to help curb sea robbery around Batam, Bintan and Singapore (*Straits Times*, 2000b). The Navy also set up an armed robbery monitoring centre in Batam. The initial intention was to register all vessels plying through the Strait of Malacca with the centre (*Straits Times*, 2000b). In order to support the Batam command centre in 2000, the Navy developed operational bases and supporting facilities in Semampir, Surabaya, Belinyu Bangka and Batam, and built two ships (Indonesian Ministry of State Secretariat, 2001, p. X-7). The Navy also carries out routine maintenance and modification of its Garret Nbell-412 helicopters and Propeller Nomad N-22 surveillance aircraft to support its maritime patrol (Indonesian Ministry of State Secretariat, 2001, p. X-7). From 2012 to 2016, Indonesia has allocated funds in its budget to build ninety-one patrol boats (Bappenas, 2013, p. 4).

Responding to the increase of reported sea-robbery incidents from 2012 to 2014 on 1 December 2014, the Indonesian navy launched the Western Fleet Quick Response (WFQR) to intercept perpetrators of armed-robbery attacks against ships. The WFQR involves the five main naval bases in the western part of Indonesia: Belawan, Mentawai, Jakarta, Tanjung Pinang and Pontianak. As part of the WFQR, counter-sea-robbery teams from each naval base are put on stand-by in a number of designated areas. In order to protect the Straits of Malacca and Singapore, the Tanjung Pinang Naval Base has assigned the WFQR teams to guard key points located in Karimun, Batam and Lagoi islands.

A senior Indonesian navy official claimed that 98 per cent of perpetrators of armed robbery attacks against ships are Indonesian.[45] However, he explained that the buyers of the stolen products and the 'brains' behind the armed robberies are nationals of Indonesia's neighbouring countries.[46] By 2015, the Indonesian navy had captured and prosecuted sixty-eight perpetrators of armed-robbery attacks.[47] The Indonesian national media reported that the success of the WFQR has been acknowledged by the governments of Malaysia and Singapore (*Antara*, 2015). The ReCAAP Information Sharing Centre in Singapore confirmed this. To quote the ReCAAP 2015 piracy and armed robbery against ships annual report: 'the efforts of ... the Indonesian authorities in stepping up surveillance and enhancing patrols had resulted in the quick apprehension of masterminds and perpetrators (ReCAAP, 2015, p. 24).

In recent years, the Indonesian navy has also carried out teach-in activities in coastal areas that are known as the sea robbers' home towns. The purpose of such activities is to advise local residents on the legal punishment for committing armed-robbery attacks against ships. The navy has also encouraged societal actors including local youth groups and religious figures to provide information pertaining to activities related to armed-robbery attacks against ships in their neighbourhood.[48] In Riau Islands Province, which borders the Straits of Malacca and Singapore, the navy and the local government authorities have ordered all boat owners to register and paint their boats a designated colour: white for boats in Batam and yellow for boats from Tanjung Balai Karimun.[49]

The details of Indonesia's national initiatives to deal with sea robbery can be seen in Table 1.1.

These initiatives to counter armed robbery against ships generate high economic costs. Figure 1.4 shows that, even prior to the launch of international initiatives dealing with armed robbery against ships in 2004, Indonesia had allocated substantial resources to tackle this issue (Indonesian Ministry of State Secretariat, 2001, p. X6–7; Bappenas, 2011).

This is also confirmed by Admiral Edhi Nuswantoro and two MoD officials who are in charge of planning defence expenditure. They claim that Indonesia has long allocated substantial resources from its national budget to halt armed robbery against ships, particularly in the Straits of Malacca and Singapore, despite most vessels passing through the Straits not being bound for Indonesian ports (Nuswantoro, 2005, p. 5).[50] As explained earlier, this resource allocation has been used to: purchase fuel, surveillance and patrol devices; develop and maintain the information sharing centre and naval operation bases; finance maritime patrols; and fund welfare improvement programs for areas surrounding important waterways (Bakorkamla, 2004, pp. 8–12; Indonesian Ministry of State Secretariat, 2001, p. X-6; Nuswantoro, 2005; Sondakh, 2004, pp. 23–26).[51] A major operation to counter sea robbery, such as Octopus, for instance, absorbs enormous resources as it takes up to three months and involves ninety patrol boats and naval ships, four planes, two helicopters, and 2,973 personnel including marine and infantry units, amphibious scouts, frogman teams, and intelligence teams (*Jakarta Post*, 2005). The government also bears the cost of conducting routine patrols most of which were established before 1998, such as 'Operasi Kamla', 'Operasi Hiu Macan', and 'Operasi Sepanjang Tahun' (Bakorkamla, 2004, pp. 8–12).[52] Each operation involves between five and seven boats and three aircraft (Sondakh, 2004, p. 23).

As a result, when the international community began to pay greater attention to the vulnerability of maritime transport plying through Indonesian waters after 9/11, at national level Indonesian maritime agencies already had mechanisms to counter sea robbery in place. As seen in Table 1.1, Indonesian maritime agencies have been carrying out various unilateral patrols throughout the year and established a 'welfare program' which aims to improve the local economic conditions of the regencies which border Indonesian strategic sea lanes. An Indonesian navy official claimed that the government dissuasion program through empowering the locals has been very effective in reducing armed robbery at sea (Ho, 2007, p. 211).[53] The IMB 2005 Piracy and Armed Robbery against Ships report

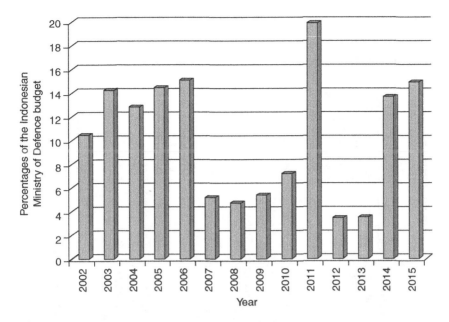

Figure 1.4 The Indonesian ministry of defence maritime security budget (percentages of total ministry of defence budget).

Source: adapted from Badan Perencanaan Pembangunan Nasional, 2011–15.

validated this claim. The IMB complimented Indonesia for its efforts to police the Strait of Malacca in several ways, including increasing unilateral patrols on the Indonesian side of the strait and intensive bilateral patrols with Malaysia that have caused a dramatic reduction in armed robbery (IMB, 2005, p. 31).

Dealing with international concerns over armed robbery against ships, the Indonesian government maintained its stance that responsibility to patrol the Straits lies solely with the littoral states and conveyed the suggestion to Malaysia and Singapore that they should conduct round-the-clock coordinated patrols (Ong-Webb, 2007, p. 88).[54] Thus, as part of the response, the Indonesian Chief of the Armed Forces, together with his Malaysian and Singaporean counterparts, launched coordinated naval patrols in 2004 and the Eyes in the Sky (EiS) air patrol in 2005 under the initiative known as the MSP agreement. In a bid to improve Straits security, the three littoral states took a further step by inviting Thailand to take part in MSP (Boey, 2006). On 21 April 2006, Indonesia, Malaysia and Singapore signed the Terms of References and Standard Operating Procedure of the Malacca Straits Patrol, which links the naval and EiS air patrols. In comparison to other forms of cooperation agreement signed in the past, the MSP agreement will allow one country's patrol vessels to cross over to other country's territorial waters in the event of hot pursuit, as long as the patrol vessel does not open fire or conduct other military actions (Raymond, 2007, p. 74).

Table 1.1 Indonesia's national initiatives to address armed robbery against ships

Initiative	Frequency	Duration	Location	Government agency
Octopus Operation (Operasi Gurita)	Five times a year	30–90 days	The Strait of Malacca and Singapore; eastern part of Indonesia; and waters surrounding Anambas	Led by the Indonesian Maritime Security Coordinating Board and involves the navy, the marine police, customs, the Ministry of Marine Affairs and Fisheries (KKP) and the air force
Bakorkamla Routine Patrol	Once every three months	30 days	All Indonesian sea lanes. The Batam work unit covers archipelagic sea lane I; Manado work unit covers archipelagic sea lane II; and Ambon work unit covers archipelagic sea lane III	Maritime Security Coordinating Board
Operasi SepanjangTahun	Every day	365 days, 24-hour patrol	Indonesian waters with particular emphasis in the Strait of Malacca	Navy
Operasi Kamla	Every day	365 days, 24-hour patrol	Strait of Malacca	Navy, marine police, customs, KKP
Operasi Trisila	Once a year	90 days	Indonesian waters	Navy
Operasi SatuanTugasMuaraPerairan (SatgasMupe)	n/a	n/a	Waters surrounding Aceh (northern end of the Strait of Malacca)	Navy
Operasi SatgaslaKoopslihkam	Bi-annual	180 days	The northern end of the Strait of Malacca (from Sabang to North of Aceh)	Navy
Air Patrol	Every day	365 days	Strait of Malacca	Air force (west squadron)
Stand-by Air Force	Every day	365 days	Tanjung Pinang, Belawan and Sabang (near the Strait of Malacca)	Air force (west squadron)

Search and Rescue Units Air Patrol	n/a	n/a	Tanjung Pinang, Belawan, Dumai and Mentigi	Search and rescue units Army
Deployment of armed forces at islands bordering key waterways	Every day	365 days	The designated points of deployment along the Strait of Malacca are (1) Sabang; (2) Lhokumawe (which covers the waterways of Pidie-Lokhsumawe, Jamboaye, Tanjung Peureula and Tanjung Tamiang); (3) Belawan (which covers the waterways of Tanjung Tamiang, Belawan, Pulau Berhala and Pulau Pandang); (4) Tanjung Balai Asahan (which covers the waterways of Pulau Pandang, Tanjung Balai Asahan-Jemur-Bagan siapi-api); (5) Dumai; (6) Iyu Kecil (the area of coverage is Iyu Kecil waterway); (7) Tanjung Balai Karimun (which covers the Philips Strait); (8) Tolop; (9) Sambu; (10) Batam; and (11) Tanjung Pinang	
Operation Bakti (poverty reduction program in areas that border key sea lanes)	n/a	n/a	Regencies of Rokan, Hilir, Bengkalis, Siak, Palawan, Indragiri Ilir and Karimun which border the Straits of Malacca and Singapore are the key priority areas (Ho, 2007, p. 211). Second in the welfare program's priority list are other regencies that border the Straits of Lombok and Sunda (Ho, 2007, p. 211)	Navy

Sources: Badan Koordinasi Keamanan Laut (2004, 2010); Ho (2007, 2011); Nuswantoro (2005); Sondakh (2004).

48 *Maritime security and Indonesia*

The MSP initiative implies a willingness to strengthen measures to counter sea robbery at a practical level. This was confirmed in an interview with a government official from the Singapore Maritime and Port Authority. He claimed that cooperation between the three littoral states became stronger in 2005 and 2006.[55] Nevertheless, prior to this period there has been 'coordination between the armed forces and police of Indonesia, Malaysia and Singapore, and also informal cooperation between the three countries coast guards, police and military'.[56] A senior official from the Singapore MFA shared this opinion. She suggested that over the years Indonesia has successfully cooperated with other littoral states and this cooperation between the littoral states is still ongoing.[57] A director of an international shipping line in an interview claimed that one initiative that seemed to be effective in reducing the number of sea robberies is the agreement between the littoral states to work together to try to police the Straits of Malacca and Singapore.[58] He pointed out that 'the united pooling of resources among Singapore, Indonesia and Malaysia to secure the Strait of Malacca and Singapore has been a constructive commitment and that appears to be having benefit for all ship-owners'.[59] Indonesian participation in various maritime arrangements to address sea robbery also points to the main puzzle of this book: Indonesia is willing to cooperate through some arrangements but less inclined to take part in others.

Maritime security issues in Indonesia's archipelago

As explained in the previous section, apart from potential maritime terrorism and armed robbery against ships, Indonesia is facing various other maritime security challenges. Indonesian documents and government officials identify four main maritime issues in Indonesian waters (Dewan Maritim Indonesia, 2007a, pp. 4–4, 4–9; Indonesian Coordinating Ministry for Political, Legal and Security Affairs, 2008, pp. 51–52; Indonesian MFA, 2004, p. 3; 2009; Indonesian Ministry of State Secretariat, 2008, p. 29; Sudrajat, 2005, pp. 80–81; Suristyono, 2005, pp. 47, 70–71).[60] These are: illegal fishing, illegal migrants travelling through its waters, maritime border issues and smuggling. There is no exact priority rank among the four maritime issues. To provide a comprehensive discussion, this section explores these maritime challenges affecting Indonesian waters. Understanding maritime threats facing Indonesia and Indonesia's perception of them is important when seeking to comprehend Indonesia's reaction towards a number of cooperation initiatives in maritime security.

On the first issue, a large volume of marine products from the archipelago are illegally fished. A substantial portion of these products are fished by foreign vessels operating without permit or with a permit that has been illegally transferred from an Indonesian permit holder to foreign fishermen (Agoes, 2005, p. 43; Williams, 2007 as cited in Cribb and Ford, 2009, p. 16). The vessels captured for conducting illegal fishing in Indonesian waters from 2007 to 2015 were flagged vessels from Indonesia (448), Malaysia (84), the Philippines (58), China (31), Thailand (113), Vietnam (426), Taiwan (6) and Hong Kong (2) (Indonesian Ministry of Marine Affairs and Fisheries, 2015).

Illegal fishing has also depleted Indonesian fish stocks, although Indonesia has only used 48 per cent out of its 6.7 million tons total allowable catch (Dewan Maritim Indonesia, 2007a, 4–1, 5–7). As a consequence of illegal fishing, overfishing has become a common phenomenon in almost all the archipelagic waters (see Table 1.2). Indonesia takes part in international cooperation to address illegal fishing. Indonesia is a signatory to the 1995 *UN Fish Stocks Agreement and the Food and Agriculture Organization International Plan of Action to Deter, Prevent and Eliminate Illegal, Unreported and Unregulated Fishing* (Sodik, 2009a, p. 250; 2009b, pp. 77–78). Indonesia's participation in international arrangements to address illegal fishing suggests that Indonesia is willing to join arrangements to solve issues that it considers as prime maritime challenges.

Second, in regards to the maritime border problem, Indonesia's sensitivity over this issue is derived from its perception of threat. In 2002 in a territorial dispute with Malaysia, Indonesia lost Sipadan and Ligitan islands through an International Court of Justice decision (*Straits Times*, 2005). Due to unsettled maritime boundaries, there has been a growing concern over possible claiming of Indonesia outermost islands by neighbouring states, as shown in the Sipadan and Ligitan islands case (*Jakarta Post*, 2009). Indonesia shares a maritime border with ten countries: Malaysia, Thailand, India, Singapore, Vietnam, the Philippines, Palau, Papua New Guinea, Timor Leste and Australia (*Jakarta Post*, 2010a). Details on the status of maritime border agreements between Indonesia and its neighbouring countries can be seen in Table 1.3.

Out of Indonesia's ninety-two outermost islands, there are twenty-two islands on the border between Indonesia and Malaysia; four islands are located near the border with Singapore; two islands sit on the border between Indonesia and Vietnam; eleven islands are located near to the Philippines; seven islands are on the border between Indonesia and Palau; twenty-three islands are close to Australia; ten islands are near the border of Indonesia and East Timor; twelve islands

Table 1.2 Overfished fishery stocks in Indonesia

	Type of fishery product	Overfished areas
1	Shrimp	All Indonesian waters except from the Seram Sea to Tomini Bay, Sulawesi Sea, Pacific Ocean and Indian Ocean
2	Karang Tille Fish	Java Sea, Makasar Strait, Flores Sea, Sulawesi Sea, Pacific Ocean and Indian Ocean
3	Demersal Fish	The Strait of Malacca, Strait of Makasar and Flores Sea, Sulawesi Sea, Pacific Ocean and Arafura Sea
4	Little Pelagic Fish	The Strait of Malacca and Java Sea
5	Big Pelagic Fish	Sulawesi Sea and Pacific Ocean
6	Lobster	The Strait of Makasar and Flores Sea
7	Squid	The Strait of Malacca, Java Sea, the Strait of Makasar, Flores Sea and Arafura Sea

Source: Dewan Maritim Indonesia (2007a, pp. 5, 6, 7).

Table 1.3 Status of Indonesia's maritime boundaries agreements with neighbouring states

Neighbouring state	Status of maritime boundaries agreement			
	Territorial sea	Contiguous zone	Exclusive economic zone	Continental shelf
1 India	✗	✗	–	✓
2 Thailand	✗	✗	–	✓
3 Malaysia	✓	–	–	✓
4 Singapore	✓	✗	✗	✗
5 Vietnam	✗	×	–	✓
6 The Philippines	✗	–	–	–
7 Palau	✗	✗	–	–
8 Papua New Guinea	✓	✗	✓	✓
9 Australia	✗	✗	✓	✓
10 East Timor	–	–	–	–

Source: Dewan Maritim Indonesia (2007a, 8–3, 8–4).

Notes
✓ Indicates that maritime border agreements between the two countries have been signed or ratified.
✗ Indicates that maritime border agreements between the two countries are not required.
– Indicates that maritime border agreements have not been discussed.

are close to the border of Indonesia and India; and one island rests near to the border of Papua New Guinea (Indonesian Coordinating Ministry for Political, Legal and Security Affairs, 2007, pp. 73, 124). Indonesia categorised twelve of its outermost islands as top priority to be secured, as these islands mark Indonesian territories. These twelve outermost islands, their locations and the bordering states are outlined in Table 1.4.

Even though there has been no open border conflict, Indonesia is concerned over unsettled maritime borders with neighbouring states. Although Indonesia has accepted its loss over the Sipadan and Ligitan islands, there remain several border disputes to settle between Indonesia and Malaysia. These include the dispute over the oil-rich Ambalat Block in the Makassar Strait and the maritime border in the Strait of Malacca (*Straits Times*, 2005). Due to the bilateral nature of this issue, Indonesia mainly carries out bilateral negotiations to manage or seek a solution over maritime disputes.

Third, illegal seaborne immigration has posed a significant challenge to Indonesian authority. There are two groups of illegal immigrants that pass through Indonesian waters. The first group is illegal migrant workers from Indonesia who are trying to cross to Malaysia. The huge volume of illegal crossers from Indonesia to Malaysia has been a source of diplomatic tensions between the two governments (Cribb and Ford, 2009, p. 9). The second group of people crossing Indonesian waters is asylum seekers from South Asia and the Middle East. Indonesia, together with Malaysia, India, Thailand, and Hong Kong (China), is

Table 1.4 List of Indonesia's outermost islands

No	Name of the island	Location	Bordering state
1	Rondo	Indian Ocean (Nangroe Aceh Darussalam)	India
2	Berhala	Strait of Malacca (North Sumatera)	Malaysia
3	Nipa	Straits of Singapore (Riau Islands)	Singapore
4	Sekatung	South China Sea (Riau Island)	Vietnam
5	Marore	Sulawesi Sea (North Sulawesi)	The Philippines
6	Marampit	Sulawesi Sea (North Sulawesi)	The Philippines
7	Miangas	Sulawesi Sea (North Sulawesi)	The Philippines
8	Fani	Pacific (West Papua)	Palau
9	Fanildo	Pacific (Papua)	Palau
10	Bras	Pacific (Papua)	Palau
11	Batek	Sawu Sea (East Nusa Tenggara)	Timor Leste
12	Sebatik Island	East Kalimantan	Malaysia

Source: Indonesian Ministry of Defence (2008, pp. 48–49).

among the top fifteen United Nations High Commissioners for Refugees (UNHCR) Refugee Status Determination operations in the world in terms of applications received and decisions given (UNHCR, 2010, p. 39). In 2009 with 3,230 claims Indonesia experienced the largest increase in asylum applications in the world (UNHCR, 2010, p. 39). This statistics increased to 3,900 in 2010 (UNHCR, 2011, p. 43). According to an Indonesian navy official, groups of immigrants that frequently ply through the Strait of Malacca are mainly asylum seekers arriving from Sri Lanka.[61] In addition to asylum seekers from Sri Lanka, Indonesia has also become an important staging point for people coming from Bangladesh, Pakistan, the Middle East and Afghanistan that intend to enter Australia and New Zealand (OECD, 2003, p. 115).[62] The Indonesian provinces of East Nusa Tenggara, the Riau Islands, West Kalimantan, and North Sulawesi, particularly Miangas Island, are common corridors for illegal migrants to travel in and out of Indonesia's territory (Dewan Maritim Indonesia, 2007b, p. 33; OECD, 2003, p. 112). Indonesia cannot easily deport these immigrants because most of them are looking for asylum protection and are protected by international convention. This circumstance has burdened the Indonesian government, although the International Organization of Migrants assists with the provision of the migrants' basic needs (OECD, 2003, p. 254). More importantly, there is a growing concern that some of the asylum seekers could be members of terrorist organisations, as most of the immigrants do not carry clear identification documents.[63] Indonesia participates in international cooperation arrangements to address undocumented immigrant issues. Indonesia has ratified the *United Nations Convention against Transnational Organized Crime* and the two protocols that supplement it, the *Protocol to Prevent, Suppress and Punish Trafficking in Persons, Especially Women and Children*; and the *Protocol against the Smuggling of Migrants by Land, Sea and Air*. Indonesia attempts to address illegal seaborne immigration by taking part in these initiatives imply that this archipelagic state is willing to address issues which it considers as high priority in its national security agenda, through participation in international arrangements.

Fourth, pertaining to smuggling over a porous border, the many outlying uninhabited islands throughout the archipelago and an under-equipped law enforcement force have weakened the state's capability to control the various networks of private authority that operate across its border. This situation renders Indonesia open to the serious problem of smuggling. Most goods are smuggled across the Strait of Malacca to avoid law or tax (Valencia, 2006, p. 92). These include illicit materials such as small arms and drugs; items that weaken domestic industries (this can range from steel to second-hand clothing); goods that circumvent national tariffs, such as liquor and cigarettes; other consumer goods, such as subsidised fuel and rice; and endangered species (Cribb and Ford, 2009, p. 15; Nik and Permal, 2008, pp. 193–194). Consumer goods such as cigarettes and drugs are smuggled from Indonesia to Malaysia, but items of concern including small arms and light weapons flow in the opposite direction (*Jakarta Post*, 2010b; Nik and Permal, 2008, pp. 193–194; Valencia, 2006, p. 92; Yasin, 2007, p. 232). The arms are smuggled by boat, usually by fishing boat, from Thailand and Malaysia across the Strait of Malacca to the Indonesian province of Aceh (*Jakarta Post*, 2010b; Valencia, 2006, p. 92; Yasin, 2007, p. 232). Beside Thailand and Malaysia, arms are also smuggled by sea into the country, particularly to North Sulawesi (Miangas Island) from the Philippines and Australia (*Jakarta Post*, 2002a). Indonesian senior intelligence officers claim that smuggled weapons from these four countries have been responsible for exacerbating violent conflicts across the country (*Jakarta Post*, 2002a). Since 1998, communal conflicts and terrorist activities have flared up in a number of locations in Indonesia (*Jakarta Post*, 2002a, 2010c). Smuggling of goods also causes economic loss to Indonesia. The value of off-book trade can reach US$2 billion per year, and every year Indonesia loses US$600 million because of smuggling (Oegroseno, 2006, p. 37). Indonesia has actively taken part in a number of international arrangements to address smuggling (Indonesian MFA 2010). These include the *UN Single Convention on Narcotics*, the *UN Convention on Psychotropic Substances*, the *UN Convention against Illicit Traffic in Narcotic Drugs and Psychotropic Substances*, the *UN Convention on Transnational Organized Crime* and the *UN Program of Action to Prevent, Combat and Eradicate the Illicit Trade in Small Arms and Light Weapons in All Its Aspects/Plan of Action*. Indonesia's response to smuggling suggests that the archipelagic state is not reluctant to explore possible solutions to one of its top maritime security problems through participation in international arrangements.

Conclusion

Indonesia is important for international maritime security. The archipelagic key straits of Malacca, Lombok and Sunda are designated as part of the world sea lanes of communication. Soon after 9/11, the international community began to view the possibility of maritime terrorism and sea robbery in Indonesian waters as an international maritime security concern. A number of key international arrangements to address armed robbery against ships and prevent maritime terrorism (including the ReCAAP, the international ship and port facility security (ISPS) Code, the CSI, and the PSI), were launched few years after the 9/11 attacks.

As this chapter has demonstrated, these arrangements did not coincide with Indonesian concern over maritime terrorism and sea robbery. The maritime security arrangements to halt armed robbery against ships, such as RMSI and ReCAAP, were introduced in 2004 when Indonesia's national, bilateral and regional efforts began to show positive results and the number of incidents started to decline. In the case of maritime terrorism, when the US launched the CSI and the PSI in 2002 and 2003, partly as result of the 2002 Bali bombing, Indonesia had already set up its national mechanism to deal with terrorism. In the following years, Indonesia started to show good results in unravelling terrorist networks. More importantly, the US-led cooperation initiatives to deal with potential maritime terrorism, such as the CSI and PSI, were designed to prevent the delivery of WMD by shipping container bound for US territory. The focus of these maritime arrangements does not correspond with the way Indonesia perceives the threat posed by maritime terrorism. Indonesian concerns over maritime terrorism are more locally focused (Valencia, 2005, pp. 18, 25). They mainly concentrate on the possibility of terrorist attacks upon key waterways, ports or a neighbouring port that may block inter-island trade and international navigation.

The benefits Indonesia perceives from cooperation are further reduced because, at the same time as the 9/11 attacks raised the profile of maritime terrorism and armed robbery against ships, Indonesia was facing a range of issues in its waterways including illegal fishing, border disputes, illegal seaborne migrants, and smuggling. The government perceived these threats as more pressing in comparison to maritime terrorism and armed robbery against ships since they posed direct threats to the Indonesian economy, territorial integrity and the livelihood of Indonesian fisherman. This is a key disjuncture between Indonesia and the international maritime community and informs Indonesia's varying participation across various maritime security initiatives.

Despite Indonesia not considering armed robbery against ships and maritime terrorism as being at the top of its security agenda, Indonesia has been cooperating extensively with neighbouring states and extra-regional states through various international cooperation arrangements. Here, Indonesia's participation adds to the key puzzle of this book. Why, despite Indonesia's active engagement in some cooperation arrangements, is participation in other arrangements met with a high degree of reluctance by Indonesia? Addressing this central question forms the core of this book.

Notes

1 Interviews with a high government official at the Indonesian Ministry of Foreign Affairs (Jakarta, 26 October 2011); representatives of the Indonesian Shipowners' Association (Surabaya, 22 September 2011); and a former government official at the Indonesian Maritime Security Coordinating Board (Jakarta, 3 July 2010).
2 Interviews with a high government official at the Indonesian Ministry of Foreign Affairs (Jakarta, 26 October 2011); representatives of the Indonesian Shipowners' Association (Surabaya, 22 September 2011); and a former government official at the Indonesian Maritime Security Coordinating Board (Jakarta, 3 July 2010).
3 Interview with a high government official at the Indonesian Ministry of Transportation (Jakarta, 29 September 2011).
4 Interviews with a high government official at the Indonesian Ministry of Defence (Jakarta, 7 July 2010), and a high government official at the Indonesian Navy (Jakarta, 14 July 2010).
5 Interview with a high government official from the Indonesian navy (Jakarta, 14 July 2010).
6 Interview with a representative of the Indonesian Shipowners' Association (Jakarta, 29 June 2010).
7 Interview with a representative of a chamber of commerce in Singapore (Singapore, 18 August 2010).
8 Interview with a representative of an international re-insurance company (Singapore, 17 August 2010).
9 Interview with an international tanker operator (Singapore, 19 August 2010).
10 Interviews with an international tanker operator (Singapore, 19 August 2010); and a representative of an international re-insurance company (Singapore, 17 August 2010).
11 Interview with a representative of a non-governmental organisation that focuses on maritime security (Singapore, 12 August 2015).
12 IMO Assembly 26th Session A 26/Res.1025 *Code of Practice for the Investigation of Crimes of Piracy and Armed Robbery Against Ships*, adopted on 2 December 2009.
13 Article 34 (1) of the UNCLOS 1982.
14 Article 92 (1) of the UNCLOS 1982 states that:

> Ships shall sail under the flag of one State only and, save in exceptional cases expressly provided for in international treaties or in this Convention, shall be subject to its exclusive jurisdiction on the high seas. A ship may not change its flag during a voyage or while in a port of call, save in the case of a real transfer of ownership or change of registry.

15 Article 94 of the UNCLOS on duties of the flag state.
16 Interview with a high government official from the Indonesian navy (Jakarta, 14 July 2010).
17 Interview with a high government official at the Indonesian National Development Planning Agency (Jakarta, 28 September 2011).
18 Law No. 1 of 2002 on Combating Criminal Acts of Terrorism and Law No. 2 of 2002 on the Enforcement of Government Regulation number 1 of 2002 on Combating Criminal Acts of Terrorism.
19 Interviews with a high government official at the Indonesian Maritime Security Coordinating Board (Jakarta, 2 July 2010); a former government official at the Indonesian Maritime Security Coordinating Board (Jakarta, 3 July 2010); and a high government official at the Ministry of Transportation (Jakarta, 3 September 2010).
20 Interviews with a high government official at the Indonesian Maritime Security Coordinating Board (Jakarta, 2 July 2010); a high government official from the Indonesian navy (Jakarta, 14 July 2010); and high government officials at the Indonesian Customs and Excise, Ministry of Finance (Jakarta, 3 November 2011).

21 Interview with a high government official at the Indonesian Customs and Excise, Ministry of Finance (Jakarta, 4 November 2011).
22 Interview with high government officials at the Indonesian Customs and Excise, Ministry of Finance (Jakarta, 3 November 2011).
23 Interview with an official at the Indonesian Customs and Excise, Ministry of Finance (Jakarta, 11 October 2011).
24 Email correspondence between the International Maritime Bureau, Kuala Lumpur, and the Indonesian Marine Police Command and Info Centre, Indonesian Navy Headquarters, Jakarta Marine Police Headquarters, Bakorkamla, subject: Possible Terror Threat, Wednesday, 3 March 2010.
25 Interview with a high government official at the Indonesian Maritime Security Coordinating Board (Jakarta, 2 July 2010).
26 Interview with a high government official at the Indonesian National Development Planning Agency (Jakarta, 28 September 2011).
27 Interview with a high government official at the Indonesian National Development Planning Agency (Jakarta, 28 September 2011).
28 Interview with a high government official at the Indonesian National Development Planning Agency (Jakarta, 28 September 2011).
29 Interviews with a high government official at the Indonesian Ministry of Defence (Jakarta, 7 July 2010); and a representative of the Indonesian Shipowners' Association (Jakarta, 29 June 2010).
30 Interviews with a representative of the IMB's Piracy Reporting Centre (Kuala Lumpur, 20 July 2010); and a high government official at the Indonesian Ministry of Transportation (Jakarta, 3 September 2010).
31 Interview with a high government official from the Indonesian navy (Jakarta, 14 July 2010).
32 Interview with a high government official at the Indonesian Maritime Security Coordinating Board (Jakarta, 2 July 2010).
33 Interview with a high government official from the Indonesian navy (Jakarta, 14 July 2010).
34 Interview with a representative of the Indonesian Shipowners' Association (Jakarta, 29 June 2010).
35 Interviews with a representative of the Indonesian Shipowners' Association (Jakarta, 29 June 2010); and a high government official at the Indonesian Ministry of Defence (Jakarta, 7 July 2010).
36 Interview with a representative of the Indonesian Shipowners' Association (Jakarta, 29 June 2010).
37 Interview with a representative of the Indonesian Shipowners' Association (Jakarta, 29 June 2010).
38 Interview with a Singaporean local ship owner (Singapore, 6 August 2010).
39 Interview with a Singaporean local ship owner (Singapore, 6 August 2010).
40 Interviews with a representative of the United States Coast Guards (Singapore, 20 August 2010); and a representative of a multinational shipping line (Singapore, 11 August 2010).
41 Interview with a Singaporean official (Singapore, 11 August 2015).
42 Interview with a high government official from the Indonesian Sea and Coast Guard, the Ministry of Transportation, (Jakarta, 19 August 2015).
43 Interviews with officials from the Indonesian Sea and Coast Guard Division, and Regional and Legal Department, the Ministry of Transportation, (Jakarta, 19 August 2015).
44 Interviews with officials from the Indonesian Sea and Coast Guard Division, and Regional and Legal Department, the Ministry of Transportation, (Jakarta, 19 August 2015).

45 Interview with a high government official from the Indonesian navy, (Tanjung Pinang, 24 February 2016).
46 Interview with a high government official from the Indonesian navy, (Tanjung Pinang, 24 February 2016).
47 Interview with a high government official from the Indonesian navy, (Tanjung Pinang, 24 February 2016).
48 Interview with a high government official from the Indonesian navy, (Batam, 19 February 2016).
49 Interview with a high government official from the Indonesian navy, (Tanjung Pinang, 24 February 2016).
50 Interview with high government officials at the Indonesian Ministry of Defence (Jakarta, 24 November 2011).
51 Interview with high government officials at the Indonesian Ministry of Defence (Jakarta, 24 November 2011).
52 Interviews with a high government official at the Indonesian Ministry of Defence (Jakarta, 7 July 2010), and high government officials at the Indonesian Ministry of Defence (Jakarta, 24 November 2011).
53 Interview with a high government official from the Indonesian navy (Jakarta, 14 July 2010).
54 Interview with a high government official from the Indonesian navy (Jakarta, 14 July 2010).
55 Interview with a high government official from the Singapore Maritime Port Authority (Singapore, 6 August 2010).
56 Interview with a high government official from the Singapore Maritime Port Authority (Singapore, 6 August 2010).
57 Interview with a Singaporean high government official (Singapore, 11 August 2010).
58 Interview with a representative of a multinational shipping line (Singapore, 11 August 2010).
59 Interview with a representative of a multinational shipping line (Singapore, 11 August 2010).
60 Interviews with a high government official at the Indonesian Ministry of Defence (Jakarta, 7 July 2010); and a high government official from the Indonesian navy (Jakarta, 14 July 2010).
61 Interview with a high government official from the Indonesian navy (Jakarta, 14 July 2010).
62 Interview with a high government official at the Indonesian Ministry of Defence (Jakarta, 7 July 2010).
63 Interview with a high government official at the Indonesian Ministry of Defence (Jakarta, 7 July 2010).

References

Agoes, Etty R. (2005). 'Pengelolaan Keamanan di Selat Malaka Secara Terpadu', in *Pertemuan Kelompok Ahli Kebijakan Terpadu Pengelolaan Keamanan Selat Malaka*. Jakarta: Badan Pengkajian dan Pengembangan Kebijakan Kementerian Luar Negeri Indonesia.

Antara. (2015). 'Tim Reaksi Cepat Komando Armada Barat TNI AL Diberi Penghargaan', 11 October 2015, available from www.antaranews.com/berita/522912/tim-reaksi-cepat-komando-armada-barat-tni-al-diberi-penghargaan. Last accessed 2 March 2016.

APEC Desk of the Republic of Indonesia Customs. (2011). *Collective Action Plan*. Jakarta: The APEC Desk of the Republic of Indonesia Customs, available at www.

sjdih.depkeu.go.id/fullText/2010/219~PMK.04~2010Per.HTM. Last accessed 28 November 2011.
ASEAN. (2009). *ASEAN Statistical Yearbook 2008*. Jakarta: ASEAN Secretariat.
Australian Department of Defence. (2012). 'Minister for Defence and Minister for Defence Materiel – Joint Press Conference – Indonesia', 5 September 2012, available at www.minister.defence.gov.au/2012/09/05/minister-for-defence-and-minister-for-defence-materiel-joint-press-conference-indonesia/. Last accessed 19 October 2012.
Badan Koordinasi Keamanan Laut (Bakorkamla). (2004). 'Workshop Selat Malaka: Pola Pengamanan Selat Malaka dan Permasalahannya'. Bakorkamla: Jakarta.
Bakorkamla. (2010). *Buku Putih Bakorkamla 2009*. Jakarta: Pustaka Cakra.
Badan Perencanaan Pembangunan Nasional (Bappenas). (2011). *Sandingan Alokasi Pagu Definitif APBN Tahun 2005–2010 Berdasarkan Program Per Kementerian/Lembaga (Juta Rupiah): Kementerian Koordinator Bidang Politik dan Keamanan*. Jakarta: Direktorat Pertahanan dan Keamanan.
Bappenas. (2013). *Rancangan Rencana Kerja Pemerintah (RKP) Tahun 2013*. Jakarta: Bappenas.
BBC. (2006). 'Indonesia determined to Postpone Ratification of Malacca Strait Pact', 27 September 2006, accessed from the Newsbank database.
Boey, David. (2006). 'S'pore, KL, Jakarta Sign Anti-Piracy Pact – Defence Chiefs again Ask Bangkok to Join Patrols in Malacca Strait', *Straits Times*, 22 April, accessed from the Newsbank database.
Brodie, Ian, Theodoulou, Michael and Cobain, Ian. (2000). 'Suicide Bombers Gave Salute as They Died', *Times*, 13 October 2000, accessed from the Newsbank database.
Burton, John. (2006). 'ASIA–PACIFIC: Malacca Strait loses its War Risk Rating as Piracy Eases', *Financial Times*, 9 August, accessed from the Newsbank database.
Carana. (2004). *Impact of Transport and Logistics on Indonesia's Trade Competitiveness*, available at www.carana.com/images/PDF_car/Indonesia%20Transport%20and%20Logistics%20Report.pdf. Last accessed 20 January 2011.
Chalk, Peter. (1998a). 'Contemporary Maritime Piracy in Southeast Asia'. *Studies in Conflict and Terrorism* 21:1, pp. 87–112.
Chalk, Peter. (1998b). 'Political Terrorism in South-East Asia'. *Terrorism and Political Violence* 10:2, pp. 118–134.
Chandrasekaran, Rajiv. (2001). 'Pirates Flourish on Asian Seas – Seizure of Indonesian Freighter Illustrates Growing Anarchy', *Washington Post*, 18 June 2001. Last accessed 28 April 2011.
Chen, Jeffrey. (2007). 'The Emerging Nexus between Piracy and Maritime Terrorism in Southeast Asia Waters: A Case Study on the Gerakan Aceh Merdeka (GAM)', in *Violence at Sea Piracy in the Age of Global Terrorism*, Peter Lehr (ed.). New York: Routledge.
Chow, Jonathan T. (2005). 'ASEAN Counterterrorism Cooperation Since 9/11'. *Asian Survey* 45:2, pp. 302–321.
Clough, Patricia. (1985). 'Gaps Left in Liner Passengers' Account of Hijack Ordeal – Achille Lauro Affair', *Times*, 18 October 1985, accessed from the Newsbank database.
Coutrier, P.L. (1988). 'Living on an Oil Highway'. *Ambio* 17:3, pp. 186–188.
Cribb, Robert and Ford, Michele. (2009). 'Indonesia as An Archipelago: Managing Islands, Managing the Seas', in *Indonesia beyond the Water's Edge*. Singapore: Institute of Southeast Asian Studies.
Desk Koordinasi Pemberantasan Terorisme (DKPT). (2008). *Catatan DKPT*. Jakarta: Kementrian Koordinator Bidang Politik, Hukum dan Keamanan Republik Indonesia.

Dewan Maritim Indonesia. (2007a). *Laporan: Perumusan Kebijakan Grand Strategi Pembangunan Kelautan*. Jakarta: Sekretariat Jenderal Departemen Kelautan dan Perikanan.
Dewan Maritim Indonesia. (2007b). *Analisis Potensi Ekonomi Maritim Dalam Rangka Perumusan Kebijakan Ekonomi Maritim Indonesia*. Jakarta: Sekretariat Jenderal Departemen Kelautan dan Perikanan.
Dittmer, Lowell. (2007). 'Assessing American Asia Policy'. *Asian Survey* 47:4, pp. 521–535.
Djalal, Hasjim. (2009). 'Indonesia's Archipelagic Sea Lanes', in *Indonesia beyond the Water's Edge*. Singapore: Institute of Southeast Asian Studies.
Emmers, Ralf. (2003). 'ASEAN and the Securitization of Transnational Crime in Southeast Asia'. *The Pacific Review* 16:3, pp. 419–438.
Febrica, Senia. (2010). 'Securitizing Terrorism in Southeast Asia: Accounting for the Varying Responses of Singapore and Indonesia'. *Asian Survey* 50:3, pp. 569–590.
Greaves, Suzanne and Hill, George. (1985). 'The Times Review of 1985 ... a Year of Calamity and Hope', *Times*, 30 December 1985, accessed from the Newsbank database.
Halloran, Richard. (2003). 'Indonesia a Worrying Blip on American Radar Screens', *Straits Times*, 2 August 2003, accessed from the Newsbank database.
Ho, Joshua. (2007). 'Securing the Seas as a Medium of Transportation in Southeast Asia', in *The Security of Sea Lanes of Communication in the Indian Ocean Region*. Kuala Lumpur: Maritime Institute of Malaysia.
Indonesian Coordinating Ministry for Political, Legal and Security Affairs. (2006a). *Laporan Akuntabilitas Kinerja Tahun 2005*. Jakarta: Kementerian Koordinator Bidang Politik, Hukum dan Keamanan.
Indonesian Coordinating Ministry for Political, Legal and Security Affairs. (2006b). *Penetapan Rencana Kinerja Tahun 2006*. Jakarta: Kemenkopolhukam.
Indonesian Coordinating Ministry for Political, Legal and Security Affairs. (2007). *Kumpulan Pidato Menteri Koordinator Bidang Politik Hukum dan Keamanan Republik Indonesia*. Jakarta: Kementerian Koordinator Bidang Politik Hukum dan Keamanan Indonesia.
Indonesian Coordinating Ministry for Political, Legal and Security Affairs. (2008). *Evaluasi Pengelolaan Bidang Politik, Hukum dan Keamanan Tahun 2007*. Jakarta: Coordinating Ministry for Political, Legal and Security Affairs.
Indonesian Directorate General of Sea Transportation (DGST). (2010). *Penjagaan Laut dan Pantai (Indonesian Sea and Coast Guard)*. Jakarta: Direktorat Jenderal Perhungan Laut.
Indonesian Ministry of Defence. (2008). *Defence White Paper*. Jakarta: Ministry of Defence.
Indonesian Ministry of Foreign Affairs (MFA). (2004). *Forum Dialog ke XI Kerjasama Maritim ASEAN*. Jakarta: Badan Pengkajian dan Pengembangan Kebijakan.
Indonesian MFA. (2006). *Pertemuan Kelompok Ahli Membahas Aspek Strategis Diplomasi Kelautan Dalam Mendukung Pembangunan Nasional*. Jakarta: Indonesian MFA.
Indonesian MFA. (2009). 'Background Singkat Pembentukan ASEAN Maritime Forum', made available to author through an email correspondence with the Head of Security Division, *Directorate* of *ASEAN Political and Security Cooperation*, Heru H. Subolo (Jakarta, 26 August 2009).
Indonesian MFA. (2010). 'International Issues: Small Arms and Light Weapons', 7 July 2010, available at www.deplu.go.id/Pages/IIssueDisplay.aspx?IDP=17&l=en. Last accessed 4 May 2011.

Indonesian Ministry of Health. (2013). 'Jumlah Pengungsi akibat Korban Tsunami Mencapai 617.159 jiwa', available at www.depkes.go.id/index.php/berita/info-umum-kesehatan/668-jumlah-pengungsi-akibat-korban-tsunami-mencapai-617159-jiwa.html. Last accessed 20 May 2013.

Indonesian Ministry of Marine Affairs and Fisheries. (2015). 'Rekapitulasi Kapal Asing: Tangkapan Kapal Pengawas Berdasarkan Bendera/Kebangsaan Kapal', 19 March 2015. Data was provided to the author by the Ministry of Marine Affairs and Fisheries in April 2015.

Indonesian Ministry of State Secretariat. (2001). *Lampiran Pidato Presiden Republik Indonesia Pada Sidang Tahunan Majelis Permusywaratan Rakyat Republik Indonesia*. Jakarta: Perum Percetakan Negara.

Indonesian Ministry of State Secretariat. (2004). *Pidato Kenegaraan Presiden Republik Indonesia serta Keterangan Pemerintah Atas Rancangan Undang-Undang tentang Anggaran Pendapatan dan Belanja Negara tahun Anggaran 2005 beserta Nota Keuangannya di Depan Rapat Paripurna Dewan Perwakilan Rakyat Republik Indonesia 16 Agustus 2004*. Jakarta: Sekretariat Negara.

Indonesian Ministry of State Secretariat. (2008). *Pidato Kenegaraan Presiden Republik Indonesia Serta Keterangan Pemerintah Atas Rancangan Undang-Undang Tentang Anggaran Pendapatan dan Belanja Negara Tahun Anggaran 2009 Beserta Nota Keuangannya Di Depan Rapat Paripurna Dewan Perwakilan Rakyat 15 Agustus 2008*. Jakarta: Sekretariat Negara.

International Crisis Group (ICG). (2002). 'Indonesia Briefing: Impact of the Bali Bombing', 24 October 2002, available at www.crisisgroup.org/home/index.cfm?id=1766&l=1. Last accessed 20 August 2008.

International Maritime Bureau (IMB). (1992). *Piracy and Armed Robbery against Ships Annual Report January 1st–December 31st, 1992*. Kuala Lumpur: IMB.

IMB. (2001). *Piracy and Armed Robbery against Ships Annual Report January 1st–December 31st, 2001*. Kuala Lumpur: IMB.

IMB. (2005). *Piracy and Armed Robbery against Ships Annual Report January 1st–December 31st, 2005*. Kuala Lumpur: IMB.

IMB. (2010). *Piracy and Armed Robbery against Ships Annual Report January 1st–December 31st, 2010*. Kuala Lumpur: IMB.

IMB. (2014). *Piracy and Armed Robbery against Ships Annual Report January 1st–December 31st, 2014*. Kuala Lumpur: IMB.

IMB. (2015). *Piracy and Armed Robbery against Ships Annual Report January 1st–December 31st, 2015*. Kuala Lumpur: IMB.

International Maritime Organization (IMO). (2009). IMO Assembly 26th Session A 26/Res.1025 *Code of Practice for the Investigation of Crimes of Piracy and Armed Robbery Against Ships*, adopted on 2 December 2009.

Intertanko. (2005). 'Shipowners Challenge Malacca Strait War Risk Zone', 16 August 2005, available at www.intertanko.com/templates/Page.aspx?id=36077. Last accessed 15 November 2010.

Jakarta Post. (2002a). 'Illegal Guns Enter Indonesia Through Four Countries', 10 July 2002, accessed from the Newsbank database.

Jakarta Post. (2002b). 'Government Seek Public Support in the War on Terror', 30 September 2002b; accessed from the Newsbank database.

Jakarta Post. (2005). 'Navy Launches Operation to Secure Malacca Strait', 13 July 2005, accessed from the Newsbank database.

Jakarta Post. (2009). 'Expedition Team Sent to Observe Outermost Islands', 17 November 2009, accessed from the Newsbank database.

Jakarta Post. (2010a). 'TNI Chief Candidate Vows to Boost Security in RI Waters', 24 September 2010, accessed from the Newsbank database.

Jakarta Post. (2010b). 'Police Find it Hard to Fight Illegal Gun Trade', 26 August 2010, accessed from the Newsbank database.

Jakarta Post. (2010c). 'Terror Cell Alliance Forges New Structure and Attack Methods', 12 March 2010, accessed from the Newsbank database.

Kurniawan, Rama Anom (Directorate of Treaties for Political, Security and Territorial Affairs at the Foreign Ministry). (2008). 'Piracy an Extension of Somalia's Lawless Land', *Jakarta Post*, 17 December 2008.

Lee, Seng Kong (Senior Director Maritime and Port Authority of Singapore). (2005). 'Singapore-Flagged Ships Not the Most Hit by Pirates', *Straits Times*, 3 August 2005, accessed from the Newsbank database.

Lloyds. (2006). 'Market Removes Malacca Straits from the List', 11 August 2006, available at www.lloyds.com/News-and-Insight/News-and Features/Archive/2006/08/Market_removes_Malacca_Straits_from_the_List. Last accessed 20 October 2009.

Mak, J.N. (2007). 'Pirates, Renegades, and Fishermen: The Politics of "Sustainable" Piracy in the Strait of Malacca', in *Violence at Sea Piracy in the Age of Global Terrorism*, Peter Lehr (ed.). New York: Routledge.

Meredith. (2000). 'Indonesia Lacks Defence Funding', *Straits Times*, 24 May 2000, accessed from the Newsbank database.

National Institute for Defense Studies. (2004). 'Southeast Asia – From Regional Cooperation to Regional Integration', in *East Asia Strategic Review*. Tokyo: National Institute for Defense Studies.

Nik, Ramli Hj and Permal, Sumathy. (2008). 'Security Threats in the Straits of Malacca', in *Profile of the Straits of Malacca: Malaysia's Perspective*, H.M. Ibrahim and Hairil Anuar Husin (eds). Kuala Lumpur: Maritime Institute of Malaysia, pp. 189–199.

Nuswantoro, Laksamana Pertama Edhi [Kepala Staf Komando Armada RI Kawasan Barat]. (2005). 'Pengelolaan Keamanan Selat Malaka Secara Terpadu', in *Pertemuan Kelompok Ahli Tentang Kebijakan Terpadu Pengelolaan Keamanan Selat Malaka, Medan 19–20 Juli 2005*. Jakarta: Badan Pengkajian dan Pengembangan Kebijakan Departemen Luar Negeri.

Oegroseno, Arif Havas. (2006). 'The Straits of Malacca and Challenges Ahead: Japan's Perspective', in *Building Comprehensive Security Environment*. Kuala Lumpur: Maritime Institute of Malaysia, pp. 28–39.

Ong, Graham Gerard. (2004). 'Ships Can Be Dangerous Too: Coupling Piracy and Maritime Terrorism in Southeast Asia's Maritime Security Framework', *ISEAS Working Paper: International Politics and Security Issues Series* No. 1, available at www.iseas.edu.sg/documents/publication/ipsi12004.pdf. Last accessed 1 May 2013.

Ong-Webb, Graham Gerard. (2007). 'Piracy in Maritime Asia: Current Trends', in *Violence at Sea Piracy in the Age of Global Terrorism*, Peter Lehr (ed.). New York: Routledge.

Organization for Economic Co-operation and Development (OECD). (2003). *Migration and the Labour Market in Asia 2002: Recent Trends and Policies.* Paris: OECD Publishing.

Polner, Mariya. (2010). *WCO Research Paper No. 8: Compendium of Authorized Economic Operator (AEO) Programmes*, available at www.wcoomd.org/files/1.%20Public%20files/PDFandDocuments/research/aeo_compendium.pdf. Last accessed 11 August 2011.

Powell, Sian. (2004). 'Megawati Offers Swansong Apology', *The Australian*, 24 September 2004, accessed from the Newsbank database.

Power, Jason. (2008). 'Maritime Terrorism: A New Challenge for National and International Security'. *Barry Law Review* 10, pp. 111–133.

Quentin, Sophia. (2003). 'Shipping Activities: Targets of Maritime Terrorism'. *MIRMAL-Maritime Law Bulletin* Vol. 2, available at www.derechomaritimo.info/pagina/mater.htm. Last accessed 11 July 2011.

Rahman, Chris. (2007). 'The International Politics of Combating Piracy in Southeast Asia', in *Violence at Sea Piracy in the Age of Global Terrorism*, Peter Lehr (ed.). New York: Routledge.

Raymond, Catherine Zara. (2006). 'Maritime Terrorism in Southeast Asia: A Risk Assessment'. *Terrorism and Political Violence* 18:2, pp. 239–257.

Raymond, Catherine Zara. (2007). 'Piracy in the Waters of Southeast Asia', in *Maritime Security in Southeast Asia*, Kwa Chong Guan and John K. Skogan (eds). New York: Routledge, pp. 62–77.

Regional Cooperation Agreement on Combating Piracy and Armed Robbery against Ships in Asia (ReCAAP). (2015). *ReCAAP Annual Report*, Singapore: ReCAAP ISC, available at www.recaap.org/DesktopModules/Bring2mind/DMX/Download.aspx?Command=Core_Download&EntryId=421&PortalId=0&TabId=78. Last accessed 23 August 2016.

Rekhi, Shefali. (2006). 'Malacca Strait Security: External Powers Still Wary – Japan, India, Australia and US Could Seek Bigger Part to Play in Protecting Narrow Sea Lanes', *Straits Times*, 3 June 2006.

Renwick, Neil and Abbott, Jason. (1999). 'Piratical Violence and Maritime Security in Southeast Asia'. *Security Dialogue* 30:2, pp. 183–196.

Reuters. (2010). 'Security Raised in Malacca Strait after Terror Warning', 4 March 2010, available at www.reuters.com/article/2010/03/04/us-malacca-threat-idUSTRE62335120100304. Last accessed 15 March 2011.

Richardson, Michael. (2004). 'Securing Choke Points at Sea Against Terrorists', *Straits Times*, 19 January 2004, accessed from the Newsbank database.

Richardson, Michael. (2005). 'Aiming A Shot Across the Bow', *Straits Times*, 25 May 2005, accessed from the Newsbank database.

Singh, Bilveer. (2004). 'The Challenge of Militant Islam and Terrorism in Indonesia'. *Australian Journal of International Affairs* 58:1, pp. 47–68.

Siregar, H.B., Nasution, S., Rahman, A., Sutiarno, H.R., Munthe, M., and Purba, D.E. (2004). *Pengamanan dan Perlindungan Pulau-Pulau Terluar Pada Batas Wilayah RI Di Kawasan Selat Malaka*. Sumatera Utara: Fakultas Hukum Universitas Sumatera Utara.

Sittnick, Tammy M. (2005). 'State Responsibility and Maritime Terrorism in the Strait of Malacca: Persuading Indonesia and Malaysia to Take Additional Steps to Secure the Strait'. *Pacific Rim Law and Policy Journal* 14, pp. 743–769.

Sodik, Dikdik Mohamad. (2009a). 'IUU Fishing and Indonesia's Legal Framework for Vessel Registration and Fishing Vessel Licensing'. *Ocean Development and International Law* 40:3, pp. 249–267.

Sodik, Dikdik Mohamad. (2009b). 'Analysis of IUU Fishing in Indonesia and the Indonesian Legal Framework Reform for Monitoring, Control and Surveillance of Fishing Vessels'. *International Journal of Marine and Coastal Law* 24, pp. 67–100.

Sondakh, Bernard Kent. (2004). 'Pengamanan Wilayah Laut Indonesia'. *Indonesian Journal of International Law*, pp. 1–26.

Suchharitkul, Sompong. (2006). 'Liability and Responsibility of the State of Registration or the Flag State in Respect of Sea Going Vessels, Aircraft and Spacecraft Registered by National Registration Authorities'. *American Journal of Comparative Law* 54, pp. 409–442.

Sudrajat (Direktur Jenderal Strategi Pertahanan Kementerian Pertahanan Indonesia). (2005). 'Kebijakan Kelautan Nasional dari Perspektif Pertahanan dan Keamanan', in Laporan Kegiatan *Diskusi Panel: Mencari Format Kebijakan Kelautan Indonesia Dalam Rangka Mendukung Pembangunan dan Integrasi Nasional (Studi Kasus Kanada dan Norwegia), Surabaya, 7–8 April 2005*. Jakarta: Kementerian Luar Negeri Indonesia.

Straits Times. (2000). 'Japan keen on joint patrols to fight piracy', 18 February 2000, accessed from the Newsbank database.

Straits Times. (2000). 'Pirates Hit Straits of Malacca', 3 August 2000, accessed from the Newsbank database.

Straits Times. (2005). 'Rights to Area Come with Islands', 8 March 2005, accessed from the Newsbank database.

Straits Times. (2010). 'Piracy in Asia on the Rise – Report Shows Incidents up 60% on Last Year, while Pirates Are Becoming More Violent', 20 October 2010, accessed from the Newsbank database.

Sunday Times. (2005). ' "Big Trouble" if Terrorists Turn Tankers into Floating Bombs', 20 November 2005, accessed from the Newsbank database.

Supriyadi. (2010). 'DJBC Ikut Serta dalam Latihan Bersama TNI-Polri untuk Penanggulangan Teroris'. *Warta Bea Cukai*. Jakarta: Direktorat Jenderal Bea dan Cukai.

Suristiyono, Komisaris Besar Polisi (Wakil Direktur Polair Babinkam Polri). (2005). 'Penyelenggaraan Keamanan dan Ketertiban Di Kawasan Perairan Selat Malaka', in *Pertemuan Kelompok Ahli Tentang Kebijakan Terpadu Pengelolaan Keamanan Selat Malaka*. Jakarta: Badan Pengkajian dan Pengembangan Kebijakan Kementerian Luar Negeri.

Tan, See Seng and Ramakrishna, Kumar. (2004). 'Interstate and Intrastate Dynamics in Southeast Asia's War on Terror'. *SAIS Review* 24:1, pp. 91–105.

Times. (1985). 'Leading Article: Truck with Terrorists – Achille Lauro Hijacking Incident', 14 October 1985, accessed from the Newsbank database.

Tiribelli, Carlo. (2006). 'Time to Update the 1988 Rome Convention for the Suppression of Unlawful Acts against the Safety of Maritime Navigation'. *Oregon Review of International Law* 8:1, pp. 133–156.

United Nations Conference on Trade and Development Secretariat (UNCTAD). (2008). *UNCTAD Review of Maritime Transport 2008*, available at www.unctad.org/en/docs/rmt2008_en.pdf. Last accessed 20 October 2010.

United Nations High Commissioner for Refugees (UNHCR). (2010). *UNHCR Statistical Yearbook 2009*, available at www.unhcr.org/4ce531e09.html. Last accessed 20 March 2011.

UNHCR. (2011). *UNHCR Statistical Yearbook 2010* available at www.unhcr.org/4ef9c8139.html. Last accessed 1 June 2013.

United States Coast Guard. (2002). 'Maritime Strategy for Homeland Security', available at www.uscg.mil/history/articles/uscgmaritimestrategy2002.pdf. Last accessed 20 October 2009.

US Department of Defense (US DoD). (2005). *Annual Report to Congress: The Military Power of the People's Republic of China*, available at www.defense.gov/news/Jul2005/d20050719china.pdf-2005-07-19-. Last accessed 17 November 2010.

US DoD. (2006). *Annual Report to Congress Military Power of the People's Republic of China*, available at www.defense.gov/pubs/pdfs/China%20Report%202006.pdf – 2007-03-30. Last accessed 17 November 2010.

US DoD. (2007). *Annual Report to Congress: Military Power of the People's Republic of China*, available at www.defense.gov/pubs/pdfs/070523-china-military-power-final.pdf. Last accessed 17 November 2010.

United States Department of the Homeland Security. (2005). 'The National Strategy for Maritime Security', 20 September 2005, available at http://georgewbush-whitehouse.archives.gov/homeland/maritime-security.html. Last accessed 13 March 2011.

United States Energy Information Administration. (2012). 'World Oil Transit Chokepoints: Malacca', 22 August 2012, available at www.eia.doe.gov/cabs/world_oil_transit_chokepoints/malacca.html. Last accessed 31 May 2013.

Urquhart, Donald. (2004). 'New 16-Nation Anti-Piracy Campaign Soon in Asia – S'pore Ready to Play its Part in the New Initiative to Enhance Security', *Business Times*, 19 November 2004, accessed from the Newsbank database.

Vagg, Jon. (1995). 'Rough Seas: Contemporary Piracy in South East Asia'. *British Journal of Criminology* 35:1, pp. 63–80.

Valencia, Mark J. (2005). *The Proliferation Security Initiative Making Waves in Asia*. Adelphi Series 45. London: International Institute for Strategic Studies.

Valencia, Mark J. (2006). 'Security Issues in the Malacca Straits: Whose Security and Why It Matters?', in *Building a Comprehensive Security Environment in the Straits of Malacca: Proceeding of the MIMA International Conference on the Straits of Malacca, 11–13 October, 2004*. Kuala Lumpur: Maritime Institute of Malaysia.

Vorbach, Joseph E. (2001). 'The Vital Role of Non-Flag State Actors in the Pursuit of Safer Shipping'. *Ocean Development and International Law* 32:1, pp. 27–42.

Yasin, Mat Taib. (2007). *The Security of Sea Lanes of Communication in the Indian Ocean Region*. Kuala Lumpur: Maritime Institute of Malaysia.

Young, Adam J. and Valencia, Mark J. (2003). 'Conflation of Piracy and Terrorism in Southeast Asia: Rectitude and Utility'. *Contemporary Southeast Asia* 25:2, pp. 269–283.

2 Domestic politics

Introduction

This chapter will look at the domestic sources of Indonesia's varying participation in maritime security cooperation. Some scholarly works have used bureaucratic politics to understand Indonesia's foreign policy making (Emmerson, 1983, pp. 1220, 1223; Jackson, 1978, p. 395; 1980, pp. 10–11; Liddle, 1985, p. 70; Nabbs-Keller, 2013, pp. 56, 68; Suryadinata, 1998, pp. 48–55). Bureaucratic politics may explain Indonesia's decisions to cooperate, but this proposition has not been systematically examined. This chapter will address that gap.

The second section of this chapter will examine Indonesia's domestic political dynamics, from the country's independence through to the present Joko Widodo administration. This section will highlight which political practices have changed and which remain the same in post-authoritarian Indonesia. The third section maps the specifics of Indonesia's bureaucratic politics. Drawing on documents and interview sources, I will identify the key actors, their roles and the institutional process of Indonesia's foreign and security policy making. The section shows the limitations of a bureaucratic politics approach to understanding Indonesia's participation and non-participation in maritime security arrangements. Allison's bureaucratic politics focuses on the process of formulation and reformulation of policy decisions through the interaction of various actors' competing preferences. This section demonstrates that Indonesia has a distinct bureaucratic politics, different from Allison's focus on competing preferences of various government institutions involved in the policy process. Given the Ministry of Foreign Affairs's dominant role in Indonesia's foreign policy, competitive bargaining among self-interested actors as expected by the bureaucratic politics literature does not take place.

Domestic politics dynamics and maritime cooperation

Indonesia's post-independence political system can be divided into three different political eras (Winanti, 2011, p. 106). Each of these eras is associated with a different political system, domestic policy process and distinct foreign policy formulation (Winanti, 2011, p. 106). The first period is known as the Old Order.

Under the Soekarno administration, the Old Order system lasted from the independence of Indonesia in 1945 through to 1966. Indonesia's participation in international cooperation in the Old Order era was characterised by Soekarno's efforts to project Indonesia as a leader among Asian and African nations. Indonesia hosted the first Asia–Africa Conference in 1955 and, together with the People's Republic of China, held the Conference of New Emerging Forces in 1965 and established its headquarter in Jakarta (Suryadinata, 1998, pp. 11–12). Under Soekarno, maritime cooperation did not feature much.

The scope of maritime cooperation for the young republic was limited to the establishment of naval to naval relations and the purchase of armaments and vessels from countries such as India and the Soviet Union that had provided Jakarta with military assistance to deal with its domestic insurgency (Ahram, 2011, p. 48; Supriyanto, 2013). Indonesia and India signed a naval agreement in 1958 and conducted their first joint naval exercises in 1960 (Supriyanto, 2013). In 1958, Indonesia began to purchase ships and submarines from the Soviet Union and by 1961 it became the largest non-communist recipient of Moscow military aid (Ahram, 2011, p. 48; Kroef, 1958, p. 78).

At the beginning of the Old Order era, Indonesia adopted a constitutional parliamentary democracy. This condition changed in the late 1950s. From 1957 to 1959, Indonesia was facing a severe financial crisis and political unrest. The Indonesian government was struggling to end the Darul Islam military campaign in West Java, Aceh and South Sulawesi. At the same time, a group of dissident colonels in Sumatra and Sulawesi had been pressing for separation from Jakarta. As the crisis in Indonesia continued to unfold, Soekarno introduced the Guided Democracy system in 1959 that ended the country's parliamentary democracy system (Evans, 1989, p. 26). The guided democracy system granted Soekarno absolute power over the state's policies, including foreign and security policy making (Agung, 1973, pp. 9, 271).

The fall of Soekarno in 1966 marked the rise of the New Order era under the Soeharto regime. This authoritarian regime lasted over three decades from 1966 to 1998. During the New Order era, the executive played the central role in determining the state's foreign policy orientation (Suryadinata, 1998, p. 7). For more than thirty years, civil society organisations were systematically suppressed (Manning and Diermen, 2000, p. 7). The government banned the establishment of independent labour unions, activist student organisations and critical Non-Governmental Organisations (NGOs) to eliminate any form of organised and coordinated opposition to the regime (Weiss, 2007, p. 10). The legislative body of the Indonesian Parliament (*Dewan Perwakilan Rakyat*) had only a limited role in shaping Indonesia foreign policy. The legislators merely gave feedback and support to the executive through a hearing mechanism (Wanandi, 1988, p. 187 as cited in Suryadinata, 1998, p. 58).

In the early decades of the New Order era, the government sought to maintain a low profile foreign policy and focused on domestic economic development (Sukma, 1995, p. 304; Suryadinata, 1998, p. 12). Indonesia began to improve its foreign relations with neighbouring countries such as Malaysia and Singapore, and embarked on maritime security cooperation with them in the late 1960s. Indonesia's relations with Malaysia and Singapore had been badly affected by Soekarno's policy of confrontation from 1963 to 1966 against the British decolonisation policy of merging Sabah and Sarawak into a single country to be known as Malaysia (Kahin and Kahin, 1995, p. 221).

In the New Order era, the adoption of UNCLOS in 1994 was seen as the culmination of twenty-five years of the Indonesian government efforts. The influence of Indonesia can be seen in 'virtually every aspect of Part IV of the Convention that defined the concept of archipelagic state' (Butcher, 2009, p. 45). The Convention set out a regime of free passage through straits used for international navigation, extended the territorial sea from three nautical miles to twelve nautical miles and adopted the Exclusive Economic Zone (EEZ) (Nandan and Rosenne, 1993, pp. 283, 279). The Convention defined that the EEZ must extend no more than 200 nautical miles from the baseline where the territorial sea is measured. The UNCLOS grants Indonesia absolute power to manage and use resources in its territorial waters and sovereign power to use resources in the EEZ and continental shelf (Djalal, 1995, p. 247). The implementation of UNCLOS has increased Indonesian waters from 100,000 square kilometres to 5.8 million square kilometres (Bakorkamla, 2010, p. 5; Lubis, 2010). These include 0.8 million square kilometres of territorial waters, 2.3 million square kilometres of archipelagic waters and 2.7 million square kilometres of EEZ (Bakorkamla, 2010, p. 5).

In May 1998, the resignation of Indonesia's second president Soeharto had brought an end to the state's authoritarian political system that had lasted for more than thirty years (Elson, 2008, p. 300; Lee, 2002, p. 821; Liddle, 1999, p. 39). A year after President Soeharto stood down from presidential office, Indonesia held its first free election since 1955, and in June 1999 parliamentary elections provided fresh legitimacy to the Indonesian Parliament and the country's political system as a whole (Ruland, 2009, p. 379). The amended 1945 constitution empowered the parliament to carry out legislative, budgeting and oversight functions (Ruland, 2009, p. 379). Law No. 24, implemented in 2000, on international treaties regulates that foreign and multilateral treaties on political, peace, defence and security matters must be ratified by the parliament (Ruland, 2009, p. 380).[1] In the parliament, foreign policy issues fall under the remit of Commission I on Foreign Affairs, Defence and Information. This commission is one of the most active and vocal bodies in the parliament (Dosch, 2006, pp. 51, 57; Ruland, 2009, p. 381; Sherlock, 2003, p. 13).

Although the role of the parliament has been strengthened by a series of amendments made to the constitution of 1945, core provisions on foreign policy are unchanged (Dosch, 2006, p. 49). Article 11 of the amended constitution only requires the executive to ask for the agreement of the parliament without specifying any procedure on how it must be reached (Dosch, 2006, p. 49). Law No. 24 also provides detailed criteria for international cooperation agreements which require parliament's approval. Yet, in practice, the government decides which agreement they want to put forward to be ratified by the parliament (Parthiana,

2008, pp. 480, 484). The existing legislation required the government to seek agreement from the parliament on international agreements, particularly those related to defence and security. However, a large proportion of such agreements have been implemented at national level without prior ratification by the parliament (Juwana, 2008, p. 450; Parthiana, 2008, p. 470).

Since the 1999 election, the parliament has shown a strong interest in foreign policy. However, not every issue attracts legislators' attention. The parliament focuses on problems related to preservation of territorial integrity, including the separatist movements in Aceh, the Moluccas and West Papua, and a number of issues that reflect deep anti-Israeli and anti-American sentiments among the Moslem-majority public, such as the relations between Arab nations and Israel, responses to the 9/11 attacks and the 2002 Bali bombings (Dosch, 2006, p. 62; Indonesian Parliament, 25 September 2006, 25 January 2007, 26 February 2007, 28 May 2007, 25 June 2007, 9 July 2007; Suhartono, 2001, p. 165).[2]

Maritime security issues such as potential maritime terrorism and armed robberies against ships do not gain much attention from the parliament. The parliament tends to dedicate its attention to high profile maritime issues that provoke the electorate's nationalist sentiment, such as the Indonesia–Malaysia dispute over the Ambalat block, a maritime area in the Sulawesi Sea, or popular issues such as the trawl ban in Indonesian waters (Indonesian Parliament, 5 March 2007, 29 October 2008).[3] Analysis of Commission I parliamentary meetings and hearing reports from 2000 to 2013 and interviews with officials and experts suggest that Indonesia's participation or non-participation in maritime security initiatives was never a major agenda for parliamentary meetings (Indonesian Parliament, 2000–2013).[4] Among various maritime security initiatives, the only initiative mentioned by the parliament during a meeting with government officials was the Proliferation Security Initiative. The initiative was only mentioned in the sidelines of the discussion between the parliament and the Coordinating Ministry for Political, Legal and Security Affairs over Indonesia' counter-terrorism policies (Indonesian Parliament, 12 June 2006). The parliament has not requested any specific hearing with the government to seek an explanation regarding Indonesia's decision to join or not to join maritime security cooperation agreements.[5]

Following the political reform in 1998, NGOs, labour unions and community groups have also started to play a much more active role in foreign and security policy (Manning and Diermen, 2000, p. 1; Sherlock, 2003, p. 6). Despite the increasing involvement of civil society in politics, their participation is spread unevenly across initiatives (Winanti, 2011, p. 108).[6] NGOs tend to focus on a limited number of political issues. In the security domain, NGOs' main concerns include military businesses, human rights violations and military, police and intelligence reform.[7] Indonesian NGOs are less familiar with issues surrounding Indonesia's rejection or participation in international maritime security cooperation initiatives.[8]

In post-authoritarian Indonesia, the general public has begun to exercise its influence in the government decision-making process. As Chow explains, the

Indonesian government's foreign policy decisions could be challenged by the unlocking of 'the floodgates to expressions of public opinion on foreign and security policies brought by democratisation and decentralisation in Indonesia' (Chow, 2005, p. 310).

However, only a small fraction of the population is concerned with Indonesia's participation in maritime security cooperation initiatives. This component of society consists of a small number of private maritime stakeholders, including shippers, port operators, forwarders and ship-owners. Private actors focus primarily on cooperation initiatives that directly influence their business activities, such as the ISPS Code and the Customs–Trade Partnership against Terrorism (C-TPAT).[9] Businesses participate in these initiatives because of the demand from their foreign business counterparts, willingness to improve their level of competitiveness in the international market, and motivation to gain priority access, particularly to ports in the US.

In sum, in the reform era, although the Indonesian political system has changed drastically, the influence of societal actors including civil society, businesses, and the general public in maritime security cooperation is fairly weak.

In the absence of the involvement of Indonesian legislative and societal actors in policy making, the government plays a central role in informing Indonesia's maritime security cooperation. Since Soeharto's resignation, Indonesia has been led by five Presidents: Habibie, Abdurrahman Wahid, Megawati, Yudhoyono and, most recently, Joko Widodo (known as Jokowi). Jokowi is the only one of them who announced his administration's commitment to put maritime security concerns as a national priority soon after he took office on 20 October 2014.

On 13 November 2015 at the East Asia Summit in Nay Pyi Taw, Myanmar, Jokowi announced his administration's plan to promote Indonesia as the maritime axis of the world. The maritime axis plan is built upon five pillars (Indonesian Presidential Office, 2015): the development of Indonesia's maritime culture; the commitment to safeguard and manage marine resources, especially fishery resources; the pledge to improve Indonesia's maritime infrastructure and connectivity by developing sea ports, shipping industry and maritime tourism; diplomacy to encourage maritime cooperation between Indonesia and other countries; and the development of Indonesia's maritime defence capacity.

Despite the Jokowi administration's emphasis on the importance of maritime security cooperation, the issues of maritime terrorism and armed robbery against ships are not key concerns. The policy programmes that followed the maritime axis concept have focused heavily on efforts to address illegal fishing at the national level. During the Jokowi administration, efforts to address illegal fishing have gained momentum. The Ministry of Marine Affairs and Fisheries, led by Susi Pudjiastuti, has spearheaded policy measures to combat illegal fishing, including blowing up and sinking vessels that committed illegal fishing in Indonesian waters. For example, on 20 May 2015 Indonesia sank forty-one foreign vessels, and on 18 August 2015 the government sank another thirty-seven vessels (*Jakarta Post*, 20 May 2015).

Having discussed the dynamics of Indonesia's political process from independence to the current Jokowi administration, the next section of this chapter will turn to an explanation of the unique features of the country's bureaucratic process.

Indonesia's assigned bureaucratic politics model

Due to the centrality of government actors in Indonesia's decision-making process, a bureaucratic politics analysis that points to the importance of government actors' preferences offers a possible explanation for Indonesia's varying participation in maritime security cooperation initiatives. The bureaucratic politics approach to the analysis of foreign policy, first introduced by Allison, focuses on competitive bargaining among different actors within the government (Allison and Zelikow, 1999, p. 255; Carlsnaes, 2006, p. 338). It looks at competing preferences among self-interested actors (Allison and Zelikow, 1999, p. 255). Each actor seeks to advance his or her interests in the bargaining process (Allison and Zelikow, 1999, pp. 295, 302). Therefore, the bureaucratic politics approach suggests that cooperation is most likely to occur when it serves the interests of those governmental actors who prevail in the internal decision-making process.

Within the Indonesian government, the Indonesian MFA plays a key role in foreign policy formulation. The MFA serves as a leading institution in the negotiation of cooperation initiatives to secure strategic waterways, such as the Straits of Malacca and the state's territory in general (Indonesian Coordinating Ministry for Political, Legal and Security Affairs, 2007, p. 31; Indonesian MFA, 2005a, p. 21; 2005b, p. 19). Other government actors and businesses view the MFA as an institution that can bridge the interests of various stakeholders in the maritime policy area (Indonesian MFA, 2005b, p. 2).[10]

In post-authoritarian Indonesia, the government has issued a series of laws to provide the MFA with the authority to formulate and implement national foreign policy (Indonesian MFA, 2006, p. 13, 1 August 2009, 6 September 2009).[11] The scope of the ministry's authority includes facilitating the implementation of policy, coordinating 'between the central level and its representatives at local level' and delegating 'authority in the administration of foreign relations and implementation of foreign policy' (Indonesian MFA, 1 August 2009; 2006, p. 13). In this context, the MFA is the leading institution in international maritime security diplomacy, although other ministries have input (Indonesian Coordinating Ministry for Political, Legal and Security Affairs, 2007, p. 31; Indonesian MFA, 2005a, p. 21; 2005b, p. 19).

The MFA makes legal and political assessments of cooperation arrangements that will involve Indonesia, represents the government during negotiations at international level and organises inter-ministerial meetings to determine Indonesia's decision at national level.[12] The national deliberation meetings involve other relevant government agencies, including the MoD, the navy, the MoT, the Ministry of Marine and Fisheries, Customs and Excise and the Coordinating

70 *Domestic politics*

Ministry for Political, Legal and Security Affairs.[13] The MFA often took on the leadership by themselves. However, when international maritime security cooperation covers technical issues such as regulation of security in ports, interdiction at sea, customs laws or naval patrol coordination, the MFA is likely to share leadership both during deliberations at national level and at negotiations in international forums.

Under any circumstances where governmental actors are unable to produce a satisfactory decision through a regular inter-ministerial meeting, the contesting issue would be solved through the Coordinating Ministry for Political, Legal and Security Affairs meeting.[14] The Coordinating Ministry is an executive agency that is responsible for marshalling other ministries who are positioned under their supervision, a practice inherited from the Soeharto administration (Smith, 2001, p. 91). The Coordinating Ministry for Political, Legal and Security Affairs supervises twelve government agencies, including the MFA and the MoD. Nevertheless, instances that require a special Coordinating Ministry for Political, Legal and Security Affairs-led meeting to decide Indonesia's participation or non-participation in maritime security cooperation have not yet happened. This is mainly because the MFA has been the leading agency in Indonesia's decision-making process.

Bureaucratic politics can be a source of explanation for Indonesia's varying participation across maritime security cooperation cases, but this proposition has not been systematically tested. The next section will provide detailed analysis of Indonesia's bureaucratic politics across all maritime security cooperation cases. It will explain that Allison's model of bureaucratic politics does not reflect the domestic-politics situation in Indonesia. The lack of bureaucratic politics is because of the leading role of the MFA in foreign policy formulation. The leading role of the MFA could be seen in two ways: first, the MFA has taken the lead in national deliberation regarding Indonesia's participation in maritime security cooperation initiatives; second, although the MFA does not gain any benefits from Indonesia's participation in all cooperation cases, it still pursues the cooperation. This demonstrates that the emphasis of the bureaucratic politics approach on competing preferences among self-interested actors cannot explain the variation in Indonesia's engagement with cooperation initiatives.

The limitation of bureaucratic politics in explaining Indonesian cooperation

Given the MFA's dominant role in Indonesia's foreign policy, competitive bargaining among self-interested actors, as expected by the bureaucratic politics literature, does not take place. The MFA's leading role is apparent in cooperation initiatives that Indonesia has joined and those in which Indonesia chose not to participate.

Cooperation cases

Bureaucratic politics cannot offer a useful explanation for Indonesia's participation in maritime security cooperation because Indonesia's cooperation was not informed by a series of bargaining games between different actors to advance their personal interests (see Allison and Zelikow, 1999, p. 295). The MFA as one of the leading agencies supported Indonesia's participation in various maritime security arrangements to address maritime terrorism and armed robbery against ships despite the absence of benefits for this ministry. Cooperation activities under these initiatives, including training, military exercises, gifting of equipment and patrols, were tailored to assist the work of Indonesia's law enforcement agencies such as the navy, the MoT's coast guard unit, Customs, the Maritime Security Coordinating Board and the Marine police.

In order to prevent maritime terrorism, Indonesia has joined bilateral counter-terrorism arrangements with the US, Japan and Australia, a tri-lateral information-sharing arrangement, the BIMP EAGA (Brunei, Darussalam, Indonesia, Malaysia, the Philippines East ASEAN growth area) memoranda of understanding (MoUs) on transport of goods and sea linkages, the ASEAN convention on counter-terrorism, the ISPS Code, the WCO SAFE Framework and the APEC TRP. Bureaucratic politics cannot account for Indonesia's cooperation, as the MFA supported Indonesia's participation in these cases although none of the benefits delivered by these arrangements were beneficial for the ministry.

Indonesia's policy making on the US–Indonesia Defence Framework Arrangement was formulated by the Indonesian MoD in close coordination with the MFA. The agreement was signed in 2010. The implementation of the cooperation arrangement made maritime exercises, training, seminars and equipment available to various agencies that do not fall under the MFA remit. These non-MFA agencies include the navy, the anti-terrorism coordinating desk of the Coordinating Ministry for Political, Legal and Security Affairs, Customs, Marine police, the Maritime Security Coordinating Board and the sea and coast guard unit of the MoT (Djalal, 2009, p. 327; Indonesian Coordinating Ministry for Political, Legal and Security Affairs, 2008, p. 76; Polres Tanjung Perak, 2011).[15] Although the US Coast Guard and Naval Criminal Investigative Service (NCIS) port security training and exercises do not offer economic benefits for the MFA, these activities are beneficial for the Indonesian maritime agencies.[16] In an interview conducted in 2010, an official from the Maritime Security Coordination Board explained that, as part of the defence cooperation, a large number of aircraft provided by the US will be allocated to his institution to assist their patrol operations.[17] This suggests that the MFA as the leading negotiator did not benefit from the signing of the defence agreement with the US.

Although Indonesia and Japan have a long history of maritime cooperation, countering maritime terrorism is a new area of cooperation for the two countries (Jailani, 2005, p. 69).[18] Counter-terrorism cooperation between the two countries was formalised by the signing of the joint announcement on fighting against international terrorism on 24 June 2003. The MFA was the lead agency in the

72 Domestic politics

negotiation of the joint announcement. Officials from the MFA, Customs, the Marine police, the Maritime Security Coordinating Board and the Coordinating Ministry for Political, Legal and Security Affairs pointed out that the MFA pushed the cooperation forward, since maritime security projects with Japan are useful to build the capacity of Indonesian maritime agencies and to improve the security of Indonesian sea ports.[19] Capacity building and equipment projects provided by Japan offered tangible benefits in the form of training, exercises and equipment to various government maritime agencies, but none of them were allocated to the lead agency, the Indonesian MFA (Embassy of Japan in Indonesia, 2008, 2011).[20]

The calculation of self-interest did not take place either in the negotiation of Indonesia–Australia bilateral cooperation initiatives to address terrorism. Indonesia and Australia first signed the MoU on counter-terrorism in February 2002. The October 2002 Bali bombings that claimed the lives of 202 people, including 88 Australians, had a significant impact upon the counter-terrorism cooperation between the two states (*Jakarta Post*, 7 August 2003). The two countries extended the MoU for a further three years in February 2008 and later in February 2011 (Australian Department of Foreign Affairs and Trade, 2012). Following the establishment of the MoU on counter-terrorism, Indonesia and Australia further signed the agreement on a framework for security cooperation (Lombok Treaty) in 2006, which was ratified in February 2008, and concluded the implementation arrangement for the Lombok Treaty (Defence Cooperation Arrangement) in 2012.

Bilateral cooperation with Australia involved the MFA, the MoD, the MoT and the police. Through the signing of three bilateral arrangements with Australia – the MoU on counter-terrorism (7 February 2002), the Lombok Treaty (13 November 2006) and the Defence Cooperation Arrangement (5 September 2012) – the Indonesian MoT would gain assistance in their search and rescue operations at sea. The Indonesian police would be offered help in their investigation of terrorist attacks, financial resources to develop counter-terrorism training centres and access to various training resources from their Australian counterparts. As noted by the Australian Ministry of Defence and the Indonesian Minister of Defence Purnomo Yusgiantoro, the search and rescue issue – that is related to people smuggling and illegal immigration issues – is one of the focuses of Indonesia–Australia security cooperation (Australian DoD, 2012; *Jakarta Post*, 4 September 2012; Sekretaris Kabinet Indonesia, 2012). The search and rescue issue falls under the MoT's remit (Australian DoD, 2012). The Australian Minister of Transportation Anthony Albanese explained:

> we [the Australia government] were searching for solutions that would provide greater assistance for capacity for Indonesian maritime search and rescue services (Basarnas, Kohadnudnas) and so the range of programmes that have been agreed today, I ... will see that they ... occur
>
> (Australian DoD, 2012; Sekretaris Kabinet Indonesia, 2012)

Indonesia's agreement to join sub-regional cooperation arrangements under the BIMP-EAGA was not shaped by the competing preferences of the MFA and the MoT (Indonesian DGST, 2010, p. 1).[21] Indonesia, Brunei Darussalam, Malaysia and the Philippines launched the initiative in 1994 to address the development gap in the less-developed parts of Southeast Asia (Asian Development Bank, 2012; Dent and Richter, 2011, p. 31). Although the BIMP-EAGA was established as an economic cooperation initiative, after 9/11 attempts to strengthen both transport security and maritime borders became one of the focuses of the BIMP-EAGA (BIMP-EAGA, 2012, pp. 25, 41; *Business World*, 2006). In 2007 the member states of the EAGA signed the MoU on establishing and promoting efficient and integrated sea linkages. Following the implementation of the MoU on sea linkages, the four states launched the MoU on transit and interstate transport of goods in 2009.

The BIMP-EAGA does not provide incentives to the MFA. The cooperation arrangements under the BIMP-EAGA – the MoU on sea linkages and the MoU on transport of goods – are in line with the MoT agenda to improve maritime connectivity both between Indonesia's least-developed areas in the central and eastern part of the country and also between other countries in the sub-region (Bakti, 2010, p. 298; Indonesian DGST, 2010, p. 1; Indonesian Coordinating Ministry for Political, Legal and Security Affairs, 2007, pp. 71, 73; Indonesian MFA, 2004, p. 15; 2006, p. 6; Indonesian Ministry of Trade, 2010, pp. 35–36). The cooperation arrangements are expected to improve economic growth, address development gaps within these areas and at the same time improve the monitoring of goods transported into and out of these sub-regions (Bakti, 2010, p. 298; Indonesian DGST, 2010, p. 1; Indonesian Ministry of Trade, 2010, pp. 35–36).[22]

The cooperation outcomes of the information exchange and establishment of communication procedures agreement, the ASEAN convention on counter-terrorism, and the APEC TRP also showed that projects governed by cooperation were not dedicated to the Indonesian MFA.[23] The Philippines, Indonesia and Malaysia formalised a tripartite cooperation agreement to strengthen maritime security cooperation in the tri-border sea areas of the Sulu and Sulawesi Sea by signing the information exchange and establishment of communication procedures agreement on 7 May 2002, to which Thailand and Cambodia later acceded (Indonesian Immigration Agency, 2011; Karniol, 2005 as cited in Rosenberg and Chung, 2008, p. 60). The agreement was deliberated among the MFA, the MoD, the police, and the Coordinating Ministry for Political, Legal and Security Affairs. The cooperation projects under the information exchange agreement include information exchange, maritime exercises and training, sharing of airline passenger lists and access to databases on fingerprints. None of these projects are aimed to benefit the MFA.

In November 2007, the ASEAN member states including Indonesia signed the ASEAN convention on counter-terrorism. This agreement serves as a framework for regional cooperation to counter, prevent and suppress terrorism. Indonesia's decision to join the ASEAN convention on counter-terrorism was shaped

74 Domestic politics

through inter-ministerial meetings led by the MFA and involved stakeholders in counter-terrorism, including the national police, the MoD and the national agency for combating terrorism (Badan Nasional Penanggulangan Terrorism/ BNPT).[24] The agreed cooperation projects under the ASEAN convention on counter-terrorism cover border control, prevention of the use of false identities and travel documents, counter-terrorism exercises, exchange of intelligence information and development of regional databases.[25] These projects were designed for participating states' law enforcement agencies. As confirmed by officials from the Indonesian Maritime Security Coordinating Board, the MoD and the MFA, these activities were crucial to support the success of the work of Indonesia's law enforcement agencies to address maritime terrorism and their capacity building.[26]

The lack of tangible incentives for the MFA is apparent in the case of the APEC TRP. The APEC TRP was introduced in 2007. It is defined as a 'set of plans, procedures and arrangements developed to identify and address specific actions needed following an event that disrupts trade operations' (APEC, 2008a, p. 4). The decision-making process related to Indonesia's participation in the TRP was led by the MFA and included the Coordinating Ministry for Political, Legal and Security Affairs, the MoT and Customs.[27] The TRP programmes are designed to improve the capacity of Indonesia's maritime agencies to deal with the aftermath of terrorist attacks or natural disasters. The TRP was deemed useful to accelerate maritime trade recovery in time of crisis and, more importantly, to develop Indonesia's authorised economic operator (AEO) programme (Wibisono, 2006, p. 174).[28] As Indonesia had joined the TRP, Indonesian Customs could gain training on the AEO. The other maritime agencies, such as the MoT, the navy, the Maritime Security Coordinating Board and the Marine police, can take part in APEC training, seminars and capacity building workshops on trade recovery (APEC, 2008b, 2008c).[29]

The MFA and the MoT support for Indonesia to join the ISPS Code and the WCO SAFE Framework do not reflect a ministry calculation of self-interest, as suggested by Allison's bureaucratic politics approach. The MFA did not gain direct benefits from Indonesia's participation in the ISPS Code and the WCO SAFE Framework. The MFA and the MoT considered that Indonesia's participation in the ISPS Code was important to ensure the success of the country's international trade activities (Bakorkamla, 2010, pp. 25–26; 2004, p. 6; Sekretariat Jenderal Departemen Kelautan dan Perikanan, 2007, p. 38). The IMO's maritime safety committee and its maritime security working group developed the ISPS Code within months of the 9/11 attacks (IMO, 2003, p. 3). The code was implemented through the adoption of a new chapter, XI-2, in SOLAS entitled 'Special measures to enhance maritime security' in 2002 (IMO, 2003, p. 5). It came into force in July 2004. The ISPS Code sets a number of mandatory obligations for governments and the private sectors within its jurisdiction to improve ship and port security. Participation in the code brought advantages to the nation's transportation businesses, including port facilities and maritime carriers, since compliance with the code guaranteed that they would not be excluded from international shipping and could potentially lower their insurance premium rate.[30] The MoT, as the national designated authority for the implementation of the ISPS Code, was willing to bear the costs for promoting the initiative at national level and reviewing ports and ships ISPS Code compliance. Although there are costs incurred in meeting the ISPS requirements, the MoT deemed the expenditure a necessary economic investment.[31]

In June 2005, members of the WCO unanimously adopted the WCO SAFE Framework of Standards (WCO, 2007, p. 1). Indonesia was among the WCO members who signed the letter of intent to implement the WCO SAFE Framework (WCO, 2010, p. 4). The framework rests on the twin pillars of Customs-to-Customs network arrangements and Customs-to-Business partnerships. The second pillar of the SAFE Framework provides a global standard for commencing the AEO programme. All economic operators engaged in international trade can apply for AEO status, thus reducing their security risk if certified. The two lead agencies in Indonesia in the case of the WCO SAFE framework are the MFA and Customs. The MFA agreed with Customs that the initiative would be useful to help create an atmosphere conducive to facilitating trade between Indonesia and other WCO members.[32] By joining the framework and implementing the AEO programme, Indonesia can establish a mutual recognition agreement with other WCO members.[33] Such an agreement can facilitate the country's exports, exempt Indonesian cargos from time-consuming physical inspections and give priority status to Indonesian businesses.[34]

Given the MFA played a decisive role in informing Indonesia's cooperation to deter maritime terrorism, a question to pose is whether this is also the case for cooperation arrangements dealing with sea robbery. The findings show that the MFA supported Indonesia's participation in cooperation initiatives to counter armed robbery against ships, including the Indo-Sin Coordinated Patrol (ISCP) agreement with Singapore and the Indonesia–Malaysia Coordinated Patrol (IMCP), the Indonesia–the Philippines Defence Agreement, the Indonesia–India Defence Agreement, the MoU on maritime cooperation between Indonesia and China, the Malacca Straits patrol agreement, and the two ASEAN initiatives (the ARF statement on cooperation against piracy and other threats to maritime security, and the ASEAN maritime forum) despite the lack of incentives and the potential diplomatic challenges that the ministry had to deal with. This shows that bureaucratic politics did not have a significant bearing on Indonesia's participation in cooperation to counter armed robbery against ships. Indonesia's decision to cooperate in these initiatives to counter sea robbery was not the result of intense bargaining among self-interested government actors.

In June 1992, responding to the rise of armed robbery incidents in waters surrounding the Straits of Malacca and Singapore, Indonesia signed the ISCP agreement with Singapore and signed the IMCP agreement in the same year (Beckman, 2002, p. 330; Beckman *et al.*, 1994, p. 15; Chalk, 1998, p. 99; Singapore MoD, 27 May 2005). The lead Indonesian government actors in the two coordinated patrol arrangements with Singapore and Malaysia were the MFA and the MoD. As the vanguard of Indonesia's foreign policy, the Ministry might deem that the cross-border element of the Indonesia–Singapore and Indonesia–Malaysia coordinated patrol arrangements contradicts the principles of non-interference and sovereignty. The MFA could have asked the MoD and the Indonesian Armed Forces to continue border cooperation and carry out cross-border pursuits informally because, through this mechanism, Indonesia can still gain incentives without developing any new legal obligations. Yet, this was not the case. The MFA and the MoD agreed that, as Singapore and Malaysia bordered the Strait of Malacca and Singapore, cooperation between their navies and marine police was important to support Indonesia's attempt to halt sea robbery (Indonesian MFA, 2004, pp. 6–7; Jailani, 2005, p. 70; Oegroseno, 2006, p. 37; Sondakh, 2004, p. 22; 2006, p. 88).[35] Government officials from both ministries also highlight the benefit of bilateral cooperation with Malaysia and Singapore to deal with other maritime issues such as illegal fishing and smuggling (Indonesian Coordinating Ministry for Political, Legal and Security Affairs, 2006, p. 35; Jailani, 2005, p. 70; Oegroseno, 2006, p. 37).[36]

On 27 August 1997, the Indonesian and the Philippines MoDs enhanced security cooperation between the two countries by signing the agreement on cooperative activities in the field of defence and security. The agreement came into force after the Indonesian parliament ratified it in April 2007. Defence cooperation between Indonesia and India is formalised by the signing of the agreement on cooperative activities in the field of defence on 11 January 2001, which was ratified in 2007. During the deliberations on the Indonesia defence agreements with the Philippines and India, it is possible to imagine a scenario in which the conventional understanding of bureaucratic politics plays out. Indonesia's participation in the two initiatives was shaped by the MFA and the MoD. The MoD is highly in favour of cooperation with the Philippines and India, since the two countries shared common maritime borders with Indonesia. Cooperation between Indonesia and both states to address sea robbery and other transnational crimes is seen as an ideal solution to deal with these matters (Consulate General of India in Medan, 2012; *Hindu*, 2003, 2005; Indonesian Coordinating Ministry for Political, Legal and Security Affairs, 2008, pp. 24–25, 29; Indonesian MFA, 2004, pp. 7, 38; Nuswantoro, 2005, p. 26; *Xinhua*, 2004).[37] In line with the bureaucratic politics argument, it could be argued that the MFA would be expected to oppose the MoD decision to negotiate the two defence agreements that include patrol arrangements or joint exercises. In the case of the defence cooperation with the Philippines, the main issue is that Indonesia and the Philippines have not settled their maritime boundaries. As archipelagic states, both countries claim EEZ up to 200 nautical miles wide in the Sulawesi Sea, despite no part of the sea reaching more than 200 nautical miles from the nearest coast (Prescott and Schofield, 2001, p. 42). The Philippines claims all waters within its treaty limits as its territorial waters (Prescott and Schofield, 2001, p. 44). Indonesia would not enter into negotiations as long as the Philippines asserted this claim because Indonesia's Pulau Miangas (Palmas Island) is located within those treaty limits (Prescott and Schofield, 2001, p. 44). Under this circumstance, the maritime agencies of Indonesia and the Philippines would be expected to cooperate to secure undefined maritime borders. The absence of clear territorial limits might cause misunderstanding or open conflict between the two countries' law enforcement agencies. In the case of the defence agreement with India, the MFA, arguably, could oppose the initiative because of India's previous attempts to get directly involved in securing the Straits of Malacca and Singapore. India's decision to deploy its naval warships in 2002 to escort merchant ships navigating through the Straits of Malacca was met with hostility by the Indonesian government. India's conduct was seen as a threat, because it could encourage other user states to take similar action and undermine Indonesia's authority (Staf Umum Operasi Markas Besar Angkatan Laut, 2004, p. 35).

In contrast to the bureaucratic politics expectation, the Indonesian MoD in close coordination with the MFA agreed to conclude the two defence agreements. Cooperation with India and the Philippines is seen as an acceptable solution to deal with sea robbery and other transnational crimes, such as smuggling of arms and illegal migration. The MoD carefully designed the type and timing of maritime patrols and exercises to complement the nation's navy, sea and coast guard (MoT) and marine police maritime patrols in the waters bordering Indonesia and these two states (Indonesian Coordinating Ministry for Legal, Political and Security Affairs, 2008, p. 29; Indonesian MFA, 2004, pp. 7, 38; Nuswantoro, 2005, p. 26; Sondakh, 2004, pp. 20–21).[38]

Cooperation to counter sea robbery between Indonesia and Japan has been governed by non-legally binding arrangements, mainly through joint statements (Japan MFA, 10 December 2003a, 10 December 2003b, 14 April 2005, 16 June 2006, 28 November 2006, 13 October 2011, 14 October 2011, 28 August 2012, 29 August 2012). In 2005, the two countries signed the joint announcement on maritime affairs. Indonesia's decision to cooperate with Japan to counter armed robbery against ships shows the limitation of the bureaucratic politics approach in understanding cooperation. The decision pertaining to this initiative was formed through an inter-ministerial meeting that was led by the MFA and involved the MoD, the MoT, the Coordinating Ministry for Political, Legal and Security Affairs, the navy, the police and the Maritime Security Coordinating Board.[39] In line with the bureaucratic politics literature, apart from the MFA, other agencies would be expected to be in favour of the joint announcement with Japan because the cooperation brought incentives to their agencies or other maritime agencies that fell under their remit. The MFA might oppose the cooperation to counter sea robbery between Indonesia and Japan. Japan is a user state that has showed a great interest in participating directly in halting sea robbery in the Straits of Malacca and Singapore. On various occasions, the Indonesian MFA has opposed the Japanese idea of joint patrols. The Japanese Prime Minister Keizo Obuchi articulated an idea to set up a regional framework to address armed robbery against ships and piracy. At the 1999 APT summit in Manila, Obuchi proposed 'a meeting of coast guards of Asian countries to discuss possible counter-measures to fight piracy' (*Straits Times*, 2000). At the 2000 APT summit in Singapore, Obuchi's successor Prime Minister Yoshiro Mori proposed a similar counter-piracy measure. Mori proposed starting a joint anti-piracy patrol at the Strait of Malacca. The parties involved would be Japan, China, South Korea and the three littoral states of Indonesia, Malaysia and Singapore (*Straits Times*, 2000). Bilateral maritime cooperation with Japan might create, for Tokyo, the opportunity for greater participation in the management of the Straits. The MFA could have refused to support the arrangement because of this potential risk and the lack of benefits of cooperation for the Ministry. Indonesia's participation in the joint announcement did not provide the MFA with any incentive.

Contrary to the bureaucratic politics argument on competition among self-interested actors, the MFA was highly in favour of the bilateral arrangement. The MFA based its policy assessment on the benefits of cooperation for the capacity-building of the country's maritime agencies (Sudrajat, 2005, p. 12).[40] In 2003 and 2004, for instance, Foreign Minister Hassan Wirajuda requested that Japan provide patrol vessels to strengthen Indonesia maritime agencies' capacity in dealing with armed robbery against ships (Japan MFA, 16 June 2006). Various cooperation activities with Japan are also designed to fill the gap in Indonesia's efforts to fight sea robbery, both in terms of equipment and human resources for various maritime agencies including the Maritime Security Coordinating Board, the marine police and the DGST (Sudrajat, 2005, p. 12).[41]

On 25 April 2005, Indonesia and China signed the Republic of Indonesia–People's Republic of China joint statement on strategic partnership, which included maritime cooperation between the two countries (Indonesian MoD, 2008, p. 148). Following the signing of the joint statement, on the same day the two governments signed the MoU on maritime cooperation (Indonesian MFA, 1 March 2007).

The MoU on maritime cooperation between Indonesia and China does not only fail to provide any incentives for the MFA but also could potentially increase China's political leverage when negotiating its EEZ with the Indonesian MFA. In 1993 China extended its claims in the South China Sea (Emmers, 2007, pp. 51–52). The EEZ China has claimed since 1993 overlaps with waters above the Indonesian Natuna gas and oil fields (Emmers, 2007, pp. 51–52; Siboro, 2011). The negotiation of the Indonesia–China MoU on maritime cooperation was led by the MFA and involved representatives of the Coordinating Ministry for Political, Legal and Security Affairs, the Ministry of Communications, the Ministry of Fisheries and Maritime Affairs, the Ministry of Defence, the navy and the marine police (Indonesian MFA, 1 March 2007). Arguably, the establishment of enterprises and joint ventures based on maritime technology and defence weaponry between Jakarta and Beijing could make any future bargaining process regarding EEZ limits more complicated for the Indonesian MFA. However, in contrast to this potential conflict, the MFA supported Indonesia's participation in the MoU. The MFA preference to support bilateral maritime cooperation with China was not consistent with the incentives offered to this individual ministry, but with the calculation of net benefits for the country as a whole. The MFA considered the benefits of cooperation for various agencies in Indonesia and held national meetings with domestic agencies to establish concrete steps to implement the cooperation programme (Indonesian Coordinating Ministry for Legal, Political and Security Affairs, 2007, p. 33; 2008, p. 28).

Indonesia, Malaysia and Singapore signed the Malacca Straits patrol (MSP) cooperation agreement on 21 April 2006 (Koh, 2006 as cited in Anwar, 2006, p. 486). The cooperation agreement governs the two ongoing cooperation activities, the Malacca Straits sea patrols (MSSP) and the EiS air patrols (Anwar, 2006, p. 486; Singapore MoD, 2008).[42] Bureaucratic politics might have had some bearing on Indonesia's behaviour towards the MSP cooperation if there were competing preferences among self-interested actors. The Indonesian MFA, MOD and navy were the key actors who negotiated the MSP cooperation arrangement. On the one hand, the MoD and the navy would be expected to support the initiative because it is in line with their interest to gain support for maritime patrols from Malaysia and Singapore. In addition, the initiative is not costly because, prior to the signing of the MSP agreement, the navy has cooperated intensively with its Malaysian and Singaporean counterparts. Therefore, the navy was not required to do more than it already was doing. On the other hand, it could be argued that the MFA might oppose it because the arrangement includes joint air and maritime patrols that could transgress Indonesian boundaries. The MSP is a precise arrangement that regulates clear procedures for coordinated sea patrols and combined air patrols including cross border pursuits.[43] This arrangement could be problematic because Indonesia still has maritime boundary disagreements to settle with Malaysia (Arsana, 2009; Dewan Maritim Indonesia, 2007, pp. 8–3, 8–4). Since the signing of the MSP agreement, a number of incidents have taken place in an overlapping area of the EEZ claimed by both Indonesia and Malaysia in the Strait of Malacca. In 2010, officials from the Indonesian Ministry for Marine and Fisheries were detained by the Malaysian law enforcement agency for alleged trespassing (Arsana, 2011, p. 2; *Xinhua*, 27 August 2010). In April 2011, an Indonesian patrolling team from the Ministry of Marine Affairs and Fisheries detained two Malaysian flagged vessels (Arsana, 2011, p. 8; Indonesian Ministry of Marine Affairs and Fisheries, 2012). This incident almost escalated to involve the military. As the Indonesian enforcement agency seized the vessels, three Malaysian Enforcement Agency and navy helicopters flying over the waters demanded the release of the Malaysian flagged vessels (Arsana, 2011, p. 8; Indonesian Ministry of Marine Affairs and Fisheries, 2012). These incidents generated more tasks for the MFA to negotiate and manage Indonesia's relations with Malaysia. In contrast to the bureaucratic politics argument, the Indonesian MFA, the MoD and the navy supported Indonesia's involvement in the MSP. They took into account the importance of securing the sea surrounding new port development areas and also the need to meet other security concerns including smuggling and illegal migration (Bakorkamla, 2010, pp. 7, 8, 13, 47, 77; Indonesian Coordinating Ministry for Political, Legal and Security Affairs, 2006, pp. 35, 39, 51; Indonesian MFA, 2007, p. 3; 2004, p. 41, 6 January 2006; Jailani, 2005, p. 60; Purnomo, 2004, p. 36; Sumaryono, 2009, p. 141; Suristyono, 2005, p. 47).[44]

80 *Domestic politics*

Regional cooperation on armed robbery against ships is primarily conducted under two ASEAN forums: the ARF and the ASEAN Maritime Forum (AMF) (Indonesian MFA, 2009, p. 1; Jailani, 2005, p. 56). The ARF and the AMF cooperation to counter sea robbery would not deliver any benefits to the MFA. At domestic level, the dialogue forums to discuss ASEAN maritime initiatives were led by the MFA and involved representatives of the navy, the MoD, the Ministry of Marine Affairs and Fisheries, and the MoT. These initiatives could potentially complicate the MFA's diplomatic efforts to manage the cooperation to deal with sea robbery, as the ARF and the AMF involve more parties including non-littoral states (*Antara*, 25 September 2006).[45] However, the MFA has been fully supportive of Indonesia's participation in the two ASEAN forums. There were no competing preferences between the MoD, the navy and the MFA. Government officials from the Indonesian MFA, the MoD, navy, the marine police and the MoT confirmed this in interviews (Indonesian MFA, 2007, p. 3).[46] As an MFA official put it, 'our main consideration is how [ASEAN] cooperation initiatives add value to our maritime security efforts, and provide benefits to Indonesian maritime agencies'.[47] Through this cooperation framework, Indonesian maritime agencies can draw on assistance from extra-regional states to deal with sea robbery and other security threats (Indonesian MFA, 2007, pp. 2–3).[48]

Non-cooperation cases

The MFA had played a central role during the negotiation of cooperation initiatives to address maritime terrorism – the SUA convention and its protocols, the CSI and the PSI – and armed robbery against ships – the RMSI, the ReCAAP, and the Defence Cooperation Agreement (DCA) with Singapore.

The SUA convention, the CSI, the PSI and the RMSI are US-led initiatives to deter maritime terrorism. The SUA convention was adopted in 1988. In comparison, the CSI, the PSI and the RMSI were only introduced after the 9/11 attacks. In the case of the SUA convention and its protocols, the CSI and the PSI, other government agencies agreed with the MFA assessment of them.[49] Therefore, Indonesia's stance on the three initiatives could be formulated in a fast manner. In the case of the SUA convention, the MoD, the Ministry of Maritime Affairs and Fisheries, the Coordinating Ministry for Political, Legal and Security Affairs and the navy were in agreement with the MFA legal interpretation of the convention and its protocols. For the MFA, the lack of clear explanation in the SUA convention and its protocols on state jurisdiction is at the heart of its concerns. The MFA was not in favour of the initiative and its protocols for two reasons. First, the Ministry perceived that the convention and its protocols could be used as a legal foundation to refer to unlawful acts at sea that take place in Indonesian waters and, therefore, provide other states with power to pursue and arrest vessels in Indonesia jurisdiction (Agoes, 2005, p. 43; Sudrajat, 2005, p. 84).[50] The issue of jurisdiction was perceived as controversial, since the SUA convention could be applied to unlawful acts that take place within Indonesia's EEZ and therefore contradict the UNCLOS. The MFA deemed that a legal precedent such as that created by the SUA convention and its protocols were harmful to Indonesia's autonomy as an archipelagic country. Second, the MFA did not see Indonesia's non-participation in the SUA convention and its protocols as a major political concern. The initiative did not provide useful advantages to Indonesian maritime law enforcement agencies. Indonesia could gain the benefits of cooperation through other counter-maritime terrorism initiatives at bilateral, regional and global level.[51]

Governmental actors involved in the national deliberation related to the CSI were the MoT and Customs. The two agencies came to agreement with the MFA to refuse Indonesia's participation in the initiative. The MFA opposed the CSI because the legal requirements under the CSI were deemed very intrusive.[52] These requirements include the placement of the US Customs team and periodic assessments in Indonesian ports. The CSI could provide benefits to the domestic constituents of Customs, particularly exporters. Customs' participation in the CSI could potentially guarantee exporters shorter waiting times at US ports or other CSI trans-shipment ports, a priority lane in the case of a terrorist attack, and no delay due to the physical inspection of cargo at US ports or at trans-shipment points. This treatment translates into lower costs for exporters. Yet, in contrast to the bureaucratic politics expectation, Indonesian Customs agreed with the MFA to refuse Indonesia's participation in the CSI. Customs deemed that there was no urgency to join the initiative for the sake of promoting the national shippers' and shipowners' interests. The businesses' export activities to the US could be made through trans-shipment via CSI ports including Singapore, Port Kelang and Tanjung Pelepas, Malaysia (*Jakarta Post*, 15 March 2003).[53]

The PSI negotiation fell under the MFA and the MoD remits.[54] In harmony with the MFA policy regarding the SUA convention, the ministries opposed the PSI. Taking part in the PSI suggests that Indonesia could be subjected to US demands to carry out interdiction upon ships plying through the archipelago's waterways and ships registered under its flag (Indonesian MFA, 2004, p. 9).[55] Such acts may create legal precedent that challenge Indonesia's rights to secure its sea lanes as granted by the 1982 Law of the Sea Convention.

The MFA and the MoD assessment of the PSI highlighted three important points: the high economic costs of the cooperation, potential challenges to current convention on the law of the sea, and lack of incentives to Indonesian maritime agencies. First, the two governmental actors' actions were consistent with the calculation of economic risks posed by the PSI. One of the main economic concerns for the two ministries was compensation for delays to shipments or damage of goods to businesses in interdiction cases. The Indonesian government was not willing to bear the additional economic costs of interdiction.[56]

Second, government officials from both ministries deemed the US-led initiative could set a legal precedent that challenged the Law of the Sea regime, in particular through the application of the PSI 'interdiction' principles (Indonesian MFA, 2006, p. 35).[57] The Law of the Sea granted Indonesia as an archipelagic state rights to manage and secure both its territorial water and its EEZ. A senior government official from the MoD involved in the decision-making process claimed that 'the Law of the Sea provides the legal foundation for Indonesia as an archipelagic state. Thus, we have to uphold it'.[58] Both the MFA and the MoD avoid creating any precedent for another country to be involved in any form of interdiction of ships in Indonesia's EEZ (Indonesian MFA, 2006, p. 35; Sumaryono, 2004, p. 42).[59]

Finally, both ministries considered that without taking part in the PSI Indonesian law enforcement agencies could gain the benefit of cooperation with the US through bilateral and regional channels (Indonesian Coordinating Ministry for Political, Legal and Security Affairs, 2008, p. 30; Indonesian Ministry of State Secretariat, 2001, p. IV-13).[60] The Indonesian MoD and other law enforcement agencies including the MoT's sea and coast guard unit, the navy, the Customs and Excise and the Maritime Security Coordination Board can gain the benefits of cooperation through bilateral cooperation with the US. This reduced the incentives to join the PSI.

The MFA and the MoD were also the government actors who shaped the Indonesian decision on the RMSI.[61] Two reasons underscored the ministries' preferences over this initiative to address armed robbery against ships. First, the MFA and the MoD suggested that the initiative was perceived as overtly militaristic. Both ministries preferred not to take part in the initiative, to avoid any possibility of the country being seen as aligning too closely with the US by the public.[62]

This decision was made when there was growing opposition against the RMSI from the public. The Indonesian parliament did not state its official position regarding the RMSI (Indonesian Parliament, 2000–2013).[63] However, members of the parliament, in particular those who are members of opposition parties, were not convinced by the US government's attempt to clarify Admiral Fargo's statement (Indonesian MoD, 2004). Amris Hassan, Chairman of Commission I (Foreign Affairs Commission), House of Representative and also a member of the opposition party, the Indonesian Democratic Party of Struggle, categorised the initiative as an act of intervention and violation of Indonesia's sovereignty (Indonesian MoD, 2004). Senior politicians in Indonesia's main Islamic party, the United Development Party (PPP), also shared this view. Aisyah Aminy, a senior politician from the PPP, warned the US not to intervene in Indonesia's sovereign territory and declared a readiness to support an increase in the military budget to improve naval capacity (Indonesian MoD, 2004).

Although the public and members of the opposition parties were not directly involved in formulating Indonesia's stance on the RMSI, their reactions to the initiative influenced government decisions. In the case of the RMSI, the societal actors, particularly members of opposition parties in the parliament, made a difference to the way the government assessed the costs and benefits of cooperation. A former government official from the MoD explained how the two ministries' preferences were also derived from careful calculations of the possible political implications that the RMSI might bring. According to him, the RMSI was overtly militaristic, and strong public opposition against the initiative suggested

Domestic politics 83

that taking part in the initiative could compromise the 'political manoeuvrability of Indonesian political leaders'.[64] Although the strong rejection by opposition parties, particularly those with a nationalist platform, were symbolic, it was important to maintain a careful balance between halting sea robbery and cooperating with foreign countries without going against the will of the public.[65] As the official put it, this was because

> states with high regional pride such as ... Indonesia ... on the one hand need US assistance but on the other hand they do not want to be assisted to such a large scale because we want to maintain the symbolic sense of pride.[66]

More importantly, the MoD and the MFA, in line with Indonesian law enforcement agencies and in particular the navy and the Indonesian Maritime Security Coordinating Board, strongly opposed the initiative because of the potential security challenges posed by militant groups to the security of the Straits (Acharya, 2007, p. 87; Bakorkamla, 2010, p. 100; BBC, 2004; Oegroseno, 2005, p. 59). As explained earlier, although US patrols in the Straits of Malacca and Singapore were not part of the cooperation activities covered by the RMSI, media reports on Fargo's comments created negative publicity in Indonesia. Despite US officials' efforts to clarify Fargo's statements, the Indonesian public believed that the US planned to send their marine forces to patrol the Straits as part of the RMSI (Acharya, 2007, p. 87; BBC, 2004; Choong, 2004; *Jakarta Post*, 20 April 2004; Medeiros, 2004). Radical factions such as the Majelis Mujahidin Indonesia stated their intention to expel American troops from the Straits of Malacca (Acharya, 2007, p. 87; Bakorkamla, 2010, p. 100; BBC, 2004). The Navy and Maritime Security Coordinating Board were concerned that taking part in the RMSI could provoke a backlash from radical elements in Indonesia and make the Straits of Malacca a more desirable target for both Al Qaeda and JI (Acharya, 2007, p. 87; Bakorkamla, 2010, p. 100; BBC, 2004; Wisnumurti, 2009, p. 347). A Maritime Security Coordinating Board document explained that the RMSI 'will create new problems, such as the rejection from groups that opposed US involvement in securing the Straits of Malacca' (Bakorkamla, 2010, p. 103).

Second, the MFA and the MoD preferred bilateral cooperation with the US rather than the RMSI because through bilateral negotiation Indonesia has a better chance of influencing the terms of agreement, which would in turn presumably contribute to generating preferable outcomes for Indonesia. As the MFA Director General of Legal Affairs and International Treaties Eddy Pratomo, confirmed, in terms of security issues Indonesia prefers technical assistance to be given through bilateral channels (Indonesian MFA, 21 September 2006). Joining the RMSI was not an immediate concern for Indonesia. The Indonesian and US security relationship had significantly improved after 9/11, three years before the RMSI was introduced. The US had provided training and equipment as part of the bilateral cooperation. Therefore, the country could gain the benefits of cooperation through existing bilateral arrangements.

84 *Domestic politics*

The central role of the MFA is most clearly shown in the negotiation of the ReCAAP agreement. The ReCAAP was established through a negotiated process which involved ten ASEAN member states, including Indonesia, three East Asian states (Japan, China and South Korea) and three South Asian states (India, Bangladesh and Sri Lanka) (Bateman, 2009, p. 118). The agreement was finalised in Tokyo on 11 November 2004 and came into effect on 4 September 2006 (ReCAAP, 2011). Competing government actors' preferences did not influence Indonesia's rejection of the ReCAAP. Rather, what mattered in the case of the ReCAAP was whose preference prevailed in informing Indonesia's decision. In this instance, the MFA preference is important in shaping Indonesia's decision not to join the ReCAAP. Both in negotiations with foreign counterparts and in formulating Indonesia's decision towards the ReCAAP, the MFA was the leading agency among governmental actors.[67] The MFA organised an interministerial meeting and invited other relevant governmental actors including the MoD, the MoT and the Coordinating Ministry for Political, Legal and Security Affairs to discuss Indonesia's position regarding the ReCAAP agreement.[68]

If the ministries had behaved as the conventional bureaucratic politics explanation would suggest, it could be argued that the MFA would have opposed the agreement because it offered no incentives to the ministry. However, although the MFA opposed the ReCAAP initiative, the MoT, the MoD, and the Coordinating Ministry for Political, Legal and Security Affairs might have supported it. This is because the cooperation initiative would not have imposed additional costs, as their associated agencies all cooperated informally with the ReCAAP ISC. Despite these expectations, the MoD and the Coordinating Ministry for Political, Legal and Security Affairs supported the MFA preference to reject Indonesia's participation in the ReCAAP. As an official from the Indonesian Ministry of Defence maintained: 'That [decision about ReCAAP] is not within our [referring to an agency that he led] scope of authority. We always follow the foreign policy formulated by the MFA. When the MFA said "this", we have to do the same'.[69] An official from the MoT confirmed this account of the internal deliberations, claiming: 'ReCAAP ... it is more a policy of the MFA ... we need to follow the guidance from the MFA. The MFA prohibited our involvement in ReCAAP'.[70]

The MFA also instructed officials from other ministries who attended ReCAAP meetings. As a government official from the Directorate of Sea Transportation, MoT suggested: 'It was the MFA that gave the note. Usually, whenever there were ReCAAP forums, they [the MFA] would provide us with a note, on what we should do'.[71] The MFA was initially enthusiastic about ReCAAP, but ultimately chose not to join the agreement. The ministry's early enthusiasm was due to seeing ReCAAP as a possible burden-sharing agreement between the user states and the littoral states of the Straits (Indonesian MFA, 2006, p. 15; Jailani, 2005, pp. 69–70; Sumaryono, 2004, p. 44).[72] The final agreement, however, did not include burden-sharing arrangements, and the MFA's enthusiasm began to diminish.[73] The MFA was further put off the ReCAAP due to its inability to get the ISC located in Indonesia. It had hoped that locating the ISC in Indonesia would both facilitate capacity building in Indonesia's maritime agencies and address Indonesia's dissatisfaction about what it considered exaggerated reporting of sea robbery and piracy incidents in regional waters by the IMB (Jailani, 2005, p. 67; Nuswantoro, 2005, p. 25; Urquhart, 2006).[74] Its concern that unfair reporting of sea robbery incidents would continue if the ISC were placed in another country was sufficient to make the Indonesian MFA consistently maintain its standpoint that, if the ISC were not placed in Indonesia, Indonesia would refuse to participate (Bradford, 2004, p. 499).[75] This was ultimately the critical sticking point. A vice-president of an NGO that specialises in maritime security in Asia confirmed Indonesia's disagreement regarding the location of the ISC. He indicated in an interview that: 'Indonesia's objection to ratifying the ReCAAP agreement derived from its dissatisfaction over the decision on ReCAAP ISC location'.[76]

The final cooperation arrangement to discuss in this section is the DCA between Indonesia and Singapore. Although the ISCP arrangement has been a success, the DCA that was signed by the two states' Ministers of Defence on April 2007 was not. If the conventional interpretation of competition among self-interested actors was to have some bearing in explaining Indonesia's non-cooperation, then from the beginning of the negotiations we would expect the two lead agencies, the MFA and the MoD, to reject the cooperation initiative. The MoD and the MFA did not obtain substantial benefits from the DCA. In the absence of the DCA, the existing links between the two armed forces would allow the Singapore armed forces to provide training assistance to their Indonesian counterparts and contribute significantly to the development and maintenance of training facilities in Indonesia (*Antara*, 22 September 2007). In contrast to the expectation of the bureaucratic politics literature, the Indonesian MFA and MoD preferred to cooperate because, by joining the DCA, Indonesia could obtain Singapore's commitment to take part in the Extradition Treaty (Indonesian Coordinating Ministry for Political, Legal and Security Affairs, 2008, p. 55; Indonesian Parliament, 21 September 2006).[77] The lack of benefits for promoting the DCA for the MFA and the MoD was even more apparent at domestic level. On the domestic front, the two ministries' preferences were met with strong opposition from the parliament. Members of parliament asserted that the terms of the agreement were highly in favour of Singapore (Deutsche Press-Agentur, 2009; *Xinhua*, 12 June 2007, 14 June 2007, 18 September 2007). Parliament members from opposition parties including the National Mandate Party, the National Awakening Party, the United Development Party, the Golkar Party and the Indonesian Democratic Party of Struggle urged the government to cancel the DCA (Indonesian Parliament, 25 June 2007, 17 September 2007; *Xinhua*, 23 February 2007, 12 June 2007, 18 September 2007).

As the issue become more politicised the Riau Islands local government officials and legislators felt it necessary to raise their objections over military exercises in their vicinity to the president, the Minister of Defence and parliament (*Antara*, 2 August 2007; Indonesian Coordinating Ministry for Political, Legal and Security Affairs, 2008, p. 24; *Xinhua*, 24 May 2007). They raised their concern that military exercises which involved the use of war equipment could harm the local population and cause environmental damage (*Antara*, 2 August 2007; Indonesian Parliament, 28 May 2007; *Xinhua*, 24 May 2007). This is despite their support of Indonesian armed forces large-scale national joint military exercises and Indonesia–Singapore bilateral routine maritime exercises that involved the use of fast patrol boats and heavy armaments in their area (*Antara*, 8 September 2012; *Antara*, 10 September 2012; *Suara Karya*, 2010).

Responding to the growing opposition at domestic level, both ministries presented the DCA as both a beneficial arrangement and a necessary trade off to gain the extradition treaty (Indonesian Democratic Party of Struggle, 2013; Indonesian Parliament, 25 June 2007; 17 September 2007). Indonesia needed the extradition treaty to prosecute businessmen that fled the country with the government bailout fund during the Asian financial crisis in 1996–97 (Indonesian Coordinating Ministry for Political, Legal and Security Affairs, 2008, p. 55; Surya Citra Televisi Liputan 6, 2007). Despite the mounting opposition, both ministries did not immediately cancel the DCA; instead they proceeded with negotiations on implementing the arrangements of the defence treaty (*Antara*, 22 September 2007; *Xinhua*, 14 June 2007). In 2007, however, Singapore's rejection of the retroactive application of the extradition treaty for fifteen years set back the negotiation of the DCA (*Antara*, 19 September 2007; Indonesian Coordinating Ministry for Political, Legal and Security Affairs, 2008, p. 55). For Indonesia, Singapore's action removed the side payment for Indonesia cooperating. The Indonesian Minister of Defence Juwono Sudarsono stated that Singapore's rejection of the retroactive application of the extradition treaty suggested that the city-state had dropped the DCA (*Jakarta Post*, 28 December 2007; Kompas, 2008). He explained that both agreements were signed as one package; thus, if one failed, the other would be discontinued (*Antara*, 8 July 2007; *Straits Times*, 26 July 2007). Indonesia decided to freeze both agreements indefinitely in late 2007 (*Jakarta Post*, 28 December 2007).

Conclusion

This chapter has explained the dynamics of Indonesia's domestic politics and the unique features of the country's bureaucratic politics process. There are two points to take away from this chapter. First, this chapter highlights the dominant role of the MFA in foreign policy making. The MFA plays a central role in negotiating cooperation arrangements at international level. At national level, the MFA organises inter-ministerial meetings, provides legal and political assessment of cooperation arrangements, and offers policy guidance to relevant authorities. The central role of the MFA is most apparent in cases where a large number of government agencies have taken part in the national deliberations, such as over the ReCAAP. The deliberation process at national level also included the MoD, the Maritime Security Coordinating Board, the MoT and the navy.

Second, this chapter brings our attention to the absence of competing preferences among self-interested actors. This is partly due to the dominant role of the MFA in foreign policy making. The lack of competitive bargaining could be seen both in cooperation and non-cooperation cases. Maritime security initiatives that Indonesia has joined include the bilateral counter-terrorism cooperation with the US, Japan and Australia, a trilateral information-sharing arrangement, the BIMP-EAGA MoUs on transport of goods and sea linkages, the ASEAN convention on counter-terrorism, the ISPS Code, the WCO SAFE framework and the APEC TRP, bilateral coordinated patrol arrangements with Singapore and Malaysia, defence arrangements with the Philippines and India, the MoU on maritime cooperation with China, the MSP agreement, the AMF and the ARF initiatives to counter sea robbery. These initiatives have provided a range of benefits, including assistance in information sharing, capacity building such as training and maritime exercises, new equipment and weaponry. None of these benefits are allocated for the MFA. Despite the absence of tangible benefits, the MFA is in favour of Indonesia's participation in these cooperation arrangements.

In terms of non-cooperation cases, other leading ministries such as the MoD in the case of the PSI and the RMSI, and the Customs in the case of the CSI, for instance, did not assess each cooperation arrangement on the basis of the benefits that they might attain. Rather, government ministries assessed each cooperation initiative according to the calculation of costs and benefits for other government agencies, Indonesian businesses and the country as a whole. As a consequence, they could easily come into agreement with the MFA to refuse Indonesia's participation in these initiatives and decisions could be made in a fast manner.

Notes

1 Article 10(1) of the Indonesian Law No. 24/2000 on international treaties.
2 Interviews with an Indonesian foreign and security policy expert at the University of Indonesia (Depok, 11 October 2011), and an Indonesian government official (Jakarta, 4 November 2011).
3 Interviews with an Indonesian government official (Jakarta, 4 November 2011) and an Indonesian foreign and security policy expert at the University of Indonesia (Depok, 11 October 2011).
4 Interviews with an Indonesian government official (Jakarta, 4 November 2011) and an Indonesian foreign and security policy expert at the University of Indonesia (Depok, 11 October 2011); email correspondence with a former expert member of staff of the Indonesian Parliament, 24 April 2013.
5 Interview with an Indonesian government official (Jakarta, 4 November 2011).
6 Interview with an NGO representative (Jakarta, 27 October 2011).
7 Interviews with an NGO representative (Jakarta, 27 October 2011) and an Indonesian foreign and security policy expert at the University of Indonesia (Depok, 11 October 2011).
8 Interview with an Indonesian foreign and security policy expert at the University of Indonesia (Depok, 11 October 2011).
9 Interviews with representatives of Indonesian Shipowners' Association (Surabaya, 22

88 Domestic politics

September 2011), a corporate communication official of a port operator (Surabaya, 20 September 2011), a security and safety official of a port operator (Surabaya, 20 September 2011), a representative of the Indonesian Forwarders Association (Jakarta, 9 September 2011) and a representative of the Indonesian Shipowners' Association (Jakarta, 29 June 2010).
10 Interviews with a high government official at the Indonesian Maritime Security Coordinating Board (Jakarta, 2 July 2010), a government official at the Indonesian Maritime Security Coordinating Board (Jakarta, 3 July 2010), a high government official at the Indonesian Ministry of Defence (Jakarta, 7 July 2010), two high government officials at the Indonesian Ministry of Transportation (Jakarta, 3 September 2010) and two high government officials at the Ministry of Transportation (Jakarta, 7 September 2010).
11 These laws are the Presidential Regulation No. 9 of 2005 regarding the position, duties, roles, structure, and work procedure of the state ministries of the Republic of Indonesia (Articles 31 and 32), Law No. 39 of 2008 on state ministries (Article 7) and Law No. 37 of 1999.
12 Interviews with an Indonesian government official (Jakarta, 4 November 2011), a high government official at the Indonesian Ministry of Defence (Jakarta, 7 July 2010), a high government official at the Indonesian navy (Jakarta, 14 July 2010), an Indonesian security policy expert at the University of Indonesia (Depok, 11 October 2011) and an Indonesian foreign and security policy expert at the University of Indonesia (Depok, 11 October 2011).
13 Interviews with an Indonesian government official (Jakarta, 4 November 2011), a former high government official at the Ministry of Defence (Depok, 8 October 2011) and a high government official at the Indonesian Maritime Security Coordinating Board (Jakarta, 2 July 2010).
14 Interview with an Indonesian security policy expert at the University of Indonesia (Depok, 11 October 2011).
15 Interviews with a government official at the Indonesian Maritime Security Coordinating Board (Jakarta, 3 July 2010) and three high government officials at the Indonesian Ministry of Transportation (Jakarta, 3 September 2010).
16 Interviews with a security and safety official of a port operator (Surabaya, 20 September 2011), a high government official at the Indonesian Ministry of Transportation (Jakarta, 3 September 2010) and an Indonesian government official (Jakarta, 4 November 2011).
17 Interview with a government official at the Indonesian Maritime Security Coordinating Board (Jakarta, 3 July 2010).
18 Interview with a Japanese high government official at the embassy of Japan in Indonesia (Jakarta, 13 December 2011).
19 Interviews with an Indonesian government official (Jakarta, 4 November 2011), a high government official at the Indonesian Coordinating Ministry for Political, Legal and Security Affairs (Jakarta, 30 July 2010), a high government official at the Indonesian marine police (Jakarta, 2 September 2010), two high government officials at the Indonesian Ministry of Transportation (Jakarta, 3 September 2010) and a Japanese high government official at the embassy of Japan in Indonesia (Jakarta, 13 December 2011).
20 Article 4 and 5 of the Japan–Indonesia joint announcement on fighting against international terrorism (24 June 2003).
21 Interview with a high government official at the Ministry of Transportation (Jakarta, 3 September 2010).
22 Indonesian President Regulation No. 184/1998 on coordinating team and sub-team in sub-regional economic cooperation; interview with a high government official at the Ministry of Transportation (Jakarta, 3 September 2010).

Domestic politics 89

23 Annex I on projects to implement the agreement on information exchange and establishment of communication procedures.
24 Interview with an Indonesian foreign and security policy expert at the University of Indonesia (Depok, 11 October 2011).
25 Article IV of the ASEAN convention on counter-terrorism.
26 Interviews with a high government official at the Indonesian Maritime Security Coordinating Board (Jakarta, 2 July 2010), a high government official at the Indonesian Ministry of Defence (Jakarta, 7 July 2010) and a high government official at the Indonesian navy (Jakarta, 14 July 2010).
27 Interviews with an official at the Indonesian Customs and Excise, Ministry of Finance (Jakarta, 11 October 2011), a high government official at the Indonesian Customs and Excise, Ministry of Finance (Jakarta, 9 November 2011) and a high government official at the Indonesian Ministry of Foreign Affairs (Jakarta, 16 December 2011).
28 Interview with a high government official at the Indonesian Ministry of Foreign Affairs (Jakarta, 16 December 2011).
29 Interviews with a high government official at the Indonesian Ministry of Foreign Affairs (Jakarta, 16 December 2011) and a high government official at the Indonesian Customs and Excise, Ministry of Finance (Jakarta, 9 November 2011).
30 Interviews with a representative of an international insurance company (Singapore, 17 August 2010) and a high government official at the Indonesian Ministry of Transportation (Jakarta, 3 September 2010).
31 Interviews with a high government official at the Indonesian Ministry of Transportation (Jakarta, 29 September 2011), a high government official at the Indonesian Maritime Security Coordinating Board (Jakarta, 23 August 2011), a high government official at the Indonesian Maritime Security Coordinating Board (Jakarta, 2 July 2010) and a high government official at the Indonesian Ministry of Transportation (Jakarta, 3 September 2010).
32 Interviews with three high government officials at the Indonesian Customs and Excise, Ministry of Finance (Jakarta, 3 November 2011, 4 November 2011 and 9 November 2011).
33 Interview with a high government official at the Indonesian Customs and Excise, Ministry of Finance (Jakarta, 4 November 2011).
34 Interviews with three high government officials at the Indonesian Customs and Excise, Ministry of Finance (Jakarta, 3 November 2011, 4 November 2011 and 9 November 2011).
35 Interviews with a high government official at the Indonesian marine police (Jakarta, 2 September 2010), a high government official at the Indonesian Maritime Security Coordinating Board (Jakarta, 2 July 2010), a high government official at the Indonesian Ministry of Defence (Jakarta, 7 July 2010) and a high government official at the Indonesian navy (Jakarta, 14 July 2010).
36 Interviews with a high government official at the Indonesian Ministry of Defence (Jakarta, 7 July 2010) and a high government official at the Indonesian navy (Jakarta, 14 July 2010).
37 Interviews with a high government official at the Indonesian Ministry of Defence (Jakarta, 7 July 2010), a high government official at the Indonesian navy (Jakarta, 14 July 2010), a high government official at the Indonesian Coordinating Ministry for Political, Legal and Security Affairs (Jakarta, 30 July 2010), a high government official at the Indonesian Maritime Security Coordinating Board (Jakarta, 23 August 2011) and an Indonesian government official (Jakarta, 4 November 2011).
38 Interviews with a high government official at the Indonesian Ministry of Defence (Jakarta, 7 July 2010), a high government official at the Indonesian navy (Jakarta, 14 July 2010), an Indonesian government official (Jakarta, 4 November 2011) and a high government official at the Indonesian Coordinating Ministry for Political, Legal and Security Affairs (Jakarta, 30 July 2010).

90 Domestic politics

39 Interview with an Indonesian government official (Jakarta, 4 November 2011).
40 Interview with an Indonesian government official (Jakarta, 4 November 2011).
41 Interview with a Japanese high government official at the embassy of Japan in Indonesia (Jakarta, 13 December 2011).
42 Interview with a high government official at the Indonesian navy (Jakarta, 14 July 2010).
43 Interviews with a high government official at the Indonesian Ministry of Defence (Jakarta, 7 July 2010); and a high government official at the Indonesian navy (Jakarta, 14 July 2010).
44 Interviews with a government official at the Indonesian Maritime Security Coordinating Board (Jakarta, 3 July 2010) and a high government official at the Indonesian Ministry of Defence (Jakarta, 7 July 2010).
45 Interview with an Indonesian government official (Jakarta, 4 November 2011).
46 Interviews with a high government official at the Indonesian navy (Jakarta, 14 July 2010), a high government official at the Indonesian marine police (Jakarta, 2 September 2010), two high government officials at the Ministry of Transportation (Jakarta, 7 September 2010) and an Indonesian government official (Jakarta, 4 November 2011).
47 Interview with an Indonesian government official (Jakarta, 4 November 2011).
48 Interview with an Indonesian government official (Jakarta, 4 November 2011).
49 Interviews with an Indonesian government official (Jakarta, 4 November 2011), a former high government official at the Ministry of Defence (Depok, 8 October 2011) and a high government official at the Indonesian National Development Planning Agency (Jakarta, 28 September 2011).
50 Interview with an Indonesian government official (Jakarta, 4 November 2011).
51 Interviews with an Indonesian government official (Jakarta, 4 November 2011) and a former high government official at the Ministry of Defence (Depok, 8 October 2011).
52 Interview with an Indonesian government official (Jakarta, 4 November 2011).
53 Interviews with government officials at the Indonesian Ministry of Trade (Jakarta, 1 September 2010), a security and safety official of a port operator (Surabaya, 20 September 2011) and a representative of the Indonesian Shipowners' Association (Jakarta, 29 June 2010).
54 Interviews with an Indonesian government official (Jakarta, 4 November 2011) and a high government official at the Indonesian Ministry of Defence (Jakarta, 7 July 2010).
55 Interview with an Indonesian government official (Jakarta, 4 November 2011).
56 Interview with an Indonesian government official (Jakarta, 4 November 2011).
57 Interview with a former high government official at the Ministry of Defence (Depok, 8 October 2011).
58 Interviews with a high government official at the Indonesian Ministry of Defence (Jakarta, 7 July 2010) and a former high government official at the Ministry of Defence (Depok, 8 October 2011).
59 Interviews with an Indonesian government official (Jakarta, 4 November 2011), a former high government official at the Ministry of Defence (Depok, 8 October 2011) and an Indonesian foreign and security policy expert at the University of Indonesia (Depok, 11 October 2011).
60 Interviews with an Indonesian government official (Jakarta, 4 November 2011), a former high government official at the Ministry of Defence (Depok, 8 October 2011) and an Indonesian foreign and security policy expert at the University of Indonesia (Depok, 11 October 2011).
61 Interviews with a high government official at the Indonesian navy (Jakarta, 14 July 2010), a former high government official at the Ministry of Defence (Depok, 8 October 2011), two high government officials at the Ministry of Transportation (Jakarta, 7 September 2010) and an Indonesian government official (Jakarta, 4 November 2011).

Domestic politics 91

62 Interview with a former high government official at the Ministry of Defence (Depok, 8 October 2011).
63 Interviews with an Indonesian government official (Jakarta, 4 November 2011) and a former high government official at the Ministry of Defence (Depok, 8 October 2011).
64 Interview with a former high government official at the Ministry of Defence (Depok, 8 October 2011).
65 Interview with a former high government official at the Ministry of Defence (Depok, 8 October 2011).
66 Interview with a former high government official at the Ministry of Defence (Depok, 8 October 2011).
67 Interviews with a high government official at the Indonesian Maritime Security Coordinating Board (Jakarta, 2 July 2010), a government official at the Indonesian Maritime Security Coordinating Board (Jakarta, 3 July 2010), a high government official at the Indonesian Ministry of Defence (Jakarta, 7 July 2010), a high government official at the Indonesian Navy (Jakarta, 14 July 2010) and two high government officials at the Ministry of Transportation (Jakarta, 7 September 2010).
68 Interview with an Indonesian government official (Jakarta, 4 November 2011).
69 Interview with a high government official at the Indonesian Ministry of Defence (Jakarta, 7 July 2010).
70 Interview with two high government officials at the Ministry of Transportation (Jakarta, 7 September 2010).
71 Interview with a high government official at the Indonesian Ministry of Transportation (Jakarta, 3 September 2010).
72 Interviews with an Indonesian government official (Jakarta, 4 November 2011) and an Indonesian foreign and security policy expert at the University of Indonesia (Depok, 11 October 2011).
73 Interviews with an Indonesian government official (Jakarta, 4 November 2011) and an Indonesian foreign and security policy expert at the University of Indonesia (Depok, 11 October 2011).
74 Interviews with an Indonesian government official (Jakarta, 4 November 2011), a high government official at the Indonesian Maritime Security Coordinating Board (Jakarta, 23 August 2011), a high government official at the Indonesian Ministry of Transportation (Jakarta, 3 September 2010) and two high government officials at the Ministry of Transportation (Jakarta, 7 September 2010).
75 Interview with a representative of an NGO in the area of maritime security (Singapore, 6 August 2010).
76 Interview with a representative of an NGO in the area of maritime security (Singapore, 6 August 2010).
77 Interview with a former high government official at the Indonesian Ministry of Defence (Depok, 8 October 2011).

References

Acharya, Arabinda. (2007). 'Maritime Terrorist Threat in Southeast Asia', in *Maritime Security in Southeast Asia*, Kwa Chong Guan and John K. Skogan (eds). New York: Routledge.

Agoes, Etty R. (2005). 'Pengelolaan Keamanan di Selat Malaka Secara Terpadu', in *Pertemuan Kelompok Ahli Kebijakan Terpadu Pengelolaan Keamanan Selat Malaka*. Jakarta: Badan Pengkajian dan Pengembangan Kebijakan Kementerian Luar Negeri Indonesia.

Agung, Ide Anak Agung Gde. (1973). *Twenty Years Indonesian Foreign Policy 1945–1965*. The Hague: Mouton.

92 Domestic politics

Ahram, Ariel Ira. (2011). *Proxy Warriors: The Rise and Fall of State-Sponsored Militias*. Stanford, CA: Stanford University Press.

Allison, Graham and Zelikow, Philip. (1999). *Essence of Decision: Explaining the Cuban Missile Crisis*, 2nd edition. New York: Wesley Longman.

Antara. (2006) 'Indonesia Determined to Postpone Ratification of Malacca Strait Pact', 25 September 2006, accessed from the Newsbank database.

Antara. (2007). 'Indonesia Perlu Tegas atas Penolakan Revisi DCA', 8 July 2007, available at www.antaranews.com/berita/69259/indonesia-perlu-tegas-atas-penolakan-revisi-dca. Last accessed 8 May 2014.

Antara. (2007). 'Menhan: Pelaksanaan DCA Mungkin Tidak di Natuna', 2 August 2007, available at www.antaranews.com/berita/1186044439/menhan-pelaksanaan-dca-mungkin-tidak-di-natuna. Last accessed 30 January 2013.

Antara. (2007). 'Anggota DPR: Singapura Secara Faktual Telah Membatalkan DCA', 19 September 2007, available at www.antaranews.com/berita/1190136535/anggota-dpr-singapura-secara-faktual-telah-membatalkan-dca. Last accessed 28 January 2013.

Antara. (2007). 'Indonesia: Minister Says Still Chance to Review Defence Ties with Singapore', 22 September 2007, accessed from the Newsbank database.

Antara. (2012). 'LAM Natuna: PPRC Pembuktian Kekuatan Militer Indonesia', 8 September 2012, available at http://kepri.antaranews.com/berita/22148/lam-natuna-pprc-pembuktian-kekuatan-militer-indonesia. Last accessed 13 March 2013.

Antara. (2012). 'TNI Unjuk Kekuatan di Gerbang Utara Indonesia', 10 September 2012, available at http://kepri.antaranews.com/berita/22167/tni-unjuk-kekuatan-di-gerbang-utara-indonesia. Last accessed 13 March 2013.

Anwar, Dewi Fortuna. (2006). 'Resource Issues and Ocean Governance in Asia Pacific: An Indonesian Perspective'. *Contemporary Southeast Asia* 28:3, pp. 466–489.

APEC. (2008a). 'Summary of Annual Fora Report to SCE and SOM2008/SOM3/SCE/013a', available at www.apec.org/Groups/SOM-Steering…on…/~/…/08_cttf_TRP.ashx. Last accessed 11 August 2011.

APEC. (2008b). 'Singapore's Report on the APEC Capacity Building Workshop on Trade Recovery Programme 23–24 July 2008', Singapore: APEC Counter Terrorism Task Force, available at http://publications.apec.org/publication-detai.php?pub_id=156. Last accessed 18 May 2012.

APEC. (2008c) 'Transportation Working Group', available at www.apec.org/Groups/SOM-Steering-Committee-on-Economic-and-Technical-Cooperation/Working-Groups/Transportation.aspx. Last accessed 18 May 2012.

Arsana, I Made Andi. (2009). 'Mapping a Good Fence With Singapore', *Jakarta Post*, 9 February 2009, accessed from the Newsbank database.

Arsana, I Made Andi. (2011). 'Good Fences Make Good Neighbours: Challenges and Opportunities in Finalising Maritime Boundary Delimitation in the Malacca Strait between Indonesia and Malaysia', Proceeding of the 2nd CILS Conference 2011: International Conference on ASEAN's Role in Sustainable Development, 21–22 November, Yogyakarta.

Asian Development Bank, (2012). 'Brunei Darussalam Indonesia Malaysia The Philippines East ASEAN Growth Area (BIMP-EAGA)', available at http://beta.adb.org/countries/subregional-programs/bimp-eaga. Last accessed 1 February 2012.

Australian Department of Defence. (2012). 'Joint Press Conference in Indonesia', 4 September 2012, available at www.minister.defence.gov.au/2012/09/04/minister-for-defence-stephen-smith-transcript-joint-press-conference-with-indonesian-minister-for-defence-yusgiantoro-purnomo/. Last accessed 20 October 2012.

Australian Department of Foreign Affairs and Trade. (2012). 'Indonesia Country Brief', available at www.dfat.gov.au/geo/indonesia/indonesia_brief.html. Last accessed 22 October 2012.

Badan Koordinasi Keamanan Laut (Bakorkamla). (2004). 'Workshop Selat Malaka: Pola Pengamanan Selat Malaka dan Permasalahannya'. Bakorkamla: Jakarta.

Bakorkamla. (2010). *Buku Putih Bakorkamla 2009*. Jakarta: Pustaka Cakra.

Bakti, Ikrar Nusa. (2010). 'Bilateral Relations between Indonesia and the Philippines: Stable and Cooperative', in *International Relations in Southeast Asia: Between Bilateralism and Multilateralism*, N. Ganesan and Ramses Amer (eds). Singapore: ISEAS.

Bateman, Sam. (2009). 'Piracy and Armed Robbery against Ships in Indonesian Waters', in *Indonesia beyond the Water's Edge*. Singapore: ISEAS.

BBC. (2004). 'SE Asia Acts on Maritime Security', 29 June 2004, available at http://news.bbc.co.uk/1/hi/world/asia-pacific/3849217.stm. Last accessed 11 May 2013.

Beckman, Robert C. (2002). 'Combating Piracy and Armed Robbery Against Ships in Southeast Asia: The Way Forward'. *Ocean Development and International Law* 33, pp. 317–342.

Beckman, Robert C., Grundy-War, Carl and Forbes, Vivian L. (1994). 'Acts of Piracy in the Malacca and Singapore Straits'. *International Boundaries Research Unit Maritime Briefing* 1:4, pp. 1–43.

BIMP EAGA. (2012). *Implementation Blueprint 2012–2016*, available at http://bimp-eaga.org/Documents/ef4b1b8e-7291-40a5-9a0a-2d0250543801.pdf. Last accessed 6 June 2013.

Bradford, John F. (2004). 'Japanese Anti-Piracy Initiatives in Southeast Asia: Policy Formulation and the Coastal States Responses'. *Contemporary Southeast Asia* 26:3, pp. 480–505.

Business World. (2006). 'Mindanao Traders Frustrated with EAGA, Call for Timetable', 10 March 2006, accessed from the Newsbank database.

Butcher, John G. (2009). 'Becoming an Archipelagic State: The Juanda Declaration of 1957 and the "Struggle" to Gain International Recognition of the Archipelagic Principle', in *Indonesia beyond the Water's Edge*, Robert Cribb and Michelle Ford (eds). Singapore: Institute of Southeast Asian Studies.

Carlsnaes, Walter. (2006). 'Foreign Policy', in *Handbook of International Relations*, Walter Carlsnaes, Thomas Risse and Beth A. Simmons (eds). London: Sage Publications.

Chalk, Peter. (1998). 'Contemporary Maritime Piracy in Southeast Asia'. *Studies in Conflict and Terrorism* 21:1, pp. 87–112.

Choong, William. (2004). 'US: It's Not for Us to Police Malacca Straits – American Forces Will Not Step in to Pre-empt Threats, Say Top Officials', *The Sunday Times*, 6 June 2004.

Chow, Jonathan T. (2005). 'ASEAN Counterterrorism Cooperation Since 9/11'. *Asian Survey* 45:2, pp. 302–321.

Consulate General of India in Medan. (2012). '20th INDOCORPAT Indian Navy-TNI AL', available at www.congendiamedan.or.id/index.php?option=com_content&view=article&id=120&Itemid=169. Last accessed 6 October 2012.

Dent, Christopher M. and Richter, Peter. (2011). 'Sub-Regional Cooperation and Developmental Regionalism: The Case of BIMP-EAGA'. *Contemporary Southeast Asia* 33:1, pp. 29–55.

Deutsche Press-Agentur. (2009). 'Report: Indonesia-Singapore Defence, Extradition Pacts Shelved', 20 March 2009; accessed from the Newsbank database.

Dewan Maritim Indonesia. (2007). *Laporan: Perumusan Kebijakan Grand Strategi Pembangunan Kelautan.* Jakarta: Sekretariat Jenderal Departemen Kelautan dan Perikanan.

Djalal, Hasjim. (1995). *Indonesia and the Law of the Sea.* Jakarta: Centre for Strategic and International Studies.

Djalal, Hasjim. (2009). 'Regulation of International Straits'. *Indonesian Journal of International Law* 6:3, pp. 315–332.

Dosch, Jorn. (2006). 'The Impact of Democratization on the Making of Foreign Policy in Indonesia, Thailand and the Philippines'. *Journal of Current Southeast Asian Affairs* 25:5, pp. 42–70.

Elson, Robert Edward. (2008). *The Idea of Indonesia: A History.* Cambridge: Cambridge University Press.

Embassy of Japan in Indonesia. (2008). 'Japan's 545 Million Yen Grant Aid to RI to Provide Security Equipments for Main Ports', 25 June 2008, available at www.id.emb-japan.go.jp/news08_25e.html. Last accessed 20 December 2011.

Embassy of Japan in Indonesia. (2011). 'Record of Recent Major Japan-Indonesia Cooperation Projects in Maritime Security, Counter Piracy, Counter Terrorism and Improving Port Security', provided to author by a high government official of the Embassy of Japan during interview in Jakarta, 13 December 2011.

Emmers, Ralf. (2007). 'Maritime Disputes in the South China Sea: Strategic and Diplomatic Status Quo', in *Maritime Security in Southeast Asia.* New York: Routledge.

Emmerson, Donald K. (1983). 'Understanding the New Order: Bureaucratic Pluralism in Indonesia'. *Asian Survey* 23:11, pp. 1220–1241.

Evans III, Bryan. (1989). 'The Influence of the United States Army on the Development of the Indonesian Army (1954–1964)'. *Indonesia* 47, pp. 25–48.

Hindu. (2003). 'India, Indonesia Agree on Anti-Terror Measures', 3 September 2003, accessed from the Newsbank database.

Hindu. (2005). 'India Signs Maritime Accord with Thailand', 21 May 2005, accessed from the Newsbank database.

Indonesian Coordinating Ministry for Political, Legal and Security Affairs. (2006). *Penetapan Rencana Kinerja Tahun 2006.* Jakarta: Kemenkopolhukam.

Indonesian Coordinating Ministry for Political, Legal and Security Affairs. (2007). *Kumpulan Pidato Menteri Koordinator Bidang Politik Hukum dan Keamanan Republik Indonesia.* Jakarta: Kementerian Koordinator Bidang Politik Hukum dan Keamanan Indonesia.

Indonesian Coordinating Ministry for Political, Legal and Security Affairs. (2008). *Evaluasi Pengelolaan Bidang Politik, Hukum dan Keamanan Tahun 2007.* Jakarta: Coordinating Ministry for Political, Legal and Security Affairs.

Indonesian Democratic Party of Struggle. (2013). 'Kebijakan Pemerintah Yang Dikritisi, Implikasi Bagi Nasib Rakyat, Sikap Politik Fraksi PDI Perjuangan', 26 January 2013, available at www.pdiperjuangan-jatim.org/v03/?mod=release&id=9. Last accessed 27 January 2013.

Indonesian Directorate General of Sea Transportation. (2010). 'Bahan Wawancara Direktur Jenderal Perhubungan Laut dengan Staf Pengajar FISIP UI', made available to author during interview with a high government official from the Indonesian Directorate General of Sea Transportation (Jakarta, 3 September 2010).

Indonesian Immigration Agency. (2011). 'Tri-Lateral Inter-Agency Maritime Law Enforcement Workshop (TIAMLEW) III', 5 April 2011, available at www.imigrasi.go.id/index.php?option=com_content&task=view&id=517&Itemid=34. Last accessed 13 July 2011.

Indonesian Ministry of Defence. (2004). 'DPR Menentang Pengerahan Armada AS ke Selat Malaka', 26 April 2004, available at www.kemhan.go.id/modules.php?name=News&file=article&sid=5567DPR. Last accessed 10 October 2009.

Indonesian Ministry of Foreign Affairs. (2004). *Forum Dialog ke XI Kerjasama Maritim ASEAN*. Jakarta: Badan Pengkajian dan Pengembangan Kebijakan.

Indonesian MFA. (2005a). *Diskusi Panel tentang Studi Kebijakan Kelautan Indonesia Dalam Rangka Mendukung Pembangunan dan Integritas Nasional, Surabaya 7–8 April 2005*. Jakarta: Badan Penelitian dan Pengembangan Kebijakan.

Indonesian MFA. (2005b). *Pertemuan Kelompok Ahli: Kebijakan Terpadu Pengelolaan Keamanan Selat Malaka, Medan 19–20 Juli 2005*. Jakarta: Badan Penelitian dan Pengembangan Kebijakan.

Indonesian MFA. (2006). *Pertemuan Kelompok Ahli Membahas Aspek Strategis Diplomasi Kelautan Dalam Mendukung Pembangunan Nasional*. Jakarta: Indonesian MFA.

Indonesian MFA. (2006). 'Pidato Menteri Luar Negeri: Paparan Lisan Menteri Luar Negeri Republik Indonesia Dr. Hassan Wirajuda Refleksi 2005 dan Proyeksi 2006', 6 January 2006, available at www.deplu.go.id/Pages/SpeechTranscriptionDisplay.aspx?Name1=Pidato&Name2=Menteri&IDP=310. Last accessed 1 April 2011.

Indonesian MFA. (2006). 'Masyarakat Internasional Mengakui Keberhasilan Negara Pantai Dalam Mengamankan Selat Malaka', 21 September 2006, available at www.deplu.go.id/Pages/News.aspx?IDP=318. Last accessed 1 April 2012.

Indonesian MFA. (2007). *Pertemuan Kelompok Ahli: Optimalisasi Kerjasama Kelautan Intra ASEAN Melalui Pembentukan ASEAN Maritim Forum (Bandung, 21–22 Maret 2007)*. Jakarta: Badan Pengkajian dan Pengembangan Kebijakan.

Indonesian MFA. (2007). 'The 1st Technical Meeting Committee on Indonesia-China Maritime Cooperation', 1 March 2007, available at www.kemlu.go.id/Lists/News/DispForm.aspx?ID=433&l=en. Last accessed 10 July 2013.

Indonesian MFA. (2009). *ASEAN Regional Forum: The First Inter-Sessional Meeting on Maritime Security, Surabaya, Indonesia, 5–6 March 2009*. Jakarta: Directorate General of Asia Pacific and African Affairs.

Indonesian MFA. (2009). 'The Duty of the Ministry of Foreign Affairs', 1 August 2009, available at www.deplu.go.id/Pages/Polugri.aspx?IDP=3&l=en. Last accessed 3 January 2011.

Indonesian MFA. (2009). 'The Role of the Ministry of Foreign Affairs', 6 September 2009, available at www.deplu.go.id/Pages/Polugri.aspx?IDP=13&l=en. Last accessed 3 January 2011.

Indonesian Ministry of Marine Affairs and Fisheries. (2012). 'Siaran Press: Kembali Kapal Ikan Illegal Ditangkap', available at www.kkp.go.id/index.php/mobile/arsip/c/4336/KEMBALI-KAPAL-ILLEGAL-FISHING-DITANGKAP. Last accessed 21 December 2012.

Indonesian Ministry of State Secretariat. (2001). *Lampiran Pidato Presiden Republik Indonesia Pada Sidang Tahunan Majelis Permusywaratan Rakyat Republik Indonesia*. Jakarta: Perum Percetakan Negara.

Indonesian Ministry of Trade. (2010). *Draft of Indonesian President Regulation on National Logistic System Appendix Section, 9 March 2010*. This document was made available to author during an interview in Jakarta.

Indonesian Parliament. (2000–2013). 'Laporan Singkat Rapat Kerja dan Rapat Dengar Pendapat Dewan Perwakilan Rakyat Komisi I 2000–2013', available at www.dpr.go.id/id/Komisi/Komisi-I/laporan-singkat. Last accessed 24 April 2013.

96 Domestic politics

Indonesian Parliament. (2006). 'Rapat Kerja Komisi I DPR RI dengan Menkopolhukam', 12 June 2006, available at www.dpr.go.id/id/komisi/komisi1/report/2/Raker-dengan-Polhukam. Last accessed 24 April 2013.

Indonesian Parliament. (2006). 'Rapat Kerja Komisi I DPR RI dengan Menteri Pertahanan dan Panglima TNI', 25 September 2006, available atwww.dpr.go.id/id/komisi/komisi1/report/95/Rapat-Kerja-Komisi-I-DPR-RI-dengan-Menteri-Pertahanan-dan-Panglima-TNI. Last accessed 24 April 2013.

Indonesian Parliament. (2006). 'Rapat Kerja Komisi I DPR RI dengan Menteri Pertahanan dengan Sekretaris Jenderal Kementerian Luar Negeri', 21 September 2006', available at www.dpr.go.id/id/Komisi/Komisi-I/laporan-singkat. Last accessed 15 January 2013.

Indonesian Parliament. (2007). 'Rapat Kerja Komisi I DPR RI dengan Menteri Luar Negeri', 25 January 2007, available at www.dpr.go.id/id/komisi/komisi1/report/89/Rapat-Kerja-Komisi-I-DPR-RI-dengan-Menteri-Luar-Negeri. Last accessed 24 April 2013.

Indonesian Parliament. (2007). 'Rapat Kerja Komisi I DPR RI dengan Menkopolhukam', 26 February 2007, available at www.dpr.go.id/id/komisi/komisi1/report/88/Rapat-Kerja-Komisi-I-DPR-RI-dengan-Menkopolhukam. Last accessed 24 April 2013.

Indonesian Parliament. (2007). 'Laporan Singkat Rapat Kerja Komisi I DPR RI dengan Menteri Pertahanan dan Panglima TNI', 5 March 2007, available at www.dpr.go.id/id/komisi/komisi1/report/131/Rapat-Kerja-Komisi-I-DPR-RI-dengan-Menteri-Pertahanan-dan-Panglima-TNI. Last accessed 24 April 2013.

Indonesian Parliament. (2007). 'Rapat Kerja Komisi I DPR RI dengan Menteri Pertahanan dan Panglima TNI', 28 May 2007, available at www.dpr.go.id/id/komisi/komisi1/report/143/Rapat-Kerja-Komisi-I-DPR-RI-Dengan-Menteri-Pertahanan-dan-Panglima-TNI. Last accessed 24 April 2013.

Indonesian Parliament. (2007). 'Rapat Kerja Komisi I DPR RI dengan Menteri Luar Negeri', 25 June 2007, available at www.dpr.go.id/id/komisi/komisi1/report/149/Rapat-Kerja-Komisi-I-DPR-RI-Dengan-Menteri-Luar-Negeri. Last accessed 24 April 2013.

Indonesian Parliament. (2007). 'Rapat Dengar Pendapat Komisi I DPR-RI dengan Gubenur Lemhanas dan Sekjen Wantannas', 9 July 2007, available at www.dpr.go.id/id/komisi/komisi1/report/150/Rapat-Dengar-Pendapat-Komisi-I-DPR-RI Dengan-Gubernur-Lemhannas-dan-Sekjen-Wantannas. Last accessed 24 April 2013.

Indonesian Parliament. (2007). 'Rapat Kerja Komisi I DPR RI dengan Menteri Pertahanan dan Panglima TNI', 17 September 2007, available at www.dpr.go.id/id/Komisi/Komisi-I/laporan-singkat. Last accessed 15 January 2013.

Indonesian Parliament. (2008). 'Rapat Kerja Komisi I DPR RI dengan Menteri Luar Negeri', 29 October 2008, available at www.dpr.go.id/id/komisi/komisi1/report/365/Raker-Komisi-I-dengan-Menlu. Last accessed 24 April 2013.

Indonesian Presidential Office. (2015). 'Indonesia Sebagai Poros Maritim Dunia', 13 November 2015, available at www.presidenri.go.id/maritim/indonesia-sebagai-poros-maritim-dunia.html. Last accessed 4 May 2016.

International Maritime Organization (IMO). (2003). *ISPS Code*. London: IMO.

Jackson, Karl D. (1978). 'The Prospects for Bureaucratic Polity in Indonesia', in *Political Power and Communications in Indonesia*, Karl D. Jackson and Lucian W. Pye (eds). Berkeley, CA: University of California Press, pp. 395–398.

Jackson, Karl D. (1980). 'Bureaucratic Polity: A Theoretical Framework for the Analysis of Power and Communications in Indonesia', in *Political Powers and Communication in Indonesia*, Karl D. Jackson and Lucian W. Pye (eds). Berkeley, CA: University of California Press, pp. 3–22.

Jailani, Abdulkadir [Staf Direktorat Perjanjian Politik Keamanan Kewilayahan Kementerian Luar Negeri]. (2005). 'Pokok-Pokok Masalah Kebijakan Luar Negeri Tentang *Issue* Keamanan Laut dan Kewilayahan Selat Malaka', in *Pertemuan Kelompok Ahli: Kebijakan Terpadu Pengelolaan Keamanan Selat Malaka*. Jakarta: Badan Pengkajian dan Pengembangan Kebijakan Departemen Luar Negeri Republik Indonesia.

Jakarta Post. (2003). 'Customs Service Wants to Negotiate over New US Import Policy', 15 March 2003, accessed from the Newsbank database.

Jakarta Post. (2003). 'Paddy's Pub Is Back More Secure than Ever', 7 August 2003, accessed from the Newsbank database.

Jakarta Post. (2004). 'No Plan to Deploy Troops to Malacca Strait: US', 20 April 2004, accessed from the Newsbank database.

Jakarta Post. (2007). 'Domestic and Foreign Links Go Much Deeper in 2007', 28 December 2007, accessed from the Newsbank database.

Jakarta Post. (2012). 'Australia, RI Hold Inaugural Defense Talks', 4 September 2012, accessed from the Newsbank database.

Jakarta Post. (2015). 'Minister Hails Sinking of 41 Fishing Vessels', 20 May 2015, available from www.thejakartapost.com/news/2015/05/20/minister-hails-sinking-41-fishing-vessels.html. Last accessed 8 September 2015.

Japan Ministry of Foreign Affairs (MFA). (2003a). 'Record of Discussion between the Government of Japan and the Government of the Republic of Indonesia Concerning the Japan–Indonesia Partnership Programme, Tokyo', 10 December 2003, available at www.mofa.go.jp/region/asia-paci/indonesia/partner0312.pdf. Last accessed 5 October 2012.

Japan MFA. (2003b). 'Signing of the Framework Documents Concerning the Japan–Indonesia Partnership Programme', 10 December 2003b, available at www.mofa.go.jp/announce/announce/2003/12/1210.html. Last accessed 5 October 2012.

Japan MFA. (2005). 'Mr Akio Shirota, Ambassador in Charge of International Counter-Terrorism Cooperation Visits Indonesia, 14 April 2005', available at www.mofa.go.jp/announce/announce/2005/4/0414-2.html. Last accessed 5 October 2012.

Japan MFA. (2006). 'Grant Aid to Indonesia for the Project for Construction of Patrol Vessels for the Prevention of Piracy, Maritime Terrorism and Proliferation of Weapons, 16 June 2006', available at www.mofa.go.jp/announce/announce/2006/6/0616-3.html. Last accessed 5 October 2012.

Japan MFA. (2006). 'Japan–Indonesia Joint Statement Strategic Partnership for Peaceful and Prosperous Future, 28 November 2006', available at www.mofa.go.jp/region/asia-paci/indonesia/joint0611.html. Last accessed 5 October 2012.

Japan MFA. (2011). 'The Third Japan–Indonesia Ministerial Level Strategic Dialogue, (Dinner) (Overview) 13 October 2011', available at www.mofa.go.jp/region/asia-paci/indonesia/s_dialogue1110.html. Last accessed 5 October 2012.

Japan MFA. (2011). 'The Third Japan–Indonesia Ministerial Level Strategic Dialogue, 14 October 2011', available at www.mofa.go.jp/region/asia-paci/indonesia/s_dialogue1110b.html. Last accessed 5 October 2012.

Japan MFA. (2012). 'Dinner between Mr Koichiro Gemba, Minister for Foreign Affairs and Mr Djoko Suyanto, Coordinating Minister for Political, Legal and Security Affairs of the Republic of Indonesia (Overview), 28 August 2012', available at www.mofa.go.jp/announce/announce/2012/8/0828_01.html. Last accessed 5 October 2012.

Japan MFA. (2012). 'Courtesy Call on Mr Yoshihiko Noda, Prime Minister by Mr Djoko Suyanto, Coordinating Minister for Political, Legal and Security Affairs of the Republic of Indonesia, 29 August 2012', available at www.mofa.go.jp/region/asia-paci/indonesia/meeting1208_pm.html. Last accessed 5 October 2012.

Juwana, Hikmahanto. (2008). 'Catatan atas Masalah Aktual dalam Perjanjian International'. *Indonesian Journal of International Law* 5:3, pp. 443–451.

Kahin, Audrey R. and Kahin, George McT. (1995). *Subversion As Foreign Policy: the Secret Eisenhower and Dulles Debacle in Indonesia*. New York: The New Press.

Kompas. (2008). 'Singapura Tetap Berkomitmen pada Paket DCA dan ET', 8 February 2008, as cited in http://entertainment.kompas.com/read/2008/02/08/1812358/singapura.tetap.berkomitmen.pada.paket.dca.dan.et. Last accessed 14 January 2013.

Kroef, Justus M. Van Der. (1958). 'Disunited Indonesia (II)'. *Far Eastern Survey* 27:5, pp. 73–80.

Lee, Junhan. (2002). 'Primary Causes of Asian Democratization: Dispelling Conventional Myths'. *Asian Survey* 42:6, pp. 821–837.

Liddle, R. William. (1985). 'Soeharto's Indonesia: Personal Rule and Political Institutions'. *Pacific Affairs* 58: 1, pp. 68–90.

Liddle, R. William. (1999). 'Regime: The New Order', in *Indonesia Beyond Suharto: Polity, Economy, Society Transition*, Donald K. Emmerson (ed.). New York: M.E. Sharpe.

Lubis, Subaktin. (Head of the Maritime Geology Research centre, Indonesian Ministry of Energy and Mineral Resources). (2010). 'Memaknai hari Nusantara: Deklarasi Djoeanda Sebagai pilar Utama Mewujudkan Kesatuan Wilayah NKRI', 12 October 2010, available at www.mgi.esdm.go.id/content/memaknai-hari-nusantara-deklarasi-djoeanda-sebagai-pilar-utama-mewujudkan-kesatuan-wilayah-0. Last accessed 21 April 2016.

Manning, Chris and Diermen, Peter Van. (2000). 'Recent Development and Social Aspects of Reformasi and Crisis: An Overview', in *Indonesia in Transition: Social Aspects of Reformasi and Crisis*, Chris Manning and Peter Van Diermen (eds). Singapore: Institute of Southeast Asian Studies.

Medeiros, John. (2004). 'No Plans to Unilaterally Deploy US Forces to Secure Malacca Straits', *Straits Times*, 7 April 2004.

Nabbs-Keller, Greta. (2013). 'Reforming Indonesia's Foreign Ministry: Ideas, Organization and Leadership'. *Contemporary Southeast Asia* 35:1, pp. 56–82.

Nandan, Satya N. and Rosenne, Shabtai. (1993). *United Nations Convention on the Law of the Sea, 1982: A Commentary*. Dordrecht: Martinus Nijhoff.

Nuswantoro, Laksamana Pertama Edhi. (Kepala Staf Komando Armada RI Kawasan Barat). (2005). 'Pengelolaan Keamanan Selat Malaka Secara Terpadu', in *Pertemuan Kelompok Ahli Tentang Kebijakan Terpadu Pengelolaan Keamanan Selat Malaka, Medan 19–20 Juli 2005*. Jakarta: Badan Pengkajian dan Pengembangan Kebijakan Departemen Luar Negeri.

Oegroseno, Arif Havas. (2005). 'Kebijakan Luar Negeri Indonesia Tentang Selat Malaka'. *Forum Hukum* 2:3, pp. 54–62.

Oegroseno, Arif Havas. (2006). 'The Straits of Malacca and Challenges Ahead: Japan's Perspective', in *Building Comprehensive Security Environment*. Kuala Lumpur: Maritime Institute of Malaysia, pp. 28–39.

Parthiana, I Wayan. (2008). 'Kajian Akademis (Teoritis dan Praktis) atas Undang-Undang Nomor 24 Tahun 2000 Tentang Perjanjian Internasional Berdasarkan Hukum Perjanjian Internasional'. *Indonesian Journal of International Law* 5:3, pp. 460–487.

Polres Tanjung Perak. (2011). 'Antisipasi Terror di Pelabuhan', 21 June 2011, available at http://polrestanjungperak.net/index.php?option=com_content&view=frontpage&limitstart=1021. Last accessed 1 August 2011.
Prescott, Victor and Schofield, Clive. (2001). 'Undelimited Maritime Boundaries of the Asian Rim in the Pacific Ocean'. *Maritime Briefing* 3:1, pp. 1–68.
Purnomo, Y. Didik Heru. (2004). 'Pengamanan Wilayah Laut RI Bagian Barat'. *Indonesian Journal of International Law*, pp. 27–40.
ReCAAP. (2011). 'About ReCAAP', available at www.recaap.org/AboutReCAAPISC.aspx. Last accessed 9 January 2011.
Rosenberg, David and Chung, Christopher. (2008). 'Maritime Security in the South China Sea: Coordinating Coastal and User State Priorities'. *Ocean Development and International Law* 39:1, pp. 51–68.
Ruland, Jurgen. (2009). 'Deepening ASEAN Cooperation through Democratization? The Indonesian Legislature and Foreign Policymaking'. *International Relations of the Asia–Pacific* 9:3, pp. 373–402.
Sekretariat Jenderal Departemen Kelautan dan Perikanan. (2007). *Laporan Perumusan Kebijakan Kelembagaan Tata Pemerintahan di Laut*. Jakarta: Sekretariat Jenderal Departemen Kelautan dan Perikanan.
Sekretaris Kabinet Indonesia. (2012). 'RI-Australia Tingkatkan Kerjasama Keamanan Laut', 5 September 2012, available at http://setkab.go.id/berita-5570-ri-australia-tingkatkan-kerja-sama-keamanan-laut.html. Last accessed 22 October 2012.
Sherlock, Stephen. (2003). *Struggling to Change: The Indonesian Parliament in an Era of Reformasi*. Canberra: Centre for Democratic Institutions, available at https://cdi.anu.edu.au/CDIwebsite_19982004/indonesia/indonesia_downloads/DPRResearchReport_S.Sherlock.pdf. Last accessed 24 April 2013.
Siboro, Tiarma. (2011). 'ASEAN Defense Dialogue Amid "Crystalized" Border Disputes', *Jakarta Post*, 28 April 2011, accessed from the Newsbank database.
Singapore MoD. (2005). 'Closer Bonds with Project SURPIC', 27 May 2005, available at www.mindef.gov.sg/imindef/publications/cyberpioneer/news/2005/may/27may05_news2.html. Last accessed 14 November 2010.
Singapore MoD. (2008). 'Factsheet: Milestones of Malacca Strait Patrols', 28 March 2008, available at www.mindef.gov.sg/imindef/news_and_events/nr/2008/mar/28mar08_nr/28mar08_fs.html. Last accessed 26 June 2011.
Smith, Anthony L. (2001). 'Indonesia Transforming the Leviathan', in *Government and Politics in Southeast Asia*, John Funston (ed.). Singapore: Institute of Southeast Asian Studies, pp. 74–119.
Sondakh, Bernard Kent. (2004). 'Pengamanan Wilayah Laut Indonesia'. *Indonesian Journal of International Law*, pp. 1–26.
Sondakh, Bernard Kent. (2006). 'National Sovereignty and Security in the Straits of Malacca', in *Building A Comprehensive Security Environment in the Straits of Malacca*. Kuala Lumpur: Maritime Institute of Malaysia, pp. 79–110.
Staf Umum Operasi Markas Besar Angkatan Laut. (2004). 'Kerjasama Regional Maritim ASEAN Dari Perspektif Pertahanan Matra Laut', in *Forum Dialog ke XI Kerjasama Maritim ASEAN*. Jakarta: Badan Pengkajian dan Pengembangan Kebijakan Kementerian Luar Negeri, pp. 32–39.
Straits Times. (2000). 'Japan Keen on Joint Patrols to Fight Piracy', 18 February 2000, accessed from the Newsbank database.
Straits Times. (2007). 'Senior MPs Insist Indonesia Won't Ratify Defence Pact'. 26 July 2007, accessed from the Newsbank database.

Suara Karya. (2010). 'Kegiatan Militer TNI AL-AL Singapura Tingkatkan Kerja Sama', 13 April 2010.
Sudrajat. (Direktur Jenderal Strategi Pertahanan Kementerian Pertahanan Indonesia). (2005). 'Kebijakan Kelautan Nasional dari Perspektif Pertahanan dan Keamanan', in *Laporan Kegiatan Diskusi Panel: Mencari Format Kebijakan Kelautan Indonesia Dalam Rangka Mendukung Pembangunan dan Integrasi Nasional (Studi Kasus Kanada dan Norwegia), Surabaya, 7–8 April 2005*. Jakarta: Kementerian Luar Negeri Indonesia.
Suhartono. (2001). 'Hubungan Indonesia–Timur Tengah Era Pemerintahan Abdurrahman Wahid', in *Analisis Kebijakan Luar Negeri Pemerintahan Abdurrahman Wahid (1999–2000)*. Jakarta: Dewan Perwakilan Rakyat Republik Indonesia.
Sukma, Rizal. (1995). 'The Evolution of Indonesia's Foreign Policy: An Indonesian View'. *Asian Survey* 35:3, pp. 304–315.
Sumaryono, Laksmana Muda TNI Djoko. (2004). 'Kerjasama Regional Maritim ASEAN dari Perspektif Keamanan Matra Laut', in *Forum Dialog ke XI Kerjasama Maritim ASEAN*. Jakarta: Badan Pengkajian dan Pengembangan Kebijakan Departemen Luar Negeri.
Sumaryono, Djoko. (2009). 'The Indonesian Maritime Security Coordinating Board', in *Indonesia beyond the Water's Edge*. Singapore: Institute of Southeast Asian Studies.
Supriyanto, Ristian Atriandi. (2013). 'The Unfulfilled Promise of Indonesia–India Defense Ties', 31 May 2013, available from http://thediplomat.com/2013/05/the-unfulfilled-promise-of-indonesia-india-defense-ties/. Last accessed 21 April 2011.
Suristiyono, Komisaris Besar Polisi. (Wakil Direktur Polair Babinkam Polri). (2005). 'Penyelenggaraan Keamanan dan Ketertiban Di Kawasan Perairan Selat Malaka', in *Pertemuan Kelompok Ahli Tentang Kebijakan Terpadu Pengelolaan Keamanan Selat Malaka*. Jakarta: Badan Pengkajian dan Pengembangan Kebijakan Kementerian Luar Negeri.
Surya Citra Televisi (SCTV) Liputan 6. (2007). 'Menhan: Penolakan Ratifikasi Salah Kaprah', 26 June 2007, available at http://news.liputan6.com/read/143646/menhan-penolakan-ratifikasi-salah-kaprah. Last accessed 13 June 2013.
Suryadinata, Leo. (1998). *Politik Luar Negeri Indonesia di Bawah Soeharto*. Jakarta: LP3ES.
Urquhart, Donald. (2006). 'S'pore Acts on Piracy Info Centre Plan – Coastal Command Head Lt Col Teo to Lay Ground Work, Say Sources', *Business Times*, 19 January 2006, accessed from the Newsbank database.
Weiss, Meredith L. (2007). 'What a Little Democracy Can Do: Comparing Trajectories of Reform in Malaysia and Indonesia'. *Democratization* 14:1, pp. 26–43.
Wibisono, Makarim. (2006). *Tantangan Diplomasi Multilateral*. Makmur Keliat and Mohtar Mas'oed (eds). Jakarta: LP3ES.
Winanti, Poppy S. (2011). *External Pressures or Domestic Politics: Explaining Change in Developing Countries' Intellectual Property Legislation – PhD Thesis*, available at http://theses.gla.ac.uk/2794/01/Winanti.pdf. Last accessed 2 February 2012.
Wisnumurti, Nugroho. (2009). 'Maritime Security Issues in Southeast Asia: An Indonesian Perspective'. *Indonesian Journal of International Law* 6:3, pp. 333–352.
World Customs Organization (WCO). (2007). *WCO SAFE Framework of Standards*, available at www.wcoomd.org/files/1.%20Public%20files/PDFandDocuments/Procedures%20and%20Facilitation/safe_package/safe_package_I.pdf. Last accessed 11 August 2011.

WCO. (2010). 'Members Who Have Expressed their Intention to Implement the WCO Framework of Standards to Secure and Facilitate Global Trade', available from www.wcoomd.org/files/1.%20Public%20files/PDFandDocuments/Enforcement/FOS_bil_03.pdf. Last accessed 11 August 2011.

Xinhua. (2004). 'India for Joint Naval Patrols with Indonesia, Malaysia', 11 August 2004, accessed from the Newsbank database.

Xinhua. (2007). 'Indonesia May Let Singapore Bring in Friend in Military Training', 23 February 2007, accessed from the Newsbank database.

Xinhua. (2007). 'Indonesian Province Rejects Military Exercise with Singapore', 24 May 2007, accessed from the Newsbank database.

Xinhua. (2007). 'Indonesian House Factions Oppose Military Deal with Singapore', 12 June 2007, accessed from the Newsbank database.

Xinhua. (2007). 'Indonesia Calls for Talks on Military Deal with Singapore', 14 June 2007, accessed from the Newsbank database.

Xinhua. (2007). 'Indonesian Government Urged to Cancel Singapore Defense Pact', 18 September 2007, accessed from the Newsbank database.

Xinhua. (2010). 'Indonesia, Malaysia to Address Border Dispute', 27 August 2010, accessed from the Newsbank database.

3 When the hegemon is leading

Introduction

The neorealist and neoliberal hegemonic leadership concept suggests that the presence of a hegemon is sufficient to induce cooperation (Gilpin, 1975, p. 85; 1981, p. 30; Keohane, 1984, p. 49; 1982, pp. 326, 330; Krasner, 1976, p. 322; Lipson, 1984, p. 19; Strange, 1987, p. 555). As states are constrained by the international distribution of power, 'units of greatest capability set the scene of action for others as well as for themselves' (Waltz, 1979, p. 72). Gilpin and Krasner argue that the leadership of these 'units of greatest capability' is deemed a sufficient and necessary condition for cooperation. The hegemon creates and enforces rules as well as organises and controls the process of interactions among actors in the system (Gilpin, 1981, pp. 29–30). It is assumed that other states in the system cooperate because the US as a hegemonic power can actively maintain cooperation through incentives, bargaining and sanctions (Gilpin, 1975, p. 85; Krasner, 1976, p. 322). A powerful state such as the US has strong incentives to endorse cooperation arrangements with generally applicable rules that promote its interests (Byers, 2003, p. 176). Cooperation initiatives with well-crafted rules will advance US interests and at the same time constrain others from taking undesired policies and actions (Byers, 2003, p. 176).

In the immediate aftermath of the 11 September 2001 terrorist attacks, the US rapidly embarked on a global campaign against terrorism. Under this extensive global campaign, the security threat posed by terrorist attacks quickly generated a remarkable array of maritime security cooperation initiatives, agencies, strategy and programmes at global and Southeast Asian regional political levels (Jackson, 2007, p. 394). These security strategies include the implementation of the CSI, the PSI, the RMSI, the International Port Security (IPS) Programme and the C-TPAT. Nevertheless, despite US leadership in these numerous anti-maritime terrorism and sea robbery initiatives and measures, there remained a great division among countries' leaders regarding maritime security cooperation and a major contestation about how to combat maritime terrorism and armed robbery attacks against ships (see Chow, 2005, p. 306). Indonesia's varying participation in maritime security cooperation is interesting in this respect.

Indonesia presents a case study where a rising middle power has declined to join a number of maritime initiatives despite the presence of US leadership.

In this chapter, I will first explain Indonesia's close cooperation with the US at bilateral level. Second, I will explore unsuccessful cases of cooperation, including the SUA convention, the PSI, the CSI and the RMSI. Using government documents, newspaper articles and research by Indonesian scholars, I argue that US leadership was not enough to change Indonesia's calculation of gains sufficiently for it to cooperate. This chapter also examines the behaviour of the US in maritime security cooperation. Indonesia's participation in US-led initiatives was important to the US objectives of halting the proliferation and transportation of WMD and securing important sea lanes from terrorist and sea robbery attacks; yet the US did not coerce Indonesia to join cooperation initiatives that Jakarta had rejected, such as the SUA convention, the PSI, the CSI and the RMSI. Third, in order to explain US behaviour towards Indonesia, this chapter also offers a comprehensive explanation of Indonesia's cooperation in US unilateral initiatives, such as the IPS Programme and the US C-TPAT, that have sufficiently induced changes at the domestic level. These two initiatives have been set up under public–private partnership schemes that involved the US government and international shipping communities.

Fully cooperative on the bilateral front

US–Indonesia bilateral relations have gone through significant changes since the archipelagic state's independence in 1945. The two countries' foreign relations reached their lowest point during the late 1950s as the Eisenhower administration supported major rebellions in Sulawesi and Sumatra. Concern over the spread of communism had led the Eisenhower administration to deploy the largest US covert operation since World War II in Indonesia (Kahin and Kahin, 1995). Involving the Central Intelligence Agency, the US Navy and the US Air Force, the covert operation had provoked a civil war from 1957 to 1958 in various parts of Indonesia, including Sulawesi, Sumatra and the Moluccas that nearly tore the country apart (Kahin and Kahin, 1995).

The relations with the US improved as General Soeharto succeeded Indonesia's first president Soekarno in 1966. Soeharto's strong anti-communist policies facilitated a dramatic rapprochement between the two countries. The US became Indonesia's main economic and military partner. The prominence of US containment policy provided leeway for Indonesia to invade East Timor in 1975 (Murphy, 2010, p. 365). In order to halt any possibility of East Timor falling into the communist orbit when the leftist group Fretilin was expected to assume power following Portugal's sudden withdrawal, Secretary of State Henry Kissinger asked for an invasion to be carried out in a quick and efficient manner without using US military equipment (Schwarz, 2000, p. 201 as cited in Murphy, 2010, p. 365).

A change of course in Indonesia and US relations took place when Clinton assumed power in 1993. The Clinton administration's national security strategy of engagement and enlargement that focused on promoting free market democracies signalled a transformation from the anti-communist-driven foreign policy goals and missions that had tied Indonesia and the US together until the end of the Cold War (Crawford, 2004, p. 689). Clinton's emphasis on free market and democratic agendas introduced key sticking points in the US relations with Indonesia's authoritarian regime. The US began to link Indonesia's human rights record with foreign aid, military training and equipment. After Indonesian military forces opened fire on protesters in Dili in 1991, killing at least 250 people, the government violations of human rights in East Timor drew close attention from the US (BBC, 2005, 2015). The massacre turned international community opinion, including the US's, against Indonesia and in support of East Timor independence (Sterio, 2013, p. 105).

The relationship between Jakarta and Washington continued to worsen up until the post-referendum violence in East Timor in 1999. During this period, pro-Indonesian militia with Indonesian army support were believed to use terror to discourage voters and, later, to murder and reduce towns to ruin after the result of the referendum showed that the majority of the population was in favour of independence (BBC, 2015). Following the 1999 violence in East Timor, the US Congress as part of the FY2000 Foreign Operation appropriations, passed the Leahy amendment to impose restrictions on US assistance to the Indonesian armed forces (Rabasa and Haseman, 2002, p. 139). The amendment prohibited access to the US foreign military financing credits for Indonesia to purchase US military equipment and to participate in the US international military education training programme. This circumstance had a significant impact on Indonesia's defence system, since in 1999 US armaments accounted for 80 per cent of the country's defence system (*Jakarta Post*, 15 January 2007). As a consequence, these weapon systems suffered due to the US arms embargo. The ban was to be in place until the Indonesian government could bring the members of the armed forces and militia groups who perpetrated human rights violations to court, allow East Timorese displaced persons in West Timor to return to their homes and prevent militia from entering East Timor (Niksch *et al.*, 2001, p. 10). As of 2001, there had been no prosecutions against perpetrators of abuses in East Timor (Niksch *et al.*, 2001, p. 8). As a consequence, it was reported to the US Congress that Indonesia had not fulfilled any of the conditions stipulated in the Leahy amendment (Niksch *et al.*, 2001, pp. 8, 10).

The 9/11 attacks dramatically transformed the course of relations between Indonesia and the US from a series of problematic interactions into a strategic partnership. Although the US Assistant Secretary of State for East Asia and the Pacific James Kelly still criticised Indonesia in 2002 for the government's lack of progress on accountability for human rights violations perpetrated in East Timor in 1999 Indonesia and the US began to resume military cooperation (Human Rights Watch, 2015).

Indonesia–US defence and military cooperation progressed rapidly as the US Department of Defense affirmed Southeast Asia as a crucial front in the war on terror. The Principal Director for South and Southeast Asia in the US

Department of Defence Marine Brigadier General John Toolan suggested that, to win the fight against terrorism, Southeast Asia 'has emerged quietly, but it's a crucial front in the long war' (US DoD, 2007). Shortly after the 11 September attacks, Deputy Secretary of Defence Paul Wolfowitz maintained that 'there are some extremists in Indonesia. There's Lasco Jihad ... but they are not international terrorists and they are not tied to Al Qaeda. Well, I was wrong; ... every day we learn more about these connections' (US DoD, 2003). He further claimed that 'the victory over the radical Islamic threat in general and in Southeast Asia in particular will ultimately require the West to drain the swamp of disgruntled, anti-Western Muslims' (Desker and Ramakrishna, 2002, p. 167). Under this circumstance, the cooperation of Indonesia, the largest country in ASEAN with almost 90 per cent of its 250 million people who are Muslim, was deemed crucial to ensure the success of the US war on terror campaign in the region. Consequently, President Bush vowed 'to open a new era of bilateral cooperation with Indonesia' (US White House, 2001). This new era paved the way for bilateral negotiation between Indonesia and the US to improve defence and security cooperation.

Soon after 9/11, President Megawati and President Bush agreed to establish a security dialogue forum between their countries' defence establishments at their September 2001 meeting in Washington (Indonesian Embassy in Washington, 2007). As a follow up to their meeting, the two countries have established the Indonesia–US security dialogue and the US–Indonesia bilateral defence discussion before the launch of the defence arrangement. These forums are held annually to discuss a wide range of security and defence issues and plan maritime security training and exercises. Indonesia and the US also re-opened the international military education and training programme in 2003 and began to discuss cooperation in the area of military weaponry after the US lifted its arms embargo in 2005. This occurred in the years before the negotiation of the defence arrangement in 2010 (Indonesian MoD, 2003, pp. 85–86; *Jakarta Post*, 16 February 2008, 26 February 2008).

To formalise the bilateral defence cooperation, the two states signed the US–Indonesia defence framework arrangement in June 2010. The defence arrangement requires Indonesia and the US to work together to maintain regular dialogue, particularly through the Indonesia–US security dialogue and the US–Indonesia bilateral defence discussion; sustain and develop the existing education and training programmes; provide capacity building in maritime security; and ensure cooperation in the area of operational support and military supplies, including acquisition, sale and exchange of goods and services.[1]

In 2006, the US authorisation of section 1206 of Public Law 109–163 on global train-and-equip authority instructed all organisational entities within the Department of Defence to train, equip, and build maritime security capacity in foreign countries to deter terrorists (US DoD, 2011). Indonesia is one of the countries that benefits from this programme, along with the Philippines and Malaysia (Indonesian Coordinating Ministry for Political, Legal and Security Affairs, 2008, p. 76; Storey, 2009). Indonesia received US$57 million through this programme to support the establishment of an Integrated Maritime Surveillance System (IMSS) located strategically to cover the Strait of Malacca, the Strait of Makassar and the Strait of Moluccas (US DoS, 2011). The US allocated an additional US$4.6 million to guarantee the sustainability of the system until 2014 (US DoS, 2011). The IMSS is an 'integrated network of ship and shore based sensors, communications devices, and computing resources that collect, transmit, analyse and display a broad array of maritime data' (US DoS, 2011). The IMSS comprises eighteen coastal surveillance stations, eleven ship-based radars, two regional command centres, and two fleet command centres (Jakarta and Surabaya) (US DoS, 2011). The IMSS covers more than 1,205 kilometres of coastline in the Straits of Malacca and approximately 1,285 kilometres of coastline in the Sulawesi Sea (*Antara*, 2010). An Indonesian security expert confirmed that information gathered from the US-installed IMSS was also shared with the US.[2]

As of May 2015, Indonesia and the US are still in the process of negotiating the MoU on maritime cooperation and its action plan. An array of activities are covered by the agreement, including collaboration to deal with illegal, unregulated and unreported fishing, maritime infrastructure and connectivity, and maritime law enforcement and security. The last draft of the proposed MoU and its action plan is by far one of the most comprehensive and detailed maritime cooperation arrangements that Indonesia has ever discussed with an extra-regional state. Cooperative measures to address illegal fishing, for instance, will include satellite data-sharing between the two countries and possibly an invitation from the Indonesian Ministry of Maritime Affairs and Fisheries to the National Oceanic and Atmospheric Administration to embed an attaché. The terms of agreement includes transfer of equipment and training from the US to assist the Indonesian enforcement efforts. The US-proposed draft of the action plan also includes commercial deals to be signed between Indonesia and US public and private sectors to support the maritime nexus strategy. It calls on the Indonesian government to 'identify infrastructure projects that reflect priority ... and to positively entertain bids from US companies'.[3] According to the cooperation draft, in the area of maritime law enforcement and security Indonesia and the US would announce a maritime law enforcement project that incorporates a focus on 'monitoring and interdiction capacities and interagency coordination in and around the Natuna sea specifically'.[4] The agreement would support various procurement and assistance programmes to support Indonesia's enforcement efforts, including the navy's undersea surveillance capability, surveillance assets including coastal radars, manned and unmanned aerial platforms as well as ship-based assets, to form one common operating picture. It also elevates joint special maritime operation exercises involving Indonesian and the US air force, navy and marines.

In conclusion, in the aftermath of 9/11 Indonesia has cooperated extensively with the US. The two countries have cooperated closely in joint exercises, procurement of weapons and the sharing of maritime data and a common operating picture of its maritime domain. Yet, despite the extensive cooperation between the two countries, Indonesia refused to join a number of US-led initiatives. The following section will explain Indonesia's non-cooperation in various US-proposed maritime security initiatives.

Cases of non-cooperation: the hegemon did not bark

Although in the immediate aftermath of the 9/11 attacks international attention focused on the security of air transport, soon after it began to turn to the vulnerability of port facilities and marine transport to terrorist attacks (Raymond, 2006, p. 239). The US began to express its concern that 'Muslim extremists in Indonesia, Malaysia, the Philippines and Thailand' were a possible threat to world trade navigating through Southeast Asian waterways (Valencia, 2006, p. 97).

Parallel to this, the US rapidly embarked on a global campaign against terrorism. Identifying and intercepting maritime terrorist threats way before they reached the US became the goal of the US maritime strategy in the war on terror (US Coast Guard, 2002, p. i). Thus, under this extensive global campaign, the US promoted a number of international cooperation arrangements to improve the security of maritime transport. The US process of improving maritime security comprised the determination to strengthen the existing maritime conventions, such as the SUA convention and establishing new initiatives, including the PSI, the CSI, and the RMSI.

The SUA convention and its protocols

Although the danger posed by potential maritime terrorism was only widely reported by the media after the 9/11 attacks, an international convention that covered measures to deal with unlawful acts against ships, the SUA convention, had been formulated a couple of decades before (see Raymond, 2006, p. 240). It might be noted that the SUA convention itself does not explicitly articulate the term 'maritime terrorism'. However, the SUA convention was formulated against the backdrop of the terrorist hijacking of the *Achille Lauro* cruise ship in October 1985 that killed a US national. In November 1985, the maritime terrorist issue was brought to the IMO's fourteenth assembly. The US proposed the introduction of a regulation to prevent unlawful acts at sea. The proposal was supported by other states, and this led to the adoption of the SUA convention in 1988 (IMO, 2009).

The Convention requires states to criminalise unlawful acts under national legislation, cooperate in investigations and extradite or prosecute alleged offenders without delay (Roach, 2004, p. 53).[5] The SUA 1988 protocol expands the obligations of the Convention to incorporate fixed platforms such as those engaged in the exploitation of offshore oil and gas (IMO, 2009). The counter-maritime terrorism elements added within the 2005 protocol to the SUA convention take account of the use of any explosive or WMD against ships and the shipment of WMD material or technology (IMO, 2009). The 2005 protocol obliges member states to take necessary measures to enable legal entities, including companies or organisations, to be made liable and to face sanctions when a person in charge of that legal entity commits an offence (IMO, 2012).

The US played a leading role in drafting and initiating the SUA convention and its 2005 protocol. The US carried out diplomatic lobbying to promote the Convention, including in UN forums. An Indonesian official explained that one form of US diplomatic persuasion could be seen in the Washington proposal in 2009 to mention the SUA convention in Security Council Resolution no. 1907 concerning Somalia and Eritrea. Indonesia rejected the insertion of the SUA convention in the resolution.[6] Despite US leadership, Indonesia did not ratify the SUA convention. There was a concern that this Convention and its protocols could be used inappropriately to refer to unlawful acts which take place in Indonesia's EEZ and therefore, imposed limits on Indonesia's rights in securing its maritime EEZ area (Agoes, 2005, p. 43; Sudrajat, 2005, p. 84).[7] The Convention could be applied to crimes/acts of violence/piratical acts that occur within 12 nautical miles (nm) from the baseline through to the state's outer limit jurisdiction (200 nm from the baseline). Thus, the SUA convention contradicts the UNCLOS that provides the Indonesian government with the right to manage and deal with maritime issues that take place beyond its territorial waters and within its EEZ, or between 12 and 200 nm.

The CSI

The CSI was introduced by the US in 2002 and came into effect in January 2003. The main purpose of the initiative is to increase security for containerised cargo shipped to the US from around the world by targeting and pre-screening the containers before they reach US ports. As of 2013, there are fifty-eight foreign ports participating in the CSI (US CBP, 2013). The cargo transported from these ports accounts for 85 per cent of container-traffic bound for the US (US CBP, 2013). Arguably, Indonesia's participation in this initiative is of great importance for Jakarta, because the US is its second largest trading partner and a key destination for the country's top ten export commodities, including textiles, electronic products, rubber, palm oil, shoes, automotive parts, prawns, cocoa and coffee (Indonesian Ministry of Trade, 15 June 2015a; 15 June 2015b). Given that the majority of exports to the US are transported by sea, unimpeded access to US seaports is crucial to ensure the smooth transfer of goods. On average, Indonesia's exports to the US account for more than 11 per cent of the country's total exports (Indonesian Ministry of Trade, 2011).

The CSI requires the Indonesian government to allow the US CBP to place teams of US officers from both the CBP and Immigration and Customs Enforcement to work jointly with host foreign government counterparts in pre-screening containers bound for US ports, purchase pre-screening equipment and radiological and nuclear detection devices, build IT infrastructure to support the implementation of the initiative and provide a full descriptions of the cargoes 24 hours in advance of its scheduled arrival in US ports, and share critical data, intelligence and risk management information with the US CBP (Barnes and

Oloruntoba, 2005, p. 523; US CBP, 2010; 2006, pp. 19, 21–23; 2007; Rosenberg and Chung, 2008, p. 53).

The US exercised its leadership by formulating the initiative, enforcing rules and using its diplomatic persuasion. Compliance in the case of the CSI is not based only on parties' good faith but on enforceable rules. The US CBP makes regular assessments of a state's compliance with the initiative (US CBP, 2006, pp. 22, 26; 2007). Only those that meet all the minimal requirements are eligible to be part of the programme (US CBP, 2007). The US CBP and Immigration and Customs Enforcement teams deployed at the foreign ports serve as the enforcer of the initiative, because they have the authority to pre-screen high-risk cargo bound for the US. In addition to the deployment of the US Customs team to monitor compliance, the US CBP established an evaluations and assessments branch. The branch carries out periodic assessments at least every two years to investigate operational CSI ports, examine the effectiveness of the CSI programme and ensure effective coordination with foreign host governments (US DHS, 2010, p. 2). The board examines the development, examination, and administrative activities at the ports (US DHS, 2010, pp. 2, 6). Upon the completion of the port evaluation, the board submits a report, recommendations and an action plan for implementing recommendations (US DHS, 2010, p. 2). After the launch of the CSI, the US carried out diplomatic persuasion and lobbying. The US contacted a number of Indonesian government institutions, including the MFA, the MoD, the Ministry of Industry, the Customs and Excise and the MoT, and explained the benefits of incorporating Indonesian ports in the CSI (Kepabeanan Internasional, 2008, p. 50).[8] The US in particular focused its persuasion on two Indonesian government institutions that are responsible for the country's seaborne containers: the Customs and Excise and the MoT.[9] Despite the US's tireless efforts to promote the initiative, Indonesia refused to participate in the CSI. Indonesian officials highlighted concerns over potential sovereignty infringements as the main reason underpinning Jakarta's rejection of the CSI. This was despite Indonesia's close cooperation in other cooperative arrangements that have enabled Washington to access various ports in Indonesia, including the restricted areas.

The PSI

President George W. Bush announced the PSI on 31 May 2003 in Cracow, Poland. The PSI does not state fixed requirements for participating states. A state can choose to participate in various ways. These options range from taking part in PSI training exercises, identifying specific national assets that might contribute to PSI activities, providing consent to other states to board and search its flagged vessels to taking part in actual PSI operations to intercept vessels flying their flag in internal waters or territorial seas or areas beyond the territorial seas of other states that are suspected of carrying WMD-related cargoes (Nikitin, 2010, p. 2; US DoS, 2003). Member states of the PSI form the Operational Expert Group to manage cooperation activities among them (Nikitin, 2010, p. 2;

110 *When the hegemon is leading*

US DoS, 2003). This body meets periodically to 'develop operational concepts, organise the interdiction exercise programme, share information about national legal authorities, and pursue cooperation with key industry sectors' (US DoS, 2008). The group consists of experts from the defence, foreign affairs, law enforcement, transport and other agencies of PSI countries (Nikitin, 2010, p. 2; Singapore MoD, 2006; US DoS, 2008).

The US proposed the initiative; contributed military, customs, law enforcement and other security experts and assets to interdiction exercises; hosted PSI meetings, workshops and exercises with other PSI-endorsing states; and worked to improve other participants' counter-proliferation capacity (US DoS, 16 July 2013). More importantly, the US played an important role in enforcing the PSI rules. In its attempt to further operationalise the PSI and considerably enhance its reach to interdict ships with WMD cargoes, the US has concluded bilateral ship-boarding agreements with the world's important flag states (Guilfoyle, 2009, pp. 247–248). These include Antigua and Barbuda, Bahamas, Belize, Croatia, Cyprus, Liberia, Malta, Marshall Islands, Mongolia, Panama, and St. Vincent and the Grenadines (US DoS, 15 July 2013). Panama, Liberia and the Marshall Islands are the top three largest shipping registries, with Malta ranked seventh, the Bahamas eighth and Cyprus tenth (UNCTAD, 2012, p. 44). In some of these arrangements, if the participating state fails to answer the US interdiction request, the US could still proceed and board the suspected vessel within a couple of hours after the flag state received the US request.[10] The US is the only PSI member that has so far made such agreements (Guilfoyle, 2009, p. 247). These agreements show US leadership in which the government used its advantage in diplomatic and legal resources to enforce the PSI rules (Guilfoyle, 2009, p. 248). It would be highly unlikely for the participants of the PSI to refuse a US request to interdict a vessel, or for any of them to seek US agreement for them to board and inspect a US vessel (Guilfoyle, 2009, p. 248).

As Indonesia serves as one of the thirty-five top flags of registration in the world, its participation in the PSI is of great importance. As a flag state, Indonesia has exclusive jurisdiction over all vessels flying its flag on the high seas, including in stopping and interdicting suspected vessels (Suchharitkul, 2006, p. 415). The US has carried out active diplomatic persuasion to encourage Indonesia to take part in the PSI to allow a focus on the interdiction of ships suspected of transporting WMD. In March 2006, Condoleezza Rice visited Jakarta. The US Secretary of State conveyed the US request for Indonesia to take part in PSI to the Minister of Foreign Affairs Hassan Wirayuda. On 16 March 2006, the MFA spokeperson Desra Percaya stated Indonesia's rejection of the US request (*Antara*, 2006). The US principal deputy assistant to the US Secretary of State for International Security and Non-Proliferation Patricia McNerney, during her visit to discuss non-proliferation and the issue of a nuclear Iran with Indonesian officials in Jakarta in August 2006, sought to assure the Indonesian government that the initiative would not undermine the sovereignty of any country (*Jakarta Post*, 16 August 2007). Interviews confirm that US government officials from both the US Defence and State Departments engaged in diplomatic persuasion to convince Indonesian decision makers.[11] Nevertheless, despite US persuasion, Indonesia chose not to join the PSI. The Indonesian government perceived that the PSI could significantly limit Indonesia's rights in controlling security over its waters as granted by the 1982 Law of the Sea Convention, as the government would have to accede to the US and other PSI members' interdiction requests over vessels flying its flag or travelling in its waterways. Following Indonesia's rejection, the US did not make any attempt to link Indonesia's level of cooperation with the possibility of lifting the arms embargo or the delivery of the defence grant to Jakarta.

The RMSI

In 2003, the US Pacific Command, working with the Department of State, started theoretical discussions with countries in the Asia–Pacific on the development of the RMSI (ASEAN, 2004; Bateman, 2005, p. 260; USPACOM, 2004a). The initiative requires states to share information on maritime threats, standardise procedures for decision-making processes, enhance interception capacity and synchronise international cooperation among agencies and ministries in the Asia–Pacific to address armed robbery against ships, piracy and other transnational threats (USPACOM, 2004a, 2004b, p. 6). As part of the information-sharing activities, member states needed to forward maritime data to the US Pacific Command to obtain a real-time maritime picture (Boutilier, 2005, p. 27; USPACOM, 2004c). After the RMSI negotiations, Indonesia declined to join the initiative.

National and foreign media suggested that Indonesia declined to join the RMSI because of concerns that the US would send its naval vessels to patrol the Straits. In a Congressional hearing on 31 March 2004, Admiral Fargo explained that, as part of the RMSI, the US was 'looking at things like ... putting Special Operations Forces on high-speed vessels, potentially putting Marines on high-speed vessels ... to conduct effective interdiction' (US House of Representatives, 2004). His statement was quoted in various international and national media. Fargo's statement was met with strong protest from radical groups and politicians from opposition parties in Indonesia (Acharya, 2007, p. 87; Bakorkamla, 2010, p. 100; BBC, 2004; Oegroseno, 2005). Despite Fargo's comments and the media reports they produced, the US never intended to send patrols as part of the RMSI and the Indonesian government understood this.[12] A former MoD official that took part in the formulation of Indonesia's policy on the RMSI explained that the administration understood that direct patrols by the US Marines were not part of the cooperation activities that Washington offered to Indonesia.[13]

In order to clarify media reports, US officials including the US Ambassador to Indonesia Ralph L. Boyce, the US Charge d'Affaires John Medeiros and the US Defence Secretary Donald Rumsfeld explained to the media that the US had no plan to deploy troops in the Straits of Malacca as part of the RMSI (Choong, 6 June 2004; *Jakarta Post*, 2004; Medeiros, 2004). According to Ambassador

Boyce, Fargo's statement was purely hypothetical (*Jakarta Post*, 2004). The US Defence Secretary Donald Rumsfeld, during his visit to Indonesia in June 2004, felt it necessary to emphasise the US stand over RMSI. Rumsfeld suggested that there were no plans for the US to send standing forces or set up a military base in the Straits (Choong, 2004).

The US created and proposed the RMSI. The US initiated this cooperation programme partly due to perceived 'slowness in the implementation of concrete measures to address transnational maritime threats' (Ho, 2007, p. 216). The US used its diplomatic leverage to begin discussion of the RMSI with the littoral states of the Straits of Malacca and Singapore. During a meeting with Indonesian officials in 2003, the US Pacific Fleet Commander in Chief Admiral Fargo stated his concern over the security of the Straits of Malacca and Singapore, pointing out that the US government viewed the security of the Straits as a serious issue and would expect Indonesia to join the US-led initiative (Bakorkamla, 2010, p. 99; Indonesian MFA, 2004, pp. 25, 35; 2005a, p. 82; 2005b, p. 18; Jailani, 2005, p. 56; Siregar *et al.*, 2004, pp. 2–3, 13–14; Sudrajat, 2005, p. 6).[14] The US leadership was most apparent in its willingness to bear the costs to establish the RMSI. The US Department of State had proposed to allocate US$2 billion to finance the implementation of the RMSI (Kucera, 2006, p. 13 as cited in Song, 2007, p. 110). The US was willing to assist participating states in building a complete maritime picture, training their law enforcement to deal with organised crimes, and aiding the development of their national coast guard (Doughton, 2006, pp. 44–45; Ho, 2007, p. 216; Stryken, 2007, p. 135). The presence of US leadership, however, was not sufficient to ensure Indonesia's cooperation. On 16 April 2004, the Ministry of Foreign Affairs spokesperson Marty Natalegawa announced Indonesia's rejection of the RMSI (Detik News, as cited in Indonesian MoD, 2004). The Indonesian government fully understood that the deployment of US Special Forces in the Straits of Malacca and Singapore was not part of the RMSI deals offered to the littoral states (Indonesian MoD, 2004). However, playing to the domestic audience, Natalegawa stated Indonesia's rejection of the RMSI and any form of ideas, suggestions or proposals that would allow external states to safeguard the Straits of Malacca. This official position was echoed in various statements made by other Indonesian high government officials. The Indonesian chief of the navy Admiral Bernard Kent Sondakh, in his statement to the media, explained that the 'Navy was ready to contain any US intrusion into Indonesia's territory' (*Jakarta Post*, 2004). According to Sondakh, 'since Indonesia, as a littoral state has not requested any assistance to patrol the waters, no foreign forces are permitted to be sent to secure the Straits' (Indonesian MoD, 2004). A government official from the navy confirmed this. As he put it:

> Let us imagine if they informed us that there is a vessel plying through and going to be hijacked in these waters ... There is a possibility that it could be used as a motive to intervene. Therefore, we need to be cautious, not to accept that [the RMSI], because it could be used as a justification.[15]

In summary, the US exercised its leadership in promoting the SUA convention, the PSI, the CSI and the RMSI by drafting, initiating the negotiations of these initiatives, conducting diplomatic persuasion at bilateral and international levels, and, in the case of the RMSI, bearing the costs of cooperation. Despite US leadership, Indonesia decided not to join the SUA convention, the PSI, the CSI and the RMSI cooperation initiatives. In all these cases, the Indonesian government claimed that concern over sovereignty infringement was the reason underpinning Jakarta's non-participation in the SUA convention, the PSI, the CSI, and the RMSI. The government highlighted their uneasiness over potential US intrusion in their waters or vessels flying their flags in the case of the SUA convention, the PSI and the RMSI, and the placement of US officials in Indonesian territory in the case of the CSI. Indonesia's non-participation in these initiatives is puzzling since Indonesia had shared sensitive security information with the US as part of its bilateral cooperation with Washington and granted access to officials from the US Coast Guard and the Customs and the CBP agency to various ports, including restricted areas, through the US public–private partnership initiatives. The next part of this chapter will explain the extent and depth of cooperation between Indonesia and the US under the public–private partnership framework. It will also explain the implications of these initiatives in informing Indonesia's maritime security practices.

The United States unilateral initiatives: the public–private partnership model

Public–private partnerships to address the threat posed by terrorism are not something new and not unique to the US. In 2000, Japan's business federation Keidanren, which represents 1,329 Japanese companies, 109 nationwide industrial associations and 47 regional economic organisations, identified the need to strengthen information-security in facing terrorist threats (East West Institute, 2006, p. 2; Keidanren, 2015). Keidanren then initiated better cooperation among the private sector, academia and government in the area of research and development to strengthen the level of information security (East West Institute, 2006, p. 2). However, in the aftermath of 9/11, what makes the US-led public–private partnerships unique are the scope of changes that they introduce to the security of the international supply chain and the global outreach of the US-led public–private initiatives. For instance, in November 2001, when the US launched the C-TPAT, only seven major US importers joined the initiative. This number has grown to more than 10,000 certified participants across the global trade community and accounts for over 50 per cent of the value of what is imported into the US (US CBP, 2015).

The US 9/11 Commission reported that, prior to the attacks, the national strategies for transportation security and private sector emergency preparedness were non-existent (US DHS, 2012). The US 9/11 Commission immediately highlighted the need to involve the private sector in the design and implementation of security counter-measures. Security is seen as a partnership, and, therefore, transportation stakeholders are responsible for delivering their contribution to security (US 9/11 Commission, 2004).

The Department of Homeland Security emphasised the importance of partnerships between the public and private sectors to better mitigate and defend against terrorist threats (US DHS, 2011, p. 3). For this purpose, the DHS has established seventy-two fusion centres that serve as focal points to receive, analyse, gather and share threat-related information between government and private sector partners (US DHS, 2011, p. 3). Although, in the immediate aftermath of 9/11, aviation security systems received most attention, the DHS has partnered with the private sector to strengthen port and cargo security. The US public–private partnership cooperation initiatives that influence maritime and port security in Indonesia include the implementation of the USCG's International Port Security Programme and the CBP's C-TPAT. The two initiatives have enabled the US government to work closely with Indonesian-based port authorities, shipowners, importers, exporters, forwarders, licensed custom brokers and manufacturers. This section will look at the implementation of two US public–private initiatives: the IPS programme and the C-TPAT in Indonesia.

The International Port Security programme

In the field of counter-maritime terrorism, Indonesia cooperates closely with the US through the US Coast Guard IPS programme. The US Maritime Transportation Security Act of 2002 assigns the Department of Homeland Security to assess the anti-terrorism measures implemented in foreign ports and vessels. The US Coast Guard launched the IPS programme to implement the Maritime Transportation Security Act. The programme specifically targets foreign ports that are 'served by vessels that also call on the United States, foreign ports to which US vessels visit and foreign ports which are determined to be a security risk to international maritime commerce' (US Coast Guard, 15 February 2005). It uses the ISPS Code as the programme benchmark to assess the level of effectiveness of 'a country's anti-terrorism measures in its ports' and a state's provisions for ship security (US Coast Guard, 15 February 2005).

The initiative involves port visits by the US Coast Guard to foreign nations and enables foreign nations to carry out reciprocal visits to the US. The cooperation programme requires a foreign government, represented by a government agency responsible for port facility security, to provide information to the US Coast Guard team pertaining to the country's practices in securing their ports facilities and vessels flying their flags, provide access to the US team to carry out reviews on access control, restricted areas, handling of cargo, delivery of stores/supplies, security monitoring, policies and procedures as well as training and exercises in a number of port facilities that are requested by the US Coast Guard (Indonesian DGST, 2010a; US Coast Guard, 15 February 2005, 2007). Despite the reciprocal nature of this cooperation initiative, it is highly unlikely that the Indonesian government will demand access and carry out a review of US key ports.

The IPS programme obliges ports to follow 'procedures for the marking, storing, distributing and destroying sensitive security information material, which includes documents that discuss' screening and detection processes (US Coast Guard, 27 May 2004). The IPS programme requires a port facility that does not have effective anti-terrorism measures to submit a security plan for approval by the US Coast Guard, and use of a Recognized Security Organization (RSO) acceptable to the US Coast Guard to verify the port facility's implementation of the ISPS Code and additional security measures (US Coast Guard, 15 February 2005).

If the Coast Guard is unable to ascertain a country's implementation status because of being denied access to a country or specific port facilities, the Coast Guard will implement a number of measures to mitigate what they deem as 'unknown security concerns' (US Coast Guard, 15 February 2005). These measures include the issuing of a port security advisory, imposing fines, boarding vessels at sea, conducting security inspections at dock and denying access to US waters (Baldor, 2004; US Coast Guard, 15 April 2004). For port facilities, the issuance of an advisory implies that all vessels stopping at these facilities will be subjected to additional security measures when calling at US ports. If, after the issuance of the advisory, the conditions of the port facility do not improve, the US Coast Guard will issue a maritime security directive or a commandant order, which will outline measures applied on vessels coming to the US from the country of concern (US Coast Guard, 15 February 2005). These measures may include denying entry to US waters (US Coast Guard, 15 April 2004). Under the IPS programme, foreign vessels that come into the US without a security certificate and a security plan will face a fine. The US Coast Guard can issue a US$10,000 fine for violators and oblige them to comply with the security requirements within thirty days or face extra fines of up to US$25,000 (Baldor, 2004). In February and March 2004 alone, the Coast Guard had issued US$1.66 million in such fines (Baldor, 2004).

The two lead Indonesian governmental actors involved in the US-led IPS programme are the MoT and the MFA. The economic factor has been the most important factor that shaped the two ministries' decision. As an Indonesian official recalled, 'if we do not cooperate, our ships calling at US ports could be denied access and foreign ships would not visit our ports'.[16] The cooperation has taken a low-key approach and been conducted informally. Therefore, it did not generate much public attention. Indonesia consents to give access to various port facilities through correspondence with the US government.[17] The US requests access for inspection through the same mechanism.[18]

Prior to the introduction of the IPS programme, the Indonesian government has implemented the ISPS Code at its own pace. The implementation of the IPS introduces changes in port facilities that are regularly visited by vessels bound to the US, as the implementation of the Code became subject to US scrutiny. The Indonesian government needs to submit security plans and provide access to the US Coast Guard to carry out inspections. Before the IPS programme, the Indonesian DGST was the authority for issuing ISPS certificates, surveying terminal areas, and reviewing the terminal operators' organisational structure and their staff's level of understanding of the ISPS requirements and security procedures.[19] After the implementation of the IPS programme, assessment of port facilities' compliance with the ISPS Code involved verification by the US Coast Guard and also an RSO acceptable to the US Coast Guard (US Coast Guard, 15 February 2005).

Although Indonesian officials have signalled their reluctance to provide access to the US due to potential intelligence activities, as confirmed by a US official, Indonesian port administrators and port facility security officers have been very cooperative on the ground.[20] Indonesia has even provided access to its restricted areas to the US (Indonesian DGST, 2010a, p. 2).[21] As a US Coast Guard official claimed, in contrast to some Southeast Asian states that have refused US Coast Guard visits to some of their facilities, Indonesia has given access to all facilities requested.[22]

The Indonesian government has aligned its port security practices with the IPS standards and borne the economic costs incurred to improve the security of its ports. These costs cover initial expenses to purchase security equipment, train staff, install equipment, maintain or update security practices, and, in the case of non-compliance, hire an RSO to verify anti-terrorism security measures (US Coast Guard, 17 October 2012).[23] Most Indonesian ports are operated solely by a state owned company PT Pelindo or jointly between PT Pelindo with foreign investors; therefore, these parties are responsible in financing the economic costs of cooperation (US Coast Guard, 15 February 2005).[24]

The authority to monitor, review and enforce the IPS Programme lies with the US Coast Guard. In Indonesia the US Coast Guard has been visiting a number of port facilities and carrying out reviews once a year since 2005. From 2005 to 2010 the US Coast Guard has conducted six visits (Indonesian DGST, 2010a, p. 1). These included visits to five port facilities in 2005; eight in 2006; nine in 2007; three in 2008; six in 2009 and twelve in 2010 (Indonesian DGST, 2010a, p. 1). A number of port facilities have been visited twice. Out of thity-six port facilities that the US Coast Guard visited, twenty-four facilities were declared as satisfying ISPS Code requirements (Indonesian DGST, 2010a, p. 5).

In the past, the US Coast Guard has imposed sanctions on Indonesian port facilities that failed to meet sufficient anti-maritime terrorism measures (US Coast Guard, 15 February 2005).[25] In February 2008, the US Coast Guard issued an advisory to most Indonesian ports due to unsatisfactory security conditions. The US, however, exempted sixteen port facilities from the advisory (US Embassy in Jakarta, 26 February 2008). These are PT Terminal Peti Kemas Surabaya, Banjarmasin Port, PT Pertamina Unit Pemasaran III, Pertamina Unit Pengolahan V Balikpapan, Senipah Terminal Total E and P Indonesia Balikpapan, Caltex Oil Terminal Dumai, Pelindo II Conventional Terminal Jakarta, Jakarta International Container Terminal, PT Pupuk Kaltim Bontang, PT Badak Bontang, PT Indominco Mandiri Bontang, Pertamina Unit Pengolahan II Dumai, PT Pelabuhan Indonesia I Cabang Dumai, Semarang International Container

Terminal, Belawan Multi-Purpose Terminal, P.T. Multimas Nabati Asahan (US Embassy in Jakarta, 26 February 2008).

With the exception of the sixteen port facilities mentioned above, it has been reported that in most ports the US Coast Guard found inconsistent procedures for security checks prior to entering port facilities, simple and easily manipulated ID card identification systems, low compliance in providing ISPS training, drills and exercises at port facilities, and insufficient knowledge of port authorities regarding their task and function in the implementation of ISPS (Indonesian DGST, 2010a; US Embassy Jakarta, 2008).[26] An Indonesian high government official claimed this decision was unfair because at that time the US had only visited 18 out of 121 Indonesian ports that had complied with the ISPS Code.[27] As a consequence of the issuance of the advisory, any vessels calling at Indonesian ports were obliged to go through extensive security procedures before being granted permission to enter US ports. An Indonesian important port facility in Jakarta, for instance, lost millions of dollar when the US Coast Guard issued the advisory in 2008 because most of its major clients withdrew their contracts with the port facility.[28]

The Container-Trade Partnership against Terrorism (C-TPAT)

Launched in November 2001, the C-TPAT is a voluntary partnership programme between the US CBP and the business community, including shippers, carriers, consolidators, licensed customs brokers and manufacturers in improving supply chain and US border security (US GAO, 2003, p. 12).

The C-TPAT customised security requirements for each business category, including brokers, warehouses, air carriers, sea carriers, land carriers and ocean transportation intermediaries. It obliges members to participate in the CBP automated manifest system, to work with CBP in identifying security gaps and implementing security measures, receive initial and annual assessment visits by the US CBP to enhance and verify compliance to the C-TPAT and provide a detailed security profile outlining security measures implemented by the company to the CBP (UNCTAD, 2004, p. 5).[29]

At the initial stage, businesses willing to take part in the C-TPAT need to fill in the C-TPAT supply chains security profile questionnaire, submit the company's security profile and sign a C-TPAT agreement to voluntary participation (UNCTAD, 2004, p. 4). The US CBP then carries out a surveillance audit of businesses' premises to review their readiness to join the initiative. The CBP only issues C-TPAT certificates to businesses that meet the CBP security requirements.

The US CBP implements a rigorous enforcement system to ensure compliance. A C-TPAT member is subjected to the US CBP's periodic assessment or validation. Prior to on-site validation, the US Customs officials review the participant's C-TPAT security profile and supplemental information given by the participant. As part of the monitoring system, a team from US CBP conducts an annual on-site visit to evaluate the participant's security measures. The result of the CBP validation is crucial for a company's C-TPAT certificate renewal. US

CBP will remove a company that fails to meet the C-TPAT security requirements from the cooperation programme.

Businesses bear substantial economic costs to participate in the initiative. On average, a C-TPAT-certified company spends US$54,000 annually to meet C-TPAT criteria (*American Shipper*, 2007). This amount shows more than 100 per cent increase of a company's expenditure for security measures than a year before joining the C-TPAT (*American Shipper*, 2007). The costs include expenses for installing new reporting systems, new identification systems for employees and visitors, adding security personnel, carrying out periodic security training for their employees, enhancing security devices and meeting detailed security standards such as the use of fences surrounding their business premises as well as secure container seals.[30]

The C-TPAT does not require immediate government involvement in the initiative. Despite the C-TPAT's robust obligations, high level of precision and rigorous enforcement mechanisms, none of the C-TPAT requirements were addressed to the Indonesian government. Indonesian businesses that signed up to the programme were shippers, port operators, manufacturers and forwarders who were involved in exporting goods to the US, and shipping lines that are part of international major liner shipping groups.[31]

Indonesia did not experience any pressure from the US to join the initiative. The C-TPAT does not require the Indonesian government to sign up to the partnership arrangement, since it is aimed to increase cooperation between the US Customs and businesses. There has been no threat or sanction carried out by the US to push the Indonesian government to encourage business participation in the C-TPAT.[32] The US representatives merely provided explanations of C-TPAT as part of their seminars and training sessions to Indonesian officials from the Ministry of Transportation and Customs on ways to improve total supply chain security (Yulianto, 2008, pp. 53–57).[33]

The US consulted Indonesian Ministry of Transportation and Customs when the C-TPAT process began in 2002. Neither the Indonesian Customs nor the Ministry of Transportation posed any challenge to the implementation of the C-TPAT nor expressed any concern over sovereignty infringement, because the C-TPAT does not require the government's direct participation in the initiative. The US also did not pressure Indonesian businesses to join the initiative. For businesses, participation in the cooperation initiative offers high incentives. The US CBP reduces the number of CBP inspections, provides priority processing, assigns a C-TPAT supply chain security specialist, who will work with the company to validate and enhance security, offers access to the CBP importer self-assessment programme with an emphasis on self-policing, not CBP audits, and provides opportunity to attend C-TPAT training seminars (US CBP, 2009a, 2009b). As a company joins the C-TPAT, the CBP reduces the overall risk score of this company in the CBP automated targeting system (US GAO, 2003, p. 14). The low risk score lessens the likelihood of being searched for WMD material (US GAO, 2003, p. 14). What the participants won from the partnership was an assurance of access to US markets.

When the hegemon is leading 119

The participation in the C-TPAT has been led and exercised purely by the business community that sought to maintain a good business reputation and meet their American business counterparts' demands for a secure supply chain.[34] Therefore, although businesses need to make costly adjustments to take part in the C-TPAT, they deem that the economic benefits of participation far exceed the costs. For business, taking part in the C-TPAT brings immediate benefits. For port operators, taking part in the C-TPAT suggests that all cargo from their port bound to the US can be delivered directly to US ports. A very small portion of Indonesian exports to the US is transported through direct shipping. On average Indonesia's direct shipping to the US reaches less than 1 per cent of the country's total exports (Indonesian DGST, 2010b, pp. 3, 10; 2014, pp. 1–2, 3–3).

When transhipment takes place in a CSI port, containers from a C-TPAT certified port will not have to go through inspection.[35] Therefore, a C-TPAT port can guarantee clients shorter waiting times at US ports, a priority lane in the case of a terrorist attack, and no delay due to the physical inspection of cargo at the US ports or at the transhipment point, making a C-TPAT port more attractive to exporters.[36] Businesses perceived the economic costs incurred in meeting the C-TPAT obligations as an investment or business requirement.[37]

Most companies in Indonesia that take part in the C-TPAT have strong business relations with their counterparts in the US. Shippers' and carriers' participation in the C-TPAT are also required by their US business counterparts.[38] Under the C-TPAT guidelines, the US importers are required to work together with other service providers to ensure the security process and procedures of the entire supply chains. Thus, C-TPAT members not only need to ensure the security practice of their business but also to ensure that their business partners do the same (UNCTAD, 2004, p. 20). Although the nature of the initiative is voluntary, to maintain business relations with their US counterparts, participation in the C-TPAT is expected (UNCTAD, 2004, p. 21). Non-cooperation creates a competitive disadvantage for Indonesian businesses that export goods to the US (UNCTAD, 2004, p. 21).[39] As the UNCTAD Secretariat report highlighted, the US-based importers, carriers and brokers are likely to 'choose supply partners that can produce reliable and suitable information on their products, organisational structures and procedures' (UNCTAD, 2004, p. 21). Consequently, this circumstance might leave out businesses that do not implement the C-TPAT requirements (UNCTAD, 2004, p. 21).

Conclusion

This chapter has shown that, as a hegemonic country, the US has exercised its leadership in designing and promoting maritime security initiatives on an international scale. The evidence, however, shows that the presence of US leadership in the case of the SUA convention, the CSI, the PSI and the RMSI could not convince Indonesia to join these arrangements. Although the US had proposed draft of the arrangements, led the negotiation process and enforced rules in these cases, Indonesia chose not to join these arrangements. This suggests that US leadership cannot account for Indonesia's participation in cooperation arrangements.

The behaviour of the US in maritime security cooperation is also interesting to examine. Indonesia's participation in the SUA convention, the CSI, the PSI, the RMSI was important to the US objectives of halting the proliferation and transportation of WMD and securing important sea lanes from terrorist and sea-robbery attacks; yet the US did not use overt coercion to make Indonesia join these cooperation initiatives. In order to explain US behaviour towards Indonesia, this chapter has offered a comprehensive explanation of Indonesia's cooperation in US unilateral initiatives including the IPS and the C-TPAT that have received Indonesia's full cooperation and to some extent have been sufficient to induce changes at the domestic level.

The Indonesian government has been supportive towards US unilateral measures to enhance cargo and port security, including the US Coast Guard's IPS programme and the US CBP's C-TPAT. In both initiatives, the US sets the rules and standards for governments and industries to comply with. Non-participation would hinder the transport of goods bound to the US and make Indonesian ports and maritime industries less competitive in the international market.

Indonesia showed extensive cooperation over the IPS programme and the C-TPAT. The evidence showed that, in the case of the IPS programme and the C-TPAT, officials from the US Coast Guard and US CBP gained business and security-critical information and access to all ports and business premises in Indonesian territory that they requested. In order to ensure compliance with the IPS programme, Indonesian officials from the Ministry of Transportation have been working closely with representatives of the US Coast Guard, which is charged to visit Indonesian port facilities to monitor, review and enforce the standards. The C-TPAT does not require Indonesian government participation. Jakarta is aware of the C-TPAT initiative and does not hinder private sector participation in this US-led partnership.

Indonesia refused to participate in the SUA convention, the CSI, the PSI and the RMSI, partly because the Indonesian government and private sector have joined US unilateral public–private partnerships and could gain the benefits of cooperation, for instance priority handling in ports and unimpeded access to US ports by taking part in these partnerships.

The findings in this chapter add to the argument made in this book regarding the centrality of the absolute gains calculation in informing Indonesia's participation or non-participation in counter-terrorism cooperation. Despite the presence of US leadership, Indonesia did not join the SUA convention, the CSI, the PSI and the RMSI because the government and private sector cooperation in US unilateral initiatives such as the IPS programme and the C-TPAT already offered sufficient benefit. The next chapter will investigate whether the ASEAN Way as a form of shared identity informs Indonesia's decision to participate in maritime security cooperation.

Notes

1 Part B of the Indonesia–US 2010 Defence Arrangement.
2 Interview with an Indonesian foreign and security policy expert at the University of Indonesia (Depok, 11 October 2011).
3 Draft of MoU on Maritime Cooperation between Indonesia and the United States of America (2015).
4 Draft of MoU on Maritime Cooperation between Indonesia and the United States of America (2015).
5 Articles 5, 6, and 12 of SUA convention 1988.
6 Interview with an Indonesian government official (Jakarta, 4 November 2011).
7 Interview with an Indonesian government official (Jakarta, 4 November 2011).
8 Interviews with a high government official at the Indonesian Ministry of Industry, (Jakarta, 6 December 2011); high government officials at the Indonesian Customs and Excise, Ministry of Finance (Jakarta, 3 November 2011); a high government official at the Indonesian Ministry of Transportation (Jakarta, 3 September 2010); and a former high government official at the Ministry of Defence (Depok, 8 October 2011).
9 Interviews with a high government official at the Indonesian Customs and Excise, Ministry of Finance (Jakarta, 4 November 2011); high government officials at the Indonesian Customs and Excise, Ministry of Finance (Jakarta, 3 November 2011); and a high government official at the Indonesian Ministry of Transportation (Jakarta, 3 September 2010).
10 Article 4 of the PSI Ship Boarding Agreement between the US and the Government of Saint Vincent and the Grenadines; Article 4 of the PSI Boarding Agreement between the US and the Government of Antigua and Barbuda.
11 Interviews with a former high government official at the Ministry of Defence (Depok, 8 October 2011); a high government official at the Indonesian Marine Police (Jakarta, 2 September 2010); an Indonesian foreign and security policy expert at the University of Indonesia (Depok, 11 October 2011); and a high government official at the Indonesian Customs and Excise, Ministry of Finance (Jakarta, 9 November 2011).
12 Interview with a former high government official at the Ministry of Defence (Depok, 8 October 2011).
13 Interview with a former high government official at the Ministry of Defence (Depok, 8 October 2011).
14 Statement of an Indonesian navy official (keynote speaker) during Indonesian Coordinating Ministry for Political, Legal and Security Affairs Focus Group Discussion on 'deployment of armed forces personnel in special mission to secure national interests', 2 November 2011, Jakarta, Indonesia.
15 Interview with a high government official at the Indonesian navy (Jakarta, 14 July 2010).
16 Interview with a high government official at the Indonesian Ministry of Transportation (Jakarta, 3 September 2010).
17 Interviews with two high government officials at the Indonesian Ministry of Transportation (Jakarta, 3 September 2010).
18 Interviews with two high government officials at the Indonesian Ministry of Transportation (Jakarta, 3 September 2010).
19 Interview with head of communication and public relations of an international (port) terminal in Indonesia, (Surabaya, 20 September 2011).
20 Interviews with a high government official at the Indonesian Customs and Excise, Ministry of Finance (Jakarta, 4 November 2011); a high government official at the Indonesian Customs and Excise, Ministry of Finance (Jakarta, 9 November 2011); an Indonesian government official (Jakarta, 4 November 2011); an Indonesian foreign and security policy expert at the University of Indonesia (Depok, 11 October 2011); a representative of the United States Coast Guard (Singapore, 20 August 2010); and

two high government officials at the Ministry of Transportation (Jakarta, 7 September 2010).
21 Interviews with two high government officials at the Ministry of Transportation (Jakarta, 7 September 2010); two high government officials at the Indonesian Ministry of Transportation (Jakarta, 3 September 2010); and a representative of the United States Coast Guard (Singapore, 20 August 2010).
22 Interview with a representative of the United States Coast Guard (Singapore, 20 August 2010).
23 Interviews with two high government officials at the Indonesian Ministry of Transportation (Jakarta, 3 September 2010).
24 Interviews with a corporate communication official of a port operator (Surabaya, 20 September 2011); a security and safety official of a port operator (Surabaya, 20 September 2011); and a high government official at the Indonesian Ministry of Transportation (Jakarta, 29 September 2011).
25 Interviews with three government officials at the Indonesian Ministry of Transportation (Jakarta, 3 September 2010).
26 Interviews with a high government official at the Indonesian Maritime Security Coordinating Board (Jakarta, 23 August 2011); and a high government official at the Indonesian Ministry of Transportation (Jakarta, 3 September 2010).
27 Interview with a high government official at the Indonesian Ministry of Transportation (Jakarta, 3 September 2010).
28 Interview with a high government official at the Indonesian Ministry of Transportation (Jakarta, 3 September 2010).
29 Interview with a security and safety official of a port operator (Surabaya, 20 September 2011).
30 Interview with a security and safety official of a port operator (Surabaya, 20 September 2011).
31 Interviews with a representative of Indonesian Forwarders Association (Jakarta, 9 September 2011); a corporate communication official of a port operator (Surabaya, 20 September 2011); a security and safety official of a port operator (Surabaya, 20 September 2011); and representatives of Indonesian Shipowners' Association (Surabaya, 22 September 2011).
32 Interviews with a representative of Indonesian Forwarders Association (Jakarta, 9 September 2011); a corporate communication official of a port operator (Surabaya, 20 September 2011); and a security and safety official of a port operator (Surabaya, 20 September 2011).
33 Interviews with a high government official at the Indonesian Ministry of Transportation (Jakarta, 3 September 2010); and high government officials at the Indonesian Customs and Excise, Ministry of Finance (Jakarta, 3 November 2011).
34 Interviews with a representative of Indonesian Forwarders Association (Jakarta, 9 September 2011); a corporate communication official of a port operator (Surabaya, 20 September 2011); and a security and safety official of a port operator (Surabaya, 20 September 2011).
35 Interviews with a corporate communication official of a port operator (Surabaya, 20 September 2011); and a security and safety official of a port operator (Surabaya, 20 September 2011).
36 Interview with a corporate communication official of a port operator (Surabaya, 20 September 2011).
37 Interview with a security and safety official of a port operator (Surabaya, 20 September 2011).
38 Interview with a representative of Indonesian Forwarders Association (Jakarta, 9 September 2011).
39 Interview with a representative of Indonesian Forwarders Association (Jakarta, 9 September 2011).

References

Acharya, Arabinda. (2007). 'Maritime Terrorist Threat in Southeast Asia', in *Maritime Security in Southeast Asia*, Kwa Chong Guan and John K. Skogan (eds). New York: Routledge.

Agoes, Etty R. (2005). 'Pengelolaan Keamanan di Selat Malaka Secara Terpadu', in *Pertemuan Kelompok Ahli Kebijakan Terpadu Pengelolaan Keamanan Selat Malaka*. Jakarta: Badan Pengkajian dan Pengembangan Kebijakan Kementerian Luar Negeri Indonesia.

American Shipper. (2007). 'Many Companies Claim C-TPAT Security Program Generates ROI', 16 April 2007, available at www.americanshipper.com/Main/News/Many_companies_claim_CTPAT_security_program_genera_27254.aspx?taxonomy=. Last accessed 23 May 2012.

Antara. (2006). 'RI Declines to Join Proliferation Security Initiative', 17 March 2006, accessed from the Newsbank database.

Antara. (2010). 'US Envoy Dedicates Maritime Radar Equipment for Indonesia', 1 July 2010, accessed from the Newsbank database.

ASEAN. (2004). 'ASEAN–US Security: US Proposes Cooperation on Maritime Security for Asia-Pacific', 5 December 2004, available at www.aseansec.org/afp/42.htm. Last accessed 5 October 2009.

Bakorkamla. (2010). *Buku Putih Bakorkamla 2009*. Jakarta: Pustaka Cakra.

Baldor, Lolita C. (2004). 'Coast Guard Issuing More Fines As Port Security Deadline Nears', 25 March 2004, available at https://homeport.uscg.mil/cgi-bin/st/portal/uscg_docs/MyCG/Editorial/20061206/CGfines.pdf?id=866396f80278fd7b62ae4aa2622c9ac5bff8d406&user_id=2a47d4dbfd24ce2da39438e736cab2d6. Last accessed 17 October 2012.

Barnes, Paul and Oloruntoba, Richard. (2005). 'Assurance of Security in Maritime Supply Chains: Conceptual Issues of Vulnerability and Crisis Management'. *Journal of International Management* 11, pp. 519–540.

Bateman, Sam. (2005). 'Maritime Regime Building', in *The Best of Times, The Worst of Times: Maritime Security in the Asia Pacific*, Joshua Ho and Catherine Zara Raymond (eds). Singapore: World Scientific & Institute of Defence and Strategic Studies.

BBC. (2004). 'SE Asia Acts on Maritime Security', 29 June 2004, available at http://news.bbc.co.uk/1/hi/world/asia-pacific/3849217.stm. Last accessed 11 May 2013.

BBC. (2005). 'US Eases Indonesia Arms Ban', 26 May 2005, available at news.bbc.co.uk/1/hi/world/asia-pacific/4581733.stma. Last accessed 6 June 2013.

BBC. (2015). 'East Timor Country Profile – Overview', 17 February 2015, available at www.bbc.co.uk/news/world-asia-pacific-14919009. Last accessed 4 June 2015.

Boutilier, James. (2005). 'The Best of Times, the Worst of Times: The Global Maritime Outlook 2004', in *The Best of Times, The Worst of Times: Maritime Security in the Asia Pacific*, Joshua Ho and Catherine Zara Raymond (eds). Singapore: World Scientific & Institute of Defence and Strategic Studies.

Byers, Michael. (2003). 'Preemptive Self-defense: Hegemony, Equality and Strategies of Legal Change'. *Journal of Political Philosophy* 11:2, pp. 171–190.

Choong, William. (2004). 'US: It's Not for Us to Police Malacca Straits – American Forces Will Not Step in to Pre-empt Threats, Say Top Officials', *The Sunday Times*, 6 June 2004.

Chow, Jonathan T. (2005). 'ASEAN Counterterrorism Cooperation Since 9/11'. *Asian Survey* 45:2, pp. 302–321.

Crawford, Neta C. (2004). 'The Road to Global Empire: the Logic of US Foreign Policy after 9/11'. *Orbis* 48:4, pp. 685–703.
Desker, Barry and Kumar Ramakrishna. (2002). 'Forging an Indirect Strategy in Southeast Asia'. *The Washington Quarterly* 25:2, pp. 161–176.
Detik News. (2004). 'RI Tolak Pengamanan Selat Malaka oleh Pihak Asing', 16 April 2004, as cited in the Indonesian Ministry of Defence website, available at www.kemhan.go.id/modules.php?name=News&file=article&sid=5532. Last accessed 24 December 2010.
Doughton, Thomas F. (2006). 'Straits of Malacca and the Challenges Ahead: The US Perspective', in *Building a Comprehensive Security Environment in the Straits of Malacca*. Kuala Lumpur: Maritime Institute of Malaysia.
East West Institute. (2006). G8 Initiative for Public–Private Partnerships to Counter Terrorism, available at www.ewi.info/sites/default/files/ideas-files/G8%20Initiative%20for%20Public-Private%20Partnerships%20to%20Counter%20Terrorism.pdf. Last accessed 17 June 2015.
Gilpin, Robert. (1975). *US Power and the Multinational Corporation: The Political Economy of Foreign Direct Investment*. New York: Macmillan Press Ltd.
Gilpin, Robert. (1981). *War and Change in World Politics*. Cambridge: Cambridge University Press.
Guilfoyle, Douglas. (2009). *Shipping Interdiction and the Law of the Sea*. Cambridge: Cambridge University Press.
Ho, Joshua. (2007). 'Securing the Seas as a Medium of Transportation in Southeast Asia', in *The Security of Sea Lanes of Communication in the Indian Ocean Region*. Kuala Lumpur: Maritime Institute of Malaysia.
Human Rights Watch. (2015). 'East Timor', 5 June 2015, available at www.hrw.org/legacy/wr2k2/asia5.html. Last accessed 5 June 2015.
IMO. (2005). '2005 Protocol to the SUA convention', available at www.imo.org/OurWork/Security/Instruments/Pages/SUA.aspx. Last accessed 16 February 2012.
IMO. (2009). 'SUA Circular Titles', available at https://imo.amsa.gov.au/public/circular-titles/sua.html. Last accessed 6 October 2009.
Indonesian Coordinating Ministry for Political, Legal and Security Affairs. (2008). *Evaluasi Pengelolaan Bidang Politik, Hukum dan Keamanan Tahun 2007*. Jakarta: Coordinating Ministry for Political, Legal and Security Affairs.
Indonesian Directorate General of Sea Transportation (DGST). (2010a). *Kronologis Kunjungan US Coast Guard di Indonesia*. Jakarta: Direktorat Jenderal Perhubungan Laut.
Indonesian DGST. (2010b). *Data Distribusi Angkutan Ekspor dan Impor Tahun 2009*. Jakarta: Directorate General of Sea Transportation.
Indonesian DGST. (2014). *Data Distribusi Angkutan Ekspor dan Impor Tahun 2013*. Jakarta: Dirjen Perhubungan Laut.
Indonesian Embassy in Washington DC. (2007). 'Joint Statement of Indonesia and the US Security Dialogue V', 19 April 2007, available at www.embassyofindonesia.org/ina-usa/statement/jointstatementSDV.htm. Last accessed 21 March 2012.
Indonesian Ministry of Defence (MoD). (2003). *Buku Putih Pertahanan [Defence White Paper]*. Jakarta: Ministry of Defence.
Indonesian MFA. (2004). *Forum Dialog ke XI Kerjasama Maritim ASEAN*. Jakarta: Badan Pengkajian dan Pengembangan Kebijakan.
Indonesian MFA. (2005a). *Diskusi Panel tentang Studi Kebijakan Kelautan Indonesia Dalam Rangka Mendukung Pembangunan dan Integritas Nasional, Surabaya 7–8 April 2005*. Jakarta: Badan Penelitian dan Pengembangan Kebijakan.

Indonesian MFA. (2005b). *Pertemuan Kelompok Ahli: Kebijakan Terpadu Pengelolaan Keamanan Selat Malaka, Medan 19–20 Juli 2005*. Jakarta: Badan Penelitian dan Pengembangan Kebijakan.
Indonesian Ministry of Trade. (2011). 'Indonesian Export-Import Data 1996–2010', made available to author by the Ministry of Trade, 8 October 2011.
Indonesian Ministry of Trade. (2015a). 'FAQ', 15 June 2015, available at www.kemendag.go.id/id/faq. Last accessed 15 June 2015.
Indonesian Ministry of Trade. (2015b). 'Negara Tujuan Ekspor 10 Komoditi Utama', 15 June 2015, available at www.kemendag.go.id/id/economic-profile/10-main-and-potential-commodities/10-main-commodities. Last accessed 15 June 2015.
Jackson, Richard. (2007). 'Constructing Enemies: 'Islamic Terrorism' in Political and Academic Discourse'. *Government and Opposition* 12:3, pp. 394–426.
Jailani, Abdulkadir (Staf Direktorat Perjanjian Politik Keamanan Kewilayahan Kementerian Luar Negeri). (2005). 'Pokok-Pokok Masalah Kebijakan Luar Negeri Tentang *Issue* Keamanan Laut dan Kewilayahan Selat Malaka', in *Pertemuan Kelompok Ahli: Kebijakan Terpadu Pengelolaan Keamanan Selat Malaka*. Jakarta: Badan Pengkajian dan Pengembangan Kebijakan Departemen Luar Negeri Republik Indonesia.
Jakarta Post. (2004). 'No Plan to Deploy Troops to Malacca Strait: US', 20 April 2004, accessed from the Newsbank database.
Jakarta Post. (2004). 'Poles Turn to Indonesia for Partners', 15 January 2007, accessed from the Newsbank database.
Jakarta Post. (2007). 'Indonesian, US Officials Discuss Iran Resolution', 16 August 2007, accessed from the Newsbank database.
Jakarta Post. (2008). 'Indonesia May Buy US Jet Fighters', 16 February 2008, accessed from the Newsbank database.
Jakarta Post. (2008). 'US Offers Help with Defense', 26 February 2008, accessed from the Newsbank database.
Kahin, Audrey R. and Kahin, George McT. (1995). *Subversion As Foreign Policy: the Secret Eisenhower and Dulles Debacle in Indonesia*. New York: The New Press.
Keidanren. (2015). 'About Keidanren', 17 June 2015, available at www.keidanren.or.jp/en/profile/pro001.html. Last accessed 17 June 2015.
Keohane, Robert O. (1982). 'The Demand for International Regimes'. *International Organization* 36:2, pp. 325–355.
Keohane, Robert O. (1984). *After Hegemony: Cooperation and Discord in the World Political Economy*. Princeton, NJ: Princeton University Press.
Kepabeanan Internasional. (2008). 'Seratus Persen Scanning Atas Ekspor Barang ke Amerika Serikat', in *Warta Bea Cukai* 402 available at www.scribd.com/doc/7707773/Warta-Bea-Cukai-Edisi-402. Last accessed 15 March 2012.
Krasner, Stephen D. (1976). 'State Power and the Structure of International Trade'. *World Politics* 28:3, pp. 317–347.
Lipson, Charles. (1984). 'International Cooperation in Economic and Security Affairs'. *World Politics* 37:1, pp. 1–23.
Medeiros, John. (2004). 'No Plans to Unilaterally Deploy US Forces to Secure Malacca Straits', *Straits Times*, 7 April 2004.
Murphy, Ann Marie. (2010). 'US Rapprochement with Indonesia: From Problem State to Partner'. *Contemporary Southeast Asia* 32:3, pp. 362–387.
Nikitin, Mary Beth. (2010). *Congressional Research Service (CRS) Report for Congress: Proliferation Security Initiative*, available at http://assets.opencrs.com/rpts/RL34327_20100108.pdf. Last accessed 15 February 2012.

Niksch, Larry, McHugh, Lois and Margesson, Rhoda. (2001). *East Timor Situation Report: CRS Report for Congress*, available from http://fas.org/asmp/resources/govern/crs-RL30975.pdf. Last accessed 4 June 2015.

Oegroseno, Arif Havas. (2005). 'Kebijakan Luar Negeri Indonesia Tentang Selat Malaka'. *Forum Hukum* 2:3, pp. 54–62.

Rabasa, Angel and Haseman, John. (2002). *The Military and Democracy in Indonesia: Challenges, Politics and Power*. Washington: Rand Corporation.

Raymond, Catherine Zara. (2006). 'Maritime Terrorism in Southeast Asia: A Risk Assessment'. *Terrorism and Political Violence* 18:2, pp. 239–257.

Roach, J. Ashley. (2004). 'Initiatives to Enhance Maritime Security at Sea'. *Marine Policy* 28:1, pp. 41–66.

Rosenberg, David and Chung, Christopher. (2008). 'Maritime Security in the South China Sea: Coordinating Coastal and User State Priorities'. *Ocean Development and International Law* 39:1, pp. 51–68.

Singapore Ministry of Defence (MoD). (2006). 'Singapore hosts Proliferation Security Initiative (PSI) Operational Experts Group (OEG) Meeting, 25 July 2006', available at www.mindef.gov.sg/imindef/news_and_events/nr/2006/jul/25jul06_nr.html. Last accessed 16 February 2012.

Siregar, Hasnil Basri, Nasution, Sanwani, Rahman, Abdul, Sutiarno, Hasibuan Rosmi, Munthe, Makdin, Purba, Deni and Eliana. (2004). *Pengamanan dan Perlindungan Pulau-Pulau Terluar Pada Batas Wilayah RI Di Kawasan Selat Malaka*. Sumatera Utara: Fakultas Hukum Universitas Sumatera Utara.

Song, Yann-huei. (2007). 'Security in the Strait of Malacca and the Regional Maritime Security Initiative: Responses to the US Proposal', in *International Law Studies Vol. 83: Global Legal Challenges: Command of the Commons, Strategic Communications, and Natural Disasters*, Michael D. Carsten (ed.). Newport, RI: Naval War College Press. Available at www.usnwc.edu/Research--Gaming/International-Law/New-International-Law-Studies-%28Blue-Book%29-Series/International-Law-Blue-Book-Articles.aspx?Volume=83. Last accessed 20 May 2014.

Storey, Ian. (2009). 'What's Behind Dramatic Drop in S-E Asian Piracy', *Straits Times*, 19 January 2009, accessed from the Newsbank database.

Stryken, Christian-Marius. (2007). 'The US Regional Maritime Security Initiative and US Grand Strategy in Southeast Asia', in *Maritime Security in Southeast Asia*. New York: Routledge, pp. 134–145.

Suchharitkul, Sompong. (2006). 'Liability and Responsibility of the State of Registration or the Flag State in Respect of Sea Going Vessels, Aircraft and Spacecraft Registered by National Registration Authorities'. *American Journal of Comparative Law* 54, pp. 409–442.

Sudrajat (Direktur Jenderal Strategi Pertahanan Kementerian Pertahanan Indonesia). (2005). 'Kebijakan Kelautan Nasional dari Perspektif Pertahanan dan Keamanan', in Laporan Kegiatan *Diskusi Panel: Mencari Format Kebijakan Kelautan Indonesia Dalam Rangka Mendukung Pembangunan dan Integrasi Nasional (Studi Kasus Kanada dan Norwegia), Surabaya, 7–8 April 2005*. Jakarta: Kementerian Luar Negeri Indonesia.

Sterio, Milena. (2013). *The Right to Self-determination Under International Law: 'selfistans', Secession and the Rule of the Great Powers*. Abingdon, Oxon: Routledge.

Strange, Susan. (1987). 'The Persistent Myth of Lost Hegemony'. *International Organization* 41:4, pp. 551–574.

UNCTAD. (2004). *UNCTAD/SDTE/TLB/2004/1 Container Security: Major Initiatives and Related International Developments*, available at www.unctad.org/en/docs/sdtetlb20041_en.pdf. Last accessed 25 January 2012.

UNCTAD. (2012). *Review of Maritime Transport*, available at http://unctad.org/en/PublicationsLibrary/rmt2012_en.pdf. Last accessed 16 July 2013.

US 9/11 Commission. (2004). 'Seventh Public Hearing of the National Commission on Terrorist Attacks Upon the United States: Statement of James M. Loy to the National Commission on Terrorist Attacks Upon The United States, 27 January 2004', available from www.9-11commission.gov/hearings/hearing7/witness_loy.htm.

US Coast Guard. (2002). 'Maritime Strategy for Homeland Security', available at www.uscg.mil/history/articles/uscgmaritimestrategy2002.pdf. Last accessed 20 October 2009.

US Coast Guard. (2004). 'Press Release: Coast Guard to Begin International Port Security Visits', 15 April 2004, available at https://homeport.uscg.mil/mycg/portal/ep/contentView.do?contentTypeId=2&channelId=-18389&contentId=55243&programId=50389&programPage=%2Fep%2Fprogram%2Feditorial.jsp&pageTypeId=0&BV_SessionID=@@@@0102172244.1350476151@@@@&BV_EngineID=cccadfidgdflkdcfngcfkmdfhfdfgo.0. Last accessed 17 October 2012.

US Coast Guard. (2004). 'Navigation and Vessel Inspection Circular (NVIC) No. 06–03, Change 1', 27 May 2004, available at https://homeport.uscg.mil/cgi-bin/st/portal/uscg_docs/MyCG/Editorial/20061012/NVIC06-03Ch1.pdf?id=db70f1fc2bc7bcaf0e7bf37732d4bb2b076bd098&user_id=f3e0323a048c9c4431fa1032dc4787d5. Last accessed 17 October 2012.

US Coast Guard. (2005). 'Navigation and Vessel Inspection Circular (NVIC) No. 02–05', 15 February 2005, available from https://homeport.uscg.mil/cgi-bin/st/portal/uscg_docs/MyCG/Editorial/20061012/NVIC2-05_2.pdf?id=9f75e3fedc14830306cc2ce463770be203bec5cd&user_id=f3e0323a048c9c4431fa1032dc4787d5. Last accessed 17 October 2012.

US Coast Guard. (2007). 'International Port Security Program', 19 January 2007, available at https://homeport.uscg.mil/cgi-bin/st/portal/uscg_docs/MyCG/Editorial/20070119/Proceedings%20Article.pdf?id=194b7ce45859fb579e0f34d784cc115fc13a6327&user_id=2a47d4dbfd24ce2da39438e736cab2d6. Last accessed 17 October 2012.

US Coast Guard. (2012). 'Best Practice', available at https://homeport.uscg.mil/mycg/portal/ep/contentView.do?contentTypeId=2&channelId=-18389&contentId=52546&programId=50386&programPage=%2Fep%2Fprogram%2Feditorial.jsp&pageTypeId=0&BV_SessionID=@@@@1425727583.1350473505@@@@&BV_EngineID=cccdadfidhikdfgcfngcfkmdfhfdfgn.0. Last accessed 17 October 2012.

US Customs and Border Protection (US CBP). (2006). *Container Security Initiative 2006–2011 Strategic Plan. US.* Washington DC: Customs and Border Protection Office of Policy and Planning and Office of International Affairs Container Security Division, available at www.cbp.gov/linkhandler/cgov/trade/…security/…/csi_strategic_plan.pdf. Last accessed 7 May 2010.

US CBP. (2007). 'CSI Fact Sheet', 2 October 2007, available at www.cbp.gov/sp/cgov/border_security/international_activities/csi/cis_in_brief.xml. Last accessed 26 October 2009.

US CBP. (2009a). 'C-TPAT Strategic Plan', 21 October 2009, available at www.cbp.gov/linkhandler/cgov/trade/cargo_security/ctpat/what_ctpat/ctpat_strategicplan.ctt/ctpat_strategicplan.pdf. Last accessed 21 October 2009.

US CBP. (2009b). 'C-TPAT Overview', 21 October 2009b, available at www.cbp.gov/xp/cgov/trade/cargo_security/ctpat/what_ctpat/ctpat_overview.xml. Last accessed 21 October 2009.

US CBP. (2010). 'CSI In Brief', available at www.cbp.gov/xp/cgov/trade/cargo_security/csi/csi_in_brief.xml. Last accessed 8 May 2010.
US CBP. (2013). 'Container Security Initiative Ports', 3 July 2013, available at www.dhs.gov/container-security-initiative-ports. Last accessed 17 June 2015.
US CBP. (2015). 'C-TPAT: Customs–Trade Partnership Against Terrorism', 17 June 2015. Available at www.cbp.gov/border-security/ports-entry/cargo-security/c-tpat-customs-trade-partnership-against-terrorism. Last accessed 17 June 2015.
US Department of Defence (DoD). (2003). 'Deputy Secretary Wolfowitz', 28 January 2003, available at www.defenselink.mil/transcripts/transcript.aspx?transcriptid=1356. Last accessed 25 July 2008.
US DoD. (2007). 'News Briefing with Brig. Gen. John Toolan from the Pentagon', 11 April 2007, available at www.defenselink.mil/transcripts/transcript.aspx?transcriptid=3927. Last accessed 25 July 2008.
US DoD. (2011). 'Instruction Number 5111.19: Section 1206 Global Train and Equip Authority', 26 July 2011, available at www.dtic.mil/whs/directives/corres/pdf/511119p.pdf. Last accessed 5 October 2012.
US Department of Homeland Security. (2010). 'CBP's Container Security Initiative Has Proactive Management and Oversight but Future Direction Is Uncertain (Letter Report). Washington: Department of Homeland Security', available at www.oig.dhs.gov/assets/Mgmt/OIG_10-52_Feb10.pdf. Last accessed 25 April 2012.
US Department of Homeland Security. (2011). "Implementing 9/11 Commission Recommendations', available at www.dhs.gov/xlibrary/assets/implementing-9-11-commission-report-progress-2011.pdf. Last accessed 17 June 2015.
US Department of Homeland Security. (2012). 'Homeland Security Progress on 9/11 Commission Recommendations', 29 June 2012, available from www.dhs.gov/homeland-security-progress-911-commission-recommendations. Last accessed 17 June 2015.
US Department of State. (2003). 'Proliferation Security Initiative: Statement of Interdiction Principles', 4 September 2003, available at www.state.gov/t/isn/c27726.htm. Last accessed 15 February 2012.
US Department of State Archive. (2008). 'Proliferation Security Initiative Frequently Asked Questions, 26 May 2008', available at http://2001-2009.state.gov/t/isn/rls/fs/105217.htm. Last accessed 17 February 2012.
US Department of State. (2011). 'DoD-funded Integrated Maritime Surveillance System', 18 November 2011, available at www.state.gov/r/pa/prs/ps/2011/11/177382.htm. Last accessed 21 March 2012.
US Department of State. (2013). 'Ship Boarding Agreement', available at www.state.gov/t/isn/c27733.htm. Last accessed 15 July 2013.
US Department of State. (2013). 'Proliferation Security Initiative', available at www.state.gov/t/isn/c10390.htm. Last accessed 16 July 2013.
US Embassy in Jakarta. (2008). 'US Coast Guard Issues Advisory to Indonesia on Port Security', 26 February 2008, available at http://jakarta.usembassy.gov/pr_02262008.html. Last accessed 20 September 2011.
US General Accounting Office. (2003). 'GAO-03–770 Container security: Expansion of key Customs Programs will require greater attention to critical success factors', available at www.gao.gov. Last accessed 25 January 2012.
US House of Representatives. (2004). 'H.A.S.C. No. 108–21: Hearings on National Defense Authorization Act for Fiscal Year 2005-H.R. 4200 and Oversight of Previously Authorized Programs before the Committee on Armed Services House of

Representatives', 31 March 2004, available at http://commdocs.house.gov/committees/security/has091000.000/has091000_0.HTM. Last accessed 5 February 2011.
US Pacific Command (USPACOM). (2004a). 'The Regional Maritime Security Initiative', available at www.pacom.mil/rmsi/. Last accessed 5 October 2009.
USPACOM. (2004b). 'United States Pacific Command Strategy for Maritime Security', available at www.pacom.mil/rmsi/RMSI%20Strategy%20Nov%2004.pdf. Last accessed 5 October 2009.
USPACOM. (2004c). '"Blue Top" Document on the Regional Maritime Security Initiative', available at www.pacom.mil/rmsi/. Last accessed 21 October 2009.
US White House. (2001). 'US and Indonesia Pledge Cooperation', 19 September 2001, available at www.whitehouse.gov/news/releases/2001/09/20010919-5.html. Last accessed 20 July 2008.
Valencia, Mark J. (2006). 'Security Issues in the Malacca Straits: Whose Security and Why It Matters?' in *Building a Comprehensive Security Environment in the Straits of Malacca: Proceeding of the MIMA International Conference on the Straits of Malacca, 11–13 October, 2004*. Kuala Lumpur: Maritime Institute of Malaysia.
Waltz, Kenneth N. (1979). *Theory of International Politics*. New York: McGraw-Hill.
Yulianto, Agus. (2008). 'C-TPAT'. *Warta Bea Cukai* 402, available at www.scribd.com/doc/7707773/Warta-Bea-Cukai-Edisi-402. Last accessed 15 March 2012.

4 When shared identity does not matter

Introduction

The role of shared identity in informing states' cooperation is one of the core features of constructivism. The so-called 'ASEAN spirit' or the 'ASEAN Way' has been deemed as the norm that helps to advance cooperation among Southeast Asian countries. The 'ASEAN Way' highlights the importance of consensus and accommodation in resolving conflict among member states and promoting security cooperation among them (Acharya, 1992; 1995; 1997, pp. 328–329; 1998, p. 80; 2004, pp. 249, 256; Acharya and Tan, 2006, pp. 42, 53; Ball, 1993, p. 53; Johnston, 1999, pp. 294–295). It serves as a collective identity for the ASEAN states. The ASEAN Way proposition echoed the constructivist argument that states that share similar identities are more likely to cooperate with each other. Following this line of thought, as an ASEAN member Indonesia should be more likely to cooperate with other ASEAN member states. This chapter will examine whether or not the ASEAN Way as a shared identity informed Indonesia's participation or non-participation in maritime security cooperation.

This chapter questions the dominant view among scholars that the ASEAN Way, as a form of shared identity among Southeast Asian states, plays an important role in shaping cooperation. This chapter challenges theoretically the constructivist argument that states which share similar identities are more likely to cooperate with each other. Constructivism deems that these states develop a collective identity that refers to positive identification with the well-being of others. This positive identification then leads to a greater propensity to cooperate for the well-being of all.

The next section in this chapter will familiarise readers with the notion of the ASEAN Way, which emphasises the role of consensus and accommodation in settling disputes and advancing security cooperation among ASEAN member states. It will explain the development of the ASEAN Way concept. This section will account for the interplay between the ASEAN Way as shared identity and the processes and interactions between Southeast Asian countries in forming communities. The third section will examine the explanation suggested by the literature on the importance of shared identity in informing cooperation to assess the reasons underpinning Indonesia's participation in maritime security cooperation. It will argue that shared identity did not inform Indonesia's decision to cooperate or not cooperate in maritime security. To support this argument, I will explain Indonesia's cooperation and non-cooperation when dealing with fellow ASEAN states and non-ASEAN states.

The ASEAN Way

As a shared identity, the ASEAN Way grew as a result of a 'gradual process of diplomatic rapprochement' between the five founding members of the organisation: Indonesia, Malaysia, the Philippines, Singapore and Thailand (Acharya and Johnston, 2007, p. 34). The development of the ASEAN Way identity is shaped by the historical experiences and interactions of Southeast Asian states in various Non-Aligned Movement summits (Intan, 2015, p. 11; Masilamani and Peterson, 2015, p. 17). The movement emerged out of the Asian–African conference held in Bandung in 1955 (Indonesian MFA, 2014). The key principles upheld by twenty-nine leaders of newly independent states in Asia and Africa at the conference were: political self-determination, mutual respect for sovereignty, non-aggression, non-interference in internal affairs and equality (US DoS, 2016). Southeast Asian states adhered to this set of 'Bandung injunction' norms and subsequently adopted them as their distinct approach within ASEAN (Acharya, 2009 as cited in Intan, 2015, p. 11).

Acharya notes that the distinctive notion of the ASEAN Way focuses on reliance on consultation, consensus and quiet diplomacy in reaching collective goals among member states rather than formal and legalistic procedures (Acharya, 2011, p. 206; Acharya and Johnston, 2007, p. 245). If member states cannot reach an agreed decision over an important matter, ASEAN would not take a joint position over such an issue and member states would simply 'agree to disagree and go their separate ways' (Narine, 1998, p. 34). The informality of the ASEAN Way is reflected in the member states' decision to keep the ASEAN bureaucratic apparatus relatively small, despite the burgeoning number of informal and formal meetings (Acharya, 2011, p. 207).

There are six core norms embedded within the concept of the ASEAN Way. These are sovereign equality; non-use of force and peaceful settlement of disputes; non-interference and non-intervention; non-involvement of ASEAN in addressing unresolved disputes between its members; quiet diplomacy; and mutual respect and tolerance (Narine, 1997, p. 964 as cited in Masilamani and Peterson, 2015, p. 32). ASEAN has stipulated these norms in three major documents: the 1967 Bangkok declaration, the 1971 zone of peace, freedom and neutrality declaration (ZOPFAN) and the 1976 treaty of amity and cooperation (TAC) (Acharya, 1992, p. 11; Masilamani and Peterson, 2015, p. 25).

The 1967 declaration, which marked the establishment of ASEAN, noted that acceptance of the ASEAN Way norms is crucial to ensure ASEAN membership because the organisation is only 'open for participation to all states in the Southeast Asian region subscribing to the principles' (ASEAN, 8 August 1967). The

Declaration points out that ASEAN states 'are determined to ensure their stability and security from external interference in any form or manifestation' (ASEAN, 1967). The 1971 ZOPFAN declaration reiterated the centrality of the ASEAN Way as working guidelines for the organisation. The document repeats ASEAN states' 'commitment to the principle in the Bangkok declaration which established ASEAN in 1967' (ASEAN, 1967).

Article 2 of the TAC obliges contracting parties to adhere to the ASEAN Way's fundamental principles:

> (a) mutual respect for the independence, sovereignty, equality, territorial integrity and national identity of all nations; (b) the right of every State to lead its national existence free from external interference, subversion or coercion; (c) non-interference in the internal affairs of one another; (d) settlement of differences or disputes by peaceful means; (e) renunciation of the threat or use of force.
>
> (ASEAN, 1976)

The ASEAN Way principle of peaceful settlement of disputes is echoed throughout Chapter IV of the treaty. Article 14 of the TAC calls for the development of a high council to settle disputes through regional process; however, this regional dispute settlement mechanism has never been invoked. ASEAN states tend to resolve issues related to maritime boundaries or territorial dispute by involving an independent third party outside of ASEAN. This could be seen from the decision of Indonesia and Malaysia to resolve the dispute over the Sipadan and Ligitan islands through the International Court of Justice (ICJ) in 2002 (*Straits Times*, 2005). Singapore and Malaysia also decided to settle the sovereignty dispute over Pedra Branca/Pulau Batu Puteh, Middle Rocks and South Ledge through the ICJ in February 2003 (Singapore Ministry of Foreign Affairs, 2003). The dispute over the Spratly and Paracel islands in the South China Sea, which involves China and ASEAN states including Malaysia, Brunei, Vietnam and the Philippines, has continued to generate concerns over potential open conflict (Coquia, 1990, p. 120). Yet, no claimant states have resorted to the development of a high council to resolve territorial disputes in the South China Sea. Rather, on 22 January 2013, the Philippines notified Beijing that the archipelagic state was seeking international arbitration to rule on China's unlawful acts in the disputed areas in the South China Sea.

The ASEAN Way and history of maritime security cooperation in ASEAN

ASEAN is portrayed in the academic literature as an example of an emerging or a nascent security community in the international system (Acharya, 2001, p. 208; Chau, 2008, p. 627; Eaton and Stubbs, 2006, p. 140). The organisation was born 'when the region was on the verge of a war' (Khoman, 1986, p. 9). The British plan to expand the state of Malaya and incorporate Sabah and Sarawak into 'a single entity to be known as Malaysia' by 16 September 1963 was met with fierce opposition from the Philippines and Indonesia (Kahin and Kahin, 1995, p. 221). This development locked the Philippines and Malaysia into a territorial dispute over Sabah (Narine, 1998, p. 33). The Indonesian government under the banner of confrontation policy or *konfrontasi* sent small military units across the border into Sarawak, landed paratroopers on the Malay peninsula in August 1964, and raided Malaysian and British warships navigating off the Indonesian coast (Kahin and Kahin, 1995, p. 222; Khoman, 1986, p. 9). Acting as a peace broker, Thailand coined the idea of forming a new regional organisation to bring reconciliation and pursue friendly cooperation between the conflicting partners. Thailand's proposal gained support from the neighbouring countries' foreign ministers. As a result ASEAN was established on 8 August 1967 (Flores and Abad, 1997).

Against the backdrop of inter-state conflicts among the founding countries, the ASEAN Way emphasised equality, non-interference and informality as the acceptable approach and code of conduct guiding states' interactions. ASEAN was not established to serve as a security organisation. The 1967 ASEAN declaration focuses on efforts to encourage collaboration in various fields, ranging from economic, social, cultural, technical, scientific and administrative fields to Southeast Asian studies (ASEAN, 1967). The organisation's objective is confined merely to maintaining 'regional peace and stability' (ASEAN, 1967). The declaration does not mention security cooperation as the aim of the organisation. Rather, the objective to 'accelerate the economic growth, social progress and cultural development' is put as the first aim and purpose of ASEAN (ASEAN, 1967). Yet, despite the Bangkok declaration's emphasis on economic cooperation, ASEAN's annual ministerial meetings were always attended by foreign ministers (Colbert, 1986, p. 196). Regular meetings among economic ministers and discussion of ASEAN economic programmes only started in March 1976 (Colbert, 1986, p. 196). This shows the political nature of ASEAN from its nascent years.

ASEAN assumed a greater political and security role following Vietnam's occupation of Cambodia in December 1978 (Colbert, 1986, p. 200). The Vietnam–Cambodia conflict dominated the ASEAN political and security agenda from 1978 to 1990 (Narine, 1998, p. 34). Khong and Nesadurai claim that accommodative diplomacy prescribed by the ASEAN Way approach had facilitated ASEAN member states to reach a concerted position on the conflict despite their differences over the nature of the threat and the way to address it (2007, p. 35). ASEAN states backed by China and the US opposed Vietnam's invasion of Cambodia (Narine, 1998, p. 34). The ASEAN Way principles enabled ASEAN to sustain the Cambodian problem on the international agenda although the organisation had limited material capabilities and the international community showed little interest in the region (Khong and Nesadurai, 2007, p. 35). ASEAN campaigned at the UN and other international forums for over a decade to put political and economic pressure on Vietnam and, later, to set the terms for the dispute settlement (Acharya, 1992, p. 11; Colbert, 1986, p. 200). The conflict was resolved through the signing of the Paris political settlement agreement in October 1991.

Concern over Vietnamese expansion and Hanoi's military strength had increased maritime security cooperation among ASEAN member states from the late 1970s to the early 1990s. In response to the growing tension in Indochina, the ASEAN Bali Concord declaration issued in 1976 had called for continuation of bilateral cooperation between member states in security matters (ASEAN, 1976). The bilateral border security arrangements then evolved into 'an overlapping and interlocking network' of a regional security system (Acharya, 1992, p. 10; 1995, p. 191). In the late 1970s, the Philippines and Indonesia improved their border arrangements to include periodic naval exercises and patrols to address 'smuggling, piracy and illegal shipment of arms' (Acharya, 1992, p. 13). Following the Vietnam–Cambodia conflict in the late 1970s, Indonesia and Malaysia also strengthened the border coordination to deal with insurgent activities and carried out bilateral military exercises as well as intelligence exchange (Colbert, 1986, p. 208). In the 1990s, the bilateral cooperation between the two countries was extended to include coordinated naval patrols. The naval patrol arrangement signed in 1992 was geared to address the problems posed by armed robbery attacks in the Strait of Malacca. In 2004 the bilateral coordinated patrol arrangement serves as a template for Indonesia, Malaysia and Singapore to set up the most advance tri-lateral naval patrol arrangement in ASEAN. The trilateral arrangement has involved cross-border naval and air patrols to halt sea robbery attacks. It was deemed most useful by the international community in reducing the number of attacks in the early 2000s (IMB, 2005, p. 31). Indonesia, Malaysia and Singapore invited Thailand to participate in the patrol arrangement in 2007.

As shown by the Malacca Straits patrol arrangement mentioned above, on a practical level the most elaborate cooperation in ASEAN to deal with armed robbery attacks against ships and potential maritime terrorism has tended to take place at bilateral and sub-regional levels. To this day, 'no denser counter-terrorism and counter-sea robbery cooperation measures have been generated by Southeast Asian countries via ASEAN' (Chau, 2008, p. 641).

Despite the absence of a formal approach to collective security within ASEAN, scholars such as Acharya, Weatherbee, Eaton and Stubbs argue that the density and quality of interactions through ASEAN help to maintain social cohesion among member countries (Eaton and Stubbs, 2006, p. 150; Weatherbee, 1984, as cited in Acharya, 1992, p. 10). Through various mechanisms in ASEAN, member states are expected to build 'habits of working together, friendship, group loyalties, knowledge about others, convergence and mutual confidence' (see Slaughter, 1995 and Tonra, 1996, as cited in March and Olsen, 1998, p. 959). The expansion of ASEAN to incorporate the 'former pariah states of Vietnam, Laos, Cambodia and Myanmar' has been seen as a testament to the growing sense of community in the region in the 1990s (Chau, 2008, p. 627).

A leap forward in ASEAN regional security cooperation in the 1990s took place when the ASEAN Regional Forum was created. The development of the

ARF was derived from the ASEAN states' willingness to lead over cooperation with other extra-regional states on various strategic and security concerns in Southeast Asia. It was set up against the backdrop of the growing interest of some Asia–Pacific countries, including Australia, Japan and Canada, to push for the establishment of a regional security forum. In 1989–90, Gareth Evans, the Australian foreign minister, inspired by the Council for Security Cooperation in Europe proposed the establishment of a Council for Security and Cooperation in Asia (Kerr, 1994, p. 401; Narine, 2002, p. 103). The Canadian external affairs minister Joe Clark endorsed a similar regional security institution (Narine, 2002, p. 103). The Japanese foreign minister Taro Nakayama, with support from Australia and Canada, unexpectedly suggested in the ASEAN Post Ministerial Conference in 1991 that the annual meeting should be used as a regional security dialogue forum (Narine, 2002, pp. 103–104). This proposal was at first met with opposition from ASEAN states.

Although ASEAN states initially opposed the idea of a regional security forum, the process of multilateral security development within ASEAN continued to evolve. The following year, on 28 January 1992, the ASEAN heads of state announced that the organisation 'could use established fora to promote external dialogues on ... security' and for this purpose it should 'intensify its external dialogues in political and security matters by using the ASEAN Post Ministerial Conferences' (ASEAN, 1992). A year later, in July 1993, at the 26th ASEAN ministerial meeting and post-ministerial conference in Singapore, ASEAN states agreed to establish the ARF (ARF, 2011). The ARF held its first meeting in Bangkok in July 1994. The purpose of the forum is to foster dialogue on security issues in the Asia–Pacific. It consists of twenty-seven states: ten ASEAN countries and Australia, Bangladesh, Canada, China, the Democratic People's Republic of Korea, European Union, India, Japan, Mongolia, New Zealand, Pakistan, Papua New Guinea, Republic of Korea, Russia, Sri Lanka, Timor-Leste and the United States. The ARF serves as a platform for member states' foreign ministers, including those of rival states such as India and Pakistan, Japan and China, and China and the US, to discuss security matters in the region, and therefore prevent potential military escalations and miscalculations (Masilamani and Peterson, 2015, p. 22).

ASEAN ensured that state interactions in ARF are guided by the ASEAN Way approach. The ARF concept paper produced by ASEAN in 1995 laid out the ASEAN Way as the standard practice in the forum (Narine, 1998, p. 36). The concept paper points out how the ARF 'should ... try to forge a consensual approach to security issues' (ASEAN, 1995, p. 1). In order to maintain a non-legalistic approach in the ARF, 'no institutionalisation is expected nor should a Secretariat be established' (ASEAN, 1995, p. 4). The procedure of ARF meetings is 'based on prevailing ASEAN norms and practices' (ASEAN, 1995, p. 5). Therefore, in line with the ASEAN Way, decisions are only 'made by consensus after careful and extensive consultation' and voting is not allowed (ASEAN, 1995, p. 5).

Since the end of the Cold War, ASEAN has played a considerable role in promoting maritime cooperation norms in Southeast Asia through the ARF

(Bradford, 2005). Within the ARF, maritime security continues to be one of the most pressing issues and potential areas for cooperation. The problems posed by potential maritime terrorism and armed robbery against ships are primarily discussed within ARF meetings under the heading of 'counter-terrorism and transnational crimes' together with the problems posed by drug trafficking, human trafficking, arms smuggling, money laundering, and cybercrime (ARF, 2014, p. 2).

The issue of potential maritime terrorism did not receive much attention in ASEAN meetings before the 11 September 2001 terrorist attacks. There was no specific reference made about terrorism, whether in the ASEAN summit declaration, in the joint communiqué of the ministerial meetings, in the joint press statement of ASEAN–US dialogue, or in the statement of the chairman of the ASEAN regional forum (ASEAN, 2001; Chow, 2005). In the weeks and months following the 11 September 2001 attacks, however, we witnessed a speedy policy shift, as the governments of the ASEAN states took firm measures against terrorism, rapidly adopting a strong declaratory position against terrorism and implementing numerous counter-terrorism measures. Within the ARF, although not all countries were directly affected by the problem posed by terrorism, there is a strong realisation regarding the negative implications of serious maritime terrorism attacks for all (Khong and Nesadurai, 2007, p. 66). There is a shared concern that a terrorist incident in busy sea lanes such as the Straits of Malacca and Singapore would hamper trade and energy supplies for many countries in the region (Khong and Nesadurai, 2007, p. 66).

As explained in Chapter 2, ASEAN cooperation against armed robbery of ships is primarily conducted under two ASEAN forums: the ARF and the AMF (Indonesian MFA, 2009a, p. 1; Jailani, 2005, p. 56). The discussion of sea robbery in the ARF has been carried out through ad hoc activities and subsumed under general discussions on transnational crimes for some years.[1] A leap forward took place in 2003 when participating states endorsed the ARF *Statement on Cooperation against Piracy and Other Threats to Maritime Security* during the tenth ARF meeting in Phnom Penh. Since then, the ARF has conducted various meetings to discuss maritime security and carry out maritime exercises (Indonesian MFA, 2009a, pp. 14–21; Jailani, 2005, p. 69).

The AMF was established in 2005. It involves all ASEAN member states. This forum is designed to improve the region's confidence-building measures and capacity building and, in the long run, it is expected to be a maritime dispute settlement forum in the region (Indonesian MFA, 2007, pp. 2, 4; 2009b). Indonesia proposed and hosted the first AMF meeting in July 2010. In October 2012, the Expanded ASEAN Maritime Forum (EAMF) was set up to incorporate not only the ten ASEAN countries but also other participants at the East Asia Summit including Australia, China, India, Japan, New Zealand, the Republic of Korea, Russia and the US (ASEAN, 2012). It first met in October 2012 to discuss various maritime issues, ranging from capacity building to security cooperation (ASEAN, 2012). The AMF and the EAMF do not stray from the ASEAN Way norms. The word 'forum' rather than 'organisation' was carefully selected to reflect the informal nature of the AMF and EAMF. The AMF and the EAMF are intended only as forums to exchange ideas on maritime security issues, and cross-cutting problems 'such as ... illegal fishing, smuggling and maritime transportation' (ASEAN, 2007). The AMF and the EAMF also highlight 'the importance of ... consensus' (ASEAN, 2012).

ASEAN continues to provide important platforms for maritime security cooperation. Officials from ASEAN member countries attend over 300 meetings annually (Ravenhill, 2001, p. 219 as cited in Eaton and Stubbs, 2006, p. 150). In 2015 alone, issues of maritime security featured in nearly fifty informal and official meetings held by ASEAN (ASEAN, 1 June 2015, 8 September 2015). Although the majority of maritime security discussions within ASEAN take place in the AMF and EAMF meetings, in the aftermath of 9/11 maritime security concerns are also discussed in various ASEAN forums. These include the high-level dialogue on maritime security, the working group on customs transit systems, the defence senior officials meeting, the military operations meeting, the military intelligence meeting, the chiefs of defence forces meeting, the ASEAN–China joint working group on the implementation of the declaration on the conduct of parties in the South China Sea (DOC), the seminar–workshop on the implementation of the 2002 ASEAN–China DOC, the network of ASEAN defence and security institutions meeting, the senior officials meeting on transnational crime, the ministerial meeting on transnational crime, the defence ministers' meeting, and the special session, consultation, and summit between ASEAN and its partners including the US, Japan, India and the EU, to mention a few. These meetings help ASEAN member states to improve the information available to other states, build familiarity, foster transparency, reduce distrust and create habits of consultation among them. Constructivists deem that cooperation emerges because of an 'institutionalised habit' (Hurrrell, 2002, p. 55). Thus, regular interactions through various ASEAN channels are expected to develop the conditions for the institutionalised habit of cooperation among member states. Scholars such as Narine, Eaton and Stubbs, and Khong and Nesadurai noted that the accession of the US, China, Australia and the EU to the TAC in recent years has confirmed the gradual acceptance of the ASEAN Way conduct of behaviour in the region by external powers (Eaton and Stubbs, 2006, p. 147; Khong and Nesadurai, 2007, p. 37; Narine, 1998, p. 44). Narine argues that, through various cooperative forums, 'consciously or not ASEAN' tries 'to convince players ... to adopt norms and rules that reflect ASEAN's values' (Narine, 1998, p. 44).

Debunking the ASEAN Way? Cooperation with extra-regional states

A constructivist would be expected to argue that shared identity plays a central role in states' cooperation. Constructivism argues that states that share a similar identity are more likely to cooperate than those who cannot identify positively with each other. Scholars including Ball, Johnston, Acharya and Tan echo the

138 *When shared identity does not matter*

constructivist argument regarding the importance of shared identity in informing states' cooperation. They point out that ASEAN states have a sense of shared identity, often called the 'ASEAN Way' norm, that puts emphasis on the role of consensus and accommodation to settle disputes and advance cooperation on security among them (Acharya, 1992; 1995; 1997, pp. 328–329; 1998, p. 80; 2004, pp. 249, 256; Acharya and Tan, 2006, pp. 42, 53; Ball, 1993, p. 53; Johnston, 1999, pp. 294–295). Given the 'ASEAN Way' identity is believed to be embraced by ASEAN states, ASEAN membership is an appropriate proxy for shared identity. In this context, Indonesia is expected to cooperate with other ASEAN states, and to be less likely to do so with non-ASEAN states.

This section argues that the constructivist argument regarding the role of shared identity cannot account for Indonesia's varying participation across cases. Indonesia joined agreements that included non-ASEAN states, as shown in the case of bilateral arrangements with the US, Japan, Australia and India, the ISPS Code, the WCO SAFE Framework, the APEC TRP, the ARF and the AMF. It also joined agreements that exclusively involved ASEAN states, including the BIMP EAGA MoUs on sea linkages and the transport of goods, the trilateral information-sharing agreement among Indonesia, Malaysia and the Philippines, the ASEAN counter-terrorism convention, two coordinated patrol arrangements with Malaysia and Singapore, bilateral defence agreements with the Philippines, and the MSP agreement.

In a number of counter-maritime-terrorism cooperation cases, such as the three Indonesia–Australia bilateral agreements, the US-led initiatives to deal with maritime terrorism such as the C-TPAT and the IPS, and the WCO, Indonesia has cooperated closely with non-ASEAN states. As part of these cooperation initiatives, Indonesia has carried out a number of tasks that could be deemed as intrusive and could potentially breach the country's sovereignty. Indonesia decided to join the MoU on counter-terrorism, the Lombok Treaty and the implementation arrangement of the Lombok Treaty with Australia, although Australia is not a member of ASEAN. As part of the MoU on counter-terrorism, Indonesia allows the deployment of the Australian Federal Police (AFP) team, which consists of thirty personnel, to work with the Indonesian Police in investigating a range of terrorism incidents. These incidents included the 12 October 2002 Bali bombing, the 5 August 2003 Marriot hotel bombing in Jakarta, the 9 September 2004 bombing outside the Australian Embassy in Jakarta, the 1 October 2005 Bali bombing and the 17 July 2009 Marriot and Ritz Carlton hotel bombings (Australian National Audit Office, 2012, p. 58; Indonesian Coordinating Ministry for Political, Legal and Security Affairs, 2007, p. 166). As part of the 2012 defence arrangement, Indonesia also enables rapid clearance for Australian aircraft to operate in its territorial airspace and to land and refuel, and maintains coordination between the Australian Search and Rescue agency and Indonesian agencies (BASARNAS, Kohadnudnas) in maritime operations (Sekretaris Kabinet Indonesia, 2012). This cooperation continues despite diplomatic tensions caused by the Australian Navy's reported incursions into Indonesian maritime territory in January 2014.

When shared identity does not matter 139

As explained in Chapter 3, although the US is a non-ASEAN state, Indonesia cooperates extensively in the area of counter-terrorism with Washington especially through the C-TPAT and the IPS program. The Indonesian government allows the US CBP to enforce the C-TPAT rules and monitor compliance in Indonesian territory. Under the IPS program, Indonesia has had to make substantial adjustments, including providing access to restricted areas in its port facilities to the US since 2005 (Indonesian DGST, 2010, p. 2). The US Coast Guard has even visited a number of port facilities twice. Although the C-TPAT and the IPS program could be deemed as intrusive, the Indonesian government has been willing to participate.

Despite the fact that the majority of the WCO SAFE Framework's over 150 states are not members of ASEAN, Indonesia has shown its commitment to joining the framework. This is demonstrated by Indonesia's willingness to accept the SAFE Framework monitoring team. Although the SAFE Framework standards and programmes are voluntary, the WCO established a review mechanism in the form of the WCO diagnostic mission (WCO, 2007, p. 51). From 2–13 February 2009, the WCO diagnostic mission visited Indonesia to survey Indonesia's compliance with the SAFE Framework. The WCO diagnostic mission reviewed seven points concerning Indonesia's adoption of the framework. The seven points were: the Indonesian Customs future strategic plan; financial management; human resources management (recruitment system; assessment of officials' performance and training); customs enforcement; national legislation; risk management procedure; and post clearance audit (facilitation service for priority importers).[2] As part of the review, the diagnostic mission provided feedback and recommendations for Indonesia. Despite the initiative introducing a third party review mechanism involving non-ASEAN states, Indonesia was supportive of this cooperation arrangement.

Shared identity did not play a major part in cases of Indonesia's non-cooperation either. Indonesia cancelled the defence cooperation agreement with Singapore that only involved Indonesia and Singapore, both ASEAN member states. As mentioned in Chapter 2, the DCA that was signed by the two states' ministers of defence in April 2007 was not successful. The DCA required Indonesia to provide the Singaporean Armed Forces with sites for individual and joint air, land, and naval military exercises (*Xinhua*, 27 April 2007a; 27 April 2007b). The DCA was a necessary trade off to gain Singapore's approval for the extradition treaty (Indonesian Democratic Party of Struggle, 2013; Indonesian Parliament, 25 June 2007, 17 September 2007). Indonesia cancelled the agreement in 2007, after Singapore's rejection of the retroactive application of the extradition treaty for fifteen years (*Antara*, 2007; Indonesian Coordinating Ministry for Political, Legal and Security Affairs, 2008, p. 55). Indonesia also refused to participate in cooperation arrangements that were led and involved a large number of non-ASEAN states, as shown in the case of the SUA convention, the PSI, the CSI, the RMSI and the ReCAAP.

A closer observation of Indonesia's participation in maritime security arrangements shows that Indonesia is most likely to cooperate with states with which it shares common maritime boundaries. Most of these states happen to be members of ASEAN. Indonesia shares maritime boundaries in the Straits of Malacca and Singapore with Malaysia, Singapore, and Thailand. In the Sulu-Sulawesi Seas, the maritime boundaries are shared by Indonesia, the Philippines, Malaysia and Brunei Darussalam. Cooperation with these neighbouring countries is essential to secure the common boundaries. As a result, Indonesia has developed various cooperation initiatives at bilateral, sub-regional and regional levels with its neighbouring countries, such as Malaysia, Singapore and the Philippines. Maritime security cooperation among Indonesia and these neighbouring countries began many years before the international community started to pay attention to concerns posed by maritime terrorism and armed robbery against ships in the aftermath of the 9/11 terrorist attacks.

In the Straits of Malacca and Singapore, Indonesian-coordinated patrol arrangements with Malaysia and Singapore at bilateral and trilateral levels are the most advanced arrangements to counter armed robbery against ships that Jakarta has developed with its cooperation partners. The bilateral Indonesia–Singapore and Indonesia–Malaysia coordinated patrol arrangements dated back to 1992 when the first surge of sea robbery attacks took place in their common maritime boundaries along the Straits of Malacca and Singapore. The two coordinated patrol agreements allow law enforcement vessels from each state to cross boundaries when conducting hot pursuit (Singapore MoD, 2012; Sondakh, 2004, p. 23).[3] As explained in Chapter 1, in 2004 the three littoral states established a new trilateral coordinated patrol arrangement called the Malacca Straits Patrol (MSP) and invited Thailand to join. The MSP agreement incorporates cross-border air and sea patrols. Indonesia has not only participated in the initiative but also proposed the idea to Malaysia and Singapore. In 2007, Indonesia designed the standard operation procedure to enable Thailand, another country that it shares maritime boundaries with, to get involved in the MSP (*Antara*, 2005).

In the aftermath of the 9/11 attacks, the security of the Sulu and Sulawesi Seas was put under further international scrutiny. Acts of maritime terrorism in this area generated international concern. In the Sulu Sea, the Abu Sayyaf Group (ASG) and the Moro Islamic Liberation Front, both based in the southern part of the Philippines, have been accused of carrying out attacks against ships to generate income (Bakti, 2010, pp. 299–300; Storey, 2007). The waters bordering Indonesia, Malaysia and the Philippines have been viewed as gateways for terrorists travelling from one part of Southeast Asia to another. Members of the Jamaah Islamiyah, a Southeast Asian terrorist group, and other Islamic militant groups from Indonesia use this route to travel to training camps in the Philippines (Bakti, 2010, pp. 299–300). They travel from Kalimantan Timur to Sabah (Malaysia) and then proceed to Tawi-Tawi and Sulu/Mindanao (the Philippines) (Bakti, 2010, pp. 299–300). In mid-September 2013, the Moro National Liberation Front's attacks on Zamboanga City and clashes with the Philippines' military in Jolo Island have forced 30,000 civilians to flee their homes, destabilising order and security in the Sulu area (*Business World*, 2013). In March and April 2016, the ASG hijacked three vessels – a TB Henry tugboat, a Cristi barge

When shared identity does not matter 141

boat and a Brahma 12 tug boat – and held hostage fourteen Indonesian seamen (*Tribun News*, 2016), ten of whom were released in early May 2016 after the seamen's employer Patria Maritime Airlines paid a ransom of US$1.14 million (*Jakarta Post*, 2016). These circumstances put more pressure on enhancing security cooperation in the Sulu and Sulawesi Seas.

Indonesia responded to this pressure by enhancing the bilateral, trilateral and sub-regional cooperation that involved the littoral states of the Philippines, Malaysia and Brunei as they shared maritime boundaries. Cooperation with these countries was seen as the most practical solution to the problem posed by armed robbery attacks and maritime terrorism. Indonesia and the Philippines, for instance, have carried out coordinated patrols, named Corpat Philindo, to secure their boundaries in the Sulu and Sulawesi seas since 1989, before maritime terrorism received worldwide attention after the 9/11 attacks (Acharya, 1990, p. 8). Coordinated patrols enable patrol vessels from each country to cross-boundaries when pursuing perpetrators of armed robbery against ships.[4] After the 9/11 attacks, the Philippines, Indonesia and Malaysia formalised a tripartite cooperation agreement to strengthen maritime security cooperation in the tri-border sea areas of the Sulu and Sulawesi seas by signing the information exchange and establishment of communication procedures agreement on 7 May 2002, to which Thailand and Cambodia later acceded (Indonesian Immigration Agency, 2011; Karniol, 2005, as cited in Rosenberg and Chung, 2008, p. 60). The agreement aims to strengthen border control through designating entry and exit points and sea lanes, and harmonise their efforts to combat terrorism. As explained in Chapter 2, Indonesia, Brunei Darussalam, Malaysia and the Philippines then signed the MoU on establishing and promoting efficient and integrated sea linkages in 2007 and launched the MoU on transit and interstate transport of goods in 2009. The two agreements seek to improve the security of maritime trade and movement of people in the shared border areas of Indonesia, Malaysia, the Philippines and Brunei.

In sum, it can be concluded that shared identity cannot account for the full range of cases involving both Indonesia's participation and its non-participation in cooperation arrangements. This suggests that there is a need to look for the explanation for Indonesia's varying response towards international maritime security cooperation elsewhere. The next chapter will analyse the way in which the calculation of gains informs Indonesia's cooperation and non-cooperation in maritime security initiatives.

Conclusion

This chapter examined whether the ASEAN Way, which has been deemed as the norm that helps to advance cooperation among Southeast Asian countries, informs Indonesia's decision to cooperate. The evidence shows that the constructivist argument about the role of shared identity cannot account for Indonesia's participation across cooperation cases. Indonesia joined counter-maritime terrorism cooperation arrangements that involved non-ASEAN states, for

142 When shared identity does not matter

instance the three bilateral arrangements with the US, Japan and Australia, the ISPS Code, the SAFE Framework and the TRP. It also joined those that exclusively involved ASEAN states, such as the EAGA MoUs on sea linkages and transport of goods, the agreement on information exchange and the ASEAN counter-terrorism convention.

Indonesia did join cooperation arrangements to counter sea robbery which exclusively involved ASEAN states – for instance the two patrol agreements with Malaysia and Singapore, the defence arrangement with the Philippines and the sub-regional MSP agreement. However, Indonesia also joined agreements that engaged non-ASEAN states – such as the three bilateral arrangements with India, Japan, and China, the ARF and the AMF.

The constructivist argument about the role of shared identity in informing states' cooperation also could not account for Indonesia's decision not to participate in various cooperation arrangements to deal with maritime terrorism and armed robbery against ships. Indonesia's rejection of three arrangements to counter maritime terrorism – the SUA convention, the CSI and the PSI – was consistent with the constructivist expectation on the role of shared identity in informing cooperation, but only to the degree that the three initiatives were proposed by the US, which is a non-ASEAN state, and involved a large number of states, most of whom were not members of ASEAN. However, since Indonesia also cooperated with the US and other non-ASEAN states in various arrangements to counter maritime terrorism, including the WCO SAFE Framework and the APEC TRP to mention a couple, shared identity cannot account for Indonesia's decision to join or not to join an arrangement.

Shared identity also cannot explain Indonesia's non-participation in a group of cooperation arrangements that dealt with the threat of sea robbery attacks. Indonesia refused to cooperate with an ASEAN state, as shown in the case of the DCA with Singapore, and non-ASEAN states, in the case of the RMSI and the ReCAAP.

This book seeks to examine why Indonesia cooperates in some maritime security initiatives but not others. In this chapter, it has been shown that shared identity does not influence Indonesia's participation in maritime security cooperation. The next chapter examines whether a gains calculation can explain Indonesia's varying participation across maritime security cooperation arrangements.

Notes

1 E-mail correspondence with the ASEAN Secretariat security cooperation officer, ASEAN Political Security Community Department, 30 June 2010.
2 Interview with a high government official at the Indonesian Directorate of Multilateral Cooperation (the WCO Desk), Customs and Excise, Ministry of Finance, Jakarta, 3 November 2011.
3 Interview with government official at the Indonesian Directorate of International Cooperation, Maritime Security Coordinating Board (Jakarta, 3 July 2010).
4 Discussion with an official from the Philippines maritime agency (New York, 25 January 2013).

References

Acharya, Amitav. (1990). 'A Survey of Military Cooperation Among the ASEAN States: Bilateralism or Alliance?' Centre for International and Strategic Studies Occasional Paper No. 14, available at http://yciss.info.yorku.ca/files/2012/06/OP14-Acharya.pdf. Last accessed 16 January 2013.

Acharya, Amitav. (1992). 'Regional Military-Security Cooperation in the Third World: A Conceptual Analysis of the Relevance and Limitations of ASEAN (Association of Southeast Asian Nations)'. *Journal of Peace Research*, 29 February, pp. 7–21.

Acharya, Amitav. (1995). 'A Regional Security Community in Southeast Asia?'. *Journal of Strategic Studies* 18:3, pp. 175–200.

Acharya, Amitav. (1997). 'Ideas, Identity and Institution Building: From the "ASEAN Way" to the "Asia–Pacific Way"?'. *The Pacific Review* 10:3, pp. 319–346.

Acharya, Amitav. (1998). 'Culture, Security, Multilateralism: The "ASEAN Way" and Regional Order'. *Contemporary Security Policy* 19:1, pp. 55–84.

Acharya, Amitav. (2001). *Constructing a Security Community in Southeast Asia: ASEAN and the Problem of Regional Order*. London: Routledge.

Acharya, Amitav. (2004). 'How Ideas Spread: Whose Norms Matter? Norm Localization and Institutional Change in Asian Regionalism'. *International Organization* 58:2, pp. 239–275.

Acharya, Amitav. (2011). *The Making of Southeast Asia: International Relations of a Region*. Ithaca, NY: Cornell University Press.

Acharya, Amitav and Tan, See Seng. (2006). 'Betwixt Balance and Community: America, ASEAN and the Security of Southeast Asia'. *International Relations of the Asia Pacific* 6:1, pp. 37–59.

Acharya, Amitav and Johnston, Alastair Iain. (2007). *Crafting Cooperation: Regional International Institutions in Comparative Perspective*. Cambridge: Cambridge University Press.

Antara. (2005). 'Indonesia Formulating Rules for Thai Role in the Malacca Straits Patrol', 3 September 2005, accessed from the Newsbank database.

Antara. (2007). 'Anggota DPR: Singapura Secara Faktual Telah Membatalkan DCA', 19 September 2007, available at www.antaranews.com/berita/1190136535/anggota-dpr-singapura-secara-faktual-telah-membatalkan-dca. Last accessed 28 January 2013.

ASEAN. (1967). 'The Asean Declaration (Bangkok Declaration) Bangkok', 8 August 1967, available from www.asean.org/the-asean-declaration-bangkok-declaration-bangkok-8-august-1967/. Last accessed 21 May 2016.

ASEAN. (1976). 'The Declaration of ASEAN Concord, Bali, Indonesia', 24 February 1976, available at www.asean.org/?static_post=declaration-of-asean-concord-indonesia-24-february-1976. Last accessed 21 May 2016.

ASEAN. (1992). 'Singapore Declaration of 1992 Singapore', 28 January 1992, available atwww.asean.org/?static_post=singapore-declaration-of-1992-singapore-28-january-1992. Last accessed 21 May 2016.

ASEAN. (1995). 'The ASEAN Regional Forum: A Concept Paper', available at http://aseanregionalforum.asean.org/files/library/Terms%20of%20References%20and%20Concept%20Papers/Concept%20Paper%20of%20ARF.pdf. Last accessed 25 May 2016.

ASEAN. (2001). 'ASEAN Document Series from 1967–2001', available at www.aseansec.org. Last accessed 20 July 2008.

ASEAN. (2007). 'ASEAN and ARF Maritime Security Dialogue and Cooperation', 4 October 2007, available at www.un.org/depts/los/consultative_process/mar_sec_submissions/asean.pdf. Last accessed 26 May 2016.

ASEAN. (2012). 'Chairman's Statement, 3rd ASEAN Maritime Forum', 9 October 2012, available at www.asean.org/news/asean-statement-communiques/item/chairman-s-statement-3rd-asean-maritime-forum. Last accessed 15 October 2012.
ASEAN. (2015). 'ASEAN Notional Calendar 2015', 1 June 2015, available at www.asean.org/official-meetings-2015/. Last accessed 20 May 2016.
ASEAN. (2015). 'Non-Traditional Security Joint Calendar 2015', 8 September 2015, available at www.asean.org/official-meetings-2015/. Last accessed 20 May 2016.
ASEAN Regional Forum (ARF). (2011). 'About the ASEAN Regional Forum', available at http://aseanregionalforum.asean.org/about.html. Last accessed 21 May 2016.
ARF. (2014). 'ASEAN Regional Forum Work Plan for Counter Terrorism and Transnational Crime 2014–2015', available from http://aseanregionalforum.asean.org/files/References/ARF%20Work%20Plan%20on%20CTTC%202014-2015.pdf. Last accessed 21 May 2016.
Australian National Audit Office. (2012). *Audit Report No. 30 2011–12 Performance Audit: Fighting Terrorism at its Source Australian Federal Police*, available at www.anao.gov.au/~/media/Uploads/Audit%20Reports/2011%2012/201112%20Audit%20Report%20No%2030.pdf. Last accessed 19 October 2012.
Bakti, Ikrar Nusa. (2010). 'Bilateral Relations between Indonesia and the Philippines: Stable and Cooperative', in *International Relations in Southeast Asia: Between Bilateralism and Multilateralism*, N. Ganesan and Ramses Amer (eds). Singapore: ISEAS.
Ball, Desmond. (1993). 'Strategic Culture in the Asia-Pacific Region'. *Security Studies* 3:1, pp. 44–74.
Bradford, John F. (2005). 'The Growing Prospects for Maritime Security Cooperation in Southeast Asia'. *Naval War College Review* 56:3, pp. 63–86.
Business World. (2013). 'Surveil', 13 September 2013.
Chau, Andrew. (2008). 'Security Community and Southeast Asia: Australia, the US and ASEAN's Counter-Terror Strategy'. *Asian Survey* 48:4, pp. 626–649.
Chow, Jonathan T. (2005). 'ASEAN Counterterrorism Cooperation Since 9/11'. *Asian Survey* 45:2, pp. 302–321.
Colbert, Evelyn. (1986). 'ASEAN as a Regional Organization: Economics, Politics and Security', in *ASEAN in Regional and Global Context*, Jackson, Paribatra and Djiwandono (eds). Berkeley, CA: University of California.
Coquia, Jorge R. (1990). 'Maritime Boundary Problems in the South China Sea', *University of British Columbia Law Review* 24:1, pp. 117–125.
Eaton, Sarah and Stubbs, Richard. (2006). 'Is ASEAN Powerful? Neo-Realist versus Constructivist Approaches to Power in Southeast Asia'. *The Pacific Review* 19:2, pp. 135–155.
Flores, Jamil Maidan and Abad, Jun. (1997). 'The History: Founding of ASEAN', 8 August 1997, available at www.asean.org/asean/about-asean/history/. Last accessed 19 May 2016.
Hurrell, Andrew. (2002). 'International Society and the Study of Regimes: A Reflective Approach', in *Regime Theory And International Relations*, Volker Rittberger and Peter Mayer (eds). Oxford: Clarendon Press.
Indonesian Coordinating Ministry for Political, Legal and Security Affairs. (2007). *Kumpulan Pidato Menteri Koordinator Bidang Politik Hukum dan Keamanan Republik Indonesia*. Jakarta: Kementerian Koordinator Bidang Politik Hukum dan Keamanan Indonesia.
Indonesian Coordinating Ministry for Political, Legal and Security Affairs. (2008). *Evaluasi Pengelolaan Bidang Politik, Hukum dan Keamanan Tahun 2007*. Jakarta: Indonesian Coordinating Ministry for Political, Legal and Security Affairs.

Indonesian Democratic Party of Struggle. (2013). 'Kebijakan Pemerintah Yang Dikritisi, Implikasi Bagi Nasib Rakyat, Sikap Politik Fraksi PDI Perjuangan', 26 January 2013, available at www.pdiperjuangan-jatim.org/v03/?mod=release&id=9. Last accessed 27 January 2013.

Indonesian Directorate General of Sea Transportation (DGST). (2010). *Kronologis Kunjungan US Coast Guard di Indonesia*. Jakarta: Direktorat Jenderal Perhubungan Laut.

Indonesian Immigration Agency. (2011). 'Tri-Lateral Inter-Agency Maritime Law Enforcement Workshop (TIAMLEW) III', 5 April 2011, available at www.imigrasi.go.id/index.php?option=com_content&task=view&id=517&Itemid=34. Last accessed 13 July 2011.

Indonesian Ministry of Foreign Affairs (MFA). (2007). *Pertemuan Kelompok Ahli: Optimalisasi Kerjasama Kelautan Intra ASEAN Melalui Pembentukan ASEAN Maritim Forum (Bandung, 21–22 Maret 2007)*. Jakarta: Badan Pengkajian dan Pengembangan Kebijakan.

Indonesian MFA. (2009a). *ASEAN Regional Forum: The First Inter-Sessional Meeting on Maritime Security, Surabaya, Indonesia, 5–6 March 2009*. Jakarta: Directorate General of Asia Pacific and African Affairs.

Indonesian MFA. (2009b). 'Background Singkat Pembentukan ASEAN Maritime Forum', made available to author through an email correspondence with the Head of Security Division, *Directorate* of *ASEAN Political and Security* Cooperation, Heru H. Subolo (Jakarta, 26 August 2009).

Indonesian MFA. (2014). 'Gerakan Non-Blok', 28 January 2014, available from www.kemlu.go.id/id/kebijakan/kerjasama-multilateral/Pages/Gerakan-Non-Blok.aspx. Last accessed 24 May 2016.

Indonesian Parliament. (2007). 'Rapat Kerja Komisi I DPR RI dengan Menteri Luar Negeri', 25 June 2007, available at www.dpr.go.id/id/komisi/komisi1/report/149/Rapat-Kerja-Komisi-I-DPR-RI-Dengan-Menteri-Luar-Negeri. Last accessed 24 April 2013.

Indonesian Parliament. (2007). 'Report of the Working Meeting of Commission I of the Indonesian House of Representatives with the Minister of Defense and Armed Forces Commander', 17 September 2007, available atwww.dpr.go.id/id/Komisi/Komisi-I/laporan-singkat. Last accessed 15 January 2013.

Intan, Rocky. (2015). 'ASEAN's Relevance and Benefit: A Perspective from ASEAN'. *The Indonesian Quarterly* 43:1, pp. 7–20.

International Maritime Bureau. (2005). *Piracy and Armed Robbery against Ships Annual Report January 1st–December 31st, 2005*. Kuala Lumpur: IMB.

Jailani, Abdulkadir (Staf Direktorat Perjanjian Politik Keamanan Kewilayahan Kementerian Luar Negeri). (2005). 'Pokok-Pokok Masalah Kebijakan Luar Negeri Tentang *Issue* Keamanan Laut dan Kewilayahan Selat Malaka', in *Pertemuan Kelompok Ahli: Kebijakan Terpadu Pengelolaan Keamanan Selat Malaka*. Jakarta: Badan Pengkajian dan Pengembangan Kebijakan Departemen Luar Negeri Republik Indonesia.

Jakarta Post. (2016). 'Who Released the Sailors? Untold Story Behind Hostage Rescue', 4 May 2016, available at www.thejakartapost.com/news/2016/05/04/who-released-the-sailors-untold-story-behind-hostage-rescue.html. Last accessed 4 May 2016.

Johnston, Alistair Ian. (1999). 'The Myth of the ASEAN Way? Explaining the Evolution of the ASEAN Regional Forum', in *Imperfect Unions: Security Institutions over Time and Space*. New York: Oxford University Press.

Kahin, Audrey R. and Kahin, George McT. (1995). *Subversion As Foreign Policy: the Secret Eisenhower and Dulles Debacle in Indonesia*. New York: The New Press.

Kerr, Pauline. (1994). 'The Security Dialogue in the Asia-Pacific'. *The Pacific Review* 7:4, pp. 397–409.

Khoman, Thanat. (1986). 'ASEAN in a Regional and Global Context', in *Regional and Global Context*. Berkeley, CA: University of California Berkeley.

Khong, Yuen Foong and Nesadurai, Helen E.S. (2007). 'Hanging Together, Institutional Design, and Cooperation in Southeast Asia: AFTA and the ARF', in *Crafting Cooperation: Regional Institutions in Comparative Perspective*, Acharya and Johnston (eds). Cambridge: Cambridge University Press.

March, James G. and Olsen, Johan P. (1998). 'The Institutional Dynamics of International Political Orders'. *International Organization* 52:4, pp. 943–969.

Masilamani, Logan and Peterson, Jimmy. (2015). 'ASEAN's Constructive Engagement Policy'. *The Indonesian Quarterly* 43:1, pp. 21–36.

Narine, Shaun. (1998). 'Institutional Theory and Southeast Asia: The Case of ASEAN'. *World Affairs* 161:1, pp. 33–47.

Narine, Shaun. (2002). *Explaining ASEAN: Regionalism in Southeast Asia*. Boulder, CO: Lynne Rienner.

Rosenberg, David and Chung, Christopher. (2008). 'Maritime Security in the South China Sea: Coordinating Coastal and User State Priorities'. *Ocean Development and International Law* 39:1, pp. 51–68.

Sekretaris Kabinet Indonesia. (2012). 'RI–Australia Tingkatkan Kerjasama Keamanan Laut', 5 September 2012, available at http://setkab.go.id/berita-5570-ri-australia-tingkatkan-kerja-sama-keamanan-laut.html. Last accessed 22 October 2012.

Singapore Ministry of Defence. (2012). 'Fact Sheet: Indonesia–Singapore Coordinated Patrol (ISCP)', 27 May 2012, available at www.mindef.gov.sg/imindef/press_room/official_releases/nr/2012/may/11may12_nr/11may12_fs.html#.UjBduX8neCk. Last accessed 11 September 2013.

Singapore Ministry of Foreign Affairs. (2003). 'Special Agreement for Submission to the International Court of Justice of the Dispute Between Malaysia and Singapore Concerning Sovereignty Over Pedra Branca/Pulau Batu Puteh, Middle Rocks and South Ledge', 6 February 2003, available at www.mfa.gov.sg/content/dam/mfa/images/media_center/special_events/pedra_branca/specialagreement.pdf. Last accessed 23 May 2016.

Sondakh, Bernard Kent. (2004). 'Pengamanan Wilayah Laut Indonesia'. *Indonesian Journal of International Law*, pp. 1–26.

Storey, Ian. (2007). 'Triborder Sea is SE Asian Danger Zone', *Asia Times*, 18 October 2007.

Straits Times. (2005). 'Rights to Area Come with Islands', 8 March 2005, accessed from the Newsbank database.

Tribun News. (2016). 'Masih Gelap Nasib Empat WNI yang Diculik di Perbatasan Malaysia-Filipina, Belum Ada Komunikasi', 27 April 2016, available at http://jateng.tribunnews.com/2016/04/27/masih-gelap-nasib-empat-wni-yang-diculik-di-perbatasan-malaysia-filipina-belum-ada-komunikasi. Last accessed 28 April 2016.

United States Department of State. (2016). 'Bandung Conference (Asian–African Conference), 1955', 24 May 2016, available at https://history.state.gov/milestones/1953-1960/bandung-conf. Last accessed 24 May 2016.

World Customs Organization. (2007). *WCO SAFE Framework of Standards*, available at www.wcoomd.org/files/1.%20Public%20files/PDFandDocuments/Procedures%20and%20Facilitation/safe_package/safe_package_I.pdf. Last accessed 11 August 2011.

Xinhua. (2007a). 'Indonesia–Singapore Defense Cooperation to Benefit Regional Stability: Susilo', 27 April 2007, accessed from the Newsbank database.

Xinhua. (2007b). 'Indonesia–Singapore Extradition Treaty Effective for Bringing Back Fugitive Corrupters', 27 April 2007, accessed from the Newsbank database.

5 Gains and losses

Introduction

This chapter will be based theoretically on the neorealist and neoliberal debate regarding the calculation of costs and benefits. Neorealists argue that states emphasise the importance of relative gains from cooperation (Waltz, 1979, p. 105). States weigh how much they gain from the cooperation in comparison to the other (Krasner, 2002, p. 139). In contrast, for neoliberals it is absolute gains rather than relative gains that matter for states (Keohane, 1984, p. 80). States will cooperate if they would be better off than if they had not cooperated (Keohane and Martin, 1995, pp. 44–45). In this chapter, I argue that the calculation of absolute gains trumps concern over relative gains. Indonesia only chose to cooperate when the benefits of cooperation exceeded the costs.

To elaborate on the above argument, the first part of this chapter will discuss the calculation of relative gains across all cooperation initiatives dealing with maritime terrorism and sea robbery. The second part of this chapter will discuss the calculation of costs and gains in absolute terms. It will assess both the sovereignty and implementation costs brought about by various agreements. This is important, since the burgeoning literature on Indonesia's maritime security overstates the sovereignty costs. As a consequence, it overlooks Indonesia's willingness to participate in maritime security cooperation including arrangements that involve cross-border sea and air patrols and to provide other states with access to its port facilities, airspace and land territory.

Relative gains' lack of explanatory purchase

A neorealist would highlight the importance of relative gains concerns in informing Indonesia's participation. As a middle power, Indonesia would be expected to cooperate with larger states and not with near-power states. With this in mind, would it be possible to explain Indonesia's cooperation through the calculation of relative gains?

The evidence shows that Indonesia's participation in cooperation initiatives to address maritime terrorism including bilateral arrangements with the US, Japan, and Australia, the two BIMP-EAGA MoUs, a trilateral information-sharing agreement, the ASEAN Counter-Terrorism Convention, the ISPS Code, the WCO SAFE Framework and the APEC TRP is not consistent with the neorealist argument regarding the importance of concerns about relative gains. As neorealists would expect, Indonesia chose to cooperate with the US, Japan and Australia, states with larger defence capabilities than Indonesia. However, as Indonesia also decided to join cooperation arrangements that involve near-peer states such as Malaysia and Singapore, the relative gains argument offers no explanatory power to understand Indonesia's cooperation across the range of cases. These cooperation arrangements include the BIMP-EAGA MoUs, a trilateral information-sharing agreement, the ASEAN Counter-Terrorism Convention, the ISPS Code, the WCO SAFE Framework and the APEC TRP.

Indonesia's participation in the two intra-ASEAN cooperation arrangements – the BIMP EAGA MoUs and the agreement on information exchange and establishment of communication between Indonesia, Malaysia and the Philippines – confirms the absence of a calculation of relative gains particularly well. Indonesia did not opt out of the BIMP-EAGA initiatives, although they involved Malaysia, Indonesia's near-peer competitor. Indonesia would have been expected to raise concerns that the MoU on sea linkages and the transit and inter-state transport of goods could significantly favour its partners, particularly if they had better policy planning. As Elisabeth explains, Indonesia's economic policy related to the EAGA 'is more like an instant policy, intended primarily to deal with problems of economic inequality between the western and eastern regions of Indonesia' (Elisabeth, 2008, p. 44). State strategies and preparation in cooperation are particularly important, as EAGA areas have similarities in economic features. These areas offer potential bases for the oil and gas industries, plantations, agriculture, fisheries and forestry (Dent and Richter, 2011, pp. 44–45; Elisabeth, 2008, pp. 36–37). Consequently, EAGA members tend to compete for the same market (Elisabeth, 2008, p. 166). This circumstance could potentially increase Indonesia's sensitivity over relative gains concerns. Yet Indonesia not only joined the EAGA initiatives but also played an important role as a lead country (Indonesian DGST, 2010c, p. 1; Yussof and Kasim, 2003, p. 43).[1] The Indonesian MoT both chaired the sea linkages working group and hosted the 2009 BIMP-EAGA fourth transport ministers meeting at which the two initiatives were drafted and negotiated (BIMP-EAGA North Sulawesi, 2009; BIMP-EAGA, 2011; Indonesian DGST, 2010c, p. 1).[2] Indonesian officials from the BIMP-EAGA national secretariat and the MoT and government documents confirmed that Indonesia was actively involved in exploring potential cooperation activities, formulating agreement drafts, proposing new sea routes and project plans, choosing designated gateway ports and conveying its disagreement to other states' requests under the EAGA framework (Dinas Perhubungan Kalimantan Timur, 2011; Indonesian Ministry of Trade, 2010, pp. 19, 58–59).[3]

Indonesia did not oppose the agreement on information exchange with Malaysia and the Philippines. This was despite Indonesia having unsettled maritime borders with Malaysia that have generated military standoffs on a number of occasions. Rather, Jakarta was willing to increase cooperation by stepping up joint counter-terrorism efforts and sharing sensitive security information with other participating states.

Despite the ISPS Code, the SAFE Framework and the APEC TRP included Indonesia's near-peer competitors such as Malaysia, Thailand and Singapore, Indonesia chose to join these cooperation arrangements. The government did not raise any concern that the extensive requirement of the ISPS Code, the SAFE Framework or the TRP would work in favour of developed countries or neighbouring countries, including Malaysian and Singaporean ports and shipping businesses (Bakorkamla, 2004, p. 6; 2010 pp. 25–26; Sekretariat Jenderal Departemen Kelautan dan Perikanan, 2007, p. 38).[4]

In efforts to halt armed robbery attacks against ships, Indonesia has joined the coordinated patrol agreements with Singapore and Malaysia, has closely cooperated with the Philippines, Japan, India and China to address armed robbery against ships, and has taken part in the MSP agreement and ASEAN initiatives to counter sea robbery.

Indonesia's decision to join the two defence agreements with the Philippines and India and the bilateral arrangements with Japan and China meets the neorealist expectation on the importance of relative gains, insofar as the middle power Indonesia cooperated with India, Japan and China, states with larger defence capabilities in comparison to Indonesia, and the Philippines, a smaller state in comparison to Indonesia. However, the relative gains calculation cannot offer a sufficient explanation, because Indonesia does not cooperate with only larger or smaller states but also with its near-peer competitors (for instance, in the two coordinated patrol agreements, with Singapore and Malaysia).

Concern over relative gains did not inform Indonesia's decision to join the two coordinated patrol arrangements with Malaysia and Singapore, the MSP agreement or the ASEAN counter sea robbery initiatives carried out under the ARF and the AMF. Although these cooperation initiatives involved Malaysia and Singapore, two near-peer states, Indonesia chose to join these initiatives. In the case of the MSP agreement, Indonesia not only participated in the initiative but also proposed the idea to Malaysia and Singapore and, later in 2007, designed the standard operation procedure to enable Thailand, another near-peer state, to get involved in the MSP (*Antara*, 3 September 2005).[5] Indonesia did not show any sensitivity over relative gains when proposing initiatives and taking part in the ASEAN cooperation frameworks to halt sea robbery. In contrast to the neorealist expectation regarding the calculation of relative gains, Indonesia was willing to cooperate not only with larger or smaller states but also near-peer states such as Malaysia, Thailand and Singapore who also joined the ARF and the AMF.

Having discussed Indonesia's participation in maritime security cooperation to address maritime terrorism and armed robbery against ships, the next part of this chapter will look at whether Indonesia's decision not to join the SUA convention, the CSI, the PSI, the RMSI, the ReCAAP and the DCA with Singapore conforms to the neorealist expectation regarding the role of relative gains concerns.

Gains and losses 151

A neorealist would expect to see Indonesia's cooperation in the SUA convention, the CSI and the PSI, because the military capabilities of the US – the leading state in the cooperation – are much larger than those of Indonesia. Relative gains should not matter in the three cases, because the power gap between Indonesia and the US is simply too wide. Indonesia's cooperation or non-cooperation in the SUA convention, the CSI and the PSI would not be able to close the vast power gap between the two. In contrast to this expectation, Indonesia refused to participate in the Convention, the CSI and the PSI.

Indonesia's rejection of the RMSI, the ReCAAP and the DCA also did not reflect concerns over relative gains. The RMSI is an initiative which was proposed and promoted by the US. In comparison, the ReCAAP was led by Japan. Both initiatives involved various states, twenty Asia–Pacific countries in the case of the RMSI, and nineteen European and Asian countries in the ReCAAP. In comparison to those two initiatives, the DCA exclusively involved Indonesia and Singapore.

Neorealism suggests that, because of Indonesia's status as a middle power, it would be less likely to cooperate with a near-peer competitor such as Singapore. The DCA indicates that the calculation of relative gains was consistent with Indonesia's decision not to join the agreement. However, the relative gains calculation cannot offer a sufficient explanation because, as explained previously, Indonesia did cooperate with near-peer competitors (as shown in the case of the two coordinated patrol agreements with Singapore and Malaysia and the MSP agreement).

Neorealism would expect Indonesia to join the RMSI and the ReCAAP, because the two lead countries in these initiatives are larger states in comparison to Indonesia. These are the US in the case of the RMSI and Japan in the case of the ReCAAP. As the US is a much larger state, the RMSI would not materially influence the great power discrepancy between the US and Indonesia. In contrast to this expectation, Indonesia decided not to join the RMSI. Government officials and documents did not suggest that Indonesia limited its commitments to the ReCAAP because of concerns over relative gains (DKPT, 2008, p. 12; Indonesian MFA, 2006a, p. 15; Sumaryono, 2004, p. 44).[6] Rather, they cited the lack of gains in absolute terms as the main reason underlying Indonesia's decision not to sign the agreement (Bakorkamla, 2010, pp. 176–177, 181; DKPT, 2008, p. 12; Indonesian MoD, 2003, pp. 62–68; 2008, pp. 140–150; Indonesian MFA, 2006a, p. 15).

As concerns of relative gains cannot provide a satisfactory explanation for Indonesia's varying participation across maritime security cooperation, the following section will examine whether the calculation of absolute gains is a plausible explanation.

Calculating absolute gains

The neoliberal account of the calculation of absolute gains provides an explanation for Indonesia's cooperation and non-cooperation across cases. To

152 Gains and losses

demonstrate this argument, we will first analyse the calculation of absolute gains from all the cooperation arrangements dealing with maritime terrorism and armed robbery against ships which Indonesia chose to take part in. The latter part of this section will examine Indonesia's non-participation in maritime security initiatives addressing the two issues.

Cooperation cases

In terms of cooperation to counter maritime terrorism, Indonesia joined bilateral cooperation arrangements with the US, Japan and Australia, the two EAGA MoUs, the trilateral exchange of information agreement, the ASEAN Convention on Counter-Terrorism, the ISPS Code, the WCO SAFE Framework and the APEC TRP, because the benefits of cooperation exceeded the costs. From these arrangements, Indonesia could gain access to maritime security training and exercises, equipment, information sharing and in some instances support from other states' law enforcement agencies during patrols.

Indonesia and the United States bilateral cooperation

As explained in Chapter 3, Indonesia and the US signed a defence cooperation arrangement in 2010. The bilateral cooperation offers three core incentives to Indonesia. First, it ensures access for Indonesian maritime agencies to various US training and exercises programmes. A result of the negotiations was that the Indonesian military gained access to US joint programmes.[7] There are more than 100 joint programmes under the US Pacific Command's theatre security cooperation, ranging from education, training and exercises, to major foreign military sales and financing (Guenther, 2005, pp. 1–2; Laksmana, 2009). The US also includes Indonesia in its network of exercises such as the Cooperation and Readiness Afloat, the Southeast Asian cooperation against terrorism, and the cobra gold exercise (Bradford, 2008, p. 485; US DoD, 2010). The US sent its NCIS to train the Indonesian police special unit that was assigned to guard international ports including Tanjung Priok Port (Jakarta) and Tanjung Perak (Surabaya) (Polres Tanjung Perak, 2011).

Second, cooperation provides Indonesia with the equipment necessary to deal with armed robbery against ships. Under the US 2006 Global Train-and-Equip programme, Indonesia received US$57 million to support the establishment of an IMSS that covers the Strait of Malacca, the Strait of Makassar and the Strait of Moluccas (US DoS, 2011).

Finally, the cooperation arrangements provide a source of weapons and defence technology through joint research, co-production, sale and purchase of goods, exchange of goods and technology transfers. As part of the bilateral arrangement, Indonesia received nineteen patrol boats to equip its national police (US Embassy in Jakarta, 2011). These boats are deployed in Batam-Riau, Bangka Island Straits, Tarakan, Bitung, Sorong and Ternate-Sofia to help secure the Straits of Malacca and the Sulu-Sulawesi Sea (US Embassy in Jakarta, 2011).

Apart from the incentives brought about by the arrangement, the defence cooperation does not show many changes in Indonesia–US relations. The US–Indonesia defence arrangement was carefully worded to indicate the non-binding and voluntary nature of the cooperation.[8] For this purpose, the term 'participants' is used instead of 'parties', the term 'arrangement' instead of 'agreement' in the document title, and the word 'intend' instead of 'shall' that would imply duties.[9] Requirements stated under the defence framework arrangement are not compulsory and are articulated as expressions of intent between the Indonesian and the US governments. Soon after 9/11, President Megawati and President Bush agreed to establish a security dialogue forum between each country's defence establishments in their September 2001 meeting in Washington (Indonesian Embassy in Washington, 2007). As a follow up to their meeting, the two countries established the Indonesia–US security dialogue and the US–Indonesia bilateral defence discussion before the launch of the defence arrangement. These forums are held annually to discuss a wide range of security and defence issues and plan maritime security training and exercises. Indonesia and the US have also re-opened the international military education and training programme in 2003 and have begun to discuss cooperation in the area of military weaponry after the US lifted its arms embargo in 2005. This occurred in the years before the negotiation of the defence arrangement (Indonesian MoD, 2003, pp. 85–86; *Jakarta Post*, 16 February 2008, 26 February 2008).

Indonesia and Japan bilateral cooperation

The Indonesia–Japan joint announcement on fighting against international terrorism provides two benefits to Indonesia. First, Indonesia receives counter-terrorism capacity-building assistance from Japan in six cooperation areas: immigration control, aviation security, customs cooperation, export control, police and law enforcement and measures against terrorist financing.[10] The capacity building for Indonesian maritime agencies is carried out through three main programmes. The first cooperation programme is the port security management initiative. Under this programme, Japan dispatched long-term experts to assist Indonesian officials in designing port facility security plans for the state's major maritime gateways and to carry out seminars and training on seaport security. The long-term experts were experts and practitioners from the Japanese Ministry of Land Infrastructure, Transportation and Tourism, the Overseas Coastal Area Development Institute of Japan and the Japan International Cooperation Agency (Indonesian DGST, 3 September 2010e). The programme was divided into two phases. The first phase began in December 2006 and ended in May 2009. The second phase started in May 2009.

The second capacity building programme is the project on the Indonesian Maritime Security Coordinating Board structural enhancement. In order to enhance the Maritime Security Coordinating Board, Japan sent their long-term experts from May 2008 to May 2011 to conduct seminars and training for officials at the board. The third capacity-building programme was on board training seminars and combined exercises for maritime law enforcement on the occasion of a port visit by Japanese Coast Guard ships. Through this programme, the Japanese Coast Guard dispatched their patrol vessels to Indonesia to carry out on board training and seminars for Indonesian officials. Since 2002, the Japanese Coast Guard has dispatched their vessels to Indonesia seven times (Embassy of Japan in Indonesia, 2011).

Second, the cooperation provides Indonesia with equipment to address maritime terrorism. Japan equips Indonesia through three main projects. The first is for security equipment at major airports and port facilities, through which Japan provided 747 million Yen (US$7.8 million) in grant aid to improve security facilities at Indonesia's major airport and seaports (Embassy of Japan in Indonesia, 2011). Under this programme, equipment including X-ray inspection systems, metal detectors, explosive detectors and CCTV systems were installed at Soekarno Hatta, Denpasar and five other airports as well as the seaports of Tanjung Priok, Tanjung Perak and Batam (Embassy of Japan in Indonesia, 2011). The two countries signed a diplomatic note in July 2004 and the handover to Indonesia was completed in September 2005.

The second project is for the improvement of port security. This 545 million Yen (US$5.7 million) project is aimed at providing security devices such as CCTV cameras and X-ray units for the major seaports of Belawan, Dumai, Tanjung Pinang, Palembang, Teluk Bayur, Pontianak, Benoa and Makassar (Embassy of Japan in Indonesia, 2008, 2011). Indonesia and Japan signed the cooperation notes in June 2008. By August 2011 Japan had handed over the project to Indonesia.

The third project is the maritime telecommunication system development project phase IV. The cooperation arrangement between the two states was signed in March 2004. Through this arrangement, Japan provided a loan of 567 million Yen (US$5.9 million) to Indonesia to improve Indonesian search and rescue systems and piracy and maritime terrorism counter-measures (Embassy of Japan in Indonesia, 2011). This project includes the installation of the global maritime distress and safety system, a communication system for maritime safety and security navigation, and the Automatic Identification System (AIS) in coastal maritime communications stations. This project was scheduled to be completed in 2012.

The Indonesia–Japan joint announcement against terrorism shows the lack of change in cooperation between the two countries. The cooperation arrangement is only a formalisation of the ongoing cooperation activities between the two states. Most activities governed by this joint announcement, including exchange of information and capacity building, have been carried out by the two countries since 1969 (Basiron and Dastan, 2006, p. 270; Jailani, 2005, p. 69).

Indonesia and Australia bilateral cooperation

Indonesia and Australia bilateral relations benefited from the signing of the 2002 counter-terrorism MoU, the 2006 Lombok treaty and the 2012 DCA.

Counter-terrorism cooperation with Australia could bring the following five benefits. First, cooperation with Australia provides assistance to the Indonesian police to investigate terrorist attacks. As part of the bilateral cooperation, Australia has deployed its AFP team to work with the Indonesian police in investigating a range of terrorist attacks in Indonesia (Australian National Audit Office, 2012, p. 58; Indonesian Coordinating Ministry for Political, Legal and Security Affairs, 2007, p. 166).

Second, through bilateral cooperation Indonesia received Australian assistance in establishing the Jakarta Centre for Law Enforcement Cooperation (JCLEC) and the Republic of Indonesia bomb data centre in 2004 to provide training and collect, analyse and exchange intelligence information (Australia DoD, 2003, p. 9; Australian Federal Police, 2012, p. 5; Australian National Audit Office, 2012, pp. 62–65). In 2004, Australia provided AU$36.8 million (US$37.7 million) to support the JCLEC for five years and to supply and refurbish the JCLEC building, and in 2009 the Australian government continued to provide AU$26.7 million (US$27.3 million) for the next five-year period (Australian National Audit Office, 2012, pp. 64–65).

Third, Indonesia benefits from Australia's capacity-building programme in the area of military training, port security, customs and immigration, criminal intelligence and forensic science (Australian National Audit Office, 2012, p. 63).[11] Cooperation in the area of capacity building provided Indonesia with a core benefit, because the country has limited resources to improve its navy, customs, immigration and police skills and capability in prevention and investigation of terrorist attacks. The 2009 White Paper of the Indonesian Maritime Security Coordinating Board confirms that Australia assists maritime institutions through training and exchanges of personnel (Australian Embassy in Indonesia, 2007; Bakorkamla, 2010, p. 179).[12]

Fourth, the bilateral cooperation provides new equipment and access to Australia's defence technology through grants, purchase of equipment and joint production of weapons. Australian transfer of equipment to Indonesian security agencies includes the gifting of patrol vessels to the Indonesian Maritime Security Coordinating Board and four C-130 aircraft to the Indonesian Air Force (Australian DoD, 2012; Bakorkamla, 2010, p. 179; *Jakarta Globe*, 6 September 2012). Indonesia had been planning to acquire six more aeroplanes from Australia (Australian DoD, 2012; *Jakarta Globe*, 6 September 2012).

Finally, cooperation with Australia provides burden-sharing assistance to deal with illegal migration (Bakorkamla, 2010, pp. 179–180; Indonesian Coordinating Ministry for Political, Legal and Security Affairs, 2006b, p. 35).[13] To quote an MoD official involved in the decision-making process for both the 2006 Lombok treaty and the 2012 defence arrangement:

> For us [the Indonesian government] the most important issue to put forward in the bilateral arrangements is illegal migration ... their [immigrants] main country of destination is Australia, we are a transit country for immigrants coming from Afghanistan, Pakistan, Bangladesh and [other parts of] South

Asia ... their identities are unclear. We are worried that some of them are terrorists ... through the Lombok Treaty we managed to gain Australia's promise to share the costs for financing refugee camps.

(Bakorkamla, 2010, pp. 179–180; Indonesian Coordinating Ministry for Political, Legal and Security Affairs, 2006b, p. 35)[14]

At the 2012 defence arrangement negotiation, the Indonesian Minister of Defence Purnomo Yusgiantoro continued to emphasise that search and rescue matters, which are related to the issues of people smuggling and illegal immigration, were one of the focuses of Indonesia–Australia security cooperation (Australian DoD, 4 September 2012; *Jakarta Post*, 4 September 2012; Sekretaris Kabinet Indonesia, 2012).

The three cooperation arrangements between Indonesia and Australia create only weak legal obligations. They require Indonesia and Australia to cooperate only after considering the primacy of participating states' sovereignty and authority in all aspects of counter-terrorism cooperation (Australian Department of Defence, 2003, p. 8; Human Rights Law Centre, 2012; Indonesian Ministry of Technology, 2012; Saroinsong, 2008, p. 566).[15] Prior to the establishment of these agreements, the two countries had carried out cooperative security and defence activities since 1959. As part of the bilateral relations, Indonesia and Australia have conducted maritime patrols, exchanges of information, inter-agency relations and regular training and exercises (Indonesian MoD, 2003, p. 66). Various issues covered under the three agreements have been discussed and dealt with regularly through the existing defence dialogues between the two countries. The Indonesian Ministry of Defence and its Australian counterpart regularly communicate through the Indonesia–Australia defence strategic dialogue (Indonesian MoD, 2003, pp. 66–67; 2008, p. 147). The MoU on counter-terrorism, the Lombok treaty and the defence arrangement do not change any organisation and coordination practices between the two countries.[16]

Although the 2012 defence arrangement touches on the issue of providing rapid clearance for Australian aircraft to operate and land in Indonesian territory, this practice is not new. Joint maritime operations had been conducted for five years prior to the signing of the defence arrangement through the *Paket Bantuan Keselamatan Transportasi* (transportation safety assistance programme) (Indonesian Ministry of Transportation, 2012). The joint operations include allowing Australian aircraft to operate in Indonesian airspace and had been carried out by the two countries' maritime agencies in areas that bordered the eastern part of Indonesia and Australia prior to the signing of the defence arrangement in 2012 (Australian DoD, 2012; Bakorkamla, 2010, pp. 179–180).[17] Indonesia is also able to approve and finalise the rapid response of Australian planes into Indonesian airspace for joint operations and refuelling without making substantial policy changes, because the country already has a system in place. The Indonesian Minister of Defence Purnomo Yusgiantoro confirmed this. According to Yusgiantoro, Indonesia already has the required system in place because the government 'has that ... precedent with the US. Therefore' Jakarta 'can look at that and apply that to Australia. So that's the easy one' (Australian DoD, 2012).

The BIMP-EAGA sub-regional cooperation

The BIMP-EAGA 2007 MoU on establishing and promoting efficient and integrated sea linkages and its 2009 MoU on transit and interstate transport of goods bring four benefits for Indonesia. First, the two BIMP maritime initiatives provide training and exercise opportunities for Indonesian maritime agencies. These activities are necessary to ensure the success of actual coordinated border patrols, as well as customs and immigration cooperation between the maritime agencies of participating states.[18] By January 2010, under the customs, immigration, quarantine and security forum, member countries had held eleven maritime exercises to enhance coordination, partnership and improve their capacity to deter terrorism and secure their ports (*Philippine Daily Inquirer*, 2010). Second, through this cooperation, the Indonesian navy and other maritime agencies received support during patrols along the coast of Sulawesi. This included vessels and aircraft accompanying ships on patrol and coastal coordination provided by the customs, immigration and security agencies of Brunei, Malaysia, and the Philippines (*Business World*, 2004; Indonesian Coordinating Ministry for Political, Legal and Security Affairs, 2008, pp. 25, 77–78).[19] The border areas between Indonesia and these countries are often used as corridors for terrorist suspects, militant groups and smugglers to escape from or enter Indonesia (see Bakti, 2010, pp. 299–300). Third, cooperation arrangements under both MoUs fitted with pre-existing goals that the government had been unable to achieve. The cooperation enables Indonesia to achieve these policy goals without having to make significant investments. These included halting smuggling and illegal seaborne migration. Coordination and designation of points and ports of entry and exit and transit routes among the four member states assist Indonesia in monitoring the illegal movement of people and goods. The two MoUs help to identify, detect and prevent 'movement and possible apprehension of undesirable travellers' and goods (*Business World*, 2004; Indonesian MFA, 2004, p. 8; Mindanao Development Authority, 2013; UNESCAP, 2013).[20] Finally, the EAGA initiatives assist Indonesia to develop the central and eastern part of Indonesia (Bakti, 2010, p. 298; Indonesian Coordinating Ministry for Political, Legal and Security Affairs, 2007, pp. 71, 73; Indonesian DGST, 2010c, p. 1; Indonesian MFA, 2004, p. 15; 2006a, p. 6; Indonesian Ministry of Trade, 2010, pp. 35–36). This benefit does not contribute to national counter-terrorism efforts. However, for the Indonesian government the improvement of maritime connectivity in these areas is a national development priority (Bakti, 2010, p. 298; Indonesian DGST, 2010c, p. 1; Indonesian Ministry of Trade, 2010, pp. 35–36).[21]

The two EAGA agreements do not generate substantial changes to Indonesia's existing counter-terrorism cooperation. Before the launch of the two MoUs in 2007 and 2009, Indonesia had regularly held meetings and carried out joint cross-border patrol exercises with the other participating states, through bilateral

158 *Gains and losses*

and trilateral cooperation with Brunei, Malaysia and the Philippines (DKPT, 2008, p. 7; Indonesian MoD, 2003, pp. 81–82; Suryadinata, 1998, pp. 103, 108, 111–112). The MoUs are built on existing bilateral and trilateral cooperation links between member states' customs, immigration and law enforcement agencies (*Philippine Daily Inquirer*, 2005).[22] Indonesian officials confirmed that the government has long standing cooperation with the neighbouring EAGA states to curb various illicit activities, including the smuggling of goods, arms and people.[23]

The Agreement on Information Exchange and Establishment of Communication

The agreement on information exchange and establishment of communication between Indonesia, Malaysia and the Philippines yields two benefits for Indonesia. First, the agreement delivers support to Indonesian law enforcement agencies from their Malaysian and Philippine counterparts through information exchange, sharing of airline passenger lists and access to databases on fingerprints, visa waiver lists of third-country nationals and forged or fake documents (Staf Umum Operasi Markas Besar Angkatan Laut, 2004, p. 38). Second, the agreement assists Indonesia in achieving policy goals that it has not managed, particularly combating the smuggling of goods, arms and people (Indonesian MFA, 2004, p. 8). Illegal migration and smuggling of arms are seen by the Indonesian government as linked to terrorism (Indonesian MFA, 2004, p. 8).[24] Finally, this cooperation initiative provides capacity-building opportunities for Indonesian maritime agencies. These include the establishment of joint training and exercises on combating terrorism and other transnational crimes. The government views cooperation among littoral states as the most ideal form of cooperation. Joint training and exercises are expected to increase the security presence in the region and improve the degree of cooperation during maritime patrols.[25]

The information exchange agreement does not introduce significant changes to the existing counter-terrorism cooperation between Indonesia, Malaysia and the Philippines. The agreement reserves the right of each party to refuse to exchange 'any particular information or intelligence for reasons of national security, public order or health'.[26] The enforcement of rules is also made 'without reference to a third party or international tribunal'.[27] Since the early 1960s, the concept of Maphilindo (Malaysia–the Philippines–Indonesia) cooperation has been introduced (Suryadinata, 1998, p. 103). Before the establishment of this agreement in 2002, the three governments had carried out various cooperation activities in the field of maritime security (Indonesian MFA, 2011; Indonesian MoD, 2003, p. 65; 2008, p. 145; Staf Umum Operasi Markas Besar Angkatan Laut, 2004, p. 38). The agreement aims to set up formal and direct communication channels between these states to enable a rapid response and improve coordination among them.[28] It formalises and improves logistical arrangements for exchanges of information and

Gains and losses 159

communication between the three countries to uncover terrorist networks (Bakti, 2010, pp. 299–300).[29]

The ASEAN Convention on Counter-Terrorism

The ASEAN convention on counter-terrorism offered two benefits to Indonesian counter-terrorism efforts. First, through this agreement the Indonesian law enforcement agencies receive support in conducting their counter-terrorism efforts at national level. Exchanges of information and assistance to prosecute and extradite terrorist perpetrators from the ASEAN member states help Indonesia to deal with terrorism, a pre-existing policy goal in the aftermath of the 2002 Bali bombing that it had not fully achieved. Assistance from ASEAN member states is deemed highly important by the Indonesian government. In 2007 when the ASEAN convention on counter-terrorism was introduced, in spite of Indonesian law enforcement's crack down on terrorist networks and arresting a number of terrorist suspects, attacks and attempted attacks continue to occur. These included simultaneous bomb attacks at the Marriott and the Ritz Carlton Hotels in 2009; attacks on NGO workers in Aceh in March to November 2009; attacks on police stations in Bekasi and Hamparan Perak in 2010; attempts to bomb churches and police stations in Central Java in 2010; and a series of letter-bombs to public figures in 2010 (ICG, 2007, 2011; *Jakarta Post*, 3 May 2011; Jones, 6 April 2011, 4 May 2011; Lunnon and Taufiqurrohman, 2011). In several of these cases, the perpetrators only came to light when attacks or attempted attacks had taken place (ICG, 2007, 2011; Jones, 6 April 2011, 4 May 2011). As terrorist groups changed their mode of operation from large groups to small cells consisting of five to ten people, their movements have become more difficult to trace (ICG, 2011; Jones, 6 April 2011). Enhanced cooperation with neighbouring ASEAN states assists Indonesia to track terrorist movement across its borders (DKPT, 2008, p. 7).

Second, the cooperation initiative is beneficial in assisting the Indonesian police and other enforcement agencies not only in curbing terrorist activities but also other transnational crimes that Indonesia has deemed important, including smuggling and illegal seaborne migration, without having to make additional investment (Djalal, 2009, pp. 327, 331; Indonesian MFA, 2004, p. 8).[30] Indonesian officials raised concerns about the influx of refugees from the Middle East and South Asia to Indonesia. Their concern was that some of these refugees may have links with terrorist organisations.[31] Indonesia's concerns over the linkage between these two issues were taken into account, as the Convention obliges participating states to 'take appropriate measures ... before granting refugee status for the purpose of ensuring that the asylum seeker has not planned, facilitated or participated in the commission of terrorist attacks'.[32]

Following a similar pattern to other ASEAN initiatives, the ASEAN convention on counter-terrorism does not dictate how Indonesia must address the terrorist problem within its territory (see Chow, 2005, p. 319). It obliges parties to carry out their duties under this convention in 'a manner consistent with the

160 *Gains and losses*

principles of sovereign and territorial integrity'.[33] It reserves the right of each state to perform counter-terrorism actions in its own territory.[34] Before the establishment of the ASEAN counter-terrorism convention, a number of counter-terrorism institutions in the region had facilitated cooperation among states. These institutions include the Southeast Asia Regional Centre for Counter-Terrorism, which was established in Malaysia in 2003; and the JCLEC and the bomb data centre, both set up in Indonesia in 2004. These institutions serve as a regional hub to carry out counter-terrorism training, as well as monitor and disseminate intelligence information (Australian Federal Police, 2012, p. 5; Australian National Audit Office, 2012, pp. 63–65; Chow, 2005, p. 319; Southeast Asia Regional Centre for Counter-Terrorism, 2013).

The WCO SAFE Framework of Standards to Secure and Facilitate Global Trade

The SAFE Framework shows that Indonesia's behaviour towards this initiative was consistent with the neoliberal argument regarding the importance of the calculation of absolute gains. Indonesia gained two benefits by taking part in the WCO SAFE Framework. First, the SAFE Framework offers capacity building for Indonesia, particularly through training and seminars on the implementation of the AEO to customs administration and the private sectors.[35] The programme enables Customs 'to focus on high risk trade whilst facilitating legitimate trade' (Polner, 2010, p. 6). Recently 'Indonesia has been reviewing the WCO's AEO requirements'.[36] Thus, taking part in the SAFE Framework provides an opportunity for Indonesia 'to build its capacity and learning best practices from other WCO members that already run their AEO programme'.[37] In 2011, as stated in an interview with an official, to improve the security of supply chains Indonesia has been focusing on attempts to implement the AEO Programme.[38] According to a customs official, at present, although Indonesia has issued the Ministry of Finance Act No. 219/PMK.04/2010 on customs procedures for AEO, Indonesia still requires 'a detailed understanding on the implementation of the Programme, the authorisation process, the recruitment of businesses to be AEO'.[39] Second, the SAFE Framework opens up opportunities for Indonesia to develop trade and industrial collaboration with businesses from overseas. An official claimed that a number of companies in South Korea that already have AEO status have asked their customs administration about the possibility of identifying and opening trade cooperation with companies in Indonesia that have similar status.[40] This is an additional benefit that Indonesia can gain from joining the SAFE Framework.

The SAFE Framework presents non-enforceable obligations. Although the SAFE Framework is deemed a minimum threshold to be adopted by member states, it is implemented in accordance with each government's capacity and the required legislative authority without a fixed deadline (WCO, 2007, p. 4). It depends entirely on good faith compliance instead of strict provisions. All standards and programmes at national level are voluntary (WCO, 2007, p. 51). Indonesia easily met the SAFE Framework requirements, because the government customs systems were already in line with the framework, with the AEO programme as the only exception. First, to achieve the harmonisation of advance electronic cargo information, Indonesia adopted the WCO data model for its customs clearance system (APEC Desk of the Indonesian Customs, 2011, p. 19). Indonesia had launched its electronic manifest data exchange programme in 1999.[41] Second, in terms of employing a risk-management approach, Indonesia already had its risk management programme before the implementation of the WCO SAFE Framework (APEC Desk of the Indonesian Customs, 2011, p. 21).[42] As part of the risk management programme, Indonesia had been developing its national importer profiling system for a long time. Since 2009, the Indonesian Customs began to develop its profiling system for freight forwarders and exporters (APEC Desk of the Indonesian Customs, 2011, p. 21). Third, to fulfil the requirement for the non-intrusive inspection of containers and cargo, Indonesia has been using large scale X-ray, Gamma ray and High-Co container scanners in its major international ports (APEC Desk of the Indonesian Customs, 2011, p. 27). Finally, to offer incentives to businesses that adopt the requirement of the WCO supply chain security standards, Indonesia is building its AEO programme. The programme itself is still in its development stage. At national level, the government has issued the Ministry of Finance Decree No. 219/PMK 04/2010 on 9 December 2010 on the customs treatment to accompany AEO status. The Indonesian government offers a number of incentives for exporters, importers, customs brokers, carriers and warehousers that take part in the AEO programme. These include an exemption from the physical inspections of cargo, rapid transit time, access to information pertaining to AEO activities, special service when major disruptions to trade emerge and the threat level is elevated and priority status to obtain customs services and simplification of customs procedures.[43] Although at present Indonesia has not put the AEO programme into practice, Indonesia established the MITA, a facilitation programme for priority importers, in 2003 (Polner, 2010, p. 33). Indonesia is planning to expand the programme for exporters, while developing its AEO programme.[44] Thus, the only implementation costs borne by the Indonesian government were incurred from financing training, seminars and inter-agency meetings on the AEO, and the introduction of this programme to businesses since 2009.[45]

The APEC TRP

The APEC TRP provided some incentives and did not require Indonesia to do much. The APEC TRP offers two benefits. First, the APEC TRP can help Indonesia to develop its AEO programme, a mutual recognition programme that served as a means to facilitate maritime trade (Wibisono, 2006, p. 174).[46] For Indonesia, the trade facilitation programme is the main benefit sought from the TRP. The AEO programme allows Indonesia's law enforcement agencies to focus on high-risk goods. Officials confirmed that, under the TRP, Indonesia has focused its attention on implementing the AEO programme that was first introduced under the SAFE Framework.[47] Although as part of the SAFE Framework

Indonesia had started to develop the programme, Indonesia still needed further understanding on the implementation of the AEO and the establishment of this mutual recognition programme with other APEC members.[48]

Finally, the APEC TRP also offers trade-recovery capacity building for government institutions.[49] Most counter-terrorism arrangements focus on prevention of maritime terrorism. Under the TRP initiative, APEC organised and financed training and workshops on recovery programmes after a terrorist attack or a major disaster (Ho, 2009b, pp. 733–734).[50] As part of the cooperation incentives, Indonesian officials from customs, marine police, and the MoT also received training and attended workshops to implement quick responses and improve the national capability for trade resumption.[51] As an Indonesian official from the MFA explained, 'The APEC TRP has been focusing on the trade resumption programme. This is beneficial for a country such as Indonesia that had experienced terrorist attacks in the past'.[52]

The initiative does not introduce substantial changes to Indonesia's efforts in dealing with maritime terrorism. The APEC TRP does not set intrusive obligations and it is not legally binding (APEC, 2008, pp. 4–8).[53] Indonesia had decided its national point of contact, adopted national programmes to prevent terrorism, and used technology to support its cargo inspection before the TRP was introduced. The government had already appointed the MFA as the point of contact in the APEC before the TRP was launched.[54] Indonesia also has been using non-intrusive cargo inspection devices before the establishment of the TRP (APEC, 2010, p. 2).[55] Indonesia did not need to carry out extensive efforts at national level to meet the TRP requirements. Two years before the TRP was introduced, Indonesia had consented to take part in the WCO SAFE Framework. As part of the SAFE Framework, Indonesia has begun to build its preventive measures to deal with maritime terrorism and to learn about the AEO programme that is part of the APEC TRP. Indonesia had also been developing the AEO Programme before joining the APEC TRP.[56] According to the Indonesian customs' self-assessment report, even without substantial policy reform the country already met more than 80 per cent of the APEC TRP requirements (APEC Desk of the Indonesian Customs and Excise 2011: 31–32).

All the initiatives to counter maritime terrorism discussed above, including the bilateral cooperation with the US, Japan and Australia, the two EAGA MoUs, the trilateral exchange of information agreement, the ASEAN Convention on Counter-Terrorism, the WCO SAFE Framework and the APEC TRP, show the absence of substantial change. As these arrangements do not introduce many changes, it is argued that these initiatives pose low sovereignty costs. All requirements listed in the cooperation documents are already in line with policies carried out by Indonesia prior to the establishment of these arrangements. The majority of the cooperation arrangements to address maritime terrorism that Indonesia chose to join mainly institutionalise the ongoing cooperation activities that have been conducted by Indonesia and its cooperation partners for many years. The absence of substantial policy changes also implies that the economic costs of implementing these agreements are low. After the signing of these initiatives, the government conducts similar policies to those carried out before. Indonesia does not need to introduce policy change at national level and allocate extra expenses to meet cooperation requirements. Compliance is automatic, because cooperation initiatives demand very minimal changes in Indonesia's practices to counter maritime terrorism. Hence, the government does not need to adjust its policies.

In comparison to the above cooperation arrangements, the ISPS Code required Indonesia to make extra economic investment. Yet, Indonesia decided to join the initiative. The detail on this initiative is presented below.

The ISPS Code

The ISPS provides three benefits for Indonesia. First, compliance with the Code provides assurance for Indonesian ports and ships to continue to take part fully in global trade (Indonesian MFA, 2004, p. 9; IMO, 2009).[57] By taking part in the ISPS Code, Indonesian flagged ships which are equipped with the code certificate will not be banned from entering the seaports of other countries that have complied with the code requirements. Similarly, ships registered in other countries that have complied with the code can enter Indonesian international seaports, because these ports have met the IMO international security standards. Participation in the code assists Indonesia to secure ports and vessels flying its flags. In addition, acts of non-compliance would exclude Indonesian flagged ships and ports from international trade. This circumstance will jeopardise the economy, since Indonesia's export and import activities rely heavily on sea transport. Ships engaging in international trade need to comply with the ISPS Code since non-ISPS ships will be denied access to a port that has implemented the Code (Dewan Maritim Indonesia, 2007, 8–5).[58] An official from the Indonesian DGST confirmed this: 'a ship that has met the ISPS Code requirement will not dare to enter a non-ISPS port. This circumstance creates an economic loss for the port'.[59] Two representatives of a major terminal operator in Indonesia confirmed this in an interview. According to them, if a terminal had not complied with the ISPS requirement, then it would be difficult for that terminal to conduct export and import activities. Ships involved in international trade are reluctant to enter a port that has not implemented the ISPS Code.[60]

Second, compliance with the ISPS Code brings extra economic incentives for ports and vessels, because the ISPS certificate is one of the requirements demanded by marine insurance when assessing a business liability and determining the insurance premium rate.[61]

Finally, participating in the ISPS Code assists the government in establishing a sea and coast guard agency. Indonesian officials and government documents pointed out that the adoption of the ISPS Code at global level would assist with the development of Indonesia's independent sea and coast guard agency (Bakorkamla, 2004, p. 6; Dewan Maritim Indonesia, 2007, pp. 5–2; Sekretariat Jenderal Departemen Kelautan dan Perikanan, 2007, p. 38).[62] After the political reform in 1998, Indonesia planned to establish a civilian maritime agency to monitor its 17,000 islands (Bakorkamla, 2010, pp. 1, 31–35, 181).[63] Although Indonesia is the largest archipelagic country in the world, its coast guard was only established in 2014. Following the passing of Presidential Decree 178 of 2014 and Law No. 32 of 2014, the Maritime Security Coordinating Board, which has long been expected to be the core of Indonesia's sea and coast guard agency, was revitalised as the Maritime Security Agency and was assigned the tasks of a coast guard (Bakorkamla, 2010, p. 176; Bakamla, 2016). The lack of resources both in terms of human capacity and equipment was one of the main hindrances for such a development. By joining the ISPS Code, Indonesia received capacity-building support from other countries, including Japan, the US and Australia, to build its coast guard. This included experts' visits, training and seminars, as well as pledges from Japan to provide 137 patrol vessels and the US to provide 5 patrol vessels and surveillance aircraft to equip the agency (Bakorkamla, 2010, pp. 176, 181–182).[65]

The implementation of the ISPS Code brought a number of changes to Indonesian port security practices. The government has to appoint security officers for 141 international ports across the archipelago, separate international ports from other business activities that were not related to shipping, develop port security plans, monitor port security which includes the use of lighting, vehicle, waterborne patrols and automatic intrusion-detection devices and surveillance equipment, carry out training, drills and exercises on port security and establish a national system to monitor compliance. In the run up to the ISPS Code deadline, the government also allocated resources to hold coordination meetings among ministries, maritime agencies, local government and businesses to discuss Indonesia's preparation to adopt the ISPS Code (Sekretariat Jenderal Departemen Kelautan dan Perikanan, 2006, p. 102). The government also carried out a nationwide survey to test the knowledge and understanding of local governments on the code requirements and its implementation in their province (Sekretariat Jenderal Departemen Kelautan dan Perikanan, 2007, p. 38).

Despite these changes, the ISPS Code did not require Indonesia to change the structure of its governance. Indonesia did not have to subject its important decision-making on port security to external authority. The Code retains Indonesia's rights to manage its own jurisdiction (IMO, 2003, p. 38). The implementation of the ISPS relies on individual governments adopting the requirements into their own national legislation. Although the Code is developed through the IMO system, the organisation does not have the authority to monitor compliance and impose any penalties or issue a 'black list' of ports or flag states which do not comply with the Code's requirements (IMO, 2009). The Indonesian government sets its own pace for meeting the Code's requirements. Prior to the implementation of the ISPS code, Indonesia already had the DGST, the Indonesian classification bureau and the port authority (Otoritas Pelabuhan) to manage the nation's port security. These institutions were appointed to form the ISPS Code enforcement system at national level.[66]

Looking at both changes and continuities brought about by the ISPS Code, it is argued that the agreement poses low sovereignty costs. Although

Gains and losses 165

Indonesia needs to make additional adjustments to meet the ISPS Code requirements, the government holds the full authority to decide every step of the country's compliance. Indonesia also does not need to change its governance structure, because the government already has the required institutions. Despite the absence of sovereignty costs, this initiative brought high implementation costs for the Indonesian government. The costs incurred include additional expenses to purchase extra fences, install more lights, non-intrusive cargo inspection devices and surveillance equipment, as well as carry out seminars, training and drills in its international ports in various part of the archipelago (Sekretariat Jenderal Departemen Kelautan dan Perikanan, 2006, p. 102; Sekretariat Jenderal Departemen Kelautan dan Perikanan, 2007, p. 38). The initial costs to comply with the ISPS obligations for a port can range between US$3,000 and US$35,500,000 and the annual costs varies between US$1,000 and US$19,000,000 (UNCTAD, 2007, p. 5). As of 2010, there were 246 port facilities and 881 ships that had complied with the Code (APEC, 2010, p. 5; Indonesian DGST, 2010a). By December 2011, 279 port facilities and 1,509 ships had met the ISPS requirements.[67] Almost 50 per cent of the total number of ports facilities adopted the Code early or to the deadline (Indonesian DGST, 2010a). The government continues to review the progress and feasibility for the adoption of the ISPS Code in all Indonesian ports (Dewan Maritim Indonesia, 2007, pp. 5–2).

In summary, Indonesia decided to participate in the ISPS Code because the absolute gains provided by the initiative were significant. Although the initiative generated high implementation costs, it offered significant benefits in the form of assurance to Indonesian vessels and ports engaged in international trade, lower insurance premiums and assistance to set up a coast guard.

Having examined Indonesia's participation in cooperation initiatives to prevent maritime terrorism, this section will proceed with an explanation of Indonesia's participation in initiatives to deal with sea robbery attacks. Indonesia joined bilateral patrol arrangements with Malaysia and Singapore, defence agreements with the Philippines and India, bilateral arrangements with Japan and China, the Malacca patrol agreement (MSP) and regional initiatives such as the ARF and the AMF. These initiatives did not require Indonesia to do more than what it already did and provided Indonesia with burden-sharing assistance, new equipment and capacity-building programmes.

The Indonesia–Malaysia and Indonesia–Singapore coordinated patrol arrangements

The coordinated patrol agreements with Singapore and Malaysia generate three incentives for Indonesia. First, Indonesia receives support when carrying out patrols on the Sumatra coast. This includes coastal monitoring and coordination support provided from Singapore's Changi naval base and bases along the Malaysian coast. The coordinated patrol arrangement with Malaysia is particularly important to assist Jakarta in dealing with sea robberies, because of the long

166 *Gains and losses*

shared maritime borders at four locations: the Strait of Malacca, the Strait of Singapore, the Sulawesi Sea and the South China Sea (Arsana, 2011, p. 7).

Second, the arrangements with Singapore and Malaysia fitted pre-existing goals that Indonesia had been unable to achieve. These goals included reducing the number of armed robberies at sea, smuggling, particularly arms smuggling, and illegal fishing (Djalal, 2009, p. 327; Indonesian Coordinating Ministry for Political, Legal and Security Affairs, 2006b, p. 35). Before the signing of the coordinated patrol agreements, information exchange and cross-border pursuit were primarily guided by non-formal practices through navy-to-navy communication.[68] The ISCP and the IMCP provide improved procedures to coordinate actions, exchange information and carry out cross-border pursuit of sea robbers. In 1992, when these agreements were established, Indonesian armed forces were embarking on an intensive military campaign to deal with the separatist movement in Aceh, an Indonesian province at the northern end of the Strait of Malacca. Cooperation with Malaysia in particular was deemed central to ensure the success of Indonesia's national attempt to curtail arms smuggling to the Free Aceh Movement. The Indonesian Police Chief General Da'i Bachtiar claimed that some of these firearms were being smuggled by fishing boat from Malaysia across the Straits of Malacca to the Indonesian province of Aceh (Indonesian Embassy in Canberra, 2003; *Jakarta Post*, 26 August 2010; Valencia, 2006, p. 92; Yasin, 2007, p. 232). The Aceh separatist group (GAM) had been reported as carrying out sea robberies in the Strait of Malacca to support its movement in the 1990s to early 2000s (Burton, 2006; ; Chen, 2007, pp. 139, 148; Mak, 2007, pp. 206–207; Ong-Webb, 2007, p. 78; Power, 2008, p. 117; Siregar *et al.*, 2004, p. 14; Sudrajat, 2005, p. 82).[69] As a result of the Indonesia–Malaysia coordinated patrol operations from 2006 to 2013, maritime agencies from both countries had inspected 172 ships suspected of conducting illegal fishing and arrested 4 ships.[70]

Third, bilateral cooperation with Singapore and Malaysia provides opportunities to develop defence logistics through the purchase, sale and gifting of equipment. These include: Indonesia's purchase of arms from Singapore; the sale of six Indonesian-built CN-235 transport aircraft, Super Puma helicopters and Anoa 6×6 armoured personnel to Malaysia; and Jakarta's purchase of twenty Malaysian-built SME MD3–160 aerobatic trainer aircraft and military trucks; and the gifting of five patrol boats from Singapore's coast guard to Indonesia's marine police (Acharya, 2001, p. 149; *Jakarta Post*, 19 May 2011; Matthews and Maharani, 2009). Singapore's weapons exports include aircraft, artillery, missiles and ships (Matthews and Maharani, 2009). Ships and aircraft purchased or received from cooperation partners contributed to Indonesia's surveillance mission to counter sea robbery.

The two coordinated patrol arrangements are not intrusive because they rely on good faith compliance and do not introduce an independent third party to enforce rules (*Jakarta Globe*, 9 February 2012; Purnomo, 2004, p. 22; Sondakh, 2006, p. 88).[71] An Indonesian official from the Maritime Security Coordinating Board claimed that: 'before the signing of the 1992 agreement Indonesia,

Malaysia and Singapore have developed a range of formal and non-formal cooperation activities' (Sondakh, 2004, p. 22; Staf Umum Operasi Markas Besar Angkatan Laut, 2004, p. 38).[72] The only change brought about by these agreements is the formalisation of hot pursuit procedures and communication channels which enable quick response.

Defence cooperation agreements: Indonesia–the Philippines and Indonesia–India

Indonesia's cooperation in defence agreements with the Philippines and India is consistent with the neoliberal expectation regarding the calculation of absolute gains. The bilateral cooperation with both countries provides three benefits. First, the Indonesian navy, marine police, sea and coast guard receive support during patrols along both the coast of Sulawesi located near to the Philippines border and the northern end of the Straits of Malacca and Singapore, located near the Indian border. Indonesia highly valued the two countries' assistance in supporting its patrols to counter sea robbery. These included surveillance aircraft accompanying ships on patrol and coastal coordination support provided from the Philippines shore and from Indian naval and coast guard bases in the Andaman and Nicobar Islands and Port Blair (Staf Umum Operasi Markas Besar Angkatan Laut, 2004, p. 38; Sakhuja, 2007a, p. 32). In addition, the Philippines coast guard stations in Palawan and the South Western and Southern Mindanao districts, and the Indian Maritime Operation Centres and Maritime Regional Coordination Centres that are located at Mumbai, Kochi, Vishakhapatnam and Port Blair maintain communication with the Indonesian maritime centre in Batam (Philippines Coast Guard, 2013; Philippines Department of National Defense, 2013; Philippine Navy, 2011, p. 1; Sakhuja, 2007a, p. 32).[73]

Second, these cooperation initiatives allow Indonesia to achieve specific policy goals in maritime security which Indonesia had been unable to achieve, without having to make additional investments. These goals include dealing with arms smuggling, illegal fishing and illegal migration (Indonesian Coordinating Ministry for Political, Legal, and Security Affairs, 2006a, p. 67; 2006b, p. 35; 2008, pp. 24–25; Nuswantoro, 2005, p. 26; Purnomo, 2004, pp. 30, 35–36).[74] When the agreement between Indonesia and the Philippines was introduced in 1997, communal and sectarian conflicts had flared up in a number of locations in Indonesia (*Jakarta Post*, 2002, 12 March 2010). The smuggling of arms from the Philippines to the North Sulawesi (Miangas Island) has played a role in exacerbating violence in the conflicts across the country (*Jakarta Post*, 2002). A former navy official explained that 'for the MoD and the MFA cooperation with the Philippines and India is important to increase the law enforcement presence in our common maritime borders ... to deal with illegal fishing and smuggling'.[75] In terms of cooperation with India, the two navies carry out a coordinated patrol in the Andaman Sea twice a year (*Hindu*, 2003, 2005; Nuswantoro, 2005, p. 26; *Xinhua*, 2004). Each patrol involves two navy ships from each state and an aircraft (Consulate General of India in Medan, 2012). The Andaman Sea is located at the northern entrance of the Straits of Malacca and Singapore. For Indonesia, due to the proximity of the Andaman Sea with the Straits of Malacca and Singapore, the coordinated patrol is useful in supplementing Indonesia's efforts to counter sea robbery in the Straits. As confirmed by Lieutenant Colonel Warsono: 'the coordinated patrol of the Indonesian and Indian navies is expected to free the Malacca Strait from security threats, such as smuggling, illegal logging ...' (*Antara*, 27 September 2011). Closer monitoring and exchange of information between the two navies are also crucial to ensure the success of Indonesia's attempts to prevent the influx of illegal seaborne migrants from South Asia, particularly Sri Lanka, and the Middle East (Purnomo, 2004, pp. 30, 35).[76]

Third, these agreements provide Indonesia with an opportunity to develop its defence industry through joint research, sale, and exchange of goods or transfers of technology with the Philippines and India. This includes the sale of three landing platform docks, CN-235 aircraft, ammunition and assault rifles from Indonesia to the Philippines (*Kompas*, 22 March 2011). Currently, Indonesia is exploring the possibility of purchasing and jointly manufacturing missiles, submarines and aircraft carriers with India (*Antara*, 22 September 2011; Indonesian MoD, 16 October 2012; 18 October 2012; *Jakarta Post*, 3 April 2007). The manufacture of missiles and submarines is useful to develop Indonesia's military capacity, although it contributes little to the country's efforts to counter sea robbery, as that task requires more high-speed patrol boats, helicopters and surveillance aircraft to secure its sea.

These agreements do not introduce significant changes to the already ongoing cooperation. The Indonesia–Philippines and Indonesia–India defence agreements maintain 'full respect of sovereignty', create weak legal responsibility because they require parties mainly 'to endeavour', 'encourage' and 'promote' bilateral relations, and settle disputes through mutual consultation.[77] Bilateral cooperation between Indonesia and the Philippines has also been institutionalised in the form of the Indonesian and Philippines joint border committee forum since 1975. The forum covers a broad range of issues including armed robbery against ships, smuggling, illegal fishing and illegal immigration (Indonesian MoD, 2003, p. 65; *Straits Times*, 26 May 1977, as cited in Acharya, 1990, p. 8). The coordinated maritime patrol involving patrol vessels and maritime reconnaissance aircraft to secure the waterway between southern Mindanao and northern Sulawesi, for instance, has been established since 1989, many years before sea robbery received worldwide attention after the 9/11 attacks (Acharya, 1990, p. 8; Sondakh, 2004, p. 22). Similarly, prior to the signing of the defence agreement in 2001, the Indonesian and Indian defence ministries and armed forces conducted cooperative activities including seminars on sea robbery, search and rescue exercises, military exercises, navy-to-navy talks, 'Milan (Hindi for meeting)' biannual gatherings of warships, Indindo coordinated patrols in the waters between Sabang and Andaman, regular meetings and exchanges of personnel at cabinet level and regular visits between Parliaments (Ali and Pardesi, 2003; Indian Embassy in Jakarta, 2011; Indian Ministry of External Affairs,

2012; Sakhuja, 2007a, p. 31; Staf Umum Operasi Markas Besar Angkatan Laut, 2004, p. 38).[78]

Indonesia–Japan bilateral cooperation

The Indonesian government supported the country's participation in the joint announcement on maritime affairs with Japan, because the overall benefits of cooperation exceeded the costs. The joint announcement provided Indonesia with two benefits. First, the cooperation is beneficial for Indonesian maritime agencies including the navy, the MoT, the marine police and customs, because they receive capacity building and new equipment (patrol vessels and the development of a vessel traffic system) from Japan (Indonesian Coordinating Ministry for Political, Legal and Security Affairs, 2008, p. 76; Japan MFA, 2006). The joint announcement explicitly mentions 'provision of patrol boats' and other 'assistance from the Japan Coast Guard and Japan International Cooperation Agency for enhancing the capacity of the maritime law enforcement authorities of Indonesia'.[79] This form of assistance can contribute directly to Indonesia's maritime agencies' efforts in addressing sea robbery. Japan provided two grants to Indonesia. These are for the project for construction of patrol vessels for the prevention of piracy, maritime terrorism and proliferation of weapons (1,921 million Yen/US$18.6 million) in June 2006 and the project for the development of a vessel traffic service in the Malacca and Singapore Straits (1,573 million Yen/US$15.2 million in November 2008 and 1,432 million Yen/US$13.9 million in June 2010) (Embassy of Japan in Indonesia, 2010; Indonesian Coordinating Ministry for Political, Legal and Security Affairs, 2008, p. 33; Indonesian MFA, 2009a, pp. 189–190). Second, technical assistance from Japan assists Indonesia in establishing its national coast guard. The Japanese coast guard has been heavily involved in providing experts and technical assistance to the Indonesian MoT and the Maritime Security Coordinating Board to identify gaps and challenges and accelerate the process of establishing an Indonesian coast guard (Bakorkamla, 2010, p. 176).[80] The establishment of a coast guard agency in Indonesia will be expected to increase the presence of law enforcement authorities in Indonesia's vast maritime areas and improve the coordination of operations to counter sea robbery across maritime agencies.

The joint announcement on maritime affairs is not a costly cooperation. Its cooperation requirements for participating states are expressed only as 'desire' or 'intention' of both parties.[81] The announcement requires both parties to conduct various activities to maintain the safety and the security of the Straits of Malacca, but only after recognising the sovereignty and sovereign rights of Indonesia over its territorial sea and EEZ within the Straits.[82] Japan and Indonesia's cooperation to counter sea robbery existed prior to the signing of these statements. In the late 1990s, a series of armed robbery attacks on Japanese vessels, including the *Tenyu* and *Alondra Rainbow*, that were plying through the Strait of Malacca and Strait of Singapore prompted Japan to call for stronger cooperation to counter sea robbery (*Straits Times*, 2000). Before sea robbery

170 *Gains and losses*

incidents in the Straits received worldwide attention, particularly after the 9/11 attacks, Indonesia and Japan had been conducting bilateral exercises to counter sea robbery and other capacity-building programmes (Djalal, 2009, pp. 317, 327, 329; Joshi, 2007).[83]

Indonesia–China bilateral cooperation

The MoU on maritime cooperation between China and Indonesia provides four benefits to Indonesia. First, the Indonesian navy receives support during patrols along the coast of the Natuna Islands that border the South China Sea (*Jakarta Post*, 23 May 2011). In recent years there have been an increasing number of armed robberies in this area.

Second, the cooperation is beneficial for Indonesia because the cooperation assists Indonesia to achieve pre-existing goals. These goals include dealing with illegal fishing in the Indonesian waters that border the South China Sea where illegal fishing is often carried out by Chinese fishermen (*Antara*, 17 May 2005; Indonesian Coordinating Ministry for Political, Legal and Security Affairs, 2007, pp. 35–36; 2008, p. 81; *Jakarta Post*, 23 May 2011; Kustia, 2003, p. 55).[84] Indonesia detained thirty-one China-flagged vessels from 2007 to 2015.[85] In 2010, a Chinese naval vessel confronted an Indonesian patrol boat and demanded the release of a Chinese trawler that fished illegally in Natuna waters. This incident was widely reported by the media. An Indonesian official claimed that at least three such incidents between Indonesia's maritime authorities and its Chinese counterparts took place in 2010 alone, with one of them involving the shooting of an Indonesian citizen.[86] In 2013, armed Chinese vessels compelled an Indonesian maritime and fisheries ministry patrol boat to release Chinese fishermen apprehended in Natuna waters (Reuters, 2014). Most recently, in June 2016, a military standoff between the Indonesian navy and the Chinese coast guard took place in Natuna. A Chinese coast guard vessel demanded that the Indonesian navy release a China-flagged fishing vessel captured in Natuna for conducting illegal fishing (Kompas, 2016). The incident sparked diplomatic tension between the two countries. The MoU on maritime cooperation was established to facilitate discussion and ease tension.

Third, the bilateral cooperation provides an opportunity for Indonesia to improve defence technology through joint research, co-production, the sale and purchase of goods, the exchange of goods and the transfer of technology. This includes joint production of ships, shipping equipment, and short, medium and long-range rockets, as well as C-705 anti-ship missiles that can equip Indonesia's warships (*Antara*, 17 May 2005; Indonesian Coordinating Ministry for Political, Legal and Security Affairs, 2007, p. 32; *Straits Times*, 2012).[87] Although technology cooperation is useful for Indonesia because it encourages the growth of Indonesian shipping manufactures and its defence industry, it does not necessarily contribute to the government's efforts to address sea robbery. This is because the technology cooperation does not specifically target the development of the fast patrol boats or surveillance aircraft that would be most useful to deal with sea robbery. Finally, cooperation with China provides financial assistance and maritime equipment. China pledged to provide 1 billion Yuan (US$154 million) to start a fund for the maritime cooperation programme and a remote sensing satellite to monitor activities at sea for the Indonesian Maritime Security Coordinating Board (*Antara*, 2009; *China Daily*, 30 April 2011; Indonesian MoD, 2003, p. 67; Kompas, 1 May 2011). The Indonesian Head of the Maritime Security Coordinating Board claimed that 'although the satellite will be owned by the Bakorkamla' the monitoring results 'could be used by other agencies in the country' (*Antara*, 2009).

In term of costs, the MoU does not introduce significant changes to Indonesia–China cooperation. Although one of the key areas of cooperation under the MoU includes the establishment of maritime enterprises and joint ventures, the MoU is not accompanied by an obligation to make reparations or restitution when one party's breach of the agreement leads to the other's loss or injury. The agreement does not assign the functions of interpreting, implementing, amending and adding rules to the MoU to an independent third party or an international tribunal. Only the Indonesian and Chinese governments can carry out these functions.[88] Most of the activities that are covered by the agreement, such as ocean research, naval dialogue, exchange of personnel, naval visits and military exercises, began after the resumption of diplomatic relations between the two countries in December 1989 (Embassy of the People's Republic of China in Indonesia, 2004; Indonesian Coordinating Ministry for Political, Legal and Security Affairs, 2007, p. 33; Indonesian MoD, 2003, p. 67; Kustia, 2003, pp. 48–49, 52). This was many years before the establishment of the MoU on maritime cooperation in 2005.

The Malacca Straits Patrol agreement

The MSP agreement brought high incentives to Indonesia for three reasons. First, the cooperation assists Indonesia in achieving pre-existing policy goals in maritime security without having to make additional investment. These goals included halting smuggling of subsidised fuels, drugs and liquor, and illegal migration (Bakorkamla, 2010, pp. 7, 8, 13, 47, 77; Indonesian Coordinating Ministry for Political, Legal and Security Affairs, 2006b, pp. 35, 39, 51; Indonesian MFA, 2004, p. 41, 6 January 2006b, 2007, p. 3; Jailani, 2005, p. 60; Purnomo, 2004, pp. 30, 32, 36; Semedi, 2012, pp. 6–7; Sumaryono, 2009, p. 141; Suristiyono, 2005, p. 47). Second, through the MSP the Indonesian navy, particularly its western fleet and marine police, receive support during patrols along the coast of Sumatra. This includes aircraft accompanying ships on patrol and coastal coordination support provided from Singapore and Malaysia. This support is most useful to monitor the straits and track down sea robbers, in particular when hot pursuit takes place. Finally, cooperation to secure the straits is in line with Indonesia's national policy to develop ports and trading areas in the islands at the northern end of the Straits of Malacca and Singapore. These areas include Nipah Island, Sabang (Weh Island, Klah Island, Rubiah Island, Seulako

172 *Gains and losses*

Island, Rondo Island), Breuh Island, Nasi Island and Teunom Island (Indonesian MoD, 2008, p. 50; 2010).[89] A secure sea lane is important to facilitate economic activities in these areas. For the government, the success of this development project is crucial because the investment in Sabang and the surrounding area is aimed at accelerating economic growth in Aceh and is also serving as a pilot project that might be implemented in other parts of Indonesia (Indonesian Coordinating Ministry for Political, Legal and Security Affairs, 2007, pp. 121–126; Indonesian MFA, 2004, p. 15).[90] The Indonesian government valued this benefit highly, because economic development in areas close to Indonesia's key sea lanes is believed to discourage locals from resorting to sea robbery as a means to earn a living (Ho, 2007, p. 211; Sondakh, 2004, p. 24).[91]

For Indonesia, the MSP cooperation arrangement is not costly. The MSP does not introduce many changes to existing cooperation to counter sea robbery among the littoral states of the Straits of Malacca and Singapore. The MSP arrangement does not introduce intrusive obligations. It does not entail duties to make reparation or restitution if a party fails to deliver on its commitments or causes loss to the other.[92] The two activities that form the crucial parts of the MSP – the MSSP sea patrol and the EiS air patrol – had begun before the signing of the MSP in 2006. The agreement was aimed at formalising ongoing cooperation on the ground and improving information sharing between participating maritime agencies.[93] The agreement only includes the littoral states of the straits and does not include a third party to monitor cooperation, interpret rules or settle disputes (Purnomo, 2004, p. 36; Sondakh, 2004, p. 22; 2006, p. 88).

The ASEAN regional cooperation to combat sea robbery

The ASEAN regional cooperation to combat sea robbery arguably generates two benefits for Indonesia. First, cooperation provides Indonesian maritime agencies with access to capacity-building programmes including maritime exercises and training carried out as part of ARF and AMF activities. The ARF includes not only the ASEAN member states but also developed states, including the US, China, Japan, Canada, Australia and South Korea, that provide 'technical assistance and capacity-building infrastructure', extend training and offer equipment to Indonesia (ASEAN, 2003; Indonesian MFA, 2007, p. 2). Second, regional cooperation allows Indonesia to achieve specific policy goals in domestic maritime security without having to make additional investment. The AMF and the ARF forums assist Indonesia in dealing not only with the issue of armed robbery against ships but also with a number of security concerns that lie at the heart of the government's priority list, including illegal logging, illegal fishing and smuggling (Huxley, 2002, p. 72; Indonesian MFA, 2007, p. 3; 2009b; Martosetomo, 2004, pp. 28–29; Yusuf, 2004, p. 25). Indonesia's efforts to shape ASEAN initiatives to suit its security concerns are particularly apparent in the attempt to deal with the smuggling of arms. Illicit weapons are smuggled from Thailand, Malaysia, the Philippines and Cambodia to Indonesia (Martosetomo, 2004, p. 28; Yusuf, 2004, p. 25). Through regional cooperation, Indonesia receives coastal

Gains and losses 173

coordination, exchange of information and monitoring support from the participating states to halt the trafficking of firearms to its territory (Indonesian Embassy in Canberra, 2003; *Jakarta Post*, 26 August 2010).

The ARF statement and the AMF do not change Indonesia's efforts to counter sea robbery. The ARF Statement only seeks 'to encourage' parties where and when possible to take action prescribed in the statement (ASEAN, 2003). It only requires parties to take various actions to address piracy and armed attacks against ships after taking into account their sovereignty and sovereign rights. Similarly, the AMF only provides guidelines and recommendations on member states pertaining to the existing and future maritime cooperation activities that states may or may not follow (ASEAN, 2012; Indonesian MFA, 2007, p. 63). Member states use the forum only to discuss and exchange views on maritime cooperation (ASEAN, 2012). Activities mentioned in the ARF statement and the AMF arrangement have been conducted by Indonesia unilaterally, bilaterally and trilaterally with other littoral states and extra-regional states, prior to the launching of these cooperation arrangements.

Looking at Indonesia's participation in bilateral patrol arrangements with Malaysia and Singapore, defence agreements with the Philippines and India, bilateral arrangements with Japan and China, the Malacca patrol agreement and regional initiatives such as the ARF and the AMF, it can be concluded that these arrangements to counter sea robbery do not introduce much change. The lack of change suggests that the sovereignty costs of these initiatives to counter sea robbery are low, because the requirements of these initiatives are in line with the Indonesian government's existing practices to counter armed robbery against ships at domestic level. These cooperation initiatives do not require Indonesia to accept an external authority to settle disputes or regulate how Indonesia should govern its territory. The implementation costs of the initiatives to counter armed robbery against ships are also low. These arrangements do not require Indonesia to purchase new equipment or make substantial changes at national level.

In summary, absolute gains inform Indonesia's cooperation in arrangements to address maritime terrorism and armed robbery against ships. With the ISPS Code as an exception, these initiatives did not demand Indonesia to do much, and offered assistance for the government to equip and train its maritime agencies to prevent maritime terrorism, to halt armed robbery attacks against ships, and to share the burden of securing common maritime border areas. This prompts the question of whether Indonesia's non-participation in a range of maritime security initiatives is driven by concerns over absolute gains.

Non-cooperation cases

Indonesia refused to participate in three initiatives to prevent maritime terrorism: the SUA convention, the CSI and the PSI. Indonesia also rejected joining three cooperation arrangements to deal with armed robberies against ships: the RMSI, the ReCAAP and the DCA with Singapore. The empirical findings show that

174 *Gains and losses*

Indonesia's decision not to participate in these initiatives was consistent with the consideration of absolute gains, as argued by neoliberalism.

The SUA convention

The SUA convention offered low incentives for Indonesia, since it did not provide tangible economic or security incentives.[94] The incentives to join the initiative were further diminished, as Indonesia had already joined a number of anti-maritime terrorism initiatives at bilateral, sub-regional, regional and multilateral levels, including the ISPS Code, the WCO SAFE Framework, and the APEC TRP. Indonesia could gain the benefits of cooperation through these cooperation channels.

With regard to the costs of cooperation, the SUA convention and its protocols do not require Indonesia to install new security measures or purchase security devices. Indonesia's national law is already compatible with SUA obligations to criminalise unlawful acts at sea. Chapter 29 of the Statute of the Criminal Law (Article 438–479) criminalises various forms of unlawful acts at sea (Indonesian Criminal Code, 2007, pp. 145–154). In addition, Government regulation no. 1/2002, on combating criminal acts of terrorism deals with the problems of the use and transfer of WMD and terrorist acts against ships (Indonesian Ministry of Justice, 2002, pp. 23–25). Despite these elements of continuity, a careful reading of the convention shows that it would introduce substantial changes to Indonesia's policies to counter maritime terrorism.

First, the convention regulates how a state must deal with unlawful acts within its jurisdiction. Article 4 of the SUA convention suggested that this agreement applies 'if the ship is navigating or is scheduled to navigate ... beyond the outer limit of the territorial sea'.[95] Thus, the convention could be applied to crimes/acts of violence/piratical acts that occur within 12 nautical miles (nm) from the baseline through to the outer limit of the state's jurisdiction (200 nm from the baseline). This SUA convention stipulation contradicts Article 101 of the UNCLOS, which provides the Indonesian government with rights to manage and deal with maritime issues that take place beyond its territorial waters and within another country's EEZ or between 12 and 200 nm. There was a concern that this convention and its protocols could be used inappropriately to refer to unlawful acts which take place in Indonesia's EEZ and, therefore, posed limits to Indonesia's rights to secure its maritime EEZ area (Agoes, 2005, p. 43; Sudrajat, 2005, p. 84).[96] Indonesia decided not to participate in this initiative and refused any possibility of including the SUA convention in any cooperation documents, particularly drafts of UN resolutions.

Second, the convention obliges parties to accept the presence of external authority over significant decision making when disputes over interpretation and implementation of the agreement occur. The SUA convention explicitly delegates authority to settle disputes to an international tribunal.

The convention would have generated low implementation costs. This is because, at national level, Indonesia's legislation was already in line with the convention. Indonesia would not have been required to make additional investment, for example to purchase new devices, to join the agreement. Despite the low implementation costs, the SUA convention imposed high sovereignty costs. The implementation of the agreement could lessen a state's autonomy to address unlawful acts that took place within its jurisdiction.

The CSI

The CSI generated only low benefits. By participating as a CSI port, states gain economic benefits, allowing containers shipped to 'quickly enter into commerce in the United States' (Embassy of the US in Nassau, 2007). If a terrorist attack takes place, containers coming from CSI ports will be given 'special continuity considerations' and 'receive facilitated handling at ports of entry' (Rosenberg and Chung, 2008, p. 54; US CBP, 2006, p. 8). Incentives for cooperation offered by the CSI could be economically rewarding for a state that relies on containerised trade such as Indonesia. Containerised trade is very important for Indonesia's economy because more than 90 per cent of Indonesia's export cargo is carried out by sea (USAID and Senada, 2008, p. 8). The country's exports to the US are also very significant and account for 12.3 per cent of Indonesia's total exports (Indonesian Ministry of Trade, 2011).

Despite the economic incentives offered by the CSI, the Indonesian government perceived the initiative to provide fairly low incentives. This is because, even without the government participation in the CSI, containers from Indonesia can have unimpeded access to US market. The majority of Indonesian export shipments to the US are via the trans-shipment ports of Singapore and/or the Malaysian ports of Port Klang and Port Tanjung Pelepas, all of which comply with the CSI framework. The incentives for cooperation were further reduced because Indonesian businesses already follow other US security initiatives, such as the C-TPAT and the 24-hours rule (Terminal Peti Kemas Surabaya, 2013). These initiatives do not require the cooperation of the Indonesian government.

In addition, the implementation of the CSI did not impede the small amount of direct shipping from Indonesia to the US. As explained in Chapter 3, a number of port facilities that have had their security and compliance to the ISPS Code verified by the US coast guard under the IPS programme could carry out direct shipping to the US (Indonesian DGST, 2010b, pp. 3, 10; 2010d, p. 5; US Embassy Jakarta, 2008).[97] Indonesia decided not to join the CSI, as the low benefits of the initiative could not outweigh the costs.

The practice of placing the US CBP officials in Indonesia's strategic sites, such as the country's major international ports, as part of the CSI key requirements would have been the main change that the CSI could have brought.[98] Indonesian high government officials explained that, as part of this initiative, Indonesia would have needed to accept external authority in the decision-making process (Indonesian MFA, 2006a, p. 35; Jailani, 2005, p. 66).[99] As the practice of placing a team of foreign customs in a port to work together with the Indonesian officials had never existed before, the government would have

176 *Gains and losses*

needed to formulate new legislation to support its implementation and adjust its port security governance to accommodate the presence of the US CBP team (US CBP, 2007).[100] Apart from accepting the CBP team, the Indonesian government would also have needed to purchase automated advance devices to share information and target high-risk containers that met the CSI's minimal requirements. In addition, the government would also have had to ensure that CSI targeting and pre-screening of containers at the port of departure would not cause delays for shippers and compensate them if such incidents occurred.[101] The Indonesian government would have expected to spend an extra annual cost of at least US$1 million to meet the CSI pre-screening requirements for containers (*Jakarta Post*, 2003).

The changes brought by the CSI agreement would have imposed high sovereignty costs. Indonesia would have needed to accept the presence of external authority to monitor its port security. This initiative would also generate high implementation costs. If Indonesia joined the CSI, the economic burden for implementing the initiative would have rested on the Indonesian government. The government would have needed to make additional investment to purchase new equipment, train its human resources to work alongside the CBP team and prepare a compensation fund for businesses should the screening process cause them financial loss (US CBP, 2006, p. 9).[102]

The PSI

The PSI offered low incentives. The PSI provided a number of cooperation incentives including potential capacity building for Indonesian maritime agencies, eligibility to participate in PSI exercises and information sharing. However, the Indonesian government deemed that these incentives to cooperate were low, because Indonesia could reap the benefit of cooperation in halting maritime terrorism, particularly with the US, through other arrangements at bilateral and regional level, for example through the bilateral Defence Arrangement and the ARF. The benefits of cooperation were further reduced, as Indonesia has already participated in other cooperation channels that aimed to prevent proliferation of WMD. Indonesia is party to a number of multilateral initiatives designed to limit the spread of nuclear weapons, including the Convention on Offences and Certain Other Acts Committed on Board Aircraft (1963), the Convention for the Suppression of Unlawful Seizure on Aircraft (1970), the Convention for the Suppression of Unlawful Acts against the Safety of Civil Aviation (1971), the Convention on the Physical Protection of Nuclear Material (1980) and the Non Proliferation Treaty (NPT) (1970) (Indonesian MoD, 2008, pp. 10–11; Sudarman, 2010, p. 18; Wibisono, 2006, p. 289). An official from the Indonesian marine police stated: 'we already have NPT ... why do we have to take part in another cooperation arrangement?'[103] A high government official from the Indonesian Maritime Security Coordinating Board, for instance, pointed out the repetitive character of the PSI. He suggested that provisions embedded within the PSI: 'have been addressed elsewhere in other international conventions and protocols. Therefore, Indonesia did not feel compelled to take part in PSI'.[104] In addition, the PSI activities are aimed at preventing the proliferation of WMD, their delivery systems or related materials. The activities covered by the initiative, including exercises and interdiction, are designed around this purpose (US DoS, 2004). For Indonesia, the proliferation of WMD is not a priority issue and, therefore, cooperation activities designed to deal with this problem would do little to assist Jakarta in addressing its maritime security concerns.[105]

The PSI imposes high sovereignty costs because, although it does not provide mandatory requirements or require a state to accept a third party in their decision-making process, the PSI could limit Indonesia's rights in controlling security over their waters, as granted by the 1982 Law of the Sea Convention. As explained in Chapter 3, participants can choose and, therefore, limit their mode of engagement. However, as explained by Indonesian officials, government documents and security experts, if Indonesia joined the arrangement and chose not to join any interdiction activities, the government would still need to answer to the demands of its cooperation partners, primarily the US, to cooperate if suspected vessels were registered under the Indonesian flag or navigating through Indonesian waters (Indonesian MFA, 2004, p. 9).[106] Such incidents could create legal precedents that would challenge Indonesia's rights as a costal state or a flag state to maintain full control over the security of its waters and the ships registered under its flag.

In addition to the high sovereignty costs, this initiative could bring high implementation costs, particularly when a participating state received a request from another to carry out interdiction either in their waters or for vessels flying its flag. Economically, implementation of the PSI was deemed too costly by the Indonesian government, as the principal actor that would bear the cost of implementation. Interdiction might create additional economic costs, because of delays to shipments or damage of goods, particularly in the case of a false alarm (Indonesian MFA, 2004, p. 9; Nuswantoro, 2005, p. 21).[107] This concern was not unique to Indonesia; for example, in Singapore, a contracting party to the PSI, concern over this matter was carefully discussed between government and businesses.[108] One issue was potential additional costs and which stakeholder was going to pay (the government, the loading port, shipping lines or shippers) when additional expenses arose.[109] In Singapore, businesses were prepared to do their best to cooperate with any attempt to halt maritime terrorism, but shipping industries were not willing to pay all the costs. The prevailing problem in the case of interdiction is 'how the businesses should be compensated'.[110] The same issue was a concern for the Indonesian government, as hundreds of ships traverse Indonesian waters every day. If one of these ships is interdicted in Indonesian waters, the Indonesian government could be held responsible for the act (Nuswantoro, 2005, p. 21).[111] In addition, as previously explained in Chapter 2, thousands of vessels travelling around the world are registered under the Indonesian flag. Therefore, as a flag state, if Indonesia provides its consent for an act of interdiction to take place on board ships flying its flag, the government could be held responsible for economic loss caused by such an act (Indonesian MFA, 2004, p. 9; Nuswantoro, 2005, p. 21).[112] An Indonesian government official closely involved in maritime affairs explained that:

> most actions conducted under the PSI framework are based on intelligence information that is sometimes inaccurate. If an act of interdiction takes place on board a ship and the Indonesian government is charged for any delay or damage resulting from the interdiction who would compensate the shippers?[113]

The RMSI

The Indonesian government found that the RMSI only provided low absolute benefits, because the initiative offered unsubstantial benefits and the implementation of this initiative would bring high costs. The RMSI would have provided three benefits, if Indonesia had participated. First, under this programme Indonesia could receive assistance in the form of new equipment from the US. The US equipped participating countries with devices in order to build capacity in generating 'a complete operating picture of the Malacca Strait' (Doughton, 2006, p. 45). Second, the RMSI provided training, education and military exercises to assist participating countries in improving their decision-making structures, creating fast domestic and international command and control processes to provide a rapid response to maritime threats, and improving their maritime interdiction capabilities (Doughton, 2006, p. 44; Ho, 2007, p. 216; Stryken, 2007, p. 135; USPACOM, 2004a, 2004b). Finally, the RMSI would have been potentially beneficial in assisting Indonesia to develop its coast guard. The RMSI was designed to assist participating states, including Indonesia, by empowering their human resources and building their own coast guard (Doughton, 2006, p. 44). In 2004, when the initiative was introduced, Indonesia was in the process of developing the country's sea and coast guard.

Despite this, the Indonesian government found that the RMSI provided only low benefits for two reasons. First, when the US introduced the RMSI in 2004, Indonesia was consistently highlighted in various media as a dangerous area of rampant sea robberies, hijackings and maritime kidnapping (Urquhart, 2004). However, the actual number of attacks had significantly reduced by the time Indonesia declined to join RMSI. As discussed in Chapter 2, a careful reading of the statistics of armed robberies in the Straits of Malacca and Singapore between 1991 and 2010 shows that sea robbery incidents in the Straits were already in decline after 2001 (IMB, 2001–2010; Jailani, 2005, p. 68). Indonesia's actions to address armed robbery against ships which had been carried out prior to 2004 had already begun to show positive results. This temporal disjuncture between the problem of sea robbery in the straits and the launching of the RMSI reduced the benefits of Indonesia joining the initiative. Second, the incentives were further reduced because Indonesia could gain the benefits of cooperation in the form of bilateral exchanges of training and equipment with the US. As explained in Chapter 3, Indonesia and the US have intensified their bilateral security and defence cooperation since 2001. Thus, without participating in the RMSI, Indonesia can benefit from cooperating with the US via bilateral channels.

The initiative did not introduce significant changes to Indonesia's policies to deal with sea robbery in the Straits of Malacca and Singapore. The RMSI relies solely on good faith compliance and not on enforceable requirements. The initiative clearly points out the conduct of activities under the RMSI, including 'information sharing with other states or acting against a threat remains voluntary and sovereign for each participating nation' (USPACOM, 2004a, 2004d, p. 1). Therefore, the ultimate decision for a member state to join any maritime security activity including information sharing and interception of threats is entirely voluntary (USPACOM, 2004c). It did not specify any requirements for Indonesia to purchase new equipment, nor did it oblige Indonesia to undergo significant policy changes at national level (Boutilier, 2005, p. 27; USPACOM, 2004c). This leads to the conclusion that the initiative imposed only low sovereignty costs. If Indonesia participated in the RMSI, the government would carry out similar activities to those it had conducted as part of the country's policies to deal with sea robbery. Indonesia did not need to change its governance structures to counter sea robbery or accept the presence of an external authority in national decision-making processes.

The absence of substantial changes also implies that, in economic terms, the costs of implementing this initiative were low. The RMSI did not require Indonesia to make substantial adjustments or investments at domestic level to comply with the arrangement. However, despite the low economic costs, participation in the RMSI would bring high political and security costs. According to a former official who was involved in decision making on the RMSI, the MFA and the MoD were aware that direct US involvement in the Straits, as reported by the media, was not part of the RMSI, yet the misreporting of the initiative by the media had some bearing in informing the government assessment of the costs and benefits brought by the RMSI.[114] Due to the media storm generated by Admiral Fargo's comments, members of opposition parties in parliament and radical groups in Indonesia understood that direct US patrols in the Straits of Malacca and Singapore were part of the cooperation deal offered to Indonesia (Bakorkamla, 2010, p. 100; Indonesian MoD, 26 April 2004).[115] Participation in the RMSI would lessen government credibility with the electorate, reduce the space for political manoeuvre at the domestic level and could invite radical and terrorist groups to make vessels and port facilities in the Straits a target (Acharya, 2007, p. 87; Bakorkamla, 2010, p. 100; BBC, 2004).

The ReCAAP

The ReCAAP imposed low cooperation costs. The ReCAAP reserves the rights of states to exercise jurisdiction on their own territory.[116] An official from an international maritime institution confirmed that the ISC does not impinge on national authorities within their jurisdiction.[117] The agreement also obliges states to endeavour to extradite pirates or sea robbers and render mutual legal

180 *Gains and losses*

assistance in criminal matters to others, but only after considering their national laws.[118] The ReCAPP would have imposed low sovereignty costs on Indonesia had it joined. The absence of significant changes also implies that, if Indonesia joined the ReCAAP, Indonesia would not have incurred high implementation costs, as compliance would have been automatic. Yet, Indonesia refused to join the agreement.

The ReCAAP offers a number of benefits for each contracting party. The ReCAAP Information Sharing Centre (ISC) provides information on the statistics of piracy and armed robbery incidents in the region, facilitates information exchange among participating governments, and offers capacity-building programmes and joint exercises. It also enables each participating state to send their representatives to manage and oversee the work of ReCAAP.[119] Indonesia, however, found these incentives insufficient for three reasons. First, the benefits that the ReCAAP offered were not much better than the status quo (Indonesian MFA, 2006a, p. 15; Jailani, 2005, pp. 69–70; Sumaryono, 2004, p. 44).[120] At the early stage of negotiations, Indonesia was enthusiastic due to possible burden sharing in the form of the equipment and capacity building that its maritime agencies could obtain from user states of the Straits of Malacca and Singapore. The final agreement, however, did not address the problem of burden sharing.[121] Indonesia's enthusiasm was further diminished, as participating countries decided not to locate the ISC in Indonesia. Indonesia had expected that the ISC would be located in Indonesia, a country with the widest maritime territories that overlap with straits used for international navigation in Southeast Asia. For Indonesia, the establishment of the ISC in Indonesia could facilitate capacity building for its maritime agencies and address what the government considered as unfair reporting of sea robbery and piracy incidents in its waters by the IMB (Jailani, 2005, p. 67; Nuswantoro, 2005, p. 25; Urquhart, 2006).[122]

The ReCAAP would add little benefit because, critically, the Indonesian government had already secured the benefits offered by ReCAAP through bilateral cooperation with littoral and extra-regional states from the early 1990s, many years before the ReCAAP was launched (*Antara*, 25 September 2006; Indonesian MFA, 2006a, p. 15).[123] In addition, Indonesia already had anti-sea robbery centres – the rescue coordinating centre of the Maritime Security Coordinating Board and the Navy Command Centres (Puskodal) in Batam and Belawan – that served the same purpose as the ISC (Indonesian MFA, 2004, p. 8; Indonesian Ministry of State Secretariat, 2001, p. X-6; Sondakh, 2004, p. 86). Almost two years before the ReCAAP agreement came into force, Indonesia together with Malaysia and Singapore, with IMO assistance, established the Cooperative Mechanism initiative (Singapore MPA, 2012). The Cooperative Mechanism became a key cooperation institution in the Straits of Malacca and Singapore for the strait states, user states and businesses to discuss, exchange information and contribute to improving navigational safety and marine pollution control (Singapore MPA, 2012). Although the cooperative mechanism does not cover cooperation to deal with armed robbery against ships or other maritime security concerns, this initiative brings a positive impact for Indonesia's maritime security. Prior to the establishment of the cooperative mechanism, the burden for maintaining the safety of navigation and pollution prevention was left primarily to the strait states (Indonesia, Malaysia and Singapore); for example, the strait states are required to allocate resources to prevent and deal with the aftermath of accidents caused by the high volume of traffic in the Straits. The substantial burden sharing provided by user states through the cooperative mechanism means that the government can have greater flexibility to use its budget and invest more resources to improve the capacity of Indonesian maritime agencies (Jailani, 2005, p. 71; Ke, 2009, p. 91; Sakhuja, 2007b).

The second reason the benefits of ReCAAP were not appealing to Indonesia was that the problem it was intended to address was not perceived as pressing. Sea robberies in Indonesian waters and the Straits of Malacca and Singapore were already in decline by 2004, the year in which ReCAAP was signed. As a result, joining the initiative was seen by the government as a low priority, as it would not add much to what was already being done (Bakorkamla, 2010, pp. 176–177, 181; IMB, 2005, p. 28; Indonesian MoD, 2003, pp. 62–68; 2008, pp. 140–150; Lloyds, 2006).[124] Indeed, Indonesia could still cooperate through ReCAAP without formally taking part. As a government official put it, 'We can gain the same advantages from cooperation [in ReCAAP] with or without being a member'.[125] ReCAAP established links with the Indonesian Maritime Security Coordinating Board and the Ministry of Transportation, Sea and Coast Guard unit (Bradford, 2008, p. 484; Ho, 2009a, p. 433).[126] The ReCAAP ISC disseminates information to Indonesian maritime agencies including the navy, marine police and Maritime Security Coordinating Board. In return, based on Indonesia's free choice even in the absence of formal membership, Indonesian maritime agencies such as the Maritime Security Coordinating Board, the navy, and the sea and coast guard cooperate with ReCAAP. As the Indonesian director of the sea and coast guard points out: 'We exchange information through ReCAAP, even though we are not a member state ... ReCAAP also shares information with us'.[127] Shipping businesses can also attend a number of events held under the ReCAAP framework. The ReCAAP establishes cooperation with national shipping associations and regularly organises piracy and sea robbery conferences and nautical forums to engage the shipping community in the fight against sea robbery, enable exchanges of views and provide an opportunity for feedback and recommendations (ReCAAP, 2008, 2012).[128] Ever since the ReCAAP invited external participants to attend its governing council annual meeting in 2008, industry organisations such as the Federation of ASEAN Shipowners' Associations and the Asian Shipowners' Forum have sent their delegates to these events (BIMCO, 2010; ReCAAP, 2008, 2012).

The DCA between Indonesia and Singapore

Although the DCA with Singapore is not a costly cooperation, neither did the initiative offer sufficient incentives. The DCA brought low incentives for Indonesia's efforts to counter sea robbery (*Antara*, 22 September 2007; Detik News,

2007; Indonesian Democratic Party of Struggle, 2013; Poerwoko, 2007; Singapore MoD, 7 June 2001, 30 October 2001; Suryadinata, 1998, p. 102; *Xinhua*, 27 April 2007b). Even though the DCA provides a better deal for Indonesia in term of cost sharing, because Singapore agreed to finance 90 per cent of the costs for the development and maintenance of the army training ground in Baturaja (South Sumatra) and the air combat training facility in Seabu (Pekanbaru), before the signing of the agreement Singapore had already borne most of the expenditure to develop and maintain these facilities (Kristiadi, 2007; Poerwoko, 2007). The Minister of Defence confirmed this in an interview; according to him, if the agreement failed: 'it would have no implications because the two countries had already been' conducting joint exercises and cooperating for a long time before the DCA (*Antara*, 22 September 2007).

Indonesia decided to join because of the side payment of this agreement. In exchange for the DCA, the Singaporean government agreed to sign an extradition treaty that had long been desired by Indonesia (Indonesian Coordinating Ministry for Political, Legal and Security Affairs, 2008, p. 55; Indonesian Parliament, 2006; *Xinhua*, 27 April 2007b). All previous administrations had failed to secure the extradition treaty (*Jakarta Post*, 28 December 2007). During the negotiation, Indonesia and Singapore discussed the DCA and the extradition treaty as one package (Indonesian Coordinating Ministry for Political, Legal and Security Affairs, 2008, p. 55; Indonesian Parliament, 2006; *Xinhua*, 27 April 2007b). As explained in Chapter 2, Indonesia has long sought an extradition treaty with Singapore to prosecute around eighty businessmen that fled the country with government bailout funds worth US$87 billion during the Asian financial crisis (Deutsche Press-Agentur, 2007, 2009; Indonesian Coordinating Ministry for Political, Legal and Security Affairs, 2008, p. 55; Indonesian Parliament, 28 May 2007, 17 September 2007; Surya Citra Televisi (SCTV) Liputan 6, 2007; *Xinhua*, 27 April 2007a, 27 April 2007b). Following the signing of the DCA and the extradition treaty, Indonesia proposed that the implementation arrangement for the naval exercise areas (Bravo Areas) should be discussed together, in the same way that the two countries had discussed the implementation arrangements for the Alpha I and Alpha II training areas (*Antara*, 10 July 2007). During the negotiation, Singapore requested the naval training to be conducted once a month for fifteen days each; in contrast, the Indonesian Minister of Defence demanded that the frequency of training be limited to four to six times in a year, in recognition of the impact on the environment and local fishermen (Kristiadi, 2007; *Jakarta Post*, 14 December 2007). Singapore was insistent that negotiation of such an arrangement was unnecessary because Indonesia did not raise this matter prior to the signing of the DCA and the extradition treaty (Singapore MoD, 2007). Singapore's position was that the two agreements: 'were already settled, and the terms cannot be changed casually or piecemeal, without risking the whole package of the extradition treaty and DCA unravelling' (Singapore MFA, 2007). Singapore then proposed a standard operating procedure for the naval exercise area, without involving the Indonesian MoD in the negotiation (*Antara*, 10 July 2007). Indonesia's dissatisfaction continued when Singapore rejected making the extradition treaty retrospective for fifteen years, and this then led to Indonesia's decision to cancel the DCA (*Jakarta Post*, 28 December 2007; Kompas, 2008). As Singapore did not approve the retroactive application of the DCA, the city state took away the only side payment wanted by Indonesia. This led to Indonesia's subsequent rejection of the DCA.

The agreement generated low sovereignty costs. It would not have limited Indonesia's authority to govern its territory or introduced an independent third party to implement rules or resolve disputes. The DCA did not delegate authority to review, interpret rules and resolve conflict to a tribunal or an independent third party.[129]

At bilateral level, the DCA only provided a continuation of a number of activities that Indonesia and Singapore had conducted prior to the establishment of the DCA. Military exercises between the two countries had existed since 1974 when the two navies started their bi-annual military exercise, the Eagle exercise. Indonesia and Singapore military exercises also included an air force joint exercise called the Elang-Indopura (since 1980), armed forces annual exercises called SAFKAR-INDOPURA (since 1989) and the fighter weapon instructor course to train combat pilots (since 1999) (Poerwoko, 2007; Singapore MoD, 7 June 2001, 30 October 2001; Staf Umum Operasi Markas Besar Angkatan Laut, 2004, p. 38). Indonesia had also provided training areas for the Singapore armed forces before the signing of the DCA in 2007 (*Antara*, 8 July 2007; Indonesian MoD, 2003, p. 80). These areas included Baturaja as the location for army training, Kayu Ara, West Kalimantan, and Natuna, Riau Islands, as the location for naval exercises and Siabu, Riau, for air force joint exercises (*Antara*, 19 January 2006). These military exercises, held under Indonesian jurisdiction, have used combat equipment, weapons, bombs and jet fighters (Poerwoko, 2007; *Sunday Times*, 2000; Suryadinata, 1998, p. 102). Most training facilities have been built by the two countries. Indonesia and Singapore developed the air weapons range facility (1989), air combat manoeuvring range facility (1991), military training area and overland flying training area that are located in Pekanbaru Air Base (Poerwoko, 2007; Suryadinata, 1998, p. 102). Indonesia and Singapore are provided with a 40 per cent allocation to use these facilities and the remaining 20 per cent is reserved for maintenance (Poerwoko, 2007). Initially, the costs of development and maintenance of equipment were borne equally by the two states. This arrangement changed in 1995, with Singapore now responsible for 75 per cent of the costs (Poerwoko, 2007). The lack of changes also suggests that the DCA generates low implementation costs. The government is not required to make additional investment to comply with the DCA, because Indonesia's policies are already in line with the agreement's requirements.

In summary, Indonesia's decision not to join the SUA convention, the CSI, the PSI, the RMSI, the ReCAAP and the DCA with Singapore points to the role of the calculation of costs and benefits in absolute terms in informing Indonesia's cooperation. All these initiatives did not offer attractive gains for Indonesia. Among these initiatives, the SUA convention, the CSI, the PSI and the RMSI were significantly costly. The SUA convention, the CSI and the PSI could have

184 *Gains and losses*

limited Indonesia's autonomy. The CSI and the PSI would have created additional costs through compensating businesses due to shipments being delayed or damaged through interdiction activities, without providing an adequate payoff. In the case of the RMSI, the high costs of cooperation resulted from the opposition of legal societal actors and government anticipation of trouble from non-legal societal actors. Indonesia did not sign the ReCAAP, because it did not provide for burden sharing and did not locate the ISC in Indonesia, which would have addressed its long-standing concern about the misreporting of information. Since its formulation, the DCA did not offer any core benefits to support Indonesia's efforts to counter sea robbery. The only ancillary benefit sought by Indonesia from the DCA was Singapore's approval of the extradition treaty. Therefore, when Singapore refused the retroactive application of the extradition treaty, the city-state eliminated the only side payment wanted by Indonesia from the DCA

Conclusion

Across the cooperation cases examined in this chapter, Indonesia only cooperated if the benefits of cooperation outweighed the costs. This is consistent with the neoliberal argument on the role of the calculation of gains in absolute terms. Analysis of Indonesia's participation in initiatives to counter maritime terrorism, including bilateral cooperation with Japan, the US and Australia, and its participation in the BIMP-EAGA initiatives, the agreement on exchange of information and communication procedures, and the ASEAN convention on counter-terrorism, the ISPS Code, the WCO SAFE Framework and the APEC TRP shows that Indonesia's participation in these arrangements was informed by the calculation of absolute gains.

In bilateral cooperation with the US, Japan and Australia, Indonesia received additional equipment without making extra effort. This included aircraft, patrol boats and the IMSS from the US which covers all of its important straits; patrol vessels, port security equipment and a maritime communication system from Japan; and surveillance aircraft from Australia. Similarly, without having to make substantial changes, Indonesia gained enormous support from participating in the EAGA MoUs, the agreement on exchange of information and the ASEAN convention in the form of access to intelligence information; fingerprint, passenger, visa blacklist and bomb databases; coastal and naval support during patrols, and assistance to investigate and extradite perpetrators of terrorist acts.

In both the SAFE Framework and the TRP, Indonesia gained capacity-building assistance from other participants and secretariats of the WCO and APEC, while not having to do much in addition to its current practice. In the case of the SAFE Framework, Indonesia gained assistance in establishing its AEO programme. In addition, in the TRP, Indonesia received further training in establishing the AEO programme and ways to improve its trade resumption capability. In comparison to the SAFE Framework and the TRP, in the ISPS Code, Indonesia was expected to allocate more resources to improve the security of its ports and vessels, but gained a substantial payoff through the assurance of continued participation in global trade, the reduction of insurance premiums and assistance in establishing a sea and coast guard agency.

Indonesia's participation in cooperation arrangements dealing with armed robbery against ships confirmed the role of an absolute gains calculation in informing the government's decision. The two coordinated patrol agreements with Malaysia and Singapore, bilateral cooperation with India and the Philippines and the sub-regional MSP agreement provided Indonesia with high incentives as they offered burden-sharing opportunities to secure waters between Indonesia and these states without making extra investments. Indonesia gained assistance in term of training and new maritime equipment through its cooperation with Japan and China, while not having to take on additional costs, tasks or responsibilities. In the case of the ARF and the AMF, Indonesia received capacity-building assistance from ASEAN dialogue partners and coastal coordination support from other Southeast Asian member states, but did not need to make substantial changes at the domestic level to secure this support.

Indonesia's decision not to join the SUA convention, the CSI, the PSI, the RMSI, the ReCAAP and the DCA with Singapore corresponded with the absolute gains provided by these arrangements. The SUA convention, the CSI and the PSI required Indonesia to do more than it already was, but did not offer adequate compensation. The SUA convention regulated how Indonesia must act within its jurisdiction and expected it to accept the authority of an international tribunal to settle disputes, but did not provide any concrete economic or security incentives. The CSI case presented high costs, because the initiative demanded that Indonesia place a US customs team in major international ports, purchase pre-screening, radiation and nuclear detection devices and build a specific IT system, but did not offer sufficient benefits. In the case of the PSI, Indonesia was faced with risks of having its rights as a coastal or flag state changed and providing compensation to businesses in case of false alarm interdiction, while not gaining much benefit from cooperation. In both the PSI and the CSI, Indonesia could obtain the benefits of cooperation through bilateral cooperation with the US. Having reviewed Indonesia's non-cooperation in the case of the SUA convention, the CSI and the PSI, it could be concluded that neoliberalism, which would argue that cooperation can take place when the overall benefits exceed the costs, explains Indonesia's conduct towards these arrangements.

Although in the RMSI, the ReCAAP and the DCA cases Indonesia was not expected to do more than it already was, it did not receive substantial benefits. The benefits of cooperation offered by the RMSI and the ReCAAP were low because, when both initiatives were introduced, Indonesia had taken part in similar initiatives at bilateral, sub-regional and regional levels to deal with sea robbery. Similarly, the DCA added little to the benefits of cooperation that Indonesia could gain from other existing bilateral arrangements with Singapore. Singapore's decision to make the DCA non-retroactive had removed the only side payment sought from the cooperation. There was thus scant incentive for Indonesia to participate in the three initiatives.

186 Gains and losses

Indonesia's participation and non-participation in all cooperation arrangements dealing with maritime terrorism and armed robbery against ships is not consistent with the neorealist argument regarding the importance of relative gains concerns. In efforts to prevent maritime terrorism, the evidence shows that Indonesia was willing to cooperate with near-peer states such as Singapore, Malaysia and Thailand – as shown in the case of the two EAGA MoUs, the trilateral agreement on information exchange and the ASEAN Convention on Counter-Terrorism – as well as with larger states – as shown in the case of bilateral arrangements with the US, Australia and Japan. Indonesia also joined cooperation arrangements dealing with sea robbery attacks that exclusively involve larger and smaller states, for instance bilateral cooperation with Japan, India, China and the Philippines, and those that involved near-peer states such as the Indo-Singapore and Indo-Malaysia coordinated patrol agreements, the Malacca Straits patrol agreement, the ARF and the AMF.

Relative gains cannot account for the choices made by Indonesia across the six non-cooperation cases: the SUA convention, the CSI, the PSI, the RMSI, the ReCAAP and the DCA with Singapore. Power disparity between Indonesia and the US, a leading state in the SUA convention, the CSI, the PSI, and the RMSI was too vast. Indonesia's approach towards these initiatives would not make a significant difference, and yet Indonesia decided not to join the four arrangements. Indonesia did not join the ReCAAP in spite of the fact this initiative was proposed and led by Japan, a state with larger defence capabilities in comparison to Indonesia. Indonesia also refused to join the DCA that involved Singapore, a near-peer state.

Notes

1. Interview with a high government official at the Ministry of Transportation (Jakarta, 3 September 2010).
2. Interview with a high government official at the Ministry of Transportation (Jakarta, 3 September 2010).
3. E-mail correspondence with an official from the Indonesian BIMP-EAGA Secretariat, North Sulawesi, Indonesia, 6 July 2013; interview with a high government official at the Ministry of Transportation (Jakarta, 3 September 2010).
4. Interview with two high government officials at the Ministry of Transportation (Jakarta, 3 September 2010).
5. Interview with a high government official at the Indonesian navy (Jakarta, 14 July 2010).
6. Interviews with a representative of a non-governmental organisation in the area of maritime security (Singapore, 6 August 2010); a high government official at the Indonesian Maritime Security Coordinating Board (Jakarta, 2 July 2010); a high government official at the Indonesian Ministry of Transportation (Jakarta, 3 September 2010); an Indonesian government official (Jakarta, 4 November 2011); and a high government official at the Indonesian navy (Jakarta, 14 July 2010).
7. Part B, Articles 1b on Promotion of Human Resources of the Defense and Armed Forces and 1c on Capacity Building Project on Maritime Security of the Indonesia–US 2010 Defence Arrangement.
8. Interview with a former high government official at the Ministry of Defence (Depok, 8 October 2011).

Gains and losses 187

9 Indonesia–US 2010 Defence Arrangement.
10 Japan–Indonesia joint announcement on fighting against international terrorism (24 June 2003).
11 Interview with two high government officials at the Indonesian Ministry of Transportation (Jakarta, 3 September 2010); interview with an official at the Indonesian Customs and Excise, Ministry of Finance (Jakarta, 11 October 2011).
12 Interview with an official at the Indonesian Customs and Excise, Ministry of Finance (Jakarta, 11 October 2011).
13 Interviews with a high government official at the Indonesian Maritime Security Coordinating Board (Jakarta, 2 July 2010); an Indonesian Customs Official, Tanjung Priok Port (Jakarta, 11 October 2011); and a high government official at the Indonesian Ministry of Defence (Jakarta, 7 July 2010).
14 Interview with a high government official at the Indonesian Ministry of Defence (Jakarta, 7 July 2010).
15 Article 2(1) of the Lombok treaty.
16 See Article 3(11) of the Lombok treaty.
17 Interview with a high government official at the Indonesian Maritime Security Coordinating Board (Jakarta, 2 July 2010).
18 Interview with a high government official at the Indonesian Maritime Security Coordinating Board (Jakarta, 2 July 2010); discussion with a Philippines official (New York, 20 February 2013).
19 Interview with a high government official at the Indonesian Maritime Security Coordinating Board (Jakarta, 2 July 2010).
20 Interview with a high government official at the Ministry of Transportation (Jakarta, 3 September 2010).
21 Indonesian President Regulation No. 184/1998 on Coordinating Team and Sub Team in Sub Regional Economic Cooperation; email correspondence with the head of the Indonesia national secretariat for BIMP-EAGA, the Indonesian Ministry of Trade, 17 July 2013; interview with a high government official at the Ministry of Transportation (Jakarta, 3 September 2010).
22 Interview with a high government official at the Indonesian Maritime Security Coordinating Board (Jakarta, 2 July 2010).
23 Interviews with a government official at the Indonesian Maritime Security Coordinating Board (Jakarta, 3 July 2010); a high government official at the Indonesian Ministry of Defence (Jakarta, 7 July 2010); a high government official at the Indonesian navy (Jakarta, 14 July 2010); and a high government official at the Indonesian marine police (Jakarta, 2 September 2010).
24 Interview with a high government official at the Indonesian Ministry of Defence (Jakarta, 7 July 2010); and a high government official at the Indonesian navy (Jakarta, 14 July 2010).
25 Interview with a high government official at the Indonesian Maritime Security Coordinating Board (Jakarta, 2 July 2010).
26 Article 8(1) of the Agreement on Information Exchange and Establishment of Communication Procedures.
27 Article 10 of the Agreement on Information Exchange and Establishment of Communication Procedures.
28 Interview with a high government official at the Indonesian Maritime Security Coordinating Board (Jakarta, 2 July 2010); discussion with a Philippines official (New York, 20 February 2013).
29 Interview with a high government official at the Indonesian Maritime Security Coordinating Board (Jakarta, 2 July 2010); discussion with a Philippines official (New York, 20 February 2013).
30 Interview with a high government official at the Indonesian Ministry of Defence (Jakarta, 7 July 2010).

188 *Gains and losses*

31 Interviews with a high government official at the Indonesian Ministry of Defence (Jakarta, 7 July 2010); and a high government official at the Indonesian navy (Jakarta, 14 July 2010).
32 Article X of ASEAN convention on counter-terrorism.
33 Article 3 of the convention.
34 Article 4 of the convention.
35 Interview with a high government official at the Indonesian Customs and Excise, Ministry of Finance (Jakarta, 4 November 2011).
36 Interview with a high government official at the Indonesian Customs and Excise, Ministry of Finance (Jakarta, 4 November 2011).
37 Interview with a high government official at the Indonesian Customs and Excise, Ministry of Finance (Jakarta, 4 November 2011).
38 Interviews with a high government official at the Indonesian Customs and Excise, Ministry of Finance (Jakarta, 9 November 2011); and a high government official at the Indonesian Ministry of Foreign Affairs (Jakarta, 16 December 2011).
39 Interview with a high government official at the Indonesian Customs and Excise, Ministry of Finance (Jakarta, 9 November 2011).
40 Interview with a high government official at the Indonesian Customs and Excise, Ministry of Finance (Jakarta, 9 November 2011).
41 Interview with a high government official at the Indonesian Customs and Excise, Ministry of Finance (Jakarta, 4 November 2011).
42 Interviews with a high government official at the Indonesian Customs and Excise, Ministry of Finance (Jakarta, 4 November 2011); and high government officials at the Indonesian Customs and Excise, Ministry of Finance (Jakarta, 3 November 2011).
43 Indonesian Ministry of Finance Act No. 219/PMK 04/2010 on Authorized Economic Operator.
44 Interview with a high government official at the Indonesian Customs and Excise, Ministry of Finance (Jakarta, 3 November 2011).
45 Interviews with a high government official at the Indonesian Customs and Excise, Ministry of Finance (Jakarta, 3 November 2011); and a high government official at the Indonesian Customs and Excise, Ministry of Finance (Jakarta, 9 November 2011).
46 Interview with a high government official at the Indonesian Ministry of Foreign Affairs (Jakarta, 16 December 2011).
47 Interviews with a high government official at the Indonesian Ministry of Foreign Affairs (Jakarta, 16 December 2011); and a high government official at the Indonesian Customs and Excise, Ministry of Finance (Jakarta, 9 November 2011).
48 Interview with a high government official at the Indonesian Customs and Excise, Ministry of Finance (Jakarta, 9 November 2011).
49 Interview with a high government official at the Indonesian Ministry of Foreign Affairs (Jakarta, 16 December 2011); and a high government official at the Indonesian Customs and Excise, Ministry of Finance (Jakarta, 9 November 2011).
50 Interview with a high government official at the Indonesian Customs and Excise, Ministry of Finance (Jakarta, 9 November 2011).
51 Interviews with a high government official at the Indonesian Ministry of Foreign Affairs (Jakarta, 16 December 2011); and a high government official at the Indonesian Customs and Excise, Ministry of Finance (Jakarta, 9 November 2011).
52 Interview with a high government official at the Indonesian Ministry of Foreign Affairs (Jakarta, 16 December 2011).
53 Interviews with a high government official at the Indonesian Ministry of Foreign Affairs (Jakarta, 16 December 2011); and a high government official at the Indonesian Customs and Excise, Ministry of Finance (Jakarta, 9 November 2011).
54 Interview with a high government official at the Indonesian Ministry of Foreign Affairs (Jakarta, 16 December 2011).

Gains and losses 189

55 Interview with a high government official at the Indonesian Ministry of Transportation (Jakarta, 3 September 2010).
56 Interviews with a high government official at the Indonesian Customs and Excise, Ministry of Finance (Jakarta, 9 November 2011); and a high government official at the Indonesian Ministry of Foreign Affairs (Jakarta, 16 December 2011).
57 Interview with two high government officials at the Indonesian Ministry of Transportation (Jakarta, 3 September 2010).
58 Interview with a high government official at the Indonesian Ministry of Transportation (Jakarta, 3 September 2010); and a corporate communication official of a port operator (Surabaya, 20 September 2011).
59 Interview with a high government official at the Indonesian Ministry of Transportation (Jakarta, 29 September 2011).
60 Interview with a corporate communication official of a port operator (Surabaya, 20 September 2011).
61 Interviews with a representative of an international insurance company (Singapore, 17 August 2010); and a high government official at the Indonesian Ministry of Transportation (Jakarta, 3 September 2010).
62 Interview with a high government official at the Ministry of Transportation (Jakarta, 3 September 2010).
63 Interviews with a high government official at the Indonesian Maritime Security Coordinating Board (Jakarta, 2 July 2010); and a high government official at the Ministry of Transportation (Jakarta, 3 September 2010).
64 Interviews with a high government official at the Indonesian Maritime Security Coordinating Board (Jakarta, 2 July 2010); and a high government official at the Ministry of Transportation (Jakarta, 3 September 2010).
65 Interviews with a high government official at the Indonesian Maritime Security Coordinating Board (Jakarta, 2 July 2010); and a high government official at the Indonesian Maritime Security Coordinating Board (Jakarta, 23 August 2011).
66 Indonesian Minister of Transportation Decision No. 34/2004 on the Appointment of the Directorate General of Sea Transportation as A Designated Authority in the Implementation of the ISPS Code (Jakarta, 23 January 2004); Indonesian Directorate General Sea Transportation Decision No. KL.93/1/9–04 on the Appointment of the Indonesian Classification Bureau as the Recognized Security Organisation in Shipping (Jakarta, 3 March 2004); interview with a corporate communication official of a port operator (Surabaya, 20 September 2011).
67 Interview with a high government official at the Indonesian Ministry of Transportation (Jakarta, 3 November 2011).
68 Interview with a high government official at the Indonesian Maritime Security Coordinating Board (Jakarta, 2 July 2010).
69 Interviews with a high government official at the Indonesian Ministry of Defence (Jakarta, 7 July 2010); and a representative of Indonesian Shipowners' Association (Jakarta, 29 June 2010).
70 Data provided by the Indonesian Ministry of Maritime and Fishery Affairs in March 2015.
71 Interviews with a high government official at the Indonesian Maritime Security Coordinating Board (Jakarta, 2 July 2010); a high government official at the Indonesian Ministry of Defence (Jakarta, 7 July 2010); and a high government official at the Indonesian Navy (Jakarta, 14 July 2010).
72 Interview with a high government official at the Indonesian Maritime Security Coordinating Board (Jakarta, 2 July 2010).
73 Discussion with a Philippines official (New York, 20 February 2013).
74 Interviews with a high government official at the Indonesian Ministry of Defence (Jakarta, 7 July 2010); and a high government official at the Indonesian Maritime Security Coordinating Board (Jakarta, 23 August 2011).

190 *Gains and losses*

75 Interview with a high government official at the Indonesian Maritime Security Coordinating Board (Jakarta, 2 July 2010).
76 Interviews with a high government official at the Indonesian Ministry of Defence (Jakarta, 7 July 2010); and a high government official at the Indonesian navy (Jakarta, 14 July 2010).
77 Opening paragraphs, Articles I and VIII of the India–Indonesia Agreement on Cooperative Activities in the Field of Defence and Security; opening paragraphs, Articles I and Article VIII of the Philippines–Indonesia Agreement on Cooperative Activities in the Field of Defence and Security.
78 Interview with a high government official at the Indonesian Maritime Security Coordinating Board (Jakarta, 2 July 2010).
79 Articles 2 and 4 of the Japan–Indonesia Joint Announcement on Maritime Affairs.
80 Interviews with a high government official at the Indonesian Maritime Security Coordinating Board (Jakarta, 2 July 2010); and three high government officials at the Indonesian Ministry of Transportation (Jakarta, 3 September 2010).
81 Articles 2, 3 and 4 of the 2005 Indonesia–Japan Joint Announcement on Maritime Affairs.
82 Article 3 of the 2005 Indonesia–Japan Joint Announcement on Maritime Affairs.
83 Interviews with a high government official at the Indonesian Maritime Security Coordinating Board (Jakarta, 2 July 2010); and a high government official at the Indonesian Ministry of Transportation (Jakarta, 3 September 2010).
84 Interview with a high government official at the Indonesian navy (Jakarta, 14 July 2010).
85 Data of vessels captured because of committing illegal fishing provided by the Indonesian Ministry of Maritime and Fisheries to author on 19 March 2015.
86 Interview with an Indonesian official (Jakarta, 7 April 2015).
87 Article 2(1) and 2(6) of the Indonesia–China MoU on Maritime Cooperation 2005.
88 Article 6 of the Indonesia–China 2005 MoU on maritime cooperation.
89 Interviews with a government official at the Indonesian Maritime Security Coordinating Board (Jakarta, 3 July 2010); and a high government official at the Indonesian Ministry of Defence (Jakarta, 7 July 2010); Law No. 2 of 2000 on Free Trade Area and the port of Sabang.
90 Interviews with a government official at the Indonesian Maritime Security Coordinating Board (Jakarta, 3 July 2010); and a high government official at the Indonesian Ministry of Defence (Jakarta, 7 July 2010); Law No. 2 of 2000 on Free Trade Area and the port of Sabang.
91 Interviews with a high government official at the Indonesian Maritime Security Coordinating Board (Jakarta, 2 July 2010); and a high government official at the Indonesian navy (Jakarta, 14 July 2010).
92 Interview with a high government official at the Indonesian Maritime Security Coordinating Board (Jakarta, 2 July 2010).
93 Interviews with a high government official at the Indonesian Maritime Security Coordinating Board (Jakarta, 2 July 2010); and a high government official at the Indonesian navy (Jakarta, 14 July 2010).
94 Interviews with an Indonesian security policy expert at the University of Indonesia (Depok, 11 October 2011); and an Indonesian government official (Jakarta, 4 November 2011).
95 Article 4(1) of the SUA convention 1988.
96 Interview with an Indonesian government official (Jakarta, 4 November 2011).
97 Interviews with two high government officials at the Ministry of Transportation (Jakarta, 7 September 2010); a high government official at the Indonesian Ministry of Transportation (Jakarta, 3 September 2010); and a representative of the United States Coast Guard (Singapore, 20 August 2010).

Gains and losses 191

98 Interviews with two high government officials at the Ministry of Transportation (Jakarta, 7 September 2010); a high government official at the Indonesian Maritime Security Coordinating Board (Jakarta, 2 July 2010); and an Indonesian foreign and security policy expert at the University of Indonesia (Depok, 11 October 2011).
99 Interview with a high government official at the Indonesian Coordinating Ministry for Political, Legal and Security Affairs (Jakarta, 30 July 2010).
100 Interview with a high government official at the Indonesian Coordinating Ministry for Political, Legal and Security Affairs (Jakarta, 30 July 2010).
101 Interview with a high government official at the Indonesian Customs and Excise, Ministry of Finance (Jakarta, 4 November 2011).
102 Interview with a high government official at the Indonesian Customs and Excise, Ministry of Finance (Jakarta, 4 November 2011).
103 Interview with a high government official at the Indonesian marine police (Jakarta, 2 September 2010).
104 Interview with a high government official at the Indonesian Maritime Security Coordinating Board (Jakarta, 23 August 2011).
105 Interviews with a high government official at the Indonesian Ministry of Defence (Jakarta, 7 July 2010); and a high government official at the Indonesian navy (Jakarta, 14 July 2010).
106 Interview with an Indonesian government official (Jakarta, 4 November 2011).
107 Interview with an Indonesian government official (Jakarta, 4 November 2011).
108 Interview with a high government official from the Singapore Maritime Port Authority (Singapore, 6 August 2010).
109 Interview with a high government official from the Singapore Maritime Port Authority (Singapore, 6 August 2010).
110 Interview with a Singaporean local ship owner (Singapore, 6 August 2010). General concerns about international maritime security initiatives and how business should be compensated were also raised in an interview with representatives of the Asian Shipowners' Forum (Singapore, 5 August 2010).
111 Interview with an Indonesian government official (Jakarta, 4 November 2011).
112 Interview with an Indonesian government official (Jakarta, 4 November 2011).
113 Interview with an Indonesian government official (Jakarta, 4 November 2011).
114 Interviews with a former high government official at the Ministry of Defence (Depok, 8 October 2011); a high government official at the Indonesian navy (Jakarta, 14 July 2010); and an Indonesian government official (Jakarta, 4 November 2011).
115 Interview with a former high government official at the Ministry of Defence (Depok, 8 October 2011).
116 Article 2(5) of the ReCAAP agreement.
117 Email correspondence with an official of an international maritime organisation that focuses on maritime security and the safety of navigation, 25 July 2011.
118 Article 12 and 13 of the ReCAAP agreement.
119 Article 4(4) of the ReCAAP agreement 2004.
120 Interview with an Indonesian government official (Jakarta, 4 November 2011).
121 Interviews with an Indonesian government official (Jakarta, 4 November 2011); and an Indonesian foreign and security policy expert at the University of Indonesia (Depok, 11 October 2011).
122 Interviews with an Indonesian government official (Jakarta, 4 November 2011); a high government official at the Indonesian Maritime Security Coordinating Board (Jakarta, 23 August 2011); a high government official at the Indonesian Ministry of Transportation (Jakarta, 3 September 2010); and two high government officials at the Ministry of Transportation (Jakarta, 7 September 2010).
123 Interview with an Indonesian government official (Jakarta, 4 November 2011).
124 Interview with a high government official at the Indonesian navy (Jakarta, 14 July 2010).

192 *Gains and losses*

125 Interview with a high government official at the Indonesian Maritime Security Coordinating Board (Jakarta, 2 July 2010).
126 Interviews with a high government official at the Indonesian Maritime Security Coordinating Board (Jakarta, 2 July 2010); and two high government officials at the Indonesian Ministry of Transportation (Jakarta, 3 September 2010).
127 Interview with a high government official at the Indonesian Ministry of Transportation (Jakarta, 3 September 2010).
128 Interview with a representative of a non-governmental organisation in the area of maritime security (Singapore, 6 August 2010); email correspondence with an official of an international non-governmental organisation that focuses on maritime security and the safety of navigation, 25 July 2011.
129 Section C of the Indonesia–Singapore Defence Cooperation Agreement.

References

Acharya, Amitav. (1990). *A Survey of Military Cooperation Among the ASEAN States: Bilateralism or Alliance?* Centre for International and Strategic Studies Occasional Paper No. 14, available at http://yciss.info.yorku.ca/files/2012/06/OP14-Acharya.pdf. Last accessed 16 January 2013.

Acharya, Amitav. (2001). *Constructing a Security Community in Southeast Asia: ASEAN and the Problem of Regional Order*. New York: Routledge.

Acharya, Arabinda. (2007). 'Maritime Terrorist Threat in Southeast Asia', in *Maritime Security in Southeast Asia*, Kwa Chong Guan and John K. Skogan (eds). New York: Routledge.

Agoes, Etty R. (2005). 'Pengelolaan Keamanan di Selat Malaka Secara Terpadu', in *Pertemuan Kelompok Ahli Kebijakan Terpadu Pengelolaan Keamanan Selat Malaka*. Jakarta: Badan Pengkajian dan Pengembangan Kebijakan Kementerian Luar Negeri Indonesia.

Ali, Mushahid and Pardesi, Manjeet S. (2003). 'ASEAN–India Strategic Engagement: Singapore-India Synergy', *Institute of Defence and Strategic Studies (IDSS) Commentaries*, 6 October 2003, available at www.rsis.edu.sg/publications/Perspective/IDSS372003.pdf. Last accessed 21 May 2013.

Antara. (2005). 'Indonesia, China to Sign Memorandum on Cooperation for Making Rockets', 17 May 2005, accessed from the Newsbank database.

Antara. (2005). 'Indonesia Formulating Rules for Thai Role in the Malacca Straits Patrol', 3 September 2005, accessed from the Newsbank database.

Antara. (2006). 'Indonesia, Singapore Agree on Location for Joint Military Exercises', 19 January 2006, accessed from the Newsbank database.

Antara. (2006). 'Indonesia determined to postpone ratification of Malacca Strait pact', 25 September 2006; accessed from the Newsbank database.

Antara. (2007). 'Indonesia Perlu Tegas atas Penolakan Revisi DCA', 8 July 2007, available at www.antaranews.com/berita/69259/indonesia-perlu-tegas-atas-penolakan-revisi-dca. Last accessed 8 May 2014.

Antara. (2007). 'Indonesia, Singapore Agree to Resume Talks on Defense Agreement', 10 July 2007, accessed from the Newsbank database.

Antara. (2007). 'Indonesia: Minister Says Still Chance to Review Defence Ties with Singapore', 22 September 2007, accessed from the Newsbank database.

Antara. (2009). 'China to Grant Remote Sensing Satellite to Indonesia', 22 January 2009; accessed from the Newsbank database.

Antara. (2011). 'RI Boosting International Defense Cooperation', 22 September 2011, accessed from the Newsbank database.

Antara. (2011). 'RI-India Hold Joint patrol in Malacca Strait', 27 September 2011, available at www.antaranews.com/en/news/76025/ri-india-hold-joint-patrol-in-malacca-strait. Last accessed 26 May 2013.

APEC. (2008). *APEC Trade Recovery Programme*. Singapore: APEC Counter Terrorism Task Force, available at www.iadb.org/intal/intalcdi/PE/2009/03362.pdf. Last accessed 7 June 2013.

APEC. (2010). 'APEC Counter-Terrorism Action Plan', available at http:www.apec.org/Groups/…on…/CTAP2010_INDONESIA.ashx. Last accessed 28 November 2011.

APEC Desk of the Republic of Indonesia Customs. (2011). *Collective Action Plan*. Jakarta: The APEC Desk of the Republic of Indonesia Customs, available at www.sjdih.depkeu.go.id/fullText/2010/219~PMK.04~2010Per.HTM. Last accessed 28 November 2011.

Arsana, I Made Andi. (2011). 'Good Fences Make Good Neighbours: Challenges and Opportunities in Finalising Maritime Boundary Delimitation in the Malacca Strait between Indonesia and Malaysia', Proceedings of the 2nd CILS Conference 2011: International Conference on ASEAN's Role in Sustainable Development, 21–22 November, Yogyakarta.

ASEAN. (2003). 'ARF Statement on Cooperation Against Piracy and Other Threats to Security', 17 June 2003, available at www.aseansec.org/14837.htm. Last accessed 16 May 2010.

ASEAN. (2012). 'Chairman's Statement, 3rd ASEAN Maritime Forum', 9 October 2012, available at www.asean.org/news/asean-statement-communiques/item/chairman-s-statement-3rd-asean-maritime-forum. Last accessed 15 October 2012.

Australian Department of Defence. (2003). Department of Defence Submission No. 92 to Joint Standing Committee on Foreign Affairs, Defence and Trade: 'Inquiry into Australia's Relations with Indonesia', available at www.aph.gov.au/Parliamentary_Business/Committees/House_of_Representatives_Committees?url=jfadt/reports.htm. Last accessed 21 October 2012.

Australian Department of Defence. (2012). 'Joint Press Conference in Indonesia', 4 September 2012, available at www.minister.defence.gov.au/2012/09/04/minister-for-defence-stephen-smith-transcript-joint-press-conference-with-indonesian-minister-for-defence-yusgiantoro-purnomo/. Last accessed 20 October 2012.

Australian Department of Defence. (2012). 'Minister for Defence and Minister for Defence Materiel – Joint Press Conference – Indonesia', 5 September 2012, available at www.minister.defence.gov.au/2012/09/05/minister-for-defence-and-minister-for-defence-materiel-joint-press-conference-indonesia/. Last accessed 19 October 2012.

Australian Embassy in Indonesia. (2007). 'Media Release: Australian Ambassador Welcomes Joint Air Force Exercises', 17 July 2007, available at www.indonesia.embassy.gov.au/jakt/MR07_045.html. Last accessed 30 January 2012.

Australian Federal Police. (2012). *Countering Terrorism*, available at www.afp.gov.au/policing/~/media/afp/pdf/c/countering-terrorism.ashx. Last accessed 21 October 2012.

Australian National Audit Office. (2012). *Audit Report No. 30 2011–12 Performance Audit: Fighting Terrorism at its Source Australian Federal Police*, available at www.anao.gov.au/~/media/Uploads/Audit%20Reports/2011%2012/201112%20Audit%20Report%20No%2030.pdf. Last accessed 19 October 2012.

Badan Koordinasi Keamanan Laut (Bakorkamla). (2004). 'Workshop Selat Malaka: Pola Pengamanan Selat Malaka dan Permasalahannya'. Jakarta: Bakorkamla.

Badan Keamanan Laut (Bakamla). (2016). 'Strengthen Marine Security Coordination, Bakamla RI held Forkor in Lombok', available at http://bakamla.go.id//index.php/home/artikel_lengkap_eng/2748/af14b8e3cd888bf4bdb3776deafe6a4c. Last accessed 21 November 2016.

Bakti, Ikrar Nusa. (2010). 'Bilateral Relations between Indonesia and the Philippines: Stable and Cooperative', in *International Relations in Southeast Asia: Between Bilateralism and Multilateralism*, N. Ganesan and Ramses Amer (eds). Singapore: ISEAS.

Bakorkamla. (2010). *Buku Putih Bakorkamla 2009*. Jakarta: Pustaka Cakra.

Basiron, Mohd Nizam and Dastan, Amir. (2006). *Building A Comprehensive Security Environment*. Kuala Lumpur: Maritime Institute of Malaysia.

BBC. (2004). 'SE Asia Acts on Maritime Security', 29 June 2004, available at http://news.bbc.co.uk/1/hi/world/asia-pacific/3849217.stm. Last accessed 11 May 2013.

BIMCO. (12 March 2010). 'ReCAAP Council Approves MoU with ReCAAP', available at www.bimco.org/en/News/2010/03/12_ReCAAP.aspx. Last accessed 12 May 2013.

BIMP EAGA North Sulawesi. (2009). '4th BIMP-EAGA Transport Ministers Meeting (TMM) Manado, North Sulawesi-Indonesia', 25 June 2009, available at www.bimpeaganorthsulawesi.org/show_news.php?Berita_Id=129. Last accessed 1 July 2013.

BIMP EAGA Transport Infrastructure, Information Communication Technology, Development Cluster Group. (2011). 'Transport Infrastructure, Information Communication Technology, Development Cluster Group 20th Senior Officials Meeting, Cagayan de Oro, Philippines', 19 October 2011, available at www. bimp-eaga-ocean-indonesia.com/wp-content/plugins/.../download.php?...pdf. Last accessed 1 July 2013.

Boutilier, James. (2005). 'The Best of Times, the Worst of Times: The Global Maritime Outlook 2004', in *The Best of Times, The Worst of Times: Maritime Security in the Asia Pacific*, Joshua Ho and Catherine Zara Raymond (eds). Singapore: World Scientific Publishing.

Bradford, John F. (2008). 'Shifting the Tides against Piracy in Southeast Asian Waters'. *Asian Survey* 48:3, pp. 473–491.

Burton, John. (2006). 'ASIA-PACIFIC: Malacca Strait Loses its War Risk Rating as Piracy Eases', *Financial Times*, 9 August 2006, accessed from the Newsbank database.

Business World. (2004). 'EAGA Members Agree to Conduct Joint Exercises versus Terrorism', 3 February 2004, accessed from the Newsbank database.

Chen, Jeffrey. (2007). 'The Emerging Nexus between Piracy and Maritime Terrorism in Southeast Asia Waters: A Case Study on the Gerakan Aceh Merdeka (GAM)', in *Violence at Sea Piracy in the Age of Global Terrorism*, Peter Lehr (ed.). New York: Routledge.

China Daily. (2011). 'Indonesia Wins Loans and Deals', 30 April 2011, available at www.chinadaily.com.cn/china/2011-04/30/content_12425113.htm Last accessed 26 July 2011.

Chow, Jonathan T. (2005). 'ASEAN Counterterrorism Cooperation Since 9/11'. *Asian Survey* 45:2, pp. 302–321.

Consulate General of India in Medan. (2012). '20th INDOCORPAT Indian Navy-TNI AL', available at www.congendiamedan.or.id/index.php?option=com_content&view=article&id=120&Itemid=169. Last accessed 6 October 2012.

Dent, Christopher M. and Richter, Peter. (2011). 'Sub-Regional Cooperation and Developmental Regionalism: The Case of BIMP-EAGA'. *Contemporary Southeast Asia* 33:1, pp. 29–55.

Desk Koordinasi Pemberantasan Terorisme (DKPT). (2008). *Catatan DKPT*. Jakarta: Kementrian Koordinator Bidang Politik, Hukum dan Keamanan Republik Indonesia.

Detik News. (2007). 'Isi Naskah Perjanjian Pertahanan RI dan Singapura', 28 May 2007, available at http://news.detik.com/read/2007/05/28/122524/785983/10/isi-naskah-perjanjian-pertahanan-ri-dan-singapura. Last accessed 27 January 2013.

Deutsche Press-Agentur. (2007). 'Indonesia, Singapore to Sign Long-Awaited Extradition Treaty', 27 April 2007, accessed from the Newsbank database.

Deutsche Press-Agentur. (2009). 'Report: Indonesia-Singapore Defence, Extradition Pacts Shelved', 20 March 2009, accessed from the Newsbank database.

Dewan Maritim Indonesia. (2007). *Laporan: Perumusan Kebijakan Grand Strategi Pembangunan Kelautan.* Jakarta: Sekretariat Jenderal Departemen Kelautan dan Perikanan.

Dinas Perhubungan Kalimantan Timur. (2011). 'Indonesia Ikuti BIMP EAGA Cluster Meeting', 28 June 2011, available at http://dishub.kaltimprov.go.id/dinamic.php?act=I&id=146&kategori=&cari=. Last accessed 1 July 2013.

Djalal, Hasjim. (2009). 'Regulation of International Straits'. *Indonesian Journal of International Law* 6:3, pp. 315–332.

Doughton, Thomas F. (2006). 'Straits of Malacca and the Challenges Ahead: The US Perspective', in *Building a Comprehensive Security Environment in the Straits of Malacca.* Kuala Lumpur: Maritime Institute of Malaysia.

Elisabeth, Adriana. (2008). *The Role of the Philippines in the BIMP-EAGA Growth Triangle and the Dynamics of ASEAN Political Economy*, PhD Thesis, Department of History and Politics, University of Wollongong, 2008, available at http://ru.uow.edu.au/theses/52. Last accessed 20 November 2012.

Embassy of Japan in Indonesia. (2011). 'Record of Recent Major Japan–Indonesia Cooperation Projects in Maritime Security, Counter Piracy, Counter Terrorism and Improving Port Security', provided to author by a high government official of the Embassy of Japan during interview in Jakarta, 13 December 2011.

Embassy of Japan in Indonesia. (2008). 'Japan's 545 Million Yen Grant Aid to RI to Provide Security Equipments for Main Ports', 25 June 2008, available at www.id.emb-japan.go.jp/news08_25e.html. Last accessed 20 December 2011.

Embassy of Japan in Indonesia. (2010). 'Penandatanganan dan Pertukaran Nota Diplomatik Bantuan Hibah Jepang untuk Indonesia: Proyek Pengadaan Peralatan Keamanan di Bandara dan Proyek Peningkatan Kemampuan Vessel Traffic System di Selat Malaka dan Selat Singapura Tahap ke-2', 25 June 2010, available at www.id.emb-japan.go.jp/news10_24.html. Last accessed 20 December 2011.

Embassy of the Republic of China in Indonesia. (2004). 'China and Indonesia', 21 April 2004, available at http://id.china-embassy.org/eng/zgyyn/sbgxgk/. Last accessed 26 July 2011.

Embassy of the United States in Nassau. (2007). 'CSI Scanner Unveiling Ceremony: Remarks by US Ambassador John D. Rood at the Freeport Container Port, Freeport, Grand Bahama, 11 January 2007', available at http://nassau.usembassy.gov/sp_12012007.html. Last accessed 8 May 2010.

Guenther, LCDR Darren B. (2005). *Time for a New Theater Security Cooperation Plan for Indonesia*, available at www.dtic.mil/cgi-bin/GetTRDoc?AD=ADA463963. Last accessed 6 June 2013.

Hindu. (2003). 'India, Indonesia Agree on Anti-Terror Measures', 3 September 2003, accessed from the Newsbank database.

Hindu. (2005). 'India Signs Maritime Accord with Thailand', 21 May 2005, accessed from the Newsbank database.

Ho, Joshua. (2007). 'Securing the Seas as a Medium of Transportation in Southeast Asia', in *The Security of Sea Lanes of Communication in the Indian Ocean Region*. Kuala Lumpur: Maritime Institute of Malaysia.

Ho, Joshua. (2009a). 'Short Communication: Combating Piracy and Armed Robbery in Asia: The ReCAAP Information Sharing Centre (ISC)'. *Marine Policy* 33:2, pp. 432–434.

Ho, Joshua. (2009b). 'Recovering After a Maritime Terrorist Attack: The APEC Trade Recovery Programme'. *Marine Policy* 33:4, pp. 733–735.

Human Rights Law Centre. (2012). 'Military Cooperation with Indonesia Must Be Subject to Stringent Safeguards', available at www.hrlc.org.au/content/publications-resources/hrlrc-e-bulletin/vol-78-october-2012/. Last accessed 22 October 2012.

Huxley, Tim. (2002). *Disintegrating Indonesia? Implications for Regional Security*. New York: The International Institute for Strategic Studies.

ICG. (2007). 'Indonesia: Jemaah Islamiyah's Current Status', 3 May 2007, available at www.crisisgroup.org/en/publication-type/media-releases/2007/asia/indonesia-jemaah-islamiyahs-current-status.aspx/ Last accessed 12 May 2011.

ICG. (2011). 'Indonesian Jihadism: Small Groups, Big Plans', Asia Report No. 204, 19 April 2011, available at www.crisisgroup.org/en/regions/asia/south-east-asia/indonesia/204-indonesian-jihadism-small-groups-big-plans.aspx. Last accessed 10 May 2011.

IMB. (2001). *Piracy and Armed Robbery against Ships Annual Report January 1st–December 31st, 2001*. Kuala Lumpur: IMB.

IMB. (2002). *Piracy and Armed Robbery against Ships Annual Report January 1st–December 31st, 2002*. Kuala Lumpur: IMB.

IMB. (2003). *Piracy and Armed Robbery against Ships Annual Report January 1st–December 31st, 2003*. Kuala Lumpur: IMB.

IMB. (2004). *Piracy and Armed Robbery against Ships Annual Report January 1st–December 31st, 2004*. Kuala Lumpur: IMB.

IMB. (2005). *Piracy and Armed Robbery against Ships Annual Report January 1st–December 31st, 2005*. Kuala Lumpur: IMB.

IMB. (2006). *Piracy and Armed Robbery against Ships Annual Report January 1st–December 31st, 2006*. Kuala Lumpur: IMB.

IMB. (2007). *Piracy and Armed Robbery against Ships Annual Report January 1st–December 31st, 2007*. Kuala Lumpur: IMB.

IMB. (2008). *Piracy and Armed Robbery against Ships Annual Report January 1st–December 31st, 2008*. Kuala Lumpur: IMB.

IMB. (2009). *Piracy and Armed Robbery against Ships Annual Report January 1st–December 31st, 2009*. Kuala Lumpur: IMB.

IMB. (2010). *Piracy and Armed Robbery against Ships Annual Report January 1st–December 31st, 2010*. Kuala Lumpur: IMB.

International Maritime Organization (IMO). (2003). *ISPS Code*. London: IMO.

IMO. (2009). 'FAQ on ISPS Code and Maritime Security', available at www.imo.org/newsroom/mainframe.asp?topic_id=897. Last accessed 5 October 2009.

Indian Embassy in Jakarta. (2011). 'Joint Statement: Vision for the India–Indonesia New Strategic Partnership over the Coming Decade', 25 January 2011, available at http://indianembassyjakarta.com/Joint%20Statement.pdf. Last accessed 3 October 2012.

Indian Ministry of External Affairs. (2012). 'India–Indonesia Relations August 2012', available at http://mea.gov.in/mystart.php?id=50044478. Last accessed 3 October 2012.

Indonesian Coordinating Ministry for Political, Legal and Security Affairs. (2006a).

Laporan Akuntabilitas Kinerja Tahun 2005. Jakarta: Kementerian Koordinator Bidang Politik, Hukum dan Keamanan.
Indonesian Coordinating Ministry for Political, Legal and Security Affairs. (2006b). *Penetapan Rencana Kinerja Tahun 2006*. Jakarta: Kemenkopolhukam.
Indonesian Coordinating Ministry for Political, Legal and Security Affairs. (2007). *Kumpulan Pidato Menteri Koordinator Bidang Politik Hukum dan Keamanan Republik Indonesia*. Jakarta: Kementerian Koordinator Bidang Politik Hukum dan Keamanan Indonesia.
Indonesian Coordinating Ministry for Political, Legal and Security Affairs. (2008). *Evaluasi Pengelolaan Bidang Politik, Hukum dan Keamanan Tahun 2007*. Jakarta: Coordinating Ministry for Political, Legal and Security Affairs.
Indonesian Criminal Code [Kitab Undang-Undang Hukum Pidana]. (2007). Jakarta: Permata Press.
Indonesian Democratic Party of Struggle. (2013). 'Kebijakan Pemerintah Yang Dikritisi, Implikasi Bagi Nasib Rakyat, Sikap Politik Fraksi PDI Perjuangan', 26 January 2013, available at www.pdiperjuangan-jatim.org/v03/?mod=release&id=9. Last accessed 27 January 2013.
Indonesian Directorate General of Sea Transportation (DGST). (2010a). 'Data Pelabuhan Comply ISPS Code (Data of Ports that Have Complied with the ISPS Code)'.Jakarta: Indonesian Ministry of Transportation. Data provided to author during interview with an official from the DGST.
Indonesian DGST. (2010b). *Data Distribusi Angkutan Ekspor dan Impor Tahun 2009*. Jakarta: Directorate General of Sea Transportation.
Indonesian DGST. (2010c). 'Bahan Wawancara Direktur Jenderal Perhubungan Laut dengan Staf Pengajar FISIP UI', made available to author during interview with a high government official from the Indonesian Directorate General of Sea Transportation (Jakarta, 3 September 2010).
Indonesian DGST. (2010d). *Kronologis Kunjungan US Coast Guard di Indonesia*. Jakarta: Direktorat Jenderal Perhubungan Laut.
Indonesian DGST. (2010e). 'Internal Report: Seminar Port Facility Security di Jepang', made available to author during interview with a high government official from the Indonesian DGST (Jakarta, 3 September 2010).
Indonesian Embassy in Canberra. (2003). 'Indonesia Calls', 8 May 2003, available at www.kbri-canberra.org.au/brief/2003/may/08may03.htm. Last accessed 21 January 2013.
Indonesian Embassy in Washington DC. (2007). 'Joint Statement of Indonesia and the US Security Dialogue V', 19 April 2007, available at www.embassyofindonesia.org/ina-usa/statement/jointstatementSDV.htm. Last accessed 21 March 2012.
Indonesian Ministry of Defence (MoD). (2003). *Buku Putih Pertahanan [Defence White Paper]*. Jakarta: Ministry of Defence.
Indonesian MoD. (2004). 'DPR Menentang Pengerahan Armada AS ke Selat Malaka', 26 April 2004, available at www.kemhan.go.id/modules.php?name=News&file=article&sid=5567DPR. Last accessed 10 October 2009.
Indonesian MoD. (2008). *Defence White Paper*. Jakarta: Ministry of Defence.
Indonesian MoD. (2012). 'Sekjen Kemhan Pimpin the 3rd Indonesia–India Joint Defence Cooperation Committee Meeting', 16 October 2012, available at www.kemhan.go.id/kemhan/?pg=63&id=649. Last accessed 10 January 2013.
Indonesian MoD. (2012). 'Menhan RI–India Adakan Pertemuan Bilateral Bidang Pertahanan', 18 October 2012, available at www.kemhan.go.id/kemhan/?pg=63&id=653. Last accessed 10 January 2013.

Indonesian MFA. (2004). *Forum Dialog ke XI Kerjasama Maritim ASEAN*. Jakarta: Badan Pengkajian dan Pengembangan Kebijakan.

Indonesian MFA. (2006). *Pertemuan Kelompok Ahli Membahas Aspek Strategis Diplomasi Kelautan Dalam Mendukung Pembangunan Nasional*. Jakarta: Indonesian MFA.

Indonesian MFA. (2006). 'Pidato Menteri Luar Negeri: Paparan Lisan Menteri Luar Negeri Republik Indonesia Dr. Hassan Wirajuda Refleksi 2005 dan Proyeksi 2006', 6 January 2006, available at www.deplu.go.id/Pages/SpeechTranscriptionDisplay.aspx?Name1=Pidato&Name2=Menteri&IDP=310. Last accessed 1 April 2011.

Indonesian MFA. (2007). *Pertemuan Kelompok Ahli: Optimalisasi Kerjasama Kelautan Intra ASEAN Melalui Pembentukan ASEAN Maritim Forum (Bandung, 21–22 Maret 2007)*. Jakarta: Badan Pengkajian dan Pengembangan Kebijakan.

Indonesian MFA. (2009). *ASEAN Regional Forum: The First Inter-Sessional Meeting on Maritime Security, Surabaya, Indonesia, 5–6 March 2009*. Jakarta: Directorate General of Asia Pacific and African Affairs.

Indonesian MFA. (2009). 'Background Singkat Pembentukan ASEAN Maritime Forum', made available to author through an email correspondence with the Head of Security Division, *Directorate* of *ASEAN Political and Security* Cooperation, Heru H. Subolo (Jakarta, 26 August 2009).

Indonesian MFA. (2011). 'RI-Filipina Perkuat Kerjasama Perbatasan', 16 February 2011, available at www.kemlu.go.id/perth/Pages/News.aspx?IDP=4432&l=id. Last accessed 21 March 2012.

Indonesian Ministry of Justice. (2002). *Peraturan Pemerintah Pengganti Undang-Undang Republik Indonesia Nomor 1 tahun 2002 tentang Pemberantasan Tindak Pidana Terorisme dan Peraturan Pemerintah Pengganti Undang-Undang Republik Indonesia Nomor 2 tahun 2002 tentang Pemberlakukan Peraturan Pemerintah Pengganti Undang-Undang Republik Indonesia Nomor 1 tahun 2002 tentang Pemberantasan Tindak Pidana Terorisme, Pada Peristiwa Peledakan Bom di Bali tanggal 12 Oktober 2002*. Jakarta: Departemen Kehakiman Republik Indonesia.

Indonesian Ministry of State Secretariat. (2001). *Lampiran Pidato Presiden Republik Indonesia Pada Sidang Tahunan Majelis Permusywaratan Rakyat Republik Indonesia*. Jakarta: Perum Percetakan Negara.

Indonesian Ministry of Technology. (2012). 'Indonesia–Australia Tingkatkan Kerjasama Hankam', 6 September 2012, available at www.ristek.go.id/index.php/module/News+News/id/11877/print. Last accessed 22 October 2012.

Indonesian Ministry of Trade. (2010). *Draft of Indonesian President Regulation on National Logistic System Appendix Section, 9 March 2010*. This document was made available to author during an interview in Jakarta.

Indonesian Ministry of Trade. (1996–2010). 'Indonesian Export–Import Data 1996–2010', made available to author by the Ministry of Trade, 8 October 2011.

Indonesian Ministry of Transportation. (2012). 'Pernyataan Kerjasama SAR Maritim Indonesia–Australia', 4 September 2012, available at www.dephub.go.id/read/berita/berita-umum/14553. Last accessed 22 October 2012.

Indonesian Parliament. (2006). 'Report of the Working Meeting of Commission I of the Indonesian House of Representatives with the Secretary General of the Ministry of Foreign Affairs', 21 September 2006, available at www.dpr.go.id/id/Komisi/Komisi-I/laporan-singkat. Last accessed 15 January 2013.

Indonesian Parliament. (2007). 'Rapat Kerja Komisi I DPR RI dengan Menteri Pertahanan dan Panglima TNI', 28 May 2007, available at www.dpr.go.id/id/komisi/

komisi1/report/143/Rapat-Kerja-Komisi-I-DPR-RI-Dengan-Menteri-Pertahanan-dan-Panglima-TNI. Last accessed 24 April 2013.
Indonesian Parliament. (2007). 'Report of the Working Meeting of Commission I of the Indonesian House of Representatives with the Minister of Defense and Armed Forces Commander', 17 September 2007, available at www.dpr.go.id/id/Komisi/Komisi-I/laporan-singkat. Last accessed 15 January 2013.
Jailani, Abdulkadir (Staf Direktorat Perjanjian Politik Keamanan Kewilayahan Kementerian Luar Negeri). (2005). 'Pokok-Pokok Masalah Kebijakan Luar Negeri Tentang *Issue* Keamanan Laut dan Kewilayahan Selat Malaka', in *Pertemuan Kelompok Ahli: Kebijakan Terpadu Pengelolaan Keamanan Selat Malaka.* Jakarta: Badan Pengkajian dan Pengembangan Kebijakan Departemen Luar Negeri Republik Indonesia.
Jakarta Globe. (2012). 'Singapore Presents 5 Coastal Patrol Craft to the Indonesian Marine Police', 9 February 2012, available at www.thejakartaglobe.com/archive/singapore-presents-5-coastal-patrol-craft-to-indonesian-marine-police/. Last accessed 13 December 2013.
Jakarta Globe. (2012). 'Hercules Deal Boosts Cooperation', 6 September 2012, available at www.thejakartaglobe.com/home/hercules-deal-boosts-cooperation/542598. Last accessed 10 November 2012.
Jakarta Post. (2002). 'Illegal Guns Enter Indonesia Through Four Countries', 10 July 2002, accessed from the Newsbank database.
Jakarta Post. (2003). 'Customs Service Wants to Negotiate over New US Import Policy', 15 March 2003, accessed from the Newsbank database.
Jakarta Post. (2007). 'Indonesia–India Security Pact Comes into Effect', 3 April 2007, accessed from the Newsbank database.
Jakarta Post. (2007). 'President Urged to Revoke Defense Pact with Singapore', 14 December 2007, accessed from the Newsbank database.
Jakarta Post. (2007). 'Domestic and Foreign Links Go much Deeper in 2007', 28 December 2007, accessed from the Newsbank database.
Jakarta Post. (2008). 'Indonesia May Buy US Jet Fighters', 16 February 2008, accessed from the Newsbank database.
Jakarta Post. (2008). 'US Offers Help with Defense', 26 February 2008, accessed from the Newsbank database.
Jakarta Post. (2010). 'Terror Cell Alliance Forges New Structure and Attack Methods', 12 March 2010, accessed from the Newsbank database.
Jakarta Post. (2010). 'Police Find it Hard to Fight Illegal Gun Trade', 26 August 2010, accessed from the Newsbank database.
Jakarta Post. (2011). 'Osama's Death Will Not Stop Local Radicals: Experts', 3 May 2011, accessed from the Newsbank database.
Jakarta Post. (2011). 'Malaysia, Indonesia Pace ASEAN Military Industry', 19 May 2011, accessed from the Newsbank database.
Jakarta Post, 'Indonesia, China Plan Coordinated Sea Patrols', 23 May 2011, accessed from the Newsbank database.
Jakarta Post. (2012). 'Australia, RI Hold Inaugural Defense Talks', 4 September 2012, accessed from the Newsbank database.
Japan MFA. (2006). 'Grant Aid to Indonesia for the Project for Construction of Patrol Vessels for the Prevention of Piracy, Maritime Terrorism and Proliferation of Weapons, 16 June 2006', available at www.mofa.go.jp/announce/announce/2006/6/0616-3.html. Last accessed 5 October 2012.

Jones, Sidney. (2011). 'Implications of Bin Laden's Death for Indonesia', *Jakarta Post*, 4 May 2011, accessed from the Newsbank database.
Jones, Sidney. (2011). 'Three Strategies for Jihad – and More Prevention Needed', *Tempo*, 6 April 2011, available at www.crisisgroup.org/en/regions/asia/south-east-asia/indonesia/op-eds/jones-three-strategies-for-jihad-and-more-prevention-needed.aspx. Last accessed 8 May 2014.
Joshi, Vijay. (2007). ' "Plain Sailing" for an Anti-Piracy Drill – Japan, Malaysia and Thailand Join Forces for Exercise in Strait of Malacca', *Washington Post*, 11 March 2007, accessed from the Newsbank database.
Ke, Xu. (2009). 'Myth and Reality: The Rise and Fall of Contemporary Maritime Piracy in the South China Sea', in *Maritime Security in the South China Sea: Regional Implications and International Cooperation*, Shicun Wu and Keyuan Zou (eds). Farnham, Surrey: Ashgate.
Keohane, Robert O. (1984). *After Hegemony: Cooperation and Discord in the World Political Economy*. Princeton, NJ: Princeton University Press.
Keohane, Robert O. and Martin, Lisa L. (1995). 'The Promise of Institutionalist Theory'. *International Security* 20:1, pp. 39–51.
Kompas. (2008). 'Singapura Tetap Berkomitmen pada Paket DCA dan ET', 8 February 2008, available at http://entertainment.kompas.com/read/2008/02/08/1812358/singapura.tetap.berkomitmen.pada.paket.dca.dan.et. Last accessed 14 January 2013.
Kompas. (2011). 'Alutsista Indonesia Diminati Asing', 22 March 2011, available at http://nasional.kompas.com/read/2011/03/22/16002370/Alutsista.Indonesia.Diminati.Asing. Last accessed 8 May 2014.
Kompas. (2011). 'RI–China Targetkan 80 Miliar Dollar AS', 1 May 2011, available at http://internasional.kompas.com/read/2011/05/01/15112041/RIChina.Targetkan.80.Miliar.Dollar.AS. Last accessed 26 July 2011.
Kompas. (2016). 'Kronologi Penangkapan Kapal Ikan China di Laut Natuna', 20 June 2016, available at http://nasional.kompas.com/read/2016/06/20/21301761/kronologi.penangkapan.kapal.ikan.china.di.laut.natuna. Last accessed 9 July 2016.
Krasner, Stephen D. (2002). 'Chapter 7: Sovereignty, Regimes and Human Rights', in *Regime Theory and International Relations*, Volker Rittberger and Peter Mayer (eds). Oxford: Clarendon Press.
Kristiadi, J. (2007). 'Nasib Kerjasama Pertahanan RI–Singapura', 17 July 2007, available at www.csis.or.id/Publications-OpinionsDetail.php?id=633. Last accessed 17 January 2013.
Kustia, Aa (Indonesian Ambassador for China). (2003). 'Tujuan Historis, Perkembangan dan Permasalahanya'. *Jurnal Luar Negeri* 50, pp. 47–55.
Laksmana, Evan A. (2009). 'Indonesia's Pivotal Role in the US's Grand Strategy', *Jakarta Post*, 6 October 2009, accessed from the Newsbank database.
Lloyds. (2006). 'Market removes Malacca Straits from the List', 11 August 2006, available at www.lloyds.com/News-and-Insight/News-and Features/Archive/2006/08/Market_removes_Malacca_Straits_from_the_List. Last accessed 20 October 2009.
Lunnon, Rebecca and Taufiqurrohman, Muh. (2011). 'Indonesia's Newest Jihadist Are Down, but Not For Long', *Jakarta Globe*, 29 April 2011, available at www.thejakartaglobe.com/opinion/indonesias-newest-jihadists-are-down-but-not-for-long/437958. Last accessed 1 May 2011.
Mak, J.N. (2007). 'Pirates, Renegades, and Fishermen: The Politics of "Sustainable" Piracy in the Strait of Malacca', in *Violence at Sea Piracy in the Age of Global Terrorism*, Peter Lehr (ed.). New York: Routledge.

Martosetomo, Supraprto (Kepala Pusat Pengkajian dan Pengembangan Kebijakan, Kementerian Luar Negeri Indonesia). (2004). 'Paparan Umum', in *Forum Dialog ke XI Kerjasama Maritim ASEAN*. Jakarta: Badan Pengkajian dan Pengembangan Kebijakan Departemen Luar Negeri, pp. 27–31.

Matthews, Ron and Maharani, Curie. (2009). 'Singapore's Arms Sale to UK: A Defence Export Breakthrough', 2 January 2009, available at www.rsis.edu.sg/publications/Perspective/RSIS0012009.pdf. Last accessed 10 June 2013.

Mindanao Development Authority. (2013). 'BIMP-EAGA Simplifies Port Security Rules, Sees Freer Flows of Goods and People', 18 October 2013, available at http://minda.gov.ph/site/BIMP--EAGA/news-and-events/view/BIMP-EAGA-simplifies-port-security-rules,-sees-freer-flow-of-goods-and-people. Last accessed 14 December 2013.

Nuswantoro, Laksamana Pertama Edhi (Kepala Staf Komando Armada RI Kawasan Barat). (2005). 'Pengelolaan Keamanan Selat Malaka Secara Terpadu', in *Pertemuan Kelompok Ahli Tentang Kebijakan Terpadu Pengelolaan Keamanan Selat Malaka, Medan 19–20 Juli 2005*. Jakarta: Badan Pengkajian dan Pengembangan Kebijakan Departemen Luar Negeri.

Ong-Webb, Graham Gerard. (2007). 'Piracy in Maritime Asia: Current Trends', in *Violence at Sea Piracy in the Age of Global Terrorism*, Peter Lehr (ed.). New York: Routledge.

Philippine Coast Guard. (2013). 'Ten Coast Guard Districts', available at www.coastguard.gov.ph/index.php?option=com_content&view=article&id=108&Itemid=54. Last accessed 21 May 2013.

Philippine Daily Inquirer. (2005). 'Borderless Economy in EAGA', 21 March 2005, accessed from the Newsbank database.

Philippine Daily Inquirer. (2010). 'Mindanaos Best of 2009', 9 January 2010, accessed from the Newsbank database.

Philippine Department of National Defense. (2013). 'Defense and Security Cooperation with Indonesia', available at www.dndph.org/press-releases/defense-and-security-cooperation-with-indonesia. Last accessed 21 May 2013.

Philippine Navy. (2011). 'Navy Launches Website for Inter-agency Coordination'. *Navy Today* 003–11:2, available at www.navy.mil.ph/downloads/1303842887-%20newsletter_February%202011.pdf. Last accessed 21 May 2013.

Poerwoko, F. Djoko. (2007). 'Is it Possible for Sovereignty to be Given Up?', *Straits Times*, 2 July 2007, accessed from the Newsbank database.

Polner, Mariya. (2010). *WCO Research Paper No. 8: Compendium of Authorized Economic Operator (AEO) Programmes*, available at www.wcoomd.org/files/1.%20Public%20files/PDFandDocuments/research/aeo_compendium.pdf. Last accessed 11 August 2011.

Polres Tanjung Perak. (2011). 'Antisipasi Terror di Pelabuhan', 21 June 2011, available at http://polrestanjungperak.net/index.php?option=com_content&view=frontpage&limitstart=1021. Last accessed 1 August 2011.

Power, Jason. (2008). 'Maritime Terrorism: A New Challenge for National and International Security'. *Barry Law Review* 10, pp. 111–133.

Purnomo, Y. Didik Heru. (2004). 'Pengamanan Wilayah Laut RI Bagian Barat'. *Indonesian Journal of International Law*, pp. 27–40.

ReCAAP. (2008). 'Press Release: The ReCAAP Information Sharing Centre Establishes itself as an Authority on Piracy and Armed Robbery against Ships, and Develops as the Focus of Anti-Piracy Cooperation in Asia', 28 February 2008, available at www.recaap.org/news/pdf/press/2nd%20GC%20Press%20release%20-%20revised%20%2828-2-08%29.pdf. Last accessed 10 December 2010.

202   Gains and losses

ReCAAP. (2012). 'Press Release: The Sixth Governing Council Meeting of the ReCAAP ISC', 8 March 2012, available at www.recaap.org/Portals/0/docs/News%20and%20 Press%20Releases/Press%20Release%20%282012-03-08%29.pdf. Last accessed 11 June 2013.

Reuters. (2014). 'Remote, Gas-Rich Islands on Indonesia's South China Sea Frontline', 26 August 2014, available at www.reuters.com/article/2014/08/26/us-southchinasea-indonesia-natuna-insigh-idUSKBN0GP1WA20140826#LPgJh1iqOzEe0gyz.97. Last accessed 14 November 2015.

Rosenberg, David and Chung, Christopher. (2008). 'Maritime Security in the South China Sea: Coordinating Coastal and User State Priorities'. *Ocean Development and International Law* 39:1, pp. 51–68.

Sakhuja, Vijay. (2007a). 'Sea Piracy in South Asia', in *Violence at Sea Piracy in the Age of Global Terrorism*, Peter Lehr (ed.). New York: Routledge.

Sakhuja, Vijay. (2007b). 'Who's to Pay for Smooth Sailing?', *Asia Times*, 16 May 2007, available at www.atimes.com/atimes/Southeast_Asia/IE16Ae01.html. Last accessed 30 April 2013.

Saroinsong, Willyam. (2008). 'Agreement Between the Republic of Indonesia and Australia on the Framework for Security Cooperation 2006'. *Indonesian Journal of International Law* 5:3, pp. 618–621.

Sekretariat Jenderal Departemen Kelautan dan Perikanan. (2006). *Laporan Kegiatan: Sosialisasi Nilai-Nilai Kemaritiman*. Jakarta: Sekretariat Jenderal Departemen Kelautan dan Perikanan.

Sekretariat Jenderal Departemen Kelautan dan Perikanan. (2007). *Laporan Perumusan Kebijakan Kelembagaan Tata Pemerintahan di Laut*. Jakarta: Sekretariat Jenderal Departemen Kelautan dan Perikanan.

Sekretaris Kabinet Indonesia. (2012). 'RI–Australia Tingkatkan Kerjasama Keamanan Laut', 5 September 2012, available at http://setkab.go.id/berita-5570-ri-australia-tingkatkan-kerja-sama-keamanan-laut.html. Last accessed 22 October 2012.

Semedi, Bambang. (2012). 'Pengawasan Bea dan Cukai di Wilayah Perairan Indonesia', available at www.bppk.depkeu.go.id/webbc/index.php?option=com_docman&task=doc_download&gid=435&Itemid=130. Last accessed 21 June 2013.

Singapore MoD. (2001). '1980 – Exercise Elang Indopura I', 7 June 2001, available at www.mindef.gov.sg/imindef/about_us/history/birth_of_saf/v05n06_history.html. Last accessed 18 May 2011.

Singapore MoD. (2001). 'Closing Ceremony of the 13/2001 SAFKAR INDOPURA Bilateral Exercise', 30 October 2001, available at www.mindef.gov.sg/imindef/news_and_events/nr/2001/oct/30oct01_nr2/30oct01_speech.html. Last accessed 30 October 2010.

Singapore MoD. (2007). 'Reply by Minister Teo Chee Hean on the Defence Cooperation Agreement at Parliament', 16 July 2007 available at www.mindef.gov.sg/imindef/press_room/official_releases/nr/2007/jul/16jul07_nr.print.noimg.html. Last accessed 1 July 2013.

Singapore MFA. (2007). 'MFA Spokesman's Comments – Remarks by Indonesian Minister of Defence Prof Juwono Sudarsono – Defence Cooperation Agreement', available at www.mfa.gov.sg/content/mfa/overseasmission/jakarta/press_statements_speeches_archives/2007/200706/press_200706.html, 13 June 2007. Last accessed 1 July 2013.

Singapore MPA. (2012). 'Annex A: Co-operative Mechanism on Safety of Navigation and Environmental Protection in the Straits of Malacca and Singapore', available at www.mpa.gov.sg/sites/.../annex_a_factsheet_on_co-operative_mechanism.pdf. Last accessed 24 December 2012.

Siregar, Hasnil Basri, Nasution, Sanwani, Rahman, Abdul, Sutiarno, Hasibuan Rosmi, Munthe, Makdin, Purba, Deni and Eliana. (2004). *Pengamanan dan Perlindungan Pulau-Pulau Terluar Pada Batas Wilayah RI Di Kawasan Selat Malaka*. Sumatera Utara: Fakultas Hukum Universitas Sumatera Utara.

Sondakh, Bernard Kent. (2004). 'Pengamanan Wilayah Laut Indonesia'. *Indonesian Journal of International Law*, pp. 1–26.

Sondakh, Admiral Bernard Kent. (2006). 'National Sovereignty and Security in the Straits of Malacca', in *Building A Comprehensive Security Environment in the Straits of Malacca*. Kuala Lumpur: Maritime Institute of Malaysia, pp. 79–110.

Southeast Asia Regional Centre for Counter Terrorism. (2013). 'About the Southeast Asia Regional Centre for Counter Terrorism', 12 February 2013 available at www.searcct.gov.my/index.php?option=com_content&task=view&id=760&Itemid=648. Last accessed 12 February 2013.

Staf Umum Operasi Markas Besar Angkatan Laut. (2004). 'Kerjasama Regional Maritim ASEAN Dari Perspektif Pertahanan Matra Laut', in *Forum Dialog ke XI Kerjasama Maritim ASEAN*. Jakarta: Badan Pengkajian dan Pengembangan Kebijakan Kementerian Luar Negeri, pp. 32–39.

Straits Times. (2000). 'Japan Keen on Joint Patrols to Fight Piracy', 18 February 2000, accessed from the Newsbank database.

Straits Times. (2012). 'Indonesia Hikes Defence Budget to Record $10b – Move Comes as it Seeks to Leverage Rising Economy to Overhaul Hardware', 24 August 2012, accessed from the Newsbank database.

Stryken, Christian-Marius. (2007). 'The US Regional Maritime Security Initiative and US Grand Strategy in Southeast Asia', in *Maritime Security in Southeast Asia*. New York: Routledge, pp. 134–145.

Sudarman, Suzie. (2010). *Report of Riset Unggulan Universitas Indonesia 2009: Anti Terrorism Norms and Supply Chain Security in Indonesia*. Depok: Centre for International Relations Studies.

Sudrajat (Direktur Jenderal Strategi Pertahanan Kementerian Pertahanan Indonesia). (2005). 'Kebijakan Kelautan Nasional dari Perspektif Pertahanan dan Keamanan', in Laporan Kegiatan *Diskusi Panel: Mencari Format Kebijakan Kelautan Indonesia Dalam Rangka Mendukung Pembangunan dan Integrasi Nasional (Studi Kasus Kanada dan Norwegia), Surabaya, 7–8 April 2005*. Jakarta: Kementerian Luar Negeri Indonesia.

Sumaryono, Laksmana Muda TNI Djoko. (2004). 'Kerjasama Regional Maritim ASEAN dari Perspektif Keamanan Matra Laut', in *Forum Dialog ke XI Kerjasama Maritim ASEAN*. Jakarta: Badan Pengkajian dan Pengembangan Kebijakan Departemen Luar Negeri.

Sunday Times. (2000). 'War Games with a Soft Touch', 17 September 2000, accessed from the Newsbank database.

Suristiyono, Komisaris Besar Polisi (Wakil Direktur Polair Babinkam Polri). (2005). 'Penyelenggaraan Keamanan dan Ketertiban Di Kawasan Perairan Selat Malaka', in *Pertemuan Kelompok Ahli Tentang Kebijakan Terpadu Pengelolaan Keamanan Selat Malaka*. Jakarta: Badan Pengkajian dan Pengembangan Kebijakan Kementerian Luar Negeri.

Surya Citra Televisi (SCTV) Liputan 6. (2007). 'Menhan: Penolakan Ratifikasi Salah Kaprah', 26 June 2007, available at http://news.liputan6.com/read/143646/menhan-penolakan-ratifikasi-salah-kaprah. Last accessed 13 June 2013.

Suryadinata, Leo. (1998). *Politik Luar Negeri Indonesia di Bawah Soeharto*. Jakarta: LP3ES.

Terminal Peti Kemas Surabaya. (2013). 'Company Overview', 11 May 2013, available at www.tps.co.id/Default.aspx?bahasa=ENG. Last accessed 11 May 2013.

UNCTAD. (2007). *UNCTAD/SDTE/TLB/2007/1 Maritime Security: ISPS Code Implementation, Costs and Related Financing*, available at http://unctad.org/en/docs/sdtetlb20071_en.pdf. Last accessed 3 September 2012.

United Nations Economic and Social Commission for Asia and the Pacific (UNESCAP). (2013). 'Facilitating Efficient and Secure Trade in BIMP EAGA', available at www.unescap.org/tid/projects/tfforum11_gms_ciqs.pdf. Last accessed 11 November 2013.

Urquhart, Donald. (2004). 'Malacca Straits Needs US Support – Having US Marines as an Anti-Piracy Force May Not Be a Bad Idea since the Littoral States Seem Hamstrung in Dealing with the Problem', *Business Times*, 10 April 2004, accessed from the Newsbank database.

Urquhart, Donald. (2006). 'S'pore Acts on Piracy Info Centre Plan – Coastal Command Head Lt Col Teo to Lay Ground Work, say sources', *Business Times*, 19 January 2006, accessed from the Newsbank database.

USAID and Senada. (2008). Indonesian Port Sector Reform and the 2008 Shipping Law. Jakarta: SENADA, available at http://pdf.usaid.gov/pdf_docs/PNADN188.pdf. Last accessed 7 June 2013.

US Customs and Border Protection (US CBP). (2006). *Container Security Initiative 2006–2011 Strategic Plan. US*. Washington DC: Customs and Border Protection Office of Policy and Planning and Office of International Affairs Container Security Division, available at www.cbp.gov/linkhandler/cgov/trade/…security/…/csi_strategic_plan.pdf. Last accessed 7 May 2010.

US CBP. (2007). 'CSI Fact Sheet', 2 October 2007, available at www.cbp.gov/sp/cgov/border_security/international_activities/csi/cis_in_brief.xml. Last accessed 26 October 2009.

US DoD. (2010). 'Department of Defense Bloggers Roundtable with Lieutenant General Benjamin Mixon, Commander, US Army, Pacific Via teleconference Subject: Cobra Gold 10 in Thailand', 2 February 2010, available at www.defense.gov/blog_files/blog_assets/20100202_mixon.pdf – 2010–02–02. Last accessed 10 March 2010.

US Department of State (DoS). (2004). 'Chairman's Statement at the 1st Anniversary PSI Meeting, Krakow, Poland', 1 June 2004, available at http://2001-2009.state.gov/t/isn/rls/other/33208.htm. Last accessed 10 July 2013.

US DoS. (2011). 'DoD-funded Integrated Maritime Surveillance System', 18 November 2011, available at www.state.gov/r/pa/prs/ps/2011/11/177382.htm. Last accessed 21 March 2012.

US Embassy in Jakarta. (2008). 'US Coast Guard Issues Advisory to Indonesia on Port Security', 26 February 2008, available at http://jakarta.usembassy.gov/pr_02262008.html. Last accessed 20 September 2011.

US Embassy in Jakarta. (2011). 'US Donates Patrol Boats to Indonesian National Police to Support Maritime Security', 3 June 2011, available at http://jakarta.usembassy.gov/embnews_06032011.html. Last accessed 5 November 2013.

US Pacific Command (USPACOM). (2004a) 'The Regional Maritime Security Initiative', available at www.pacom.mil/rmsi/. Last accessed 5 October 2009.

USPACOM. (2004b). 'United States Pacific Command Strategy for Maritime Security', available at www.pacom.mil/rmsi/RMSI%20Strategy%20Nov%2004.pdf. Last accessed 5 October 2009.

USPACOM. (2004c). '"Blue Top" Document on the Regional Maritime Security Initiative', available at www.pacom.mil/rmsi/. Last accessed 21 October 2009.

USPACOM. (2004d). '"Trifold" Document on the Regional Maritime Security Initiative', available at www.pacom.mil/rmsi/. Last accessed 21 October 2009.

Valencia, Mark J. (2006). 'Security Issues in the Malacca Straits: Whose Security and Why It Matters?', in *Building a Comprehensive Security Environment in the Straits of Malacca: Proceeding of the MIMA International Conference on the Straits of Malacca, 11–13 October, 2004.* Kuala Lumpur: Maritime Institute of Malaysia.

Waltz, Kenneth N. (1979). *Theory of International Politics.* New York: McGraw-Hill.

WCO. (2007). *WCO SAFE Framework of Standards*, available at www.wcoomd.org/files/1.%20Public%20files/PDFandDocuments/Procedures%20and%20Facilitation/safe_package/safe_package_I.pdf. Last accessed 11 August 2011.

Wibisono, Makarim. (2006). *Tantangan Diplomasi Multilateral.* Makmur Keliat and Mohtar Mas'oed (eds). Jakarta: LP3ES.

Xinhua. (2004). 'India for Joint Naval Patrols with Indonesia, Malaysia', 11 August 2004, accessed from the Newsbank database.

Xinhua. (2007a). 'Indonesia–Singapore Defense Cooperation to Benefit Regional Stability: Susilo', 27 April 2007, accessed from the Newsbank database.

Xinhua. (2007b). 'Indonesia–Singapore Extradition Treaty Effective for Bringing back Fugitive Corrupters', 27 April 2007b, accessed from the Newsbank database.

Yasin, Mat Taib. (2007). *The Security of Sea Lanes of Communication in the Indian Ocean Region.* Kuala Lumpur: Maritime Institute of Malaysia.

Yussof, Ishak and Kasim, Mohd Yusof. (2003). 'Human Resources Development and Regional Cooperation Within BIMP-EAGA: Issues and Future Directions'. *Asia Pacific Development Journal* 10:2, pp. 41–56.

Yusuf, Ibrahim (Kepala Badan Pengkajian dan Pengembangan Kebijakan Departemen Luar Negeri). (2004). 'Sambutan', in *Forum Dialog ke XI Kerjasama Maritim ASEAN.* Jakarta: Badan Pengkajian dan Pengembangan Kebijakan Departemen Luar Negeri, pp. 24–26.

6 Conclusion

Indonesia occupies a vitally important position in respect of global maritime security. Situated between two shipping routes connecting the Indian and Pacific Oceans and with maritime areas covering the three Sea Lanes of Communications of Malacca and Singapore, Lombok and the Sunda Straits, it exercises responsibility for a large percentage of the world's shipping trade. In one year, it is estimated that over 3 million ships pass through Indonesia's waters.[1] This makes Indonesia's role in securing shipping against piracy and armed robbery at sea of great significance. Given the economic and security significance of the issue and the cross-border nature of the problem, there have been numerous international efforts to secure the sea lanes. Strikingly, Indonesia has joined some of these maritime security arrangements, such as the MSP Agreement and the WCO SAFE Framework, but not others, like the ReCAAP and the CSI. Both the MSP Agreement and the ReCAAP are aimed at increasing coordination and information sharing among states to deal with armed robbery attacks at sea, whereas, the WCO SAFE Framework and the CSI are designed to improve port and container security and deter terrorist attacks. This prompts the motivating question of this book: why did Indonesia participate in some maritime security arrangements, but not join functionally similar ones?

This book has examined the entire population of maritime security cooperation agreements affecting Indonesia from 1988 to 2013. In doing so, it has demonstrated that most of the explanations in the existing literature over- or under- or mis-predict Indonesia's cooperation. The explanation that best fits the evidence is one that has been neglected in the literature to date: the importance of absolute gains, as stressed by neoliberal accounts of cooperation. This finding is particularly surprising, since it suggests that, contrary to what one might otherwise assume, the consideration of absolute gains trumps concern for relative gains, even in the sphere of maritime security cooperation.

Findings

This section draws together the findings of this book. For this purpose this section is divided into five sub-sections, based on five plausible explanations offered by the existing international relations literature on cooperation and bureaucratic politics. These include bureaucratic politics, hegemonic leadership, shared identity and the calculation of relative and absolute gains. The summary of evidence across cooperation cases presented in this book can be found in Table 6.1 and Table 6.2.

Bureaucratic politics: absence of competitive preferences among self-interested actors

A group of works have used bureaucratic politics to understand Indonesia's foreign policy making. Liddle, Jackson, Suryadinata, Emmerson and Nabbs-Keller point to the centrality of government actors in the decision-making process (Emmerson, 1983, pp. 1223, 1228, 1230; Jackson, 1978, pp. 10–11; Liddle, 1985; pp. 70–71; Nabbs-Keller, 2013, pp. 56, 68; Suryadinata, 1998, pp. 50–51). Given the importance of bureaucratic actors and processes in Indonesia's policy making, this book uses bureaucratic politics as a plausible explanation to account for Indonesia's varying participation across cooperation cases.

Allison's bureaucratic politics focuses on the process of formulation and reformulation of policy decisions through the interaction of various actors' competing preferences (Allison and Zelikow, 1999, p. 255). This book shows the limitation of the bureaucratic politics approach in understanding Indonesia's participation and non-participation in maritime security arrangements. It demonstrates that Indonesia has a distinct bureaucratic politics, different from Allison's focus on the competing preferences of various government institutions involved in the policy process. Chapter 2 shows that the MFA has been a leading agency in Indonesia's decision-making process. The main functions of the MFA are to make assessments of cooperation and to lead both the negotiation at international level and the formulation of policy at national level. This is solely delegated to the MFA or shared between the MFA and other agencies because the area of cooperation falls under these agencies' remits. Given the MFA's dominant role in Indonesia's foreign policy, competitive bargaining among self-interested actors as expected by the bureaucratic politics literature does not take place.

The discussion in Chapter 2 of this book also shows that Indonesia's decision to join or not to join cooperation arrangements was not informed by individual ministries' self-interest. Leading ministries did not assess each cooperation arrangement on the basis of the benefits that they might attain. Rather, government ministries assessed each cooperation initiative according to the calculation of costs and benefits for other government agencies, Indonesian businesses and the country as a whole. The MFA as one of the leading agencies supported Indonesia's participation in various maritime security arrangements, including the bilateral counter-terrorism cooperation with the US, Japan and Australia, a trilateral information sharing arrangement, the BIMP-EAGA MoUs on transport of goods and sea linkages, the ASEAN Convention on Counter-Terrorism, the ISPS Code, the WCO SAFE Framework and the APEC TRP, bilateral coordinated patrol arrangements with Singapore and Malaysia, defence arrangements with the Philippines and India, the MoU on maritime cooperation with China, the

Table 6.1 Cooperation to address maritime terrorism: variables and negotiated outcomes

Initiative	Relative gains	Shared identity	Hegemonic leadership	Absolute gains Benefits	Sovereignty costs	Implementation costs	Bureaucratic politics	Outcome
US–Indonesia Defence Arrangement	Advantage position	Not present	n/a	High	Low	Low	In favour	Cooperation
Indonesia–Japan Joint Announcement on Counter-Terrorism	Advantage position	Not present	n/a	High	Low	Low	In favour	Cooperation
Three security arrangements with Australia	Advantage position	Not present	n/a	High	Low	Low	In favour	Cooperation
Two BIMP-EAGA MoUs	Disadvantage position	Present	n/a	High	Low	Low	In favour	Cooperation
The Agreement on Information Exchange and Establishment of Communication	Disadvantage position	Present	n/a	High	Low	Low	In favour	Cooperation
The ASEAN Convention on Counter-Terrorism	Disadvantage position	Present	n/a	High	Low	Low	In favour	Cooperation

The International Ship and Port Facility Security (ISPS) Code	Disadvantage position	Not present	n/a	High	Low	High	In favour	Cooperation
The World Customs Organization (WCO) SAFE Framework	Disadvantage position	Not present	n/a	High	Low	Low	In favour	Cooperation
The Asia–Pacific Economic Cooperation Trade Recovery Programme (APEC TRP)	Disadvantage position	Not present	n/a	High	Low	Low	In favour	Cooperation
The Convention for the Suppression of Unlawful Acts (SUA) against the Safety of Maritime Navigation	Advantage position	Not present	High	Low	High	Low	Not in favour	Non-cooperation
The Proliferation Security Initiative (PSI)	Advantage position	Not present	High	Low	High	High	Not in favour	Non-cooperation
The Container Security Initiative (CSI)	Advantage position	Not present	High	Low	High	High	Not in favour	Non-cooperation

Table 6.2 Cooperation to address sea robbery: variables and negotiated outcomes

Initiative	Relative gains	Shared identity	Hegemonic leadership	Absolute gains - Benefits	Absolute gains - Sovereignty costs	Implementation costs	Bureaucratic politics	Outcome
Indonesia–Singapore Coordinated Patrol Arrangement	Disadvantage position	Present	n/a	High	Low	Low	In favour	Cooperation
Indonesia–Malaysia Coordinated Patrol Arrangement	Disadvantage position	Present	n/a	High	Low	Low	In favour	Cooperation
Indonesia–the Philippines Defence Agreement	Advantage position	Present	n/a	High	Low	Low	In favour	Cooperation
Indonesia–India Defence Agreement	Advantage position	Not present	n/a	High	Low	Low	In favour	Cooperation
Indonesia–China MoU on Maritime Cooperation	Advantage position	Not present	n/a	High	Low	Low	In favour	Cooperation
The Malacca Straits Patrol (MSP) Agreement	Disadvantage position	Present	n/a	High	Low	Low	In favour	Cooperation
The ASEAN Regional Forum (ARF) and the ASEAN Maritime Forum (AMF)	Disadvantage position	Not present	n/a	High	Low	Low	In favour	Cooperation
The Regional Maritime Security Initiative (RMSI)	Advantage position	Not present	High	Low	Low	High	Not in favour	Non-cooperation
The Regional Cooperation Agreement on Combating Piracy and Armed Robbery against Ships in Asia (ReCAAP)	Advantage position	Not present	n/a	Low	Low	Low	Not in favour	Non-cooperation
The Defence Cooperation Agreement (DCA) with Singapore	Disadvantage position	Present	n/a	Low	Low	Low	Not in favour	Non-cooperation

MSP agreement, and the AMF and ARF initiatives to counter sea robbery, despite the ministry not receiving any benefits from Indonesia's cooperation. Cooperation activities under these initiatives, including training, military exercises, gifting of equipment and patrols, were tailored to assist the work of Indonesia's law enforcement agencies such as the navy, the MoT coast guard unit, customs, the Maritime Security Coordinating Board and the marine police. None of the arrangements discussed in this book allocated incentives or resources to the MFA. The consistent feature of the MFA in all cooperation cases was also shown even in a cooperation case that involved a large number of Indonesian government actors, such as the ReCAAP. In addition to the MFA, the ReCAAP also involved the MoD, the MoT, and the Maritime Security Coordinating Board. However, as explained in Chapter 2, officials from other government agencies confirmed that the MFA played the key role in deciding Indonesia's non-participation and informing their agencies how they should engage with the ReCAAP ISC.

Hegemonic leadership: insufficient cause of cooperation

King, Byers, Stryken and Rosenberg and Chung's studies on maritime cooperation touch upon the neorealist and neoliberal hegemonic leadership argument. They draw attention to US leadership in promoting new maritime arrangements, such as the PSI and the RMSI among others, but do not assess how the US leadership informs Indonesia or other states' participation in these arrangements (Byers, 2003, pp. 171–210; 2004; King, 2005, pp. 236, 241; Rosenberg and Chung, 2008, pp. 53–54, 63–64; Stryken, 2007, pp. 136–137, 141–142). Using these scholarly works as a point of departure, this book treats hegemonic leadership as a plausible explanation to understand Indonesia's cooperation and non-cooperation.

As discussed in the Introduction, both neorealism and neoliberalism explain that, when the benefits of cooperation are insignificant, the presence of hegemonic leadership can convince states to cooperate. Contrary to this expectation, this book shows that hegemonic leadership cannot explain Indonesia's participation or non-participation in cooperation because, in a number of arrangements that involved the US including the SUA convention, the PSI, the CSI and the RMSI, the presence of US leadership was not sufficient to ensure Indonesia's cooperation (see Table 6.1 and Table 6.2). The US drafted, initiated, and actively promoted the SUA convention, the CSI, the PSI and the RMSI, both through its bilateral relations with Indonesia and its engagement in multilateral forums. In the case of the PSI, the US for instance actively enforced rules through developing various agreements with major flag-states to facilitate interdiction of vessels suspected of carrying WMD materials and conducting actual interdiction activities. In the case of the CSI, the US could place US Customs in foreign ports and bar all containers coming from non-CSI ports from entering US ports. Yet, despite the presence of strong US leadership, Indonesia decided not to join these cooperation arrangements. Thus, it would seem that the neorealist and neoliberal

212 *Conclusion*

argument on hegemonic leadership is not sufficient to explain Indonesia's decision to cooperate or not cooperate in a maritime security arrangement.

This book also raises questions about the behaviour of the US. Indonesia's participation was important to the US objectives of halting the proliferation and transportation of WMD and securing important sea lanes from terrorist and sea robbery attacks; yet, the US only provided incentives and stated its agreement to bear the enforcement costs. The question that arises from this circumstance is why the US did not use overt coercion to compel Indonesia to join initiatives such as the SUA convention, the PSI, the CSI and the RMSI. Chapter 3 explained that Indonesia's cooperation with US unilateral initiatives, such as the 24-Hours Rule, the International Port Security Programme and the US Customs-Trade Partnership against Terrorism was sufficient to induce changes at the domestic level and, therefore, US coercion in the case of the SUA convention, the PSI, the CSI and the RMSI was not required.

Shared identity: not a cause of cooperation

Constructivism argues that states that share a similar identity are more likely to cooperate than those who cannot identify positively with each other. Scholars, including Ball, Johnston, Acharya and Tan, echo the constructivist argument regarding the importance of shared identity in informing states' cooperation. They point out that ASEAN states have a sense of shared identity, often called the 'ASEAN way' norm, that puts emphasis on the role of consensus and accommodation to settle disputes and advance security cooperation among them (Acharya, 1992; 1995; 1997, pp. 328–329; 1998, p. 80; 2004, pp. 249, 256; Acharya and Tan, 2006, pp. 42, 53; Ball, 1993, p. 53; Johnston, 1999, pp. 294–295). Given the 'ASEAN way' identity is believed to be embraced by ASEAN states, ASEAN membership is an appropriate proxy for shared identity. In this context, Indonesia is expected to cooperate with other ASEAN states, and less likely to do so with non-ASEAN states.

The constructivist argument regarding the role of shared identity cannot account for Indonesia's varying participation across cases. As seen in Table 6.1 and Table 6.2, Indonesia joined agreements that included non-ASEAN states, as shown in the case of bilateral arrangements with the US, Japan, Australia and India, the ISPS Code, the WCO SAFE Framework, the APEC TRP, the ARF and the AMF; and those that exclusively involved ASEAN states, including the BIMP-EAGA MoUs on sea linkages and transport of goods, the trilateral information sharing agreement among Indonesia, Malaysia and the Philippines, the ASEAN Counter-Terrorism Convention, two coordinated patrol arrangements with Malaysia and Singapore, a bilateral defence agreement with the Philippines, and the MSP agreement. Shared identity also did not play a major part in cases that showed Indonesia's non-cooperation. Indonesia cancelled the DCA with Singapore that only involved Indonesia and Singapore, both ASEAN member states. Indonesia also refused to participate in cooperation arrangements that were led and involved a large number of non-ASEAN states, as shown in

Conclusion 213

the cases of the SUA convention, the PSI, the CSI and the RMSI. A closer observation of Indonesia's participation in maritime security arrangements shows that Indonesia is most likely to cooperate with states with which it shares common maritime boundaries. Most of these states happen to be members of ASEAN. Therefore, it is concluded that shared identity cannot account for the full range of cases involving both Indonesia's participation and non-participation in cooperation arrangements.

Relative gains concerns: lack of explanatory purchase

Both neorealism and neoliberalism argue that the state is a rational actor and, therefore, is likely to join a cooperation arrangement when the benefits of cooperation are higher than the costs. The two lines of reasoning, however, differ in their understanding of how costs and benefits are calculated. For neorealists, as explained in the Introduction, states are not only preoccupied with the total gains that they can achieve from a cooperation arrangement since they also take into account their concerns over relative gains. The existing literature does not advance the calculation of relative gains as an explanation for Indonesia's participation or non-participation in security cooperation dealing with maritime terrorism and armed robbery against ships. Despite the existing literature not making much reference to the relative gains calculation, this argument is worth considering in this book given that neorealism purports to offer its most precise explanations when investigating security cooperation (Krasner, 1992, p. 40).

A neorealist would argue that, given Indonesia is a middle power, it is likely to cooperate with larger and smaller states. Cooperation with larger and smaller states would put Indonesia in an advantageous position. This is because the power disparity between them is vast and, therefore, a cooperation arrangement would not change the power gap between them and put Indonesia in a risky situation. In contrast, neorealists would expect that a middle power such as Indonesia would be less likely to cooperate with near-peer states, because a single cooperation arrangement between Indonesia and a near-peer state can easily close the narrow power disparity between them and risk disadvantaging Indonesia.

Contrary to these expectations, Indonesia chose to cooperate with near peer-states, as well as with larger and smaller states (see Table 6.1 and Table 6.2). For instance, Indonesia was willing to join cooperation arrangements that involved near-peer states, including two coordinated patrol arrangements with Malaysia and Singapore, the MSP agreement, the AMF and ARF, the BIMP-EAGA MoUs on sea linkages and transport of goods, the agreement on the information exchange, the ASEAN Counter-Terrorism Convention, the ISPS Code, the WCO SAFE Framework and the APEC TRP. Moreover, Indonesia refused to join cooperation arrangements that were led by larger states, such as the US and Japan, for instance the SUA convention, the PSI, the CSI, the RMSI and the ReCAAP, where relative gains considerations would not be expected to matter. The only instance in which Indonesia refused to cooperate with a near-peer was

214 *Conclusion*

the DCA with Singapore. Taken as a whole, the neorealist argument regarding the role of relative gains calculation cannot explain Indonesia's cooperation or non-cooperation. In contrast to the neorealist expectation Indonesia agreed to cooperate with near-peer states as well as smaller and larger states.

The calculation of costs and benefits: absolute gains matter

As explained above, concerns over relative gains, shared identity, hegemonic leadership and bureaucratic politics cannot explain Indonesia's participation and non-participation across cooperation cases. Therefore, we need to locate the reason for Indonesia's varying cooperation elsewhere. Bradford and Sato cited the calculation of costs and benefits as the reason underpinning Indonesia's reluctance to join the ReCAAP (Bradford, 2004, p. 497; Sato, 2007, pp. 6–7). The calculation of costs and benefits in absolute terms is the final plausible explanation to consider.

The findings in this book confirm the neoliberal argument regarding the role of a calculation of absolute gains. Chapter 5 shows that the calculation of absolute gains corresponded with negotiated outcomes. Indonesia only joined cooperation initiatives where the overall benefits exceeded the costs.

Indonesia participated in bilateral cooperation with the US, Japan and Australia, the BIMP-EAGA MoUs on sea linkages and transport of goods, a sub-regional information sharing cooperation, the ASEAN Counter-Terrorism Convention, the ISPS Code, the WCO SAFE Framework, the APEC TRP, two coordinated patrol arrangements with Malaysia and Singapore, bilateral agreements with the Philippines, India, and China, the MSP sub-regional patrols, and the AMF and the ARF because the incentives offered by these initiatives exceeded the costs. Without having to do much, Indonesia gained new equipment, funds to establish counter-terrorism centres and capacity-building assistance in the form of training and exercises for its maritime agencies from bilateral cooperation with the US, Japan, Australia and China. Indonesia did not need to make significant adjustment for its maritime agencies to gain naval and aircraft surveillance support during patrols from Malaysia, Singapore, the Philippines and India.

The BIMP-EAGA initiatives, the exchange of information agreement, the ASEAN Counter-Terrorism Convention and the MSP agreement did not require Indonesia to make substantial changes at national level. Yet, these sub-regional and regional initiatives enabled Indonesia to receive enormous support from countries in the region in: investigating terrorist attacks; providing access to their fingerprint databases, lists of airline passengers, visa blacklists and intelligence information; and sharing burdens among them in dealing with armed robbery against ships and deterring maritime terrorism. The ISPS Code posed high implementation costs, because Jakarta needed to allocate additional resources to install new security devices in its international ports, carry out ISPS Code training and exercises and review ports and ships compliance to the Code. Nevertheless, the payoff that Indonesia gained from making these additional investments was high. This was because Indonesian ports and ships were not excluded from international trade, and the government received assistance to establish a sea and coast guard. As the ISPS Code was one of the requirements demanded by marine insurance companies, compliance with the Code also provided the additional economic benefit of avoiding an increase in insurance premiums. Cooperation in the WCO SAFE Framework and the APEC TRP was even more straightforward for Indonesia, because these initiatives provided high incentives and generated low costs. From both initiatives, Indonesia gained capacity-building programmes from other member states and secretariats of the WCO and the APEC to develop its own trade facilitation and recovery programme, while not having to do much more than what it already did.

Indonesia's reluctance to join some maritime security cooperation arrangements also confirms the neoliberal argument regarding the importance of the calculation of absolute gains. Indonesia did not join three arrangements dealing with maritime terrorism – the SUA convention, the PSI and the CSI – and three arrangements to address sea robbery – the RMSI, the ReCAAP and the DCA – because these initiatives did not offer sufficient absolute gains. The Indonesian government deemed that participation in these initiatives was redundant because Indonesia could gain the benefits offered by the initiative, including exchange of intelligence information, new equipment and capacity-building assistance, through its participation in other maritime arrangements. Some of these arrangements, including the SUA convention, the RMSI, the PSI and the CSI, also brought high costs. The SUA convention would have regulated how Indonesia must deal with unlawful acts that occur in parts of Indonesia's maritime jurisdiction and required Jakarta to accept external authority over dispute settlement without offering tangible economic and security benefits. The RMSI would have been costly for Indonesia because of problems caused by the rejection of the agreement from some Parliament members and security risks posed by radical groups. The PSI and the CSI would have imposed even higher costs in comparison to the SUA convention and the RMSI. The PSI would have compromised Indonesia's rights as a coastal or flag state since under this initiative Jakarta would have been subjected to other participants' demands for access when an act of interdiction took place in Indonesian waters or was carried out against vessels registered under the Indonesian flag. In addition, when a false interdiction takes place, the Indonesian government faces the risk of compensating businesses for any loss and delay suffered by them. Indonesia felt that bearing such costs were unnecessary because Jakarta can gain the incentives of cooperation offered by the PSI, particularly in term of new equipment and capacity-building training and exercises, through bilateral cooperation with the US. The CSI would have required Indonesia to change its legislation to accommodate the presence of external authority in its ports, accept external authority over significant decision making in relation to port and container security and invest more resources to purchase new security devices that met the cooperation standard. At the same time, the high costs of the cooperation would not have been met with sufficient benefits. The main advantage of the CSI is to ensure unimpeded access to US ports. Indonesia can gain this benefit of cooperation by trans-shipping its containers bound to the US through Singapore and Malaysia CSI ports, a practice that has been conducted for many years by Indonesian businesses.

Across the cooperation cases presented in Chapter 5, the calculation of absolute gains was not influenced by societal actors, with the RMSI the only exception. In the case of the RMSI, because of popular sentiment against the initiative, societal actors which included Parliament members and radical groups rejected the agreement, and this influenced the government's assessment of the costs and benefits posed by the initiative. Having surveyed the calculation of absolute gains in all cooperation cases discussed in this book, it is concluded that Indonesia's decision to participate in some cooperation arrangements and not to participate in others is consistent with the absolute gains calculation.

Conclusion

The main findings of this book confirm the neoliberal account of the role of the calculation of absolute gains in international cooperation. This book, therefore, offers three major contributions. First, given the importance of absolute gains across cooperation cases, this book shows that even in maritime security cooperation relative gains concerns did not matter. Although the neorealists claim that the calculation of relative gain would have better explanatory purchase in explaining security issues, the findings presented in this book contradict this expectation. Only the calculation of absolute gains can explain Indonesia's cooperation and non-cooperation in maritime arrangements.

Second, by focusing solely on explaining Indonesia's decision to join or not to join a cooperation arrangement, this book has met its main purpose to seek the causes underlying Indonesia's participation in maritime security arrangements. As a result, this book also offers a conceptual discussion of the reasons underlying middle-power participation or non-participation in cooperation agreements. The international relations cooperation literature tends to focus on cooperation between major powers (see Axelrod, 1981; Axelrod and Keohane, 1985; Gowa, 1986; Grieco, 1988; Jervis, 1978, 1988; Keohane, 1984; Krasner, 1982; Lipson, 1984; Martin and Simmons, 1998; Mearsheimer, 2001; Moravcsik, 1993; Oye, 1985; Singer, 1958; Snidal, 1985, 1991; Waltz, 1979). Little attention has been given to the study of middle-power participation in cooperation arrangements, some of which they have little influence on. This book has provided a starting point for a new research agenda to search for the reasons underpinning middle-power participation in cooperation arrangements. Most literature on middle powers focuses on explaining traditional middle-power leadership at international organisations such as the United Nations (Behringer, 2005; Chapnick, 1999, 2000; Fox, 1980; Glazebrook, 1947; Granatstein, 1973, 2011; Higgott and Cooper, 1990; Holmes, 1976; Ravenhill, 1998). These works primarily centre on Canadian and Australian foreign policy. Very little attention has been given to discussing the behaviour of emerging middle powers such as Indonesia. The existing studies on emerging middle powers show a lack of theoretical discussion on factors that inform states' decisions in approaching different cooperation settings (see Efstathopoulos, 2011; Jordaan, 2003; Neufeld, 1995; Pfister, 2005; Ping, 2005; Westhuizen, 1998). By systematically testing international relations arguments on why a state cooperates, this book has filled the gap left both by the current international relations literature on cooperation and the middle-power literature.

Finally, the evidence in the empirical chapters that supports the role of absolute gains in informing Indonesia's cooperation also dismisses scholarly arguments which state that Indonesia was reluctant to participate in maritime cooperation during the early years following 9/11, particularly between 2001 and 2004. This study demonstrates that Indonesia cooperated when the benefits of cooperation exceeded the costs. Indonesia does take part in maritime cooperation and has been a willing participant and aspiring leader in establishing various arrangements. Indonesia has been less willing to commit itself to some arrangements because the incentives offered by these do not outweigh the costs. Indonesia can gain the benefits offered by a number of arrangements including the SUA convention, the PSI, the CSI, the RMSI and the ReCAAP through other cooperation channels.

Future work

This chapter has dealt with the main question of this book, why Indonesia joined some maritime security arrangements but refused to participate in others. In addressing this question, this book has revealed several further questions that warrant attention, and would thus provide fruitful lines for further inquiry.

First, why does Indonesia choose different forms of agreement across cases? The form of agreement refers to the design of the cooperation arrangement that can range from non-legally binding joint announcement to formal treaty that calls for parliamentary ratification. The question of why Indonesia chooses certain forms of cooperation that entail particular cooperative activities and levels of political commitment rather than others at a given time is a question that will be addressed in my future research.

Second, why did Malaysia and Singapore join the CSI when Indonesia did not? Why did Singapore choose to participate in the SUA convention, the PSI and the ReCAAP and supported the RMSI when Indonesia and Malaysia did not? This book does not seek to compare Indonesia's varying participation in international cooperation with the policies of other littoral states in responding to maritime security arrangements. It focuses solely on investigating Indonesia's participation in maritime security arrangements. Nevertheless, this book opens the way to embark upon a systematic comparison of the participation of the littoral states of the Straits of Malacca and Singapore in maritime security arrangements in the future, using the plausible explanations that I have developed in this book.

It would be useful to test whether these explanations hold across countries or if they are unique to Indonesia. Some of the alternative explanations offered in this book, including relative gains, hegemonic leadership and shared identity, apply in the same way to these countries as Indonesia. In term of relative gains, Malaysia and Singapore have relatively similar defence capabilities as Indonesia. Therefore, they would be expected to cooperate with larger or smaller states but avoid cooperation with their near-peer competitors. Given Indonesia, Malaysia and Singapore have cooperated among themselves to address maritime terrorism and sea robbery, this argument offers no explanatory power. With regards to hegemonic leadership, the US leadership was also present in the case of the SUA convention, the PSI, the CSI and the RMSI. Despite a constant presence of US leadership, the negotiated outcome varied across cases and countries. Singapore supported all of these US-led initiatives and Malaysia opposed most of them, with the CSI as the only exception. This implies that the hegemonic leadership argument cannot hold across cases. Finally, in terms of shared identity the three states are all ASEAN states. Since Malaysia and Singapore cooperated with non-ASEAN states as well as ASEAN states, shared identity cannot account for their cooperation or non-cooperation. Taken as a whole, since relative gains, shared identity and hegemonic leadership arguments apply to Malaysia and Singapore exactly as they do to Indonesia, these three arguments can be rejected. Therefore, future inquiry can focus on assessing the role of the absolute gains calculation and bureaucratic politics in informing Singapore and Malaysian cooperation or non-cooperation.

Third, to what extent does Indonesia comply with the requirements of cooperation initiatives that it has chosen to join? This book does not seek to test the degree of compliance, implementation and enforcement displayed by Indonesia towards cooperation arrangements dealing with maritime terrorism and armed robbery against ships. The level of compliance of the Indonesian government and businesses with a number of cooperation arrangements, including the ISPS Code, the WCO SAFE Framework, and the APEC TRP, at domestic level is beyond the scope of this book, but this line of enquiry can be developed further in the future.

In this book the question of why Indonesia chose to cooperate with some initiatives but not others was addressed. It has been shown that Indonesia has been willing to make compromises in allowing cross-border maritime and air patrols and enabling its cooperation partners' aircraft to enter its airspace, land and refuel in its territory to enable the success of cooperation. This is in contrast to most academic works that cited concerns over sovereignty infringement as the main impediment for Indonesia's participation in maritime security arrangements. Indonesia chose to cooperate when the benefits of an initiative outweighed the costs. This is important, not just to the academic exercise of trying to understand middle-power cooperation in international relations, but also to those involved in the design, negotiation and decisions on international cooperation agreements that involve middle powers. It is vital that negotiators and policy makers understand that, in order to achieve success, the absolute gains should be sufficient to entice a state to cooperate.

Note

1 This figure is an estimate generated from data of vessels navigating through Indonesian waters on 12 December 2013, 08:30 GMT. As shown by the live marine traffic map (available at www.marinetraffic.com/en/), there were 1,735 vessels plying through Indonesian waters at this time. This number only includes ships that are fitted with AIS transponders. According to IMO regulations (Regulation 19 of SOLAS Chapter V), the AIS is only required to be fitted aboard ships of 300 gross tonnage and upwards engaged on international voyages. Therefore, this figure does not include vessels below 300 gross tonnage involved in international shipping.

References

Acharya, Amitav. (1992). 'Regional Military-Security Cooperation in the Third World: A Conceptual Analysis of the Relevance and Limitations of ASEAN (Association of Southeast Asian Nations)'. *Journal of Peace Research February* 29, pp. 7–21.

Acharya, Amitav. (1995). 'A Regional Security Community in Southeast Asia?'. *Journal of Strategic Studies* 18:3, pp. 175–200.

Acharya, Amitav. (1997). 'Ideas, Identity and Institution Building: From the "ASEAN Way" to the "Asia–Pacific Way"?' *The Pacific Review* 10:3, pp. 319–346.

Acharya, Amitav. (1998). 'Culture, Security, Multilateralism: The "ASEAN Way" and Regional Order'. *Contemporary Security Policy* 19:1, pp. 55–84.

Acharya, Amitav. (2004). 'How Ideas Spread: Whose Norms Matter? Norm Localization and Institutional Change in Asian Regionalism'. *International Organization* 58:2, pp. 239–275.

Acharya, Amitav and Tan, See Seng. (2006). 'Betwixt Balance and Community: America, ASEAN and the Security of Southeast Asia'. *International Relations of the Asia Pacific* 6:1, pp. 37–59.

Allison, Graham and Zelikow, Philip. (1999). *Essence of Decision: Explaining the Cuban Missile Crisis*, 2nd edition. New York: Wesley Longman.

Axelrod, Robert. (1981). 'The Emergence of Cooperation among Egoists'. *American Political Science Review* 75:2, pp. 306–318.

Axelrod, Robert and Keohane, Robert O. (1985). 'Achieving Cooperation under Anarchy: Strategies and Institutions'. *World Politics* 38:1, pp. 226–254.

Ball, Desmond. (1993). 'Strategic Culture in the Asia–Pacific Region'. *Security Studies* 3:1, pp. 44–74.

Behringer, Ronald M. (2005). 'Middle Power Leadership on the Human Security Agenda'. *Cooperation and Conflict* 40:3, pp. 305–342.

Bradford, John F. (2004). 'Japanese Anti-Piracy Initiatives in Southeast Asia: Policy Formulation and the Coastal States Responses'. *Contemporary Southeast Asia* 26:3, pp. 480–505.

Byers, Michael. (2003). 'Preemptive Self-defense: Hegemony, Equality and Strategies of Legal Change'. *Journal of Political Philosophy* 11:2, pp. 171–190.

Byers, Michael. (2004). 'Policing the High Seas: The Proliferation Security Initiative'. *The American Journal of International Law* 98:3, pp. 526–545.

Chapnick, Adam. (1999). 'The Middle Power'. *Canadian Foreign Policy* 7:2, pp. 73–82.

Chapnick, Adam. (2000). 'The Canadian Middle Power Myth'. *International Journal* 55:2, pp. 188–206.

Efstathopoulos, Charalampos. (2011). 'Reinterpreting India's Rise through the Middle Power Prism'. *Asian Journal of Political Science* 19:1, pp. 74–95.

Emmerson, Donald K. (1983). 'Understanding the New Order: Bureaucratic Pluralism in Indonesia'. *Asian Survey* 23:11, pp. 1220–1241.

Fox, Annette Baker. (1980). 'The Range of Choice for Middle Powers: Australian and Canada Compared'. *Australian Journal of Politics and History* 26:2, pp. 193–203.

Glazebrook, G. De T. (1947). 'The Middle Powers in the United Nations System', *International Organizations* 1:2, pp. 307–315.

Gowa, Joanne. (1986). 'Anarchy, Egoism, and Third Images: The Evolution of Cooperation and International Relations'. *International Organization* 40:1, pp. 167–186.

Granatstein, J.L. (1973). *Canadian Foreign Policy Since 1945: Middle Power or Satellite?* 3rd Edition. Toronto: The Copp Clark Publishing Company.

Granatstein, J.L. (2011). 'Can Canada Have a Grand Strategy?', presented at a Grand Strategy Symposium, 6–7 April 2011, at the Canadian Forces College, Toronto, available at www.cdfai.org/PDF/Can%20Canada%20Have%20a%20Grand%20Strategy.pdf. Last accessed 26 April 2013.

Grieco, Joseph M. (1988). 'Anarchy and the Limits of Cooperation: A Realist Critique of the Newest Liberal Institutionalism'. *International Organization* 42:3, pp. 485–507.

Higgott, Richard A. and Cooper, Andrew Fenton. (1990). 'Middle Power Leadership and Coalition Building: Australia, the Cairns Group and the Uruguay Round of Trade Negotiations'. *International Organization* 44:4, pp. 589–632.

Holmes, John W. (1976). *Canada: A Middle-Aged Power*. Ottawa: McClelland and Stewart Ltd. and The Institute of Canadian Studies, Carleton University.

Jackson, Karl D. (1978). 'The Prospects for Bureaucratic Polity in Indonesia', in *Political Power and Communications in Indonesia*, Karl D. Jackson and Lucian W. Pye (eds). Berkeley, CA: University of California Press, pp. 395–398.

Jervis, Robert. (1978). 'Cooperation under the Security Dilemma'. *World Politics* 30:2, pp. 167–214.

Jervis, Robert. (1988). 'Realism, Game Theory and Cooperation'. *World Politics* 40:3, pp. 317–349.

Johnston, Alistair Ian. (1999). 'The Myth of the ASEAN Way? Explaining the Evolution of the ASEAN Regional Forum', in *Imperfect Unions: Security Institutions over Time and Space*. New York: Oxford University Press.

Jordaan, Eduard. (2003). 'The Concept of a Middle Power in International Relations: Distinguishing Between Emerging and Traditional Middle Powers'. *Politikon* 30:2, pp. 165–181.

Keohane, Robert O. (1984). *After Hegemony: Cooperation and Discord in the World Political Economy*. Princeton, NJ: Princeton University Press.

King, John. (2005). 'The Security of Merchant Shipping'. *Marine Policy* 29, pp. 235–245.

Krasner, Stephen D. (1982). 'Regimes and the Limits of Realism: Regimes as Autonomous Variables'. *International Organization* 36:2, pp. 497–510.

Krasner, Stephen D. (1992). 'Realism, Imperialism and Democracy: A Response to Gilbert'. *Political Theory* 20:1, pp. 38–52.

Liddle, R. William. (1985). 'Soeharto's Indonesia: Personal Rule and Political Institutions'. *Pacific Affairs* 58: 1, pp. 68–90.

Lipson, Charles. (1984). 'International Cooperation in Economic and Security Affairs'. *World Politics* 37:1, pp. 1–23.

Martin, Lisa L. and Simmons, Beth A. (1998). 'Theories and Empirical Studies of International Institutions'. *International Organization* 52:4, pp. 729–757.

Mearsheimer, John J. (2001). *The Tragedy of Great Power Politics*. New York: W.W. Norton & Company.
Moravcsik, Andrew. (1993). 'Armaments among Allies European Weapons Collaboration, 1975–1985', in *International Bargaining and Domestic Politics: Double Edged Diplomacy*. Berkeley, CA: University of California Press.
Nabbs-Keller, Greta. (2013). 'Reforming Indonesia's Foreign Ministry: Ideas, Organization and Leadership'. *Contemporary Southeast Asia* 35:1, pp. 56–82.
Neufeld, Mark. (1995). 'Hegemony and Foreign Policy Analysis: The Case of Canada as Middle Power'. *Studies in Political Economy* 48, pp. 7–29.
Oye, Kenneth A. (1985). 'Explaining Cooperation under Anarchy'. *World Politics* 38:1, pp. 1–24.
Pfister, Roger. (2005). *Apartheid South Africa and African States: from Pariah to Middle Power, 1961–1994*. London: Tauris Academic Studies.
Ping, Jonathan H. (2005). *Middle Power Statecraft: Indonesia, Malaysia and the Asia Pacific*. Aldershot: Ashgate.
Ravenhill, John. (1998). 'Cycles of Middle Power Activism: Constraint and Choice in Australian and Canadian Foreign Policies'. *Australian Journal of International Affairs* 52:3, pp. 309–327.
Rosenberg, David and Chung, Christopher. (2008). 'Maritime Security in the South China Sea: Coordinating Coastal and User State Priorities'. *Ocean Development and International Law* 39:1, pp. 51–68.
Sato, Yoichiro. (2007). 'Southeast Asian Receptiveness to Japanese Maritime Security Cooperation', The Asia-Pacific Center for Security Studies, Honolulu, available at www.dtic.mil/cgi-bin/GetTRDoc?AD=ADA472466. Last accessed 7 December 2013.
Singer, David J. (1958). 'Threat-Perception and the Armament-Tension Dilemma'. *The Journal of Conflict Resolution* 2:1, pp. 90–105.
Snidal, Duncan. (1985). 'Coordination versus Prisoners' Dilemma: Implications for International Cooperation and Regimes'. *American Political Science Review* 79:4, pp. 923–942.
Snidal, Duncan. (1991). 'Relative Gains and the Pattern of International Cooperation'. *American Political Science Review* 85:3, pp. 701–726.
Stryken, Christian-Marius. (2007). 'The US Regional Maritime Security Initiative and US Grand Strategy in Southeast Asia', in *Maritime Security in Southeast Asia*. New York: Routledge.
Suryadinata, Leo. (1998). *Politik Luar Negeri Indonesia di Bawah Soeharto*. Jakarta: LP3ES.
Waltz, Kenneth N. (1979). *Theory of International Politics*. New York: McGraw-Hill.
Westhuizen, Janis Van Der. (1998). 'South Africa's Emergence as a Middle Power'. *Third World Quarterly* 19:3, pp. 435–455.

Index

Page numbers in *italics* denote tables, those in **bold** denote figures.

9/11 3, 29, 37, 44, 52, 73, 83, 105, 153, 217; aftermath 106, 113–14, 137; US 9/11 Commission 113–14
9/11 attacks 15n2, 25, 28, 53, 74, 80, 104, 141, 168, 170; aftermath 26–7, 30, 107, 140; responses to 67

Abbot, J. 31
Abbot, K.W. 8
absolute gains 7, 165, 173–4, 206, *208*, *210*; calculation 4, 11, 15, 120, 148, 151–2, 160, 167, 184–5, 207, 214–16, 218; role of 217; *see also* relative gains
Aceh 46, *51*, 52; attacks on NGO workers in 159; Darul Islam military campaign 65; economic growth 172; military operations 43; people killed 41; separatist movements 15n2, 40, 67, 166
Aceh separatist group 40, 166
Acharya, A. 5–6, 130–4, 137–8, 141, 166, 168, 212
Agoes, E.R. 48, 80, 108, 174
Ahram, A.I. 65
air patrols 46–7; cross-border 13, 15, 79, 134, 148, 218; EiS 45, 79, 172
Allison, G. 10, 14, 64, 69–71, 74, 207
Ambalat Block 50, 67
American Shipper 118
Anggoro, K. 12
Antara 43, 80, 85–6, 106, 110, 139–40, 150, 168, 170–1, 180–3
anti-communist policies 103–4
anti-piracy patrol 77–8
Anwar, D.F. 79
APEC TRP 2, 71, 73–4, 87, 138, 142, 149–50, 152, 161–2, 174, 184, 207, *209*, 212–15, 218

Arafuru Sea 33
archipelagic country 81, 164; state 36, 52, 66, 76, 81–2, 103, 132
archipelagic sea lanes 12; sea lanes I, II and III 33, *46*
archipelagic waters 29, 66; illegal fishing 49; key straits 52
armed robbery against ships 1, *2–3*, 12, 14, 25–6, 48, 54n12, 68, 78, 136, 168, 172, *210*, 214; addressing 71, 82, 111, 178; annual report 43–4; attacks 29–30, **31**, **32**, 40–1, 102, 134, 141, 169; cooperation to counter 75, 77, 80, 140, 142, 150, 152, 173, 180, 185–6, 213, 218; halting 53; increase in 36; international concerns 45; national initiatives *46*; at sea 3, 31, 41–2, 44, 206; spate of 42
Arsana, I Made Andi 79, 166
ASEAN (Association of Southeast Asian Nations) 28, 105, 111, 131–3, 142n1, 172; ASEAN–China DOC 137; ASEAN–US dialogue 136; Bali Concord declaration 134; cooperation frameworks 150; counter-terrorism convention 2, 71, 73–4, 87, 89n25, 138, 142, 152, 159–60, 162, 184, 186, 188n32, 207, *208*; dialogue partners 185; Federation of ASEAN Shipowners' Associations 181; forums 80; initiatives 75; intra-ASEAN cooperation arrangements 149; maritime security cooperation 132; member states *2–3*, 6, 11, 15, 73, 84, 130, 133–4, 136, 139–40, 159, 172, 212; political and security agenda 133; Post Ministerial Conference 135; regional security cooperation 134, 172

Index 223

ASEAN Bali Concord declaration 134
ASEAN Maritime Forum (AMF) *3*, 75, 80, 87, 136–8, 142, 150, 165, 172–3, 185–6, *210*, 211–14
ASEAN Plus Three (APT) 30; summit 77
ASEAN Regional Forum (ARF) 80, 134–6, 138, 142, 150, 165, 172, 176, 185–6, *210*, 212–14; Statement on Cooperation against Piracy *3*, 5, 75, 87, 136, 173, 211
ASEAN Way 5, 14–15, 120, 130–3, 135–8, 141, 212; Counter-Terrorism Convention 2, 138, 142, 149, 160, 212–14; member states 212–13
Asia–Africa Conference 65
Asia-Pacific Economic Cooperation (APEC) 165, 184, 215; Desk of the Indonesian Customs 38–9, 74, 161–2; members 162
Asia-Pacific Economic Cooperation Trade Recovery Programme (APEC TRP) *2*, 71, 73–4, 87, 138, 142, 149–50, 152, 161–2, 174, 184, 207, *209*, 212–15, 218
Asian Development Bank 73
Asian Shipowners' Forum (ASF) 181, 191n110
Australian Department of Defence (DoD) 28, 72, 155–7
Australian Department of Foreign Affairs and Trade 72
Australian Federal Police (AFP) 138, 155, 160
Authorised Economic Operator (AEO) 74; programme 75, 160–2, 184
Automatic Identification System (AIS) 154, 219n1
Axelrod, R. 4, 216

Badan Koordinasi Keamanan Laut (Bakorkamla) 47
Badan Nasional Penanggulangan Terrorism (BNPT) 74
Badan Perencanaan Pembangunan Nasional (Bappenas) 37, 39, 43, 44
Bakorkamla 28, 35–7, 44, *46*, 55n24, 66, 74, 79, 83, 111–12, 150–1, 155–6, 163–4, 169, 171, 179, 181, 193
Bakti, I.N. 8, 73, 140, 157, 159
Baldor, L. 115
Bali bombings 15n2, 28, 37, 53, 67, 72, 138, 159
Ball, D. 5–6, 130, 137–8, 212
Banda Sea 33
Bateman, S. 12–13, 84, 111

BBC 41, 83, 104, 111, 179
Beckman, R.C. 75
Behringer, R.M. 5, 216
bilateral 183; defence agreements 138, 212; efforts against armed robbery 53; exchanges of training 178; patrols 45, 87, 140, 165, 173; relations 154, 156, 168, 211; ship-boarding agreements 110; US–Indonesia defence discussion 105, 153
bilateral arrangements 142, 148, 150; against armed robbery 40; with Australia *2*, 72; border security 5, 134; counter-terrorism 71; Defence 176; patrol 165, 173; US defence 31
bilateral cooperation 152–5, 157–8, 162, 166–70, 180, 184–6, 214–15; with Australia 72; counter-terrorism 87, 207; with Malaysia and Singapore 76; maritime 12, 78; security and defence 178–9; sub-regional 141; with US 14, 82–3, 103, 113
bilateral maritime security issues 30; anti-terrorism initiatives 81, 174; cooperation 12; cooperation with Japan and China 78; exercises to counter sea robbery 170; Indonesia–Singapore exercises 86; negotiations over disputes 50
BIMP-EAGA *see* Brunei Darussalam–Indonesia–Malaysia–the Philippines East ASEAN Growth Area
Bingley, B. 12–13
Boutilier, J. 111, 179
Bradford, J.F. 7, 12–13, 85, 136, 152, 181, 214
Brunei Darussalam–Indonesia–Malaysia–the Philippines East ASEAN Growth Area (BIMP-EAGA) 71, 73, 87, 138, 148–9, 157, 184, 186n3, 187n21, 207, *208*, 212–14
bureaucratic politics 9, 71, 75, 84, *208*, *210*, 214, 218; approach 5, 10–11, 14, 69–70, 74; argument 76, 78–9; expectation 77, 81, 85; limitations of 14, 64, 70, 77, 207; literature 14, 64, 70, 77, 85, 207; process 86
Burton, J. 40, 166
Bush, President G.W. 105, 109, 153
Business World 73, 140, 157
Byers, M. 9, 102, 211

Carana 1, 33, 35
Carlsnaes, W. 10, 69
Central Intelligence Agency (CIA) 103

Chalk, P. 3, 25, 27, 30–1, 43, 75
Chapnick, A. 5, 216
Chen, J. 40–1, 166
Choong, W. 83, 111–12
Chow, J.T. 39, 67–8, 102, 136, 159–60
Clinton, President B. 103–4
coast guard 48, 71, 181; of Asian countries 30, 77; Chinese 170; Indian 167; Indonesian Sea and Coast Guard 38, 42, 55n42, 55n43, 55n44, 112, 163–5, 167, 178, 185, 215; Japanese 154, 169; MoT unit 82, 211; Philippines 167; Singapore 166; US 27, 55n40, 107, 113–17, 120, 121n20, 122n21, 122n22, 139, 175, 190n97
Cold War 104, 135
Conference of New Emerging Forces 65
Consulate General of India in Medan 76, 167
Container Security Initiative (CSI) *2*, 9, 13–14, 27–8, 53, 80, 87, 102–3, 107–8, 113, 120, 139, 142, 150–1, 173, 176, 183–6, 206, *209*, 212–13, 215, 217–18; ports 81, 109, 119, 175, 211, 216
Convention for the Suppression of Unlawful Acts against the Safety of Maritime Navigation (SUA convention) 1, 2, 12–14, 32, 80–1, 103, 107–8, 113, 119–20, 139, 142, 150–1, 173–5, 183, 185–6, 211–13, 215, 217–18; Articles 121n5, 190n95
cooperative 13, 116; activities 76, 156, 168, 190n77, 217; arrangements 1, 109; on the bilateral front 103; forums 137; measures 33, 106; mechanism 180–1
coordinated patrols *3*, 41, 45, 167; agreements 138, 140, 150–1, 165–6, 185–6; Andaman Sea 167; arrangements 75–6, 138, 140, 207, *210*, 212–14; bilateral arrangements 87, 134; *Corpat Philindo* 141; *Indindo* 168; Indonesia–Malaysia (IMCP) 3, 75–6, 134, 165–6; Indo-Sin (ISCP) *3*, 75–6, 87, 165; Malacca Strait 41, 45, 140, 168
counter-piracy measures 30, 77
counter-terrorism 139; ASEAN convention 71, 73–4, 87, 89n25, 138, 142, 149, 152; bilateral arrangements 71; capacity-building assistance 153; cooperation 134; Coordinating Body 40; joint efforts 150; measures 28, 40, 136; MoU 72, 138, 154; policies 67; training exercises 37–8; units 39

counter-terrorism ASEAN Convention on 152, 159–60, 162, 184, 186, 188n32, 207–8, 212–14; bilateral cooperation with US 207; MoU 154, 156; national efforts 157; Southeast Asia Regional Centre 160
counter-terrorism cooperation 71–2, 120, 157–8; with Australia 155–6; bilateral with US 87, 207
Coutrier, P.L. 11, 33
Cribb, R. 48, 50, 52
Customs and Border Protection (CBP) 9, 108–9; agency 113; automated manifest system 117; inspections 118; team 176
Customs–Trade Partnership Against Terrorism (C-TPAT) 68, 102–3, 113–14, 117–20, 138–9, 175
cybercrime 136

deaths 4; sentence 28; *see also* killed
Defence Cooperation Agreement (DCA) *3*, 80, 85–6, 139, 142, 150–1, 154, 173, 181–6, 192n129, *210*, 212, 214–15
Dent, C.M. 73, 149
Desk Koordinasi Pemberantasan Terorisme (DKPT) 27–8, 36, 38–9, 151, 158–9
Desker, B. 13, 105
Detik News 112, 181
Deutsche Press-Agentur 85, 182
Dewan Maritim Indonesia 28, 36, 41, 48, *49*, *50*, 51, 79, 163, 165
Directorate General of Sea Transportation (DGST) 38, 73, 78, 114–17, 119, 139, 149, 153, 157, 163–5, 175, 189n66
Djalal, H. 7, 12, 33, 66, 71, 159, 166, 170
domestic politics dynamics 64, 86
Dosch, J. 10, 66–7
Doughton, T.F. 112, 178
drugs 52, 171; trafficking 136

East Africa piracy 12, 25
East Timor 49, *50*, 103–4
East Timorese displaced persons 104
East West Institute 113
Efstathopoulos, C. 5, 217
Eisenhower administration 103
Elisabeth, A. 8, 149
Embassy of Japan in Indonesia 72, 154, 169
Emmers, R. 39, 78
Emmerson, D.K. 5, 9, 11, 64, 207
Exclusive Economic Zone (EEZ) 66, 76, 78–82, 108, 169, 174

Expanded ASEAN Maritime Forum (EAMF) 136–7
extra-regional states 2–3, 30, 33, 53, 80, 106, 135, 173; cooperation with 137, 180
extradite 107, 159, 179, 184; extradition treaty 85–6, 139, 182–4
Eyes in the Sky (EiS) air patrols 45, 79, 172

Febrica, S. 28
foreign policy 66–7; analysis 5, 10, 69; Canadian and Australian 5, 216; formulation 10, 64, 69–70, 84; goals 104; Indonesia's 9–10, 14, 64–5, 68, 70, 75, 207; making 9, 64, 86–7, 207
Fox, A.B. 5, 216
Frigo, M. 5

Gerakan Aceh Merdeka (GAM) 40–1, 166
Gilpin, R. 8, 102
Glazebrook, G. De T. 5, 216
Gowa, J. 4, 216
Granatstein, J.L. 5, 216
Greaves, S. 27
Grieco, J.M. 4, 6, 216
Gross Domestic Product (GDP) 5
Guilfoyle, D. 110

Halimi, A.-L. 5
hegemon 8, 11, 14, 102, 107
hegemonic leadership 8–9, 11, 102, 207, *208*, *210*, 211–12, 214, 218
Higgott, R.A. 5, 216
hijackings 4, 25, 27, 36, 107, 112, 140, 178
Hindu 76, 167
Ho, J. 4, 7, 13, 33, 44, *47*, 112, 162, 172, 178, 181
Holmes, J.W. 5, 216
hostage 141; taking 36
Huang, V. 12–13
human rights Indonesia's record 104; Law Centre 156; violations 67, 104
Human Rights Watch 104
human trafficking 136

illegal fishing 28, 48–9, 53, 68, 76, 106, 137, 166–8, 170, 172, 190n85
illegal immigration 72, 156, 168
illegal migrants/immigrants 28, 48, 50–1
IMB Piracy Reporting Centre 41, 55n30
Indian Ocean 11–12, 206; Indonesian islands *51*; overfished *49*; piracy 25; shipping routes 33, 41

Indonesia: importance in maritime security 14, 26, 33, 35
Indonesia–Malaysia Coordinated Patrol *3*, 75–6, 140, 165–6, *210*
Indonesia–Singapore Coordinated Patrol (ISCP) 3, 75, 85, 165–6, 210
Indonesian armed forces 76, 86, 104, 166
Indonesian Coordinating Board for Maritime Security 16n5, 36–7, 40, *46*, 54n1, 54n2, 54n19, 54n20, 55n25, 55n32, 71–2, 74, 77–8, 82–3, 86, 88n10, 88n13, 88n15, 88n17, 89n26, 89n31, 89n35, 89n37, 90n44, 91n67, 91n74, 122n26, 142n3, 153, 155, 164, 166, 169, 171, 176, 180–1, 186n6, 187n13, 187n17–187n19, 187n22, 187n23, 187n25, 187n28, 187n29, 189n63–189n65, 189n68, 189n71, 189n72, 189n74, 190n75, 190n78, 190n80, 190n83, 189n89, 190n90, 190n91, 190n92, 190n93, 191n98, 191n104, 191n122, 192n125, 192n126, 211
Indonesian Coordinating Ministry for Political, Legal and Security Affairs 10, 28, 37, 39, 48, 50, 67, 69, 70–4, 76–80, 82, 84–6, 88n19, 89n37, 89n38, 105, 121n14, 138–9, 155–7, 166–7, 169–72, 182, 191n99, 191n100
Indonesian Democratic Party of Struggle 82, 85–6, 139, 182
Indonesian Directorate General of Sea Transportation (DGST) 38, 73, 78, 114–17, 119, 139, 149, 153, 157, 163–5, 175
Indonesian Embassy in Washington DC 105, 153
Indonesian Immigration Agency 73, 141
Indonesian maritime jurisdiction 33, 35, 215
Indonesian Ministry of Defence (MoD) 9, 10, 16n4, 16n5, 16n6, 27–8, 33, 37, 44, **45**, *51*, 54n4, 55n29, 55n35, 56n50, 56n51, 56n52, 56n60, 56n62, 56n63, 69–87, 88n10, 88n12, 88n13, 89n26, 89n35, 89n36, 89n37, 89n38, 90n43, 90n44, 90n49, 90n51, 90n54, 90n57, 90n58, 90n59, 90n60, 90n61, 91n62, 91n63, 91n64, 91n65, 91n66, 91n67, 91n69, 91n77, 105, 109, 111–12, 121n8, 121n11, 121n12, 121n13, 151, 153, 155–6, 158, 167–8, 171–2, 176, 179, 181–3, 186n8, 187n13, 187n14, 187n23, 187n24, 187n30, 188n31, 189n69, 189n71, 189n74, 190n76, 190n89, 190n90, 191n105, 191n114, 191n115, 211

226 Index

Indonesian Ministry of Foreign Affairs (MFA) 10–11, 28, 33, 48, 52, 54n1, 54n2, 69–73, 76–85, 89n27, 89n28, 89n29, 112, 131, 136, 151, 157–9, 163, 169, 171–3, 175, 177, 180, 188n38, 188n46, 188n47, 188n49, 188n51, 188n52, 188n53, 188n54, 189n56

Indonesian Ministry of Health 41

Indonesian Ministry of Marine Affairs and Fisheries *46*, 48, 68, 79–80

Indonesian Ministry of State Secretariat 28, 43–4, 48, 82, 180

Indonesian Ministry of Trade 73, 90n53, 108, 149, 157, 175, 187n21

Indonesian Ministry of Transportation (MoT) 16n6, 38, 54n3, 54n19, 55n30, 55n42, 55n43, 55n44, 69, 71–5, 77, 80–2, 88n10, 88n15, 88n16, 88n19, 88n21, 88n22, 89n30, 89n31, 90n46, 90n61, 91n67, 91n70, 91n71, 91n74, 109, 115, 118, 120, 121n8, 121n9, 121n16, 121n17, 121n18, 121n20, 122n21, 122n23, 122n24, 122n25, 122n26, 122n27, 122n28, 122n33, 149, 156, 162, 169, 181, 186n1, 186n2, 186n3, 186n4, 186n6, 187n11, 187n20, 187n21, 189n55, 189n57, 189n58, 189n59, 189n61, 189n62, 189n63, 189n64, 189n67, 190n80, 190n83, 190n97, 191n98, 191n122, 192n126, 192n127, 211

Indonesian Parliament 10, 15n2, 65–7, 82, 85–6, 87n4, 139, 182

Indonesian Presidential Office 68

Indonesian waters 44; act of interdiction 177, 215; armed robbery attacks 1, 12, 25, 30, **31**, 32, 40–2, *46*, 53, 181; asylum seekers and illegal immigrants 50; illegal fishing 48, 68, 170; implementation of UNCLOS 66; overfishing *49*; possibility of terrorist attack 27, 36; sea lane for the oil trade 35; trawl ban 67; unlawful acts at sea 80; US warships patrolling 13; vessels navigating 219n1

Indonesian waterways 12, 27–8, 30, 32, 35–7, 40–1, 44, *47*, 53, 69, 81, 107, 111

Information Sharing Centre (ISC) 43, 84–5, 179–81, 184, 211

Initiatives, US unilateral 14, 103, 113, 120, 212

insurgent activities 134; domestic insurgency 65

Integrated Maritime Surveillance System (IMSS) 106, 152, 184

International Convention for the Safety of Life at Sea (SOLAS) 2, 74, 219n1

international cooperation 4–6, 10, 13, 29, 49, 65, 111, 216–17; agreements 32, 66, 218; arrangements 27, 51, 53, 107; Indonesian Directorate 142n3; Japan Agency 153, 169

International Crisis Group (ICG) 37, 159

International Maritime Bureau (IMB) 1, 12, 25, **31**, **32**, 39–40, 45, 55n24, 85, 134, 178, 180–1; Piracy and Armed Robbery against Ships report 44; Piracy Reporting Centre 41, 55n30

International Maritime Organization (IMO) 25, 29, 54n12, 74, 107–8, 163–4, 180, 219n1

international maritime security 26, 33, 36, 52; concern 53; cooperation 3, 67, 70, 141; diplomacy 10, 69; initiatives 191n110

International Port Security (IPS) 14, 138, 212; Programme 102–3, 114–16, 120, 139, 175; standards 116

International Ship and Port Facility Security (ISPS) 2, 53, *208*; certificates 115, 163; Code 68, 71, 74–5, 87, 114–15, 138, 142, 149–50, 152, 163–5, 173–5, 184, 189n66, 207, *208*, 212–15, 218; Code compliance 75, 116, 163, 175; requirements 75, 116, 163, 165; training 117, 214

Intertanko 42

ISPS Code 68, 71, 74–5, 87, 114–17, 138, 142, 149–50, 152, 163–5, 173–5, 184, 189n66, 207, 208, 212–15, 218

Jackson, K.D. 9, 11, 64, 207

Jailani, A. 71, 76, 79–80, 84–5, 112, 136, 154, 171, 175, 178, 180–1

Jakarta Centre for Law Enforcement Cooperation (JCLEC) 155, 160

Jakarta Post 1, 5, 39, 42, 44, 49, 52, 68, 72, 81, 83, 86, 104–5, 110–12, 141, 153, 156, 159, 166–8, 170, 173, 176, 182–3

Jamaah Islamiyah (JI) 28, 83, 140

Japan Ministry of Foreign Affairs (MFA) 77–8, 169

Jervis, R. 4, 216

Johnston, A.I. 5–6, 130–1, 137–8, 212

Joint War Committee (JWC) 42

Jordaan, E. 5, 217

Juwana, H. 10, 67

Kahin, A.R. 66, 103, 133
Keidanren 113
Keohane, R.O. 4, 7–8, 102, 148, 216
Kepabeanan Internasional 109
killed 41; American passenger 27; Bali bombing 28; seamen 32; US national 107
King, J. 9, 211
Kompas 86, 168, 170–1, 183
Krasner, S.D. 4, 6, 8, 102, 148, 213, 216
Kristiadi, J. 8, 182

Laksmana, E.A. 5, 152
Liddle, R.W. 9, 11, 64, 66, 207
Lipson, C. 4, 9, 102, 216
littoral states 13, 25, 28–30, 41, 45, 48, 78, 80, 84, 112, 140–1, 158, 172–3, 217
Lloyds 42, 181
Lombok Strait 33
Lombok treaty 2, 72, 138, 154–6; Articles 187n15, 187n16

Mak, J.N. 13, 40, 166
Makassar Strait 33, 50
Malacca Patrol Agreement (MPA) 165, 173
Malacca Straits Patrol (MSP) 1, 3, 45, 48, 75, 79, 87, 134, 138, 140, 142, 150–1, 171–2, 185–6, 206, 210, 211–14
Malacca Straits Sea Patrol (MSSP) 79, 172
Malaysia 2–3, 13, 30, 40, 51, 81, 105, 140, 217; ASEAN Way 131; BIMP EAGA 71, 73; closure of ports 4; coordinated patrols 41, 45, 48, 75–9, 87, 134, 142, 150–1, 157–8, 165, 171, 173, 185–6, 207, 210, 213–14; Enforcement Agency 79; foreign relations 65–6; government 42–3; information exchange 149; information sharing 138, 212; maritime boundaries agreement 50; Muslim extremists 27, 107; pollution prevention 181; ports 175, 216; smuggling 52, 166, 172; Southeast Asia Regional Centre for Counter-Terrorism 160; territorial dispute 49–50, 67, 132–3
Malaysia cooperation 218; activities 167; arrangements 149; cooperative mechanism 180; maritime security 141; partners 7
Malaysian 166; Chief of Armed Forces 45; cooperation or non-cooperation 218; government 42; law enforcement agencies 79, 158; naval bases 165; navy cooperation 79; ports and shipping businesses 150, 175; warships raided 133

Manning, C. 65, 67
Maphilindo cooperation 158
maritime community 25; international 29, 53
maritime cooperation 1, 6, 12–13, 26, 32, 64–5, 68, 71, 173, 211, 217; bilateral 78; MoU 3, 75, 87, 106, 121n3, 121n4, 170–1, 190n87, 190n88, 207, 210; norms in Southeast Asia 135; programme fund 171
maritime kidnapping 178
maritime security 7, 11, 30, 68, 80, 137, 148, 158, 177, 179, 191n110, 191n117, 192n128; Agency 164; arrangements 14, 36, 53, 64, 71, 139, 206–7, 212–13, 216–18; capacity building 105, 186n7; challenges 3, 31, 48; diplomacy 10, 69; directive 115; improving 107; Indonesian ministry of defence budget 45; international 26, 33, 36, 52–3; measures 4; NGO 54n11, 85, 91n75, 91n76, 186n6, 192n128; policy 9, 37; policy goals 167, 171–2; projects with Japan 72; threats 1, 3, 12, 28, 75, 136; training 152–3; working group 74
maritime security cooperation 1, 5, 11–13, 15, 26, 120, 140, 150–1, 206, 215–16; in ASEAN 132, 134, 137; Indonesia's participation 36, 64–6, 68–71, 130–1, 142, 148; international 3, 67, 70; literature on 12; participation in 102; tripartite agreement 73, 141; US behaviour 9, 14, 103
maritime security Indonesian Coordinating Board 16n5, 36–7, 40, 46, 54n1, 54n2, 54n19, 54n20, 55n25, 55n32, 71–2, 74, 77–8, 82–3, 86, 88n10, 88n13, 88n15, 88n17, 89n26, 89n31, 89n35, 89n37, 90n44, 91n67, 91n74, 122n26, 142n3, 153, 155, 164, 166, 169, 171, 176, 180–1, 186n6, 187n13, 187n17–187n19, 187n22, 187n23, 187n25, 187n28, 187n29, 189n63–189n65, 189n68, 189n71, 189n72, 189n74, 190n75, 190n78, 190n80, 190n83, 190n89, 190n90, 190n91, 190n92, 190n93, 191n98, 191n104, 191n122, 192n125, 192n126, 211
maritime security initiatives 3, 9, 35, 48, 53, 67, 87, 107, 113, 119, 141–2, 152, 173; international initiatives 191n110; Regional Initiative 210

maritime terrorism *2–3*, 4, 7, 11–12, 14–15, 26, 28–9, 37, 40, 68, 71, 74–5, 80, 138, 140–1, 148, 150, 165, 169, *208*, 213, 215, 218; anti-maritime terrorism 102, 116, 174; attacks 1, 3, 25, 27, 36, 39; counter initiatives 81, 114, 141–2, 152, 154, 162–3, 184; deterring 214; halt 176–7; potential 48, 53, 67, 107, 134, 136; prevent 173, 186

maritime transport 33, 44, 137; security 27, 107; US Security Act 114

Martin, L.L. 4, 7, 148, 216

Mearsheimer, J.J. 4, 216

Medeiros, J. 83, 111

media 11, 25, 27, 42–3, 83, 107, 111–12, 170, 178–9

Megawati, President 68, 105, 153

Memorandum of Understanding (MoU) Australia *2*; BIMP EAGA *2*, 71, 73, 87, 138, 141–2, 148–9, 152, 157–8, 162, 184, 186, 207, *208*, 212–14; on counter-terrorism 72, 138, 154, 156; on Maritime Cooperation *3*, 75, 78, 106, 121n3, 121n4, 170–1, 190n87, 190n88, 207, *210*

military training 104, 155, 183

Ministry of Defence (MoD) 9–10, 37, 69–70, 73–4, 78, 211; Australian 72; Philippines 76; Singapore 75, 79, 110, 140, 182–3; *see also* Indonesian Ministry of Defence (MoD)

Ministry of Foreign Affairs (MFA) 9; Indonesian 9–11, 28, 33, 48, 52, 54n1, 54n2, 69–87, 89n27, 89n28, 89n29, 109–10, 112, 115, 131, 136, 151, 157–9, 162–3, 167, 169, 171–3, 175, 177, 179–80, 188n38, 188n46, 188n47, 188n49, 188n51, 188n52, 188n53, 188n54, 189n56, 207, 211; Japan 77–8, 169

Ministry of Marine Affairs and Fisheries *46*, 48, 68, 79, 80

Ministry of Transportation (MoT) 10, 37–8, 69, 84, 86; Australian 72; *see also* Indonesian Ministry of Transportation

Mitra Utama (MITA) 40, 161

Mo, J. 13

Moluccas civil war 103; Sea 33; separatist movements 15n2, 67; Strait of 106, 152

money laundering 136

Moravcsik, A. 4, 216

MSP agreement 45, 79, 87, 138, 140, 142, 150–1, 171, 206, 211–14; sub-regional 185

Murphy, A.M. 103

Murphy, M. 12–13

Muslim 105; extremists 27, 107

Nabbs-Keller, G. 9–11, 64, 207

Nasrun, R.A. 12

National Institute for Defense Studies 28

Natuna Sea 33, 106

Naval Criminal Investigative Service (NCIS) 71, 152

neighbouring states 15, 49, *50*, 53

Neufeld, M. 5, 217

New Order era 65–6

Nik, R.H. 52

Nikitin, M.B. 109–10

Niksch, L. 104

Noer, J.H. 4

non-ASEAN states *2*, 15, 131, 138–9, 141–2, 212, 218

non-cooperation 1, 7, 12–13, 15, 80, 85, 87, 107, 119, 139, 173, 185–6, 209–10, 212; Indonesia's 131, 141, 151, 211, 214, 216; Singapore and Malaysian 218

Non-Governmental Organisation (NGO) 29, 42, 54n11, 65, 67, 85, 87n6, 87n7, 91n75, 91n76, 159, 186n6, 192n128

non-proliferation 110; treaty (NPT) 176

Nuswantoro, L.P.E. 44, *47*, 76–7, 85, 167, 177–8, 180

Oegroseno, A.H. 35, 52, 76, 83, 111

oil 1, 36, 149; Ambalat Block 50; Chinese imports 33; drilling companies 28; fields 78; Middle East exports 11, 33, 36; offshore 107; palm 108; spills 12; supply 33; trade 11, 35

Ong-Webb, G.G. 27, 40, 45, 166

Operation Bakti *47*

Organization for Economic Co-operation and Development (OECD) 51

Oye, K.A. 4, 216

Pacific Ocean 11, 33, *49*, 206

Papua *51*; New Guinea 49, *50*, 135; West separatist movement 15n2, 40, 67

Parthiana, I.W. 10, 66–7

People's Republic of China 65; Embassy 171; Republic of Indonesia–People's Republic of China joint statement on strategic partnership 78

Pfister, R. 5, 217

Philippines, the 2, 4, 42, 48–9, *50*, *51*, 52, 76–7, 105, 132–3, 158, 187n18, 187n28, 187n29, 189n73, 212; arms smuggling

172; ASEAN Way 131; bilateral cooperation 185–6; coast-guard officials 30; cooperation initiatives 140; cooperation partners 7; coordinated patrols 141, 150, 157, 214; defence agreements *3*, 75, 165, 167–8, 173, 190n77, 207, *210*; defence arrangements 87, 142; East ASEAN growth area 71, 73; information-sharing agreement 138, 149; maritime agency 142n4; Muslim extremists 27, 107; naval exercises and patrols 134; territorial dispute 132–3; waterway 33
Ping, J.H. 4–5, 217
piracy *3*, 12, 29–30, 43, 77, 111, 134, 136, 154, 173, 181, 206, *210*; attacks 25; cooperation against 75; IMB Reporting Centre 41, 44, 55n30; incidents 85, 180; prevention 169; *see also* anti-piracy, counter-piracy
Polner, M. 39, 160–1
Polres Tanjung Perak 71, 152
Power, J. 26–7, 40, 166
Prescott, V. 76
Proliferation Security Initiative (PSI) *2*, 9, 13–14, 27–8, 53, 67, 80–2, 87, 102–3, 107, 109, 111, 113, 119–20, 139, 142, 150–1, 173, 176–8, 183–6, *209*, 211–13, 215, 217–18; Ship Boarding Agreement 110, 121n10
public–private partnership 103, 113–14; US unilateral120
Purdjianto, T.E. 12
Purnomo, Y.D.H. 12, 79, 166–8, 171–2

rapprochement 103, 131
Raustiala, K. 8
Ravenhill, J. 5, 137, 216
Raymond, C.Z. 13, 27, 45, 107
Regional Cooperation Agreement on Combating Piracy and Armed Robbery against Ships in Asia (ReCAAP) *3*, 7, 12–13, 32, 53, 80, 84, 86, 139, 142, 150–1, 173, 179, 181, 183–6, 206, *210*, 213, 215, 217; Articles 191n116, 191n118, 191n119; Information Sharing Centre (ISC) 43, 85, 180–1, 211; reluctance to sign 214
Rekhi, S. 30–1
relative gains 6–7, 11, 186, 206, *208*, *210*, 216, 218; calculation 15, 148–51, 207, 213–14
Renwick, N. 31
Reuters 12, 39, 170

Richardson, M. 25, 37
Roberts, C.B. 5
Rosenberg, D. 9, 13, 73, 109, 141, 175, 211
Ruland, J. 10, 66
Russia 135–6

Sato, Y. 7, 214
Sawu Sea 33, *51*
Sea Lanes of Communication (SLOC) 3–4, 41, 52, 206
sea robbers 25, 29, 171; cross-border pursuit of 166; extradition 179; murdered by 32
sea robbery 1, 4, 7, 11–12, 15, 40, 43; attacks 14, 32, 103, 140, 165, 186, 212; attempts to halt 76–7, 83, 134; discussion in ARF 136; efforts to address 170–1; efforts to fight 78; GAM 166; incidents in the Straits 178–9; Indonesian responses 36, 41, 44; in Indonesian waters 53, 181; international community response 29–30; reported incidents 31, 85, 180; threat of 25–6, 42, 142
sea robbery, countering 44, 48, 75, 87, 102, 166, 168–9, 173, 179, 181, 184, 215; bilateral exercises 170; cooperation 77, 80, 134, 142, 148, 150, 172, 185, *210*, 211, 218; patrols 30, 167
Sekretaris Kabinet Indonesia 72, 138, 156
Seram Sea 33, *49*
shared identity 6, 14–15, 120, 139, 140–1, 207, *208*, *210*, 213–14, 218; ASEAN membership proxy for 138, 212; role in informing state cooperation 130–1, 137, 142
Sherlock, S. 10, 66–7
Shie, T.R. 12–13
shipping routes 33, 35, 206
Singapore closure of ports 4; cooperation partner 7; Defence Cooperation Agreement *3*; Indonesia–Singapore Coordinated Patrol Arrangement *3*; Ministry of Foreign Affairs 1; Straits 3, 11–12
Singapore Ministry of Defence (MoD) 75, 79, 110, 140, 182–3
Singapore Ministry of Foreign Affairs (MFA) 1, 48, 132, 182
Singer, D.J. 4, 216
Singh, B. 28, 37, 39
Siregar, H.B. 40, 112, 166
Sittnick, T.M. 12–13, 39, 42

smuggling 28, 48, 52–3, 76, 79, 134, 137, 157–9, 168, 171; arms 77, 136, 166–7, 172; of migrants 51; people 72, 156
Snidal, D. 4, 8, 216
Soeharto, President 66, 103; administration 70; regime 65; resignation 68
Soekarno, President 103; administration 65; policy of confrontation 66
Sondakh, B.K. 8, 12, 36–7, 44, *47*, 76–7, 112, 140, 166–8, 172, 180
South China Sea 33, 40–1, *51*, 78, 166; declaration on the conduct (DOC) 137; illegal fishing 170; territorial disputes 132
Soviet Union 65; *see also* Russia
Staf Umum Operasi Markas Besar Angkatan Laut 77, 158, 167, 169, 183
Storey, I. 105, 140
Strait of Makassar 106, 152
Strait of Malacca 25, 31, 35–6, 39–43, 45, *46–7*, 48, *49*, 50, *51*, 52, 76, 78–9, 106, 134, 152, 166, 169
Strait of Moluccas 106, 152
Strait of Sunda 3, 33, 35
Straits of Malacca and Singapore 3, 11–12, 28–30, **31**, **32**, 33, 36–7, 41–4, *47*, 48, 75, 77, 83, 112, 136, 140, 167–8, 171–2, 178–81, 217
Straits Times 30, 42–3, 49–50, 77–8, 86, 132, 168–70
Strange, S. 9, 102
Stryken, C.-M. 8–9, 13, 112, 178, 211
Suchharitkul, S. 35, 110
Sudrajat 40, 48, 78, 80, 108, 112, 166, 174
Suhartono 10, 67
Sulawesi Sea 31, 33, 42, *49*, *51*, 67, 73, 76, 106, 140–1, 152, 166
Sulu Sea 4, 73, 140–1, 152
Sumaryono, Djoko 79, 171
Sumaryono, Laksmana Muda TNI Djoko 82, 84, 151, 180
Sunda Straits 33, 41, 206
Sunday Times 25, 183
Suppression of Unlawful Acts against the Safety of Maritime Navigation (SUA) 1, 2; convention 12–14, 32, 80–1, 103, 107–8, 113, 119–20, 139, 142, 150–1, 173–5, 183, 185–6, *209*, 211–13, 215, 217–18; Articles 121n5, 190n95
Supriyanto, R.A. 65
Suristiyono, K.B.P. 171
Surya Citra Televisi (SCTV) Liputan 86, 182
Suryadinata, L. 9, 11, 64–5, 158, 182–3, 207

Tan, S.S. 5, 37, 130, 137–8, 212
Terms of References and Standard Operating Procedure of the Malacca Straits Patrol (MSP agreement) 45, 79, 87, 138, 140, 142, 150–1, 171, 185, 211–14
territorial disputes 49, 132–3
terrorism ASEAN measures against 136; C-TPAT 117; fight against 105; global campaign against 27, 102, 107; Indonesia–Japan joint announcement 154; international 2, 71, 88n20, 153, 187n10; Southeast Asian cooperation against 152; US Customs–Trade Partnership against 9, 14, 68, 212; war against 39
terrorism threats 28, 36, 38
terrorist activities 39, 52, 159; acts 26, 174, 184; attacks 12, 14, 27–9, 36, 39, 53, 72, 74, 81, 102–3, 107, 119–20, 136, 140, 155, 162, 175, 206, 212, 214; financing 153; groups 29, 36, 140, 159, 179; hijacking 4, 27, 36, 107; networks 53; organisations 51, 159; suspects 28, 157; threats 27, 107, 113–14
terrorist threats 113–14; maritime 27, 107
terrorists 27–8, 36–8, 156; Abu Sayaff Group 4; gateways for 140; international 105
The Brunei Darussalam–Indonesia–Malaysia–the Philippines East ASEAN Growth Area MoU on Sea Linkage 2
Timor Leste 49, *51*, 135
Timor Sea 33
Tiribelli, C. 26–7
trafficking 136; of firearms 173; in persons 51
transnational crimes 51–2, 76–7, 136–7, 158–9; threats 111–12
treaty/treaties 4, 8, 217; of amity and cooperation 131; ASEAN 132; defence 86; extradition 85–6, 139, 182–4; international 54n14, 66, 83, 87n1; limits 76; Lombok 2, 72, 138, 154–6, 187n15, 187n16; making 10; non-proliferation (NPT) 176; Philippines 76
Treaty of Amity and Cooperation (TAC) 131–2, 137

United Nations Conference on Trade and Development Secretariat (UNCTAD) 35–6, 110, 117, 119, 165
United Nations Convention on the Law of the Sea (UNCLOS) 35, 66, 80, 108, 174; Articles 54n13, 54n14, 54n15

Index 231

United Nations High Commissioner for Refugees (UNHCR) 51
United States (US) 114, 135, 175; bilateral cooperation 152; Coast Guards 55n40, 121n20, 122n21, 122n22, 190n97; cooperation partners 7; Energy Information Administration 12; MoU on Maritime Cooperation 121n3, 121n4; unilateral initiatives 113
United States (US) 9/11 Commission 113
United States (US) Coast Guard 27, 55n40, 71, 107, 113–17, 120, 121n20, 122n21, 122n22, 139, 175, 190n97
United States (US) Customs and Border Protection (US CBP) 9, 108–9, 113–14, 117–18, 120, 139, 175–6
United States (US) Department of Defense (US DoD) 33, 104–5, 152
United States (US) Department of Homeland Security 1, 33, 35, 114
United States (US) Energy Information Administration (EIA) 12, 33, 37
United States (US) Regional Maritime Security Initiative (RMSI) *3*, 9, 13–14, 30–2, 53, 80, 82–3, 87, 102–3, 107, 111–13, 119–20, 139, 142, 150–1, 173, 178–9, 183–6, *210*, 211–13, 215–18
United States (US) unilateral initiatives 14, 103, 113, 120, 212
United States (US) unilateral public–private partnerships 120
Urquhart, D. 25, 85, 178, 180

Vagg, J. 31, 43

Valencia, M.J. 12–13, 25, 27, 42, 52–3, 107, 166
vessels sunk 68

Waltz, K.N. 4, 6, 102, 148, 216
war against terrorism 27, 39, 104–5, 107; civil 103; Cold 104, 135; equipment 86; risk zone 42; World War II 103
Weapons of Mass Destruction (WMD) 9, 37, 53, 109–10, 174, 176–7; materials 13, 107, 118, 211; transportation of 14, 103, 120, 212
Wendt, A. 6
West Timor 104
Westhuizen, J. van der 5, 217
Wibisono, M. 74, 161, 176
Winanti, P.S. 64, 67
Wisnumurti, N. 12, 83
World Customs Organization (WCO) *2*, 38, 138, 161, 184, 215; AEO requirements 160; Desk 142n2; diagnostic mission 139; members 75
World Customs Organization SAFE Framework of Standards to Secure and Facilitate Global Trade (WCO SAFE Framework) 1, *2*, 71, 74–5, 87, 138–9, 142, 149, 152, 160–2, 174, 184, 206–7, *209*, 212–15, 218

Xinhua 76, 79, 85–6, 139, 167, 182

Yasin, M.T. 52, 166
Young, A.J. 25, 42

Taylor & Francis eBooks

Helping you to choose the right eBooks for your Library

Add Routledge titles to your library's digital collection today. Taylor and Francis ebooks contains over 50,000 titles in the Humanities, Social Sciences, Behavioural Sciences, Built Environment and Law.

Choose from a range of subject packages or create your own!

Benefits for you
- Free MARC records
- COUNTER-compliant usage statistics
- Flexible purchase and pricing options
- All titles DRM-free.

REQUEST YOUR FREE INSTITUTIONAL TRIAL TODAY

Free Trials Available
We offer free trials to qualifying academic, corporate and government customers.

Benefits for your user
- Off-site, anytime access via Athens or referring URL
- Print or copy pages or chapters
- Full content search
- Bookmark, highlight and annotate text
- Access to thousands of pages of quality research at the click of a button.

eCollections – Choose from over 30 subject eCollections, including:

Archaeology	Language Learning
Architecture	Law
Asian Studies	Literature
Business & Management	Media & Communication
Classical Studies	Middle East Studies
Construction	Music
Creative & Media Arts	Philosophy
Criminology & Criminal Justice	Planning
Economics	Politics
Education	Psychology & Mental Health
Energy	Religion
Engineering	Security
English Language & Linguistics	Social Work
Environment & Sustainability	Sociology
Geography	Sport
Health Studies	Theatre & Performance
History	Tourism, Hospitality & Events

For more information, pricing enquiries or to order a free trial, please contact your local sales team:
www.tandfebooks.com/page/sales

 | The home of Routledge books

www.tandfebooks.com